THE BRITISH GENERAL
ELECTION OF 1950

THE BRITISH
GENERAL ELECTION
OF 1950

By
H. G. NICHOLAS

*Fellow of Exeter College, Oxford, and Faculty Fellow
of Nuffield College, Oxford*

With an Appendix by
D. E. BUTLER
Student of Nuffield College, Oxford

LONDON
MACMILLAN & CO. LTD
1951

" The strife of the election is but human nature applied to the facts of the case."

ABRAHAM LINCOLN, *Reply to a Serenade, November 10, 1864*

PRINTED IN GREAT BRITAIN

PREFACE

THE credit for this study, in its inception, promotion, and financing is due to Nuffield College, Oxford. To the Warden and Fellows, for their generosity and encouragement throughout, I owe warm thanks; I am similarly indebted to the staff of the College for their kind and ready assistance. For leave of absence during the election campaign my thanks are due to the Rector and Fellows of Exeter College, Oxford.

Any General Election study must owe a heavy debt to Mr. R. B. McCallum and Miss Alison Readman, whose *British General Election of* 1945 first raised the seed from which this (and, it is to be hoped, later) crops could alone be grown. What I owe to these pioneers is evident on every page. I count myself most fortunate, too, in having enjoyed the services of Mr. David Butler, a veteran of the earlier venture. He has been responsible for the appendix on pp. 306 to 333, for assistance and advice on every statistical item, and for the collection of much valuable material used elsewhere in the book. But more than that, there is hardly a page in the present volume which has not benefited by his rigorous but always constructive criticisms.

It is obvious that the collection and ordering of material for a study of this kind must always be a task which far exceeds the capabilities of one pair of hands. It has been my great good fortune to have had my range of observation widened and my burden lightened by the assistance of an exceptional number of interested and assiduous scholars and students. Space forbids the listing of all the helpful people up and down the country who placed the findings of their industry and curiosity so readily at my disposal. I am, however, particularly indebted to Mr. R. S. Milne of the University of Bristol; Mr. Roderick Ross of the University College of the South-West at Exeter; Mr. Peter Richards of the University College, Southampton; Miss Jean Stott of Liverpool University; Mr. Peter Campbell of the University of Manchester; Mr. Galpin of Pembroke College, Cambridge; Mr. Ivor Gowan of the University of Nottingham; Mr. Peter Bromhead of the University of Durham; Mr. Edward Hughes of King's College, Newcastle; Mr. Heath of the University of Edinburgh; Mr. Rose of the University of Aberdeen; Mr. Basil Chubb of Trinity College, Dublin; Mr. Stansfield Turner, U.S.N., Mr. A. B. Evans and Mr. J. H. D. Page all of Exeter College, Oxford; Mr. G. F. Hourani of Balliol College, Oxford; Mr. Mansell-Moullin of Brasenose College, Oxford; Miss Janet Parkin and Mr. W. E. Warrington. I am also indebted to Mr. Mark Benney of the London School of Economics and to Mr. S. B. Chrimes and his colleagues at the University of Glasgow for giving me access to work undertaken by them on the election and separately published by them elsewhere.

For work on the press I am particularly indebted to Dr. Charles Higbie, who directed and supervised the analysis of the British press. With him worked Mr. D. Samuel and Mr. C. L. Burns of Balliol College; Mr. D. V. Grossman and Mr. S. N. M. Moxley of New College; Mr. J. F. S. Russell of Magdalen College; Mr. K. Mackenzie of Queen's College and Mr. A. P. B. Hewitt of Manchester College, all of Oxford University. Overseas I owe especial thanks to Professor Crisp of the University of Canberra, Australia, and Mr. Donald Gardner of the Canadian Institute of International Affairs, Toronto.

What I owe to the parties, the candidates and the agents is as real as it is obvious. Without their willingness to co-operate, such a study as this would be quite impossible, and I am very grateful to them for their readiness in granting me such generous facilities for observation and inquiry. Since I have sometimes had occasion to refer critically to the press, I particularly welcome the opportunity of acknowledging here the debt—so pervasive as sometimes to pass unnoticed—which this volume owes to the daily chroniclers of our times. That it is the press which has so often provided the instruments for its own reproof and correction is the ultimate—and perhaps the only necessary—evidence of its indispensability.

To the journals and organisations which have allowed me to reproduce their cartoons and posters I am especially grateful, as also to the British Broadcasting Corporation for permission to use the material quoted on pp. 127 to 129, and to Mr. Silvey of their Audience Research Department for his advice and help. I am also much obliged to Dr. Henry Durant for access to the findings of the British Institute of Public Opinion and advice on their interpretation.

It remains for me to thank Miss Stephen for her manifold services throughout the campaign, Miss Potter of the Oxford School of Geography for her execution of the maps and diagrams, and Miss Alexander and Miss Davies for their invaluable secretarial assistance.

Finally it should be made clear that just as the views expressed in this study are my own, so also is the responsibility for any errors or omissions.

H. G. Nicholas.

Nuffield College,
  10th September, 1950.

CONTENTS

LIST OF PLATES AND MAPS

CHAPTER I

THE LAW AND THE CAMPAIGN

THE legal framework within which the British General Election of February 1950 took place did not differ in essentials from that described by R. B. McCallum and Alison Readman in Chapter II of *The British General Election of 1945*.[1] Nevertheless there were certain changes introduced by the passage of the Representation of the People Act in July 1948 and largely incorporated in a consolidating act, the Representation of the People Act, 1949, which modified the existing law in several important respects. For a full exposition and examination of these, students of election law are referred to the professional treatises on the subject; here the object is simply to set out briefly the main changes in the law as they affected the conduct and outcome of the general election.

The Representation of the People Act combined in one measure certain changes in the franchise, an extensive scheme of redistribution and several modifications in the law relating to the conduct of elections. Mr. Chuter Ede, who as Home Secretary was the parent of the Bill, claimed for his offspring when he introduced it to the House of Commons: "This Bill completes the progress of the British people towards a full and complete democracy, begun by the great Reform Bill of 1832. From now on every citizen of full age will have a vote, and only one vote. This Bill wipes out the last of the privileges that have been retained by special classes in the franchise of this country. It arranges for a complete redistribution of seats."[2] Critics of the Bill complained variously that in too many respects it was a "disenfranchising" measure or that its appearance of egalitarianism was illusory because it ignored the principle of "one vote one value".

The Act abolished the two remaining forms of plural voting: the business premises vote and the university graduates vote. The first was numerically insignificant; it was estimated that the number of voters affected by it was under 70,000. However,

---

[1] Hereafter referred to as *McCallum and Readman*.
[2] House of Commons Debates, February 16th, 1948, c. 839.

there were a few constituencies at the heart of the great cities where it was concentrated in sufficient strength to constitute a sizeable Conservative asset, even if not, generally speaking, large enough to turn defeat into victory. Only in the City of London was it a dominant factor.

The university vote was of more consequence. The 12 university seats, at the Dissolution of the 1945 Parliament, were held as follows :

Independents	. .	5
Conservative	. .	5
Liberal	. . .	1
National	. . .	1

Furthermore, one of the Independents, Sir Arthur Salter, and the solitary " National ", Sir John Anderson, had both held office in Mr. Churchill's " Caretaker " Government of 1945 and qualified thereby, in the opinion of many judges, for the Conservative label. Sir Arthur Salter and his fellow Independent at Oxford, Sir Alan Herbert, both publicly announced their intention of voting Conservative in 1950, while at the same time remaining Independents. Mr. Kenneth Lindsay, the Independent member for the Combined English Universities, offered his services to the Labour Party, which accepted them. On an extreme calculation in each direction it might therefore be concluded that the abolition of university representation cost the Conservatives 8 seats, Labour 1 and the Liberals 1. Excessive reliance ought not, however, to be placed on such computations. The Independents concerned were independent not only in their refusal of a party whip, but also in the freedom they enjoyed and exercised to speak and vote against any party proposal. Moreover, the most truly independent of them had the independence which comes of never having their political and parliamentary thinking conditioned by party allegiance.

The number of university graduates to lose a vote by the abolition of these seats was 228,769. Of the 12 sitting members only 4 sought re-election elsewhere, all of them Conservative— Mr. Kenneth Pickthorn (Cambridge), Mr. H. G. Strauss (Combined English), Mr. Walter Elliot (Scottish) and Professor D. L. Savory (Belfast). All were successful. The Conservative Party pledged itself, if returned to power, to restore the university vote, and the pledge was incorporated in the party's election manifesto. It did not, however, excite much attention during the campaign.

Redistribution, combined with the abolition of the business premises vote, involved one notable break with tradition. The City of London, already shrunk by depopulation to a figure far below any other constituency (its electorate numbered only 10,830 in 1945), was further enfeebled by the loss of the business vote, which made up two-thirds of its total. It was therefore, despite determined protests, merged with the City of Westminster to make one constituency returning only one member in place of its own previous two and Westminster's two.

The Act also put an end to the few remaining two-member constituencies. Including the City of London, there were 12 such boroughs in England and Scotland and 3 counties in Northern Ireland. Each of these was broken into two single-member constituencies. The split as such hardly worked to the benefit of either party, but in one or two instances it may have reduced the chances of a weak candidate riding in on a strong one's coat-tails. It is certainly interesting that whereas in each of the 11 boroughs * in 1945 the party that topped the poll also carried the second seat, in 1950 3 of them were split between Labour and Conservatives. The comparison, however, cannot be pushed too far, since boundary revision introduced incalculable variables at the same time.

Over the country at large the effects of redistribution were considerable. Only 80 constituencies escaped untouched, and of those which were affected many were so extensively re-drawn as to be in effect, though not always in name, new constituencies. Although regard was paid wherever possible to considerations of historical continuity, the shifts of population since 1918 (the date of the last redistribution) had been so extensive that if anything approaching equality was to be achieved wide changes were inevitable. For party organisers these changes meant a great deal of labour and planning, re-grouping their ward organisations and revising their campaign tactics to take account of new and often only half-predictable shifts in their voting strength. For electoral statisticians, in the press and elsewhere, it meant an interruption in one of the oldest of British post-election pursuits, the analysis of the returns of each party's " gains and losses " of seats.

* The City of London is excluded as non-comparable.

It was as if Wisden had had to adjust itself to the introduction of a seven-ball over.

There was a good deal of debate over the precise effect of redistribution upon the fortunes of the parties. There is no doubt that the distribution of seats in 1945 favoured Labour owing to the movements of population since the boundaries were last drawn in 1918. The average constituency returning a Labour member had only 51,000 electors, while the average constituency returning a Conservative had 57,000. The redistribution which took place under the Act of 1948 was bound to have an adverse effect upon the fortunes of the Labour Party. It is an open question how great was this effect. During the debates on the Bill Mr. Churchill and other Conservative speakers referred to the 35 seats which Labour would lose through redistribution. Labour organisers subsequently spoke of its costing them 30 seats. A careful constituency by constituency survey leads to the conclusion that if the election had been fought on the old boundaries Labour would have won at least 25 more seats than they actually did. The inquiries into the relation of seats to votes in the appendix to *McCallum and Readman* and in pp. 327–333 *infra* suggest that on balance there was a bias in the electoral system in favour of Labour in 1945 and in favour of the Conservatives in 1950. The net change in the bias appears to have been about 40 seats; there is no doubt that redistribution was by far the most important factor in any such change. All in all it is not unreasonable to suppose that, of Labour's drop of 79 seats since 1945, changes in constituency boundaries, as distinct from any loss of votes, accounted for between 25% and 50%.

The bulk of these boundary revisions were already embodied in the Bill when it came before the House for its Second Reading, but at the Committee Stage the Government introduced amendments to give a total of 17 extra seats to certain large towns. These were fiercely attacked by the Opposition front bench as constituting a partisan attempt to make good the losses which Labour had sustained by the revisions already accepted. In view of the stir this occasioned at the time, it is interesting to see how these new seats went in 1950. Of the 8 seats created by dividing the boroughs with an electorate of over 80,000, 2 went to the Conservatives and 6 to Labour. With a very slight swing to the Conservatives the result would have levelled out at 4–4.

Of the 9 seats allotted to the larger boroughs, 3 certainly went to the Conservatives and 3 to Labour; the remaining 3 cannot be calculated with confidence, but it is quite probable that the division for the whole 9 was 5–4 in favour of Labour. *In toto*, then, the creation of the 17 extra seats may have led to a net gain of about 5 for Labour.

In addition to revising boundaries, the Act also transferred a few constituencies from the Borough into the County category or vice versa. In so doing it had regard to a criterion of population density, now for the first time consciously applied by the Boundary Commissioners. In general, county constituencies were those in which there were less than four persons per acre.[1] The main practical importance attaching to the distinction was in the determination of the permitted total of expenses (see *infra*).

The total number of seats under the new Act was 625 compared with 640 in 1945. England had 506 of these (compared with a previous 510), Wales 36 (previously 35), Scotland 71 (unchanged), and Ulster 12 (unchanged). The total electorate on the October 1949 Register (on which the election was fought) was 34,410,306, of whom 28,372,971 were in England, 1,802,222 in Wales, 3,370,028 in Scotland and 865,085 in Ulster. The figures in 1945 were: total electorate (excluding University electors) 32,836,419, in England 26,969,611, in Wales 1,756,885, in Scotland 3,332,742 and in Ulster 777,181. From a comparison of these figures it will be seen that, despite an increase of 1,403,360 electors, England had 4 fewer seats than in 1945, and that in a smaller House of Commons. Only Ulster sustained a comparable increase in population, and her strength in the House remained the same.[2] The justification given for the seemingly disparate treatment of England on one hand and Wales and Scotland on the other was the hardship that would be imposed on the latter by reducing their large or scattered areas to a system of representation based solely on size of population. If Mid-Wales or the Highlands were to be accorded only the representation to which their electorate entitled them, the few remaining constituencies would be so vast in area as to lose all sense of community and become quite unmanageable for the members who represented them. Nevertheless the practical consequence was a tilting of

[1] House of Commons Debates, April 26th, 1948, c. 60.
[2] Excluding the theoretically non-territorial university seat which she lost.

the balance of representation, not only in favour of the country as against the town—the average county constituency's size (in Great Britain) being 52,575 as against the average borough's 56,529—but also in favour of the remote and incidentally Celtic periphery against the centre.

In 1945, plural voters apart, the only persons entitled to vote by post or proxy were persons on the " service register ", i.e. those absent from home owing to some form or another of national service duties. Under the 1948 Act provision was made for the compilation by each local Registration Officer of an " absent voters' list ", which contains not only service voters but also several other categories of persons eligible to vote by post or proxy. These include persons whose occupation by its " general nature " would prevent them voting in person, or whose particular duties in connection with the election might have a similar effect. Most importantly, it includes " those unable or likely to be unable by reason either of blindness or any other physical incapacity, to go in person to the polling station or, if able to go, to vote unaided ". Of secondary importance are those who could only reach the polling-station by means of a sea or air journey (e.g. in such constituencies as the Western Isles). Finally persons who have changed their address can vote by post—providing the change takes them outside their previous borough, urban district or parish.

The total number of persons eligible under one or other of these categories is obviously quite considerable, and it might reasonably have been anticipated that, although the service voters would be fewer than in 1945, the total number of postal or proxy voters would exercise a considerable effect on the election. Furthermore, since inclusion on the absent voters' list was necessarily dependent, not upon the Registration Officer's initiative, but on that of the voter, there was obviously scope here for party enterprise and assiduity in getting any of their eligible supporters registered. In varying degrees all parties were alive to this, but without doubt it was the Conservatives who in the vast majority of constituencies made the most of the opportunities so afforded. They took pains to find out where their potential postal voters were, then to get them registered, and finally to circularise every postal voter with election literature timed, so far as possible, so that its arrival synchronised with that of the ballot paper he had to complete. Thus in Truro it was claimed by the Conservatives that " of over 1400 postal voters, applications for over 1200 were made through Conservative branch offices ". It is doubtful if there was a single locality in Britain where Labour or the Liberals could claim to have done as much for even half of the postal voters in a constituency.

In all, in February 1950, Returning Officers issued postal voting papers to 505,702 electors, or 1·5% of the registered electorate. Of these, 93·2% or 471,088 were returned correctly and included in the count as valid votes; these amounted to 1·6% of all valid votes. Of the 409,000 papers returned in England and Wales, about 9,000 were rejected as invalid.* Most of these were rejected because the witness had failed to record his address. Some Returning Officers insisted on observance of this technicality, while others did not. In Manchester, for instance, only 14 out of 2,998 ballots returned were rejected (0·5%). But in Liverpool 267 out of 3,048 were rejected (8·8%), almost twenty times as many. In the Wythenshawe division of Manchester not one out of 524 was cast out, while in the Exchange division of Liverpool 76 out of 262 were excluded from the count.

The use made of the postal vote varied greatly. There were on the average 756 valid postal votes per constituency. But there were wide extremes. At one end was the remarkable figure of 7,323 in Fermanagh and South Tyrone. At the other was the mere 91 in the Bridgeton division of Glasgow. A list of the constituencies where the vote was highest and where it was lowest is given at the top of following page. The area where most use was made of the postal vote appears to be the Highlands, where 2·9% of all votes counted came by post; next came the West of England, where the percentage was 2·8 (1,254 per constituency). The area where the postal vote was least used was Manchester, where it contributed only 0·6% of the total vote.

The postal vote was, as might be expected, particularly used in the most straggling constituencies. In the 126 largest in area, 2·2% of the electorate had postal facilities. In the other 497 seats

---

* This proportion (2·2%) compares well with the voting performance of at least one university which employs the postal ballot for the election of its governors. In the last four elections for vacancies on the Hebdomadal Council at the University of Oxford the average proportion of invalid votes was 2·9%.

Seat	Postal electors	Valid votes	% of all votes
Highest			
Winchester	2,249	2,056	3·7
East Grinstead	2,147	2,000	3·7
Honiton	2,006	1,941	4·2
Hampstead	1,835	1,730	3·0
North Cornwall	1,706	1,590	4·3
Merioneth	1,089	1,036	4·2
Banff	1,822	1,361	5·7
Caithness	1,071	908	4·7
Lanark	1,737	1,563	4·0
Fermanagh and South Tyrone .	7,826	7,323	11·8
Mid-Ulster	6,957	5,950	9·5
South Down	3,192	2,758	4·5
Londonderry	3,077	2,824	4·8
Lowest			
Liverpool, Scotland	128	93	0·2
Hexham	128	122	0·4
Glasgow, Bridgeton . . .	115	91	0·3
Glasgow, Gorbals	136	111	0·3

the figure was only 1·3%. In the 20 very largest, as many as 3·3% were postal electors.

A majority of the postal vote undoubtedly went to the Conservatives. On this point all observers agree, and Labour organisers not least amongst them. In the Yorkshire area Labour estimated that if, even in the last month before the election, they had given as much attention to the postal vote as had the Conservatives, they might have won three more seats. These impressions are confirmed by the much greater use made of the postal vote in constituencies which returned Conservatives than in those which returned Labour members. On the average, 983 postal votes were counted in the former to only 498 in the latter. In some places the contrast was even more extreme. In the 12 London constituencies which returned Conservatives postal votes averaged 1,119. In the 31 which returned Labour members the average was only 490. In Bristol the figures were 1,044 and 441.

These are only very rough pointers to the Conservative leanings on the postal vote. Exactly how it divided cannot of course be known, any more than one can say how many postal voters would have contrived to vote in the ordinary way if postal facilities had not been available. One can only calculate how many seats the

Conservatives would owe to the postal vote if certain assumptions about their majority are made:

Conservative majority among postal voters	Seats owed to postal vote	Effect of abolition of the postal vote on seats in Parliament			
		Con.	Lab.	Lib.	Others
100%	18	280	332	10	3
60%	13	285	327	10	3
50%	12	286	326	10	3
30%	11	287	325	10	3
20%	10	288	324	10	3
10%	5	293	319	10	3
0%	0	298	315	9	3

These are the seats involved:

Seat	Conservative majority	Valid postal votes	Conservative majority as % of postal vote
Stroud . . .	28	1,630	1·7
Spelthorne . . .	31	792	3·9
York	77	972	7·9
Pudsey . . .	64	797	8·0
North Dorset . .	97 *	1,041	9·3
Shipley . . .	81	694	11·7
Chislehurst . . .	167	1,204	13·9
Peterborough . .	144	954	15·1
West Woolwich . .	139	863	16·1
Bexley . . .	133	752	17·7
Bromsgrove . . .	190	724	26·2
Lanark . . .	685	1,563	43·8
Scotstoun . . .	239	414	57·7
Carlton . . .	395	567	64·7
North Somerset . .	903	1,395	69·7
Colchester . . .	931	1,144	81·4
Taunton . . .	1,372	1,562	87·8
Bury and Radcliffe .	780	833	93·6

* Over Liberal.

It is very hard not to believe that the Conservatives owe at least 10 seats to the introduction of the postal vote.

Finally, it is perhaps worth recording that, while 93·2% of all those to whom postal ballots were sent cast valid votes, in seats won by Conservatives the figure was 94·5 and in seats won by Labour only 91·0. This suggests that not only is the postal vote in some sense an electoral "bonus for literacy", but also that it is a bonus from which Conservatives win the greater advantage.

From a technical point of view arrangements for the postal vote worked well.   No doubt the generally early date for closing the absent voters' register resulted in some late invalids and absentees failing to secure their postal votes in time.   Moreover, there was excessive variation in the fixing of the date, some Returning Officers making it February 3rd and others entertaining applications a good deal later.   No doubt also there were instances of voters whose ballot papers failed to reach them, or did not reach them in time.   But these would seem to have been few.   The application forms and the postal voting papers themselves were criticised as unduly cumbersome.   So they were; at the same time, the low incidence of spoilt votes suggests that the actual consequences were not serious.   Undoubtedly the postal vote as such can be criticised on the grounds that, as an eminent Labour organiser remarked, " every vote cast by post is a vote cast out of secrecy ".*   Nevertheless its successful employment in 1950 undoubtedly justifies its retention.   For many voters it makes voting easier and for some it alone makes it possible.

No feature of the Representation of the People Bill excited stronger feelings than the clause, not introduced until the report stage, limiting and controlling the use of motor vehicles to take voters to the polls.   The *hire* of vehicles for this purpose had long been unpopular; the new Act now forbade the use beyond a certain maximum of even freely donated motor vehicles and required that each vehicle be registered with the Returning Officer.   The limits imposed were very strictly drawn—one car for every 1,500 electors in county constituencies and one for every 2,500 in boroughs.   It was made illegal for any person, whether a party worker or not, to give lifts " with a view to supporting or opposing the candidature of any individual as against any other or others ".   The only exceptions permitted were lifts given to members of the motorist's own " household " (defined as persons who slept under his roof the night before the poll).

The clause was avowedly a party measure, aimed at rectifying the advantage which Labour felt that Conservatives enjoyed by being able to employ more cars on polling day than their rivals. Unfortunately the advantage it sought to offset was one difficult

* Cf. Lord Shepherd in House of Lords Debates, July 5th, 1948, c. 313.

to control by legislation. In a society in which motor-cars were rarities such legal restrictions would be easy to apply; in a society like that of the United States, in which car ownership is all but universal, they are superfluous. The Britain of 1950 would appear to have reached the half-way stage of evolution at which the difficulties of applying such legislation outweigh its theoretical advantages. There is always some difficulty in prohibiting a practice whose illegality consists entirely in the agent's intention. But where that intention depends upon collusion with another agent (the voter receiving the lift) before it is likely to be put into effect the difficulties are sensibly increased. It is impossible to state with confidence how far the law was violated on February 23rd. From the fact that the Director of Public Prosecutions had received only one complaint of an infringement up to March 13th it is reasonable to assume that it was pretty generally respected. If so, however, it is certain that its observance depended on the law-abiding character of the party agents and their subordinates, and not upon its enforceability. A complaint made after the election by Mr. Wigg, M.P. for Dudley, is interesting evidence not so much of the extent as of the ease with which the law can be evaded:

> " In my constituency, we were limited to 28 and beyond that we did not go, and each of those motor cars had a registration number. My political opponents apparently did not see it that way. We noticed that as polling day went on, they seemed to have more than 28 cars in use, but for some extraordinary reason, which we never understood, these motor cars, or many of them, did not draw up at the polling stations. The electors were inconvenienced by being dumped in back streets about 200 yards away from the polling stations." *

The effectiveness of these restrictions in realising the Labour Party's objective in imposing them varied a good deal, quite apart from any instances of evasion. In a good many constituencies Labour was well off for cars and could have used more than the permitted total. In several areas a respectable tradition of Labour supporters riding to the polls in Conservative cars came to an abrupt and inconvenient end. In rural constituencies all

* House of Commons Debates, March 31st, 1950, c. 810.

parties undoubtedly suffered inconvenience; if Labour, as the pedestrian party, had fewer of its supporters seduced by Conservative lifts, so Conservatives, as owner-drivers, found greater ease in getting themselves and their " households " to the polls. Probably the Liberals, as the marginal party with the loosest organisation, suffered more than either. The much-publicised use of horse-drawn transport (on which the law placed no restrictions) was more effective as an advertisement and a protest (" Labour's horse-and-buggy election ") than as a serious supplement to the motor-car; many agents discovered with a shock that the countryside's reserves of ponies and traps have been severely depleted by rural mechanisation.

Considering the novelty of these regulations their administration passed off fairly smoothly. But one widespread misunderstanding caused some trouble on polling day. The police in many areas did not appreciate that registered cars were fully entitled to carry party favours, and started to ban their employment. Speedy instructions from Whitehall ordered them to desist, but not before a certain amount of flurry and agitation had been occasioned.

It was the claim of the Bill's proponents than any obstacles placed in the way of voting by these restrictions on transport would be more than offset by the new facilities for postal voting and the increased number of polling districts. One of the oldest complaints in rural areas was the distances voters sometimes had to cover in order to reach the poll. The Act did not transfer from local authorities their existing responsibility for the provision of polling places, but it emphasised more clearly than before their obligation to provide enough. Every parish, or in Scotland every electoral division, should, " in the absence of special circumstances ", constitute a polling district. Furthermore, any interested authority, or any 30 electors in a constituency, could petition the Home Secretary and through him obtain further facilities if they made out a convincing case. Several such petitions were made and acted upon before February 1950. The result was a very considerable increase in the facilities for voting in rural areas, even if the expense of providing them was sometimes high (e.g. in parts of the Western Highlands the cost was estimated at 10s. for each registered voter). For party organisers, however, this sometimes created new problems, since each polling place ideally requires its own committee room on polling day, with all that that implies in terms of organisation, staffing and expense. Rural police forces, obliged by law to post a policeman at every polling place, also often found that this strained their resources to the limit. In some towns, short of available premises, mobile polling stations were used.

Of more doubtful advantage was a novel provision of the Act imposing on Returning Officers the responsibility for issuing to each elector a polling card notifying him of his registered number and instructing him how, where and when to vote. Previously it had been left to the parties each to circularise the electorate with this information, a task which they turned to their own advantage by printing the particulars on a card tinted with the party colours, or bearing party slogans and indicating by a cross opposite their candidate's heavily printed name where they wished the voter to cast his vote. With the imposition of this duty on the Returning Officer went a clause forbidding the issuance of " any poll card or document so closely resembling an official poll card as to be calculated to deceive ". This led the cautious *Parker* [1] to suggest " that an election agent would be well advised not to issue any poll cards ", since " it is difficult to see " how he could usefully issue one " which might not be held to resemble " the official form. A similar view appears to have been held by *Wooding's*,[2] while the Labour Party's official *Conduct of Parliamentary Elections* was even more emphatic :

> " On legal opinion it is thought that information as to the polling day, hours of poll, place of voting, and the electoral number may be given (if desired) on a Candidate's Election Address as this production cannot be held to be an official document.
>
> " A subsequent leaflet could be issued to call attention to the official poll card or to the information given in the Election Address and could request voters to give their numbers or addresses to the checker at the gate of the polling station on leaving.
>
> " . . . In no case should a *card* of any sort be issued in this connection." [3]

---

[1] *Parker's Election Agent and Returning Officer*, 5th ed., 1950, p. 148.
[2] *Wooding's Conduct and Management of Parliamentary Elections*, 10th ed., 1949, p. 29.   [3] 3rd ed., 1949, p. 133.

This point was obviously considered most important by the author, who devoted a special appendix to its treatment. The Conservative *Parliamentary Election Manual*, however, made no reference to the possible illegality of a non-official poll card, and the omission is indicative of a different interpretation of the law. Already at the Bradford by-election of December 1949 the Conservatives had issued one of their own, and in February 1950 they did the same in a good many constituencies, including the Cities of London and Westminster, within whose purlieus the very embodiments of law and propriety might be held to reside. Such cards, though cast in the traditional form, were, however, careful to add, " You will receive an *official poll card* from the Returning Officer ", or some such clearly distinguishing form of words. Even so, by no means all Conservative candidates interpreted the law in this way. A common protest on election addresses (even of members of the Conservative " Shadow Cabinet ") ran as follows : " I am sorry that owing to a *Socialist* Government law we cannot send you a voting card showing your voting number. . . ."

Such discrepancies in interpretation, coupled with the fact that some Returning Officers did not succeed in issuing all their poll cards in time, led to a good deal of criticism of the value of this provision.   Many agents viewed the party poll card as a link between candidate and voter almost as valuable as the election address (and sometimes more valuable, since its surrender to " tellers " at polling-stations made the recognition of supporters especially easy).   They regarded the official poll card, devoid as it was of candidate's names and of party labels, as a wholly inadequate substitute.   Certainly if parties for these reasons are going to continue issuing their own, the official card would appear to be an unjustifiable public expense.

The substitution of the official for the party poll card was linked in the minds of the authors of the Bill with another clause, that which imposed lower limits on permitted election expenditure. These limits were agreed upon by the national agents of all three major parties in modification (owing to a rise in costs) of an earlier all-party agreement embodied in the 1944 recommendations of the Speaker's Conference. They constituted a considerable reduction on previously permitted limits. Previously in counties the maximum was 6*d.* for each elector plus £75 for the agent's fee, and in boroughs 5*d*. plus £50. The Speaker's Conference substituted for counties £450 plus 1½*d*. for each elector, and for boroughs £450 plus 1*d*. (the agent's fee to be included in these totals, but not the £100 allowance for the candidate's personal expenses). The Act in its final form retained the basic figure of £450, but increased the *per capita* allowance to 2*d*. in counties and 1½*d*. in boroughs. The effect may be illustrated as follows :

.	1945 limit	Proposed new limit	Enacted new limit
County Constituency with electorate of 40,000 .	£1,075	£700	£786 6*s*. 8*d*.
County Constituency with electorate of 50,000 .	£1,325	£762 10*s*. 0*d*.	£866 13*s*. 4*d*.
County Constituency with electorate of 60,000 .	£1,575	£825	£950
County Constituency with electorate of 70,000 .	£1,825	£887 10*s*. 0*d*.	£1,033 6*s*. 8*d*.
Borough Constituency with electorate of 40,000	£883 6*s*. 8*d*.	£616 13*s*. 4*d*.	£700
Borough Constituency with electorate of 50,000	£1,091 13*s*. 4*d*.	£658 6*s*. 8*d*.	£762 10*s*. 0*d*.
Borough Constituency with electorate of 60,000	£1,300	£700	£825
Borough Constituency with electorate of 70,000	£1,508 6*s*. 8*d*.	£741 13*s*. 4*d*.	£887 10*s*. 0*d*.

It will be apparent that even at the finally enacted figure these allowances constituted a considerable reduction on 1945 maxima. Even if £50 be allowed for the relief made available by the provision of an official polling card, that is more than offset by the rise in printing costs (estimated at one-third above 1945 figures), quite apart from the increase in other types of expenses. Obviously therefore an agent accustomed to budgeting up to his old maximum could only keep within his new by conducting a much cheaper campaign. This in fact was what was done. The Conservative *Parliamentary Election Manual* gives comparative tables of typical budgets of the pre-1939–45 period and post-1948. (These are given at the top of following page.) The most conspicuous difference is the reduction in the estimate for paid employment—24% in the first and 14% in the second. By contrast printing and stationery, though absolutely less, bulk proportionately larger in a modern budget—45% instead of 30%.

	County, %	Borough, %
Pre-war		
Fee of Election Agent (in addition to £75 in Counties, and £50 in Boroughs) . .	4	3
Paid employment	24	24
Printing and stationery	30	30
Advertising and billposting . . .	10	10
Postages, telegrams, telephones . .	6	3
Rooms for public meetings . . .	6	9
Committee rooms	6	7
Miscellaneous	7	7
Emergencies	7	7
	100%	100%
Post-1948		
Paid employment	14	14
Printing and stationery	45	45
Advertising and billposting . . .	10	10
Postages, telegrams, telephones . .	5	4
Rooms for public meetings . . .	5	5
Committee rooms	4	5
Speakers	3	3
Miscellaneous	7	7
Emergencies	7	7
	100%	100%

An examination of the published returns of election expenses suggests that in the majority of constituencies and amongst all parties printing and stationery was by far the largest single item. The official sub-head, "Printing, Stationery" (which in these returns covers also advertising, postage and telegrams), accounted for 61% of the total. It varied little between one part of the country and another, although in London the proportion reached 70% while in Wales it was only 56%. The returns show expenditure divided thus : *

Total	Agents	Clerks, etc.	Printing, stationery, etc.	Public meetings	Committee rooms	Miscel- laneous matters	Personal expenses
£1,170,114 100·0%	90,536 7·7	65,321 5·6	714,858 61·1	67,425 5·8	53,895 4·6	114,057 9·7	64,022 5·5

* Four candidates are not included in this or subsequent expense calculations —two Liberals who failed to make a return of their expenditure and the two Conservatives in Northern Ireland who were returned unopposed.

The proportion of expenditure devoted to these various items did not seem to vary markedly between the parties. There were, however, as the following table shows, considerable discrepancies between the totals :

	Average per candidate						% of permitted maximum					
	Con.	Lab.	Lib.	Com.	Other	All	Con.	Lab.	Lib.	Com.	Other	All
England .	793	706	464	255	449	641	94	83	55	31	55	76
Wales . .	713	719	570	287	245	630	86	86	67	35	30	75
Scotland .	701	628	361	240	240	545	88	79	46	30	33	68
N. Ireland .	561	322	—	—	393	456	93	54	—	—	64	75
U.K. .	777	694	459	254	359	628	93	83	55	31	46	75

It will be seen that expenditure fell below the national average in Scotland and in Northern Ireland, in the latter largely owing to the lower maximum imposed by law.*

In all, Conservative candidates spent £478,738 or 10d. per vote received. Their Labour rivals spent £428,447 or 8¼d. per vote. The Liberals spent £217,291 or 1s. 9½d. per vote. The Communists spent £25,377 or just 6s. per vote. In all £1,169,936 was spent in soliciting votes. This works out at 1s. 2d. per vote. Of course for a few candidates the tariff rose to a fantastic level. The Socialist Party of Great Britain's candidate in North Paddington spent £481 and received only 192 votes, while five other candidates, including two Communists, spent more than £1 for every vote they won. At the other extreme the record is easily held by Mr. John Parker at Dagenham, who won 43,300 votes for an expenditure of £228—little more than 1d. a vote.

Mr. Parker had by far the lowest expenditure of any Labour or Conservative candidate—only 25% of the permitted maximum. All but half a dozen Labour candidates spent at least 50% of their legal maximum, and only one Conservative (fighting the forlorn hope of East Rhondda) fell below that level. Among other parties, however, small expenditures were normal. There were even a few candidates who spent less than £100 apiece, though Major Sleigh who championed the cause of Scottish Nationalism in Edinburgh Central on a budget of £33 was quite exceptional.

* In Northern Ireland there is no " basic " £450 allowance. There is only an allowance of 2d. for every entry in the Electoral Register.

The Liberal in North Battersea who spent only £70 was easily the most economical in his party, and there were few Communists who spent as little as the £101 on which their candidate fought Sparkbrook.

The Conservative and Labour candidates tended in most seats to run close to the legal maximum and a few exceeded it. The record expenditures were the £1,046 reached by the Labour candidate in Midlothian and the £1,045 reached by the Conservative candidate in Stroud and Thornbury. The Liberal in Wells spent £980, the highest figure for his party. Mr. Piratin in Stepney topped the Communist totals with a modest £640. Commander King-Hall's attempt to win Bridgwater as an Independent cost £904. Of 1,864 candidates, 4 returned expenses beyond the permitted maximum; two of these were Conservatives (at York and East Willesden) and two were Labour (at Batley and Morley and Southampton (Itchen)). There were also four returns which exactly equate with the permitted maxima (exclusive of the allowance for candidates' personal expenses) and two which were just £1 below it.

This suggests that candidates and agents found it more practicable than some had expected to operate within the new maxima. This held true even of the counties, where the greatest difficulty had been anticipated. Thus in the 15 constituencies in Great Britain where expenditures of £1,000 or over were permitted only two candidates (the Labour and the Conservative in Barnet) availed themselves of the opportunity to spend up to four figures (exclusive of their personal expenses).

It is worth investigating whether any factors were obviously linked to variations in expenditure. Parties seem to put more into seats they win than seats they lose. The Labour Party averaged £659 in their successful contests and only £594 in their unsuccessful ones. The Conservatives' variation was slightly less— £730 for a win and £677 for a defeat. The Liberals with £733 and £454 show a much sharper contrast. Further light is shed by a study of the 20 safest seats for each party and of the 20 most marginal.

In the 20 seats where the Conservatives had the largest majority over Labour they spent 92% of the maximum while Labour spent only 67%. The 20 seats where Labour secured its largest majorities over the Conservatives show a different picture. The

ERRATA

Page 18, Lines 13 -16 should read :-

"Of 1,864 candidates, 2 returned expenses beyond the permitted maximum; one was the Conservative at East Willesden, and the other was the Labour candidate at Batley and Morley."

Nicholas:-
The British General Election of 1950

Conservatives spent 75% of the legal limit and Labour 78%. In the 20 seats where the fewest votes divided the major parties both sides, as might be expected, spent most heavily. The Conservatives virtually spent the permitted maximum while Labour spent 88% of it.

Although the discrepancy is not very great, the broad picture that emerges is of Conservative candidates spending almost all that they were allowed to in all but the most hopeless seats, while Labour candidates tended generally to spend less, particularly in seats where the issue was not in doubt. As for the Liberals, their expenditure fluctuated more from one constituency to another than any other party's. Over the country as a whole, as the table above shows, they spent only 55% of the permitted amount. But in the 20 seats where they fared best the average expenditure rose from £459 to £738, or 92% of the legal limit. This suggests that they may have been fairly successful in concentrating their expenditure where it would do most good, though it may merely reflect the financial self-sufficiency (or -insufficiency) of strong (or weak) constituency organisations.[1]

It is an interesting comment on the foresight of legislators that the clause in the 1948 Act which occasioned most perturbation both before and during the election was one which went through virtually without debate during the passage of the Bill itself. The clause in question ran :

> " No expenses shall, with a view to promoting or procuring the election of a candidate at an election, be incurred by any person other than the candidate, his election agent and persons authorised in writing by the election agent on account :—
>
> (a) of holding public meetings or organising any public display ; or
>
> (b) of issuing advertisements, circulars or publications ; or
>
> (c) of otherwise presenting to the electors the candidate or his views or the extent or nature of his backing or disparaging another candidate." [2]

[1] A significant sidelight, incidentally, is thrown on Liberal organisational weakness (see further, pp. 33–34) by the fact that 151 (or almost one-third of their candidates) returned no expenditure whatever on election agents or sub-agents. Of these 151, 117 were contesting county constituencies whose scattered character made the employment of sub-agents particularly desirable.

[2] R.P.A., 1948, Section 42(1).

No allusion to this clause was made by either of the Government spokesmen at the second reading. At the Committee and the Report stages it occasioned virtually no comment. It had its origins in a similar clause in the 1918 Act, which laid an identical prohibition on the practices mentioned in items (*a*) and (*b*); the 1948 provision merely extended the prohibition to cover any other type of propaganda (other than by the press, which was specifically exempted).

At the Committee stage some discussion arose as a result of an amendment moved by Mr. Gallacher (Communist) to enable a political party to incur expenses in an election where they were not putting up a candidate. Rejecting the amendment, Mr. Ede said that the existing law had been operative since 1918,

"... and it arises from the activities of parties, such as the Tariff Reform League, and other organisations, in the early years of this century, which used to go to by-elections and general elections to support Liberal or Conservative candidates, as the case might be, carrying on an intensive campaign for those candidates. But, they said they were not members of either the Liberal or the Conservative Party and, therefore, their expenses could not be charged against the candidate. This is the mischief aimed at by the Clause we have now under discussion and if, in fact, a person goes down to advocate the views of some other political party, he does not incur liability unless he recommends his hearers to vote for or against one of the candidates at an election."

He concluded :

" All of us, and anyone who has had experience of fighting an election, knows well what is aimed at." *

In the whole debate on this clause there was no suggestion that it constituted any significant departure from existing practice, and the official Opposition moved no amendment and voiced no criticism either then or later.

The party manuals of election law in their post-1948 editions made due note of the change in the previously existing law without suggesting that it had any especial significance. The prescient

* House of Commons Debates, April 20th, 1948, c. 1757–8.

Parker devoted considerable space to its exposition but came to a guarded conclusion:

> "This section . . . appears to be designed to restrict expenditure by 'outsiders' in support of a particular candidate at an election and to allow such expenditure only under conditions which ensure that any of the expenses specified will be subject to the control of the election agent concerned and will be treated as election expenses. The meaning and scope of the section will, no doubt, in due course, be the subject of judicial decision." *

Hence the invocation of this section of the Act by Mr. Herbert Morrison, in reference to propaganda by industries threatened with nationalistion, provoked widespread surprise and lively controversy. For its effect upon the conduct of the early stages of the election campaign the reader is referred to p. 71. ff.

It says much for the training and conduct of all who took part in the 1950 election that despite the novelties and the occasional spinosities of the 1948 Act, the election was carried out with so few contraventions of the law. Indeed, with one or two exceptions, such cases as did come before the courts arose out of alleged contraventions of what had been standard legal practice well before 1948. But even these were not the result of misbehaviour by the parties as such, but only by individuals acting in ignorance or from misguided zeal. In general it may be said of the general election of 1950, no less than of its predecessor, that its officials were competent and its participants law-abiding.

* *Op. cit.*, p. 309.

CHAPTER II

PARTY ORGANISATION

THE 1945 election caught all three major party organisations in varying degrees of unpreparedness. By contrast 1950 gave ample warning of approach and enabled the two strong parties, Labour and Conservative, to bring their organisations to a pitch of preparedness which probably has no equal in the history of British politics. There is no such thing as complete preparedness, in politics or in war, and each side remained convinced that if only it had had a little more time or a little more money this or that omission might have been corrected, this or that weakness eliminated. But, so far as the resources and the human limitations of each side permitted, 1950 was a fully planned and fully organised election. The parties might differ in their attitude to a planned economy. They were at one in their addiction to planned electioneering.

A full picture of the role of party organisation in the election would need to begin with a detailed description of the structure, the staffing and the financing of the central offices of each party. No such depiction will be attempted here, if only for the sufficient reason that the information publicly available is wholly inadequate for such a task. But also it may be fairly argued that the role of the central offices, though vitally important for the election, goes far beyond it, and that their story belongs properly to the whole history of party warfare since 1945, which it is no part of the business of this study to describe. British electoral law draws a distinction between those portions of a party's expenditure which are related to the propagation of its general political views in time of electoral " peace " and those which are directed to securing the victory of candidates in the electoral " war ". On the basis of an analogous distinction, this chapter will confine itself to an examination of party organisation in the constituencies and of central office operations in relation to the campaign in the field.

The most evident and probably the most important development in party electoral organisation in 1950, compared with previous general elections, was in the recruitment and training of constituency agents. The election agent is a distinctive figure in

British political life and one whose history well deserves writing. His ancestry goes back to shady beginnings in the service of aristocratic borough patrons, but today he enjoys the esteem which attaches to a profession and accompanies legal recognition. A passage in Wooding's *Conduct and Management of Parliamentary Elections* well describes his qualifications :

> " It is not sufficient that he should have a thorough knowledge of election law ; he must possess capacity, initiative, and good judgment, and be able to combine tact with firmness ; he ought to have a thorough knowledge of current politics, and should be intimately acquainted with the practical details of electoral work. Nothing can legally be done without his sanction, and where large bodies of workers exist there is danger of conflict and confusion, unless the agent is a man of ability and resource. He will occasionally be urged by over-zealous partisans to resort to extravagant and even questionable methods ; and he must, therefore, be a man possessing the necessary firmness of character, not only to resist such importunities, but to prevent others from resorting to improper practices. To the qualities already named should be added the very desirable ones of energy and force of character sufficient to make his personal influence effective in connection with the minutest details of the work and the smallest actions of his many helpers. It is not, of course, contended that the most perfect election agent can ensure victory under all conditions ; but in a closely-contested election a good agent may win, while an indifferent or inexperienced man would most probably lose." *

The establishment of one of these paragons in each of the parliamentary constituencies of the country has become one of the ideal goals of party endeavour. In this the role played by the central offices is crucial. The problem for each was essentially the same. An agent works for, as well as in, a constituency ; " strong " constituencies can best afford an agent, but it is " weak " constituencies which will probably most need one. Only the central organisation can resolve the discrepancy between means and need. But in doing this it must also have a care

* *Woodings*, 10th edition, page 17.

C

that it does not offend local susceptibilities or stifle local enterprise. Each party solved the problem in its own way.

There can be no doubt that by February 1950 the Conservative Party had the largest and most highly trained agency organisation of any party. Between October 1945 and February 1950 the number of fully qualified Conservative agents was more than doubled. In England and Wales by the time of the general election 527 out of the 542 constituencies had full-time party officials in charge. The regions least strongly organised were the north-western area and Wales. Of these 527, 428 were fully qualified agents, 46 were " Certificated Organisers " and the remaining 53 were unqualified organisers. For Scotland similarly precise figures are not available, but there were only a few constituencies which did not have a full-time organising secretary or agent.

The different terms employed for the various grades of party officials reflect different levels of training and proficiency and indicate, incidentally, how much the political worker's occupation has acquired the internal differentiation proper to a profession. The lowest rung of the profession is occupied by the uncertificated organiser. Next comes his certificated counterpart. Then comes the Certificated Agent. In large cities with an organisation embracing several constituencies there will be a Chief Agent, while at the Regional level there will be a Central Office Agent and at the Central Office itself the General Director.

The Committee on Party Organisation which the Conservative Party set up in 1947 did at first consider a plan for " some form of central employment of agents " designed to secure that hypothetically ideal distribution of professional workers which electoral strategy might dictate. But it became " perfectly clear . . . that such a plan was not going to commend itself to general opinion in the party ",* and it was accordingly dropped. Instead efforts were concentrated on the establishment *pari passu* of professional standards of proficiency and professional levels of remuneration and social security. The Central Office already conducted courses of training, culminating in examinations, for would-be organisers and agents, at the end of which certificates were awarded. These examinations are the responsibility of an

* *Report* of the 69th Annual Conference at Llandudno, October 6th–9th, 1948, p. 35.

Examination Board, which is composed of an equal number of representatives from the National Union, the Agents' Society and the Central Office.

After 1948 an age limit for entry of 23 was imposed and the periods of training at each stage were extended. A scale of minimum salaries was drawn up, according to which a certificated organiser would be paid £400 p.a., or £450 if in sole charge of a constituency, and a certificated agent £500 on first appointment and £600–£800 after experience of a general election and not less than 2 years in charge of a constituency, rising by annual increments of £25. A superannuation scheme, with joint payments by agent and constituency association on a 50 : 50 basis, had been in existence since 1927. Although at the Llandudno Conference of 1948 Mr. Henry Brooke had still to regret that there were " a few " constituency associations which were " not contributing the employer's share towards the Agents' Superannuation Fund ", the vast majority of constituencies accepted both the revised scales and the superannuation obligations.

The result of this was to make possible the creation of a national force of full-time political workers who, though locally employed, were centrally trained and had a highly developed awareness of serving in a national organisation. They had a guaranteed and reasonable level of pay, and contracts which encouraged them to think of themselves as permanent party organisers between as well as during elections. Finally, they had an interest in adding to their experience and expertise in the prospects of moving from a poor to a better constituency or in securing increments or promotion within their own constituency or outside. To add that they have their own association,* their own monthly journal and even, upon occasion, their own internal altercations, is merely to indicate that they have acquired the foibles as well as the functional characteristics which accompany professional status.

The degree of completeness and complexity which Conservative organisation can reach is best illustrated by the example of Birmingham. Here, in the home of Joseph Chamberlain, where no false modesty debars the frank employment of the term " political machine ", the city Unionist Association can claim " that in no other large centre are the forces of the Conservative and Unionist Party so closely co-ordinated to provide such a

* The National Society of Conservative and Unionist Agents.

powerful organisation ; its strength and efficiency are the envy of our friends and the constant despair of our opponents ".* The senior official of the organisation is the Chief Agent.

> " Administrative and financial matters are dealt with by the Secretary. The very extensive Women's Organisation is under the supervision of the Women's Organiser, while the Young Unionist movement also has its own organiser. There is a Publicity Officer responsible for press and public relations work. . . . The important work of political educa- tion . . . is in the hands of a Political Education officer. Special organisational matters . . . are dealt with by the Organisation Officer."

Each of the 13 Birmingham divisions has its own full-time certi- ficated agent with secretarial assistance. Similarly all but one or two of the 38 wards of the city has its organiser, generally certificated ; these work under the divisional agents. At a similar level there are 30 or more full-time " missioners " or paid canvassers and subscription collectors.

Such an organisation is not typical. It represents in British politics the equivalent of a Cook County rather than an Erie County machine. A more representative sample of Conservative organisation is perhaps afforded by the East Midlands Area, which covers 42 constituencies, divided about equally into safe Con- servative, safe Labour, and marginal seats. In each of these there was a full-time agent, and in 14 of them there was a deputy agent or a women's organiser. In one city—Nottingham—which has 4 divisions, there was a Chief Agent as well. Most constituencies had enjoyed the services of an agent for at least two years before the general election, but in the three months immediately pre- ceding it no fewer than 10 constituencies had experienced a change of agent—an interesting sidelight on the mobility of the pro- fession. At the Area headquarters a staff was maintained to co- ordinate and assist the officials in the constituencies. This in- cluded a Central Office Agent and Deputy Agent, an Area Educa- tion Officer, an Area Publicity Officer, an Organiser for the Young Conservatives, a Tutor in Public Speaking, and an Area Labour Organiser, with a staff of five secretaries and a telephonist.

The East Midlands organisation may also give an indication

* *Birmingham Unionist Association Year Book*, 1949.

of the type of man which the Conservative Party has recruited for its constituency agents. They tend somewhat to fall into two groups: the pre-war and the post-war. The first are the old, experienced hands, of whom there were 12 (all but one over 50 years of age). The post-war recruits contained about 10 who were still in their twenties and about twice that number who were mostly in their early thirties. 26 of the 43 were fighting a parliamentary election for the first time, though most of them had had a mild baptism of fire in municipal contests. 8 were women. They had nearly all received a secondary education; about a quarter of them had been educated at one of the smaller public schools and one was a graduate of London University. Three or four had experience of mining or industry, and might be said to have a working-class background.

Investigation of a sample of 76 Conservative election agents drawn from all parts of England and Wales reveals similar results. 70 of them were working as full-time agents before the election, 6 were merely *ad hoc*. 36 had had previous experience of fighting in either a general or a by-election, though of the remainder 8 had seen action in local government elections. Few had had any legal or political experience outside their work as agents; the figure of 17 for this was probably a generous estimate. About two-thirds had been resident in or near their constituency before 1950. 70 were men, 6 women. Of those whose ages could be established, 11 were in the twenties, 22 in the thirties (mostly early thirties), 14 in the forties, 12 in the fifties and 3 in the sixties.* As far as education was concerned, secondary school men predominated, numbering 44. 14 had been at a public school, 4 at a university. Of the remainder, the majority appear to have received elementary schooling only. Though precise figures were not obtainable a very high percentage had seen service in the armed forces, frequently holding commissioned rank. Of the post-war recruits, a great many, probably a majority, came out of the services in 1945 and 1946, and took up political work either directly or else after a fairly brief experience of some other job which they found less to their taste. One might almost say that the typical Conservative agent is either a young man of 35 or less who has held a wartime commission,

---

* Though this perhaps is also an appropriate spot in which to do honour to the 72-year-old veteran in a constituency on Tyneside.

or else a retired regular service officer who finds that the work provides an agreeable outlet for his energies, a practical application of his political convictions and a useful supplement to his pension. But, of course, a service background is by no means universal. Other occupations from which agents had been recruited included school teaching, organising secretaryships, rubber planting and radiography.

The Labour Party's electoral organisation shows several interesting differences from that of the Conservatives. Its agency strength, in the first place, was less. For the 1945 election the party succeeded in mustering about 250 paid agents, but these were largely temporary recruits who fell away after the election was over. Labour's problem, like that of the Conservatives, was to make the conditions of employment attractive enough to win and keep a sizeable, permanent, full-time force. The report that the Executive presented to the party's annual conference at Margate in May 1947 said: " There are approximately 150 full-time Labour agents in the country. . . . Clearly the present scale of progress in the appointment of paid, full-time agents is quite inadequate to improve the striking power of the Party between now and the next General Election." To meet this situation it went on to make some financial recommendations which are discussed later in this chapter. As the result of the financial stimulus which followed on the acceptance of these recommendations, the Executive was able to report at Blackpool in June 1949 that " there has been a net increase in full-time agencies since 1948 " of 79 and, notably, that " 69 full-time agents are working in rural and semi-rural districts ".[1] By November 1949 there were 245 full-time agents. By the eve of the election there were 279 [2] for England, Wales and Scotland.

The inferiority in numbers which this still represented compared with Conservative strength was in some degree made up by the greater powers of direction which Transport House possessed over its limited forces. This is fairly clearly demonstrated in the geographical disposition of full-time Labour agents. The London Region had the greatest concentration, where more than two-thirds of the London Boroughs were looked after by full-

[1] *Report*, p. 10.
[2] Of these, 51 were financed by trade unions and served mostly in constituencies where there was a union-sponsored candidate.

timers. In the Eastern, South-Western and Southern Regions about half the constituencies were thus taken care of—representing Labour's solicitude for its marginal areas. East and West Midlands were only a little less well covered. The weakest regions were Yorkshire, Scotland and Wales, areas with more than the average number of seats which from Labour's point of view were either safe or else inexpugnable. Of course local zeal and enterprise accounted for a good deal, but the fact that full-time agents were operating in 101 of the 115 seats which Labour regarded as marginal indicates clearly that Transport House used the powers at its disposal to place them where they would do most good.

These powers were only partly financial—the supplementing of salaries and, as in the Conservative Party, the maintenance of a contributory pensions scheme, partly financed by headquarters. They were also constitutional, reflecting the generally closer-knit organisation of the Labour Party. Although the initiative in appointing an agent will generally come from the constituency party, all appointments have to be approved by the National Executive before they become valid. There is a standard form of contract of employment, based upon a " national agreement " negotiated by a regularly constituted " Adjustments Board ". This Board, which exists " to consider the relations of constituency agents with the Labour Party ", consists of four representatives of the National Executive, including the National Agent, who acts as secretary, and three representatives of the National Union of Labour Organisers and Election Agents. This is the body which makes recommendations concerning recruitment, training and qualifications and which between October 1947 and March 1948 negotiated a revised salary scale for agents binding on all constituency employers. The minimum salary for a full-time qualified agent was fixed at £400 p.a., with annual increments of £25 rising to £475 p.a., any advance beyond that to be by agreement between the constituency party and the agent. Further promotion, as in the Conservative Party, proceeds via the regional organisation to the post of District Organiser, reaching the eventual apex of the pyramid in the post of National Agent. Occasionally, though not often, an agent may move from behind the scenes to the footlights and himself become a candidate. Instances among Labour M.P.'s are Mr. Watkins of Brecon and Radnor, and Mr. Dye of South-West Norfolk. Less differentiated than the Conservatives, the Labour Party has only this one grade of qualified agent, but before this is attained more than one requirement has to be satisfied. The entrant must first secure his diploma, awarded on the satisfactory completion of a correspondence course in party organisation and electoral law and the passing of a written examination. Later, after practical experience of constituency work as an unqualified but active agent, an agent will be expected to take a more advanced course and further examination leading to the award of an Agents Grade A Certificate. At that stage he becomes entitled to membership of the Agent's Union and remuneration at the union rate of £400 p.a.

As might be expected from the nature of the party's membership and the relatively modest scale of pay, the average candidate for agent's work in the Labour Party is poorer and less well educated than his Conservative opposite number. It is a tribute to the care and skill of the party officials responsible that they have devised a form of instruction and training which enables such entrants to master the essentials of organisation and the often abstruse technicalities of electoral law in their spare time and in their own homes. The study courses are indeed a model of simplification and clarity. The party may also provide (and subsidise attendance at) week-end courses designed to give practical training and opportunities for discussion.

The result of this effort at recruitment, training and organisation in perhaps the best-manned Labour area, the County of London, was as follows. Of its 43 constituencies, 29 had full-time agents. In addition there were 3 organisers, one of them a woman, operating in the area under the direction of the party headquarters. The 14 constituencies which had no full-time agents were manned by volunteers. Most of the full-timers were working-class party members and active trade unionists, the majority of whom had fought in the war. There was a small core of 6 " experienced " agents—i.e. who had fought elections before the war. 9 were in their thirties or twenties. 23 were fighting a parliamentary election for the first time. 4 were women.

As another example of Labour organisation, this time in an area of relative Labour weakness (15 members of the 1945 Parliament out of a possible 43), one might take the South-Western Region. Here assiduous effort had raised the number of full-time agents to 21. In 2 constituencies there were full-time secretaries who acted as election agents. Finally in 5 others there were agents who, though part-time, were in receipt of a regular stipend. Furthermore, in the one big town in the area—Bristol—there was a full-time chief agent. With one exception the full-time agents were all men. It is of incidental interest that 15 of the marginal 22 constituencies in this area had full-time Labour agents.

An examination of a nation-wide sample of 56 full-time Labour agents may fill out this picture a little further. 48 were men, 8 women.* Of 31 whose ages were known, 11 were in their twenties and 4 in their thirties (representative, probably, of the post-war recruits); 9 were over 40 and 7 over 50. Elementary education exceeded secondary in the proportion of 5 to 1. Ruskin College, if one may judge from the presence of three of its ex-members in this sample, has contributed as much to the education of Labour agents as to the education of Labour candidates. Experience in public life outside agency work and routine party activity was not common, but 18 men or women had been in local government or had held some executive post in their trade union, 16 had had experience of fighting parliamentary elections and 11 of municipal elections. Only 17 were resident in their constituency before their appointment as agents.

There is much diversity in the occupational backgrounds of Labour agents. There are one or two areas where a single occupation has almost a monopoly, such as Durham, where the dominance of mining shows itself as much in the agents as in the candidates; 7 out of 11 agents encountered there were or had been colliery workers. But this is exceptional, and beyond a natural predominance of manual or minor clerical occupations there is little pattern that can be discerned. Ex-insurance agents are fairly often encountered; so are draughtsmen and accountants. It is not uncommon amongst full or part-timers to meet with trade union officials, but despite the overlap of interest between unionism and Labour, there is enough difference in the kind of work involved to make joint (or even consecutive) tenure of such posts difficult. The majority, of course, of the full-timers have made, or intend to make, political work their life's main occupation. The part-timers, as might be expected, show even greater

---

* The total of women agents, full-time and part-time, for the whole country was 49—about 1 in 12.

occupational diversity.   In one large urban agglomeration the occupational role of volunteer agents read as follows : two insurance agents, drapery shop assistant, retired analytical chemist, clerk in engineering firm, dairyman, printer, milk roundsman, private detective, factory hand, housewife, electrician, retired sales executive.   In fact the volunteer Labour agent is as varied as the Labour Party member.   He is, in fact, simply a party member with a gift (wherever possible) for organisation.

A treatment of Labour Party electoral organisation which stopped here would, while being formally fairly complete, remain, in fact, considerably misleading.   It is frequently alleged by Conservatives that the reason they require to employ a full-time staff so much larger than that of their rivals is that behind the thin red line of Labour's regular troops there are the ubiquitous guerillas of the trade unions.   The financial assistance which can be furnished by trade unions (as by any other organisation) at election times is very strictly controlled by law and, valuable though this is, it is not here that their distinctive electoral contribution is to be found.   It lies rather in the service rendered by a full-time, nation-wide, permanent " going concern " which has its roots in the needs and circumstances of half the electorate's everyday life, with an economic and social function of its own apart from politics, yet so interpenetrated with a loyalty to the Labour Party that to place its membership and its organisation at the service of the party at election times is an act of historical and temperamental, if not of logical, necessity.   Thus even the political levy, for all that its incidence and employment are closely regulated by law, has an influence over and above the financial ; as has been well pointed out : " The very fact that a man has not contracted out makes him feel he has to support the man and the party, the expenses of which his contribution has helped to defray." *

It is a consequence of this unforced and natural intimacy of the Labour Party and the unions that one cannot isolate, much less measure statistically, the aid in terms of organisation that the one derives from the other.   But perhaps one instance may serve to indicate something of the form and extent which this aid may assume.   In Birmingham Labour had no full-time agents, and the paid staff for the whole city consisted only of a Chief Organ-

* Sir Percy Harris, *The Contemporary Review*, April, 1950.

iser, an assistant and a couple of secretaries. But a joint Trade Union and Labour Party Liaison Committee was set up for the election campaign, on which sat full-time organisers representing all the unions operating in Birmingham. This committee held lunch-hour meetings in every factory of any size, produced and sold throughout the workshops a distinctive red " victory badge ", raised an election fund and from the offices of the trade unions supplied a squad of voluntary typists who were at the disposal of candidates and agents every evening throughout the campaign. The practical value of this kind of collaboration and aid is obviously considerable, but the psychological impetus and stimulus which it affords is probably more important still.

Measured by the side of its rivals, the Liberal Party organisation presented an unimpressive appearance. Lacking the financial resources of the Conservatives or the backing of any such para-political group as the trade unions, it was unusually dependent upon unpaid, amateur and often makeshift assistance. Moreover, the very nature and tradition of the party induced a greater aversion to central direction and a lesser esteem for the beauties and benefits of organisation than could be found elsewhere. This reflected itself most blatantly in the strength and efficiency of its agency force.

At first sight, and in relation to the 475 seats which the party was contesting, the figures look quite good. The number of agents in October 1949 was 140, about half of whom had their agent's certificate. By the end of November the figure had been increased to 170 and by the beginning of January to 210. During the actual election period the party had 350 agents who were in receipt of pay for their services. The remainder of their seats were manned by volunteers, and there were even instances where the candidates acted as their own agents, as in three constituencies in Glasgow. Nevertheless, it is not unfair to describe these figures as a misleading index of strength. While there was an invaluable core of agents who were experienced campaigners and possessed of a professional skill quite the equal of their Labour or Conservative opponents, the majority of the 350 had neither a comparable training, experience nor organising ability. The party had its recommended scale of salaries—a minimum of £400 p.a., with an addition of £50 for holders of an agent's certificate

—but it had neither the power to impose acceptance of this on constituency associations nor the finance to supplement adequately whatever they might be able to provide.   Thus it was by no means uncommon, although frowned on by headquarters, for constituency associations to employ agents in whole or in part on a commission basis, proportionate to their success in increasing the membership or raising subscriptions.   Moreover, though there existed, as in the other parties, an Agent's Society, membership of it was not compulsory, and by the nature of things it could not impose conditions of employment upon either the headquarters or the constituencies.   Consequently, despite the issuance in May 1948 of a " Liberal Agents' Charter ", the majority of agents were employed upon whatever terms were agreed between themselves and their constituency associations, often with a contract of strictly limited duration, not infrequently of only a month's duration.   Finally, all too few even of the 140 full-time agents who were operating in October 1949 had been functioning in their constituencies long enough to have built up a really efficient organisation by Nomination Day.   Many, of course, had to improvise at the last minute.

As might be expected, few generalisations about an agency force so diverse and so recruited can usefully be made.   Inspection of a sample of 66 Liberal Party agents yields only limited information.   Of these, only 11 were full-time before 1950.   13 were women—a higher percentage than in other parties.   8 were in their twenties, 15 in their thirties, 16 in their forties, 4 in their fifties and 6 over 60 ; the remaining 17 could not be placed. Two-thirds had had a secondary education (3 had been public-school men), 11 had gone to a university and 9 had left school at 14.   About one-sixth of them had fought a parliamentary election before, though 7 had been in local government fights.   The overwhelming majority (as might be expected of a largely volunteer force) were local residents.   They were of all occupations, with no particular group dominant—unless it was the small retail business man or the retired professional man.   The younger men (and several of the women) had nearly all been war-time commissioned officers or N.C.O.s.

It can hardly be doubted that it is the recruitment and maintenance of a permanent field force of organisers, agents, etc., such as I have been describing that constitutes the major financial problem for a modern party. Election expenses have been successively scaled down by law until they are now fixed at what is an extremely modest limit. Moreover, a parliamentary election campaign, if a proper amount of enthusiasm is evoked, can be made self-supporting, or even positively profitable, by a constituency association which uses it as an excuse for a fund-raising drive. But the maintenance of a fully-trained field force in the constituencies, with permanent offices for them to work in and the necessary tools for their job—the whole operating even in electoral " peace-time " and ready for complete mobilisation whenever electoral " war ", either parliamentary or municipal, threatens—this is the load which most constituencies find too heavy to carry unaided and for which central offices distribute the bulk of the funds they succeed in raising.

The Conservatives, in considering this problem after the setback of 1945, encountered it in the context of an additional problem peculiar to themselves. It had long been a matter for complaint in the party that well-to-do aspirants to Parliament had, in effect, been able to buy themselves a candidacy by generous subscription to a needy constituency, and the party by successive stages was seeking to eliminate the abuse and to make its parliamentary candidacies a career open to the talents. Thus in 1944 the following principles were laid down :

(a) That the annual subscription of an M.P. or a candidate to his constituency association should not normally exceed £100.

(b) That at least 50% of the sum necessary to defray election expenses should be raised from constituency sources.

(c) That if either (a) or (b) were violated (without valid reasons) the Standing Advisory Committee (by which every " official " Conservative Candidate must be approved) should withhold its approval of the candidate adopted.

Nevertheless, in 1948 it was necessary for Mr. Henry Brooke to tell the party at the Annual Conference at Llandudno * that " there are still too many constituencies—not by any means a majority, but still too many—which do not summon for interview with the selection committee anyone who does not promise in

* *Report*, p. 36.

advance to contribute half the election expenses . . . and to pay £100 a year towards the association ; or if they do interview him they make it all too clear to him early in the interview that money counts ". To correct this state of affairs the conference accepted with a few dissentients the recommendations of the Committee on Party Organisation " that candidates should be relieved of all responsibility for election expenses, that M.P.s should be permitted to contribute annually to their Association up to a maximum of £50, and that in the case of candidates the subscriptions should in no case exceed £25 per annum ". It should, however, be noted that this had effect only in respect of candidates selected after December 31st, 1948. Its impact, therefore, on the 1950 election was not very great, since, as Mr. Brooke pointed out, " the vast majority of constituencies " had " already chosen their candidates ". Nevertheless, with the exception of certain candidates who had already promised to pay half their election expenses, it would appear as if the great majority of candidates went into the election free of any considerable financial commitments to their constituency associations.

The corollary of these restrictions on private subsidy was, of course, that the strong should help the weak, and that the Central Office should be the organising agency for this political application of the principle of social solidarity. Logically, therefore, the Conference at the same time accepted the accompanying recommendations on party finance. These were that the constituency associations should carry the whole of their candidate's election expenses, that they should contribute annually on a " voluntary quota " basis towards the Central Fund of the party, and that they should only be permitted themselves to apply for grants from the Central Fund " on strict proof " that they had made every effort to raise the necessary funds themselves. Finally, it was accepted that the Party Treasurer should publish an annual financial statement—though this has not yet been acted on by the Central Office. Their failure to do so, incidentally, makes impossible any computation of the aid given by the Central Fund towards constituency costs. It is known that it is the practice to assist (usually via the Area organisation) weak constituencies, particularly so as to enable them to support a full-time agent, but how often this occurs and at what cost is not made public.

In the Labour Party the equivalent of the well-to-do candidate has been the well-to-do union, and here the problem has been how to prevent the union contributions, welcome though they are, from swamping the initiative and independence of the divisional labour parties. The previously accepted solution of this problem (and the one still obtaining when the 1945 election was held) was embodied in the so-called "Hastings Agreement" of 1933. Briefly, this provided that in divisions "fathered" by "affiliated trade unions" the union grant towards the running expenses should not exceed £200 per annum for a borough, and £250 per annum for a county, while their contribution towards election expenses should similarly be limited to "80% of 60% of that part of the legal maximum which is based on the number of electors in the constituency". The new system of computing election expenditure and the new limits imposed by the 1948 Act would have made some change in the Hastings Agreement necessary in any event, but the new burdens of the party's organisation also played their part in inducing change. As the National Executive put it in their report to the Party's Annual Conference at Scarborough in May 1948 : [1]

"Owing to the increase in agents' salaries, and the increased cost in the maintenance of Constituency Party organisation, the National Executive Committee consulted with the Affiliated Trade Unions. . . . The National Executive Committee proposed, and the Unions have agreed to recommend the proposal that the annual grant should be raised . . . to £250 (in Boroughs) and £300 (in Counties). Consideration was also given to the increased cost of Elections and the proposed reduction of the maximum amount that could be spent at Parliamentary Elections under the Representation of the People Bill. The Unions agreed to a proposal that in future, instead of paying up to 80 per cent. of 60 per cent. of the legal maximum, they would pay up to 80 per cent. of the legal maximum."

Since there are 140 constituencies with trade-union-sponsored candidates [2] and full-time agents in 51, this assistance was substantial and welcome.

Where a divisional party is not so sponsored, and yet needs aid

[1] P. 10.
[2] Besides a further 36 sponsored by the Co-operatives under similar conditions.

either to maintain an agent or to fight an election, Transport House will help it so far as the one's deserts and the other's facilities permit. To stimulate the employment of full-time agents, the party has maintained a system of grants-in-aid, contributing 30% or 50% of an agent's stipend for a three-year period, to enable him to get on his feet and the constituency to become self-supporting. During 1948 " grants were made . . . to Constituency Labour Parties amounting to £2,485 ".* Subsequent figures have not yet been published. Similarly, contributions towards the cost of constituencies' election campaigns were made from a General Election Fund opened in 1949.

For Liberals the problem was never one of circumscribing the financial influence of affiliated organisations, because their party has had none. Nor, though there are well-to-do individual party members, was the party at all embarrassed in 1950 by the risk of wealth being preferred to worth ; there were candidacies available for all who were prepared to come forward and fill them. The party's organisational problems have boiled down to one, and that one both simple and serious—lack of money. It was this which placed a limit on the number of seats they could contest and on the number of paid workers, agents and others, which they could employ. Figures of the headquarters' campaign expenditure are not yet available, but the official returns of election expenses made by Liberal candidates indicate that they had less money to spend in the constituencies during the campaign than either of their rivals. There can be no doubt that pre-election expenditure on constituency organisation was similarly modest. Occasional *ad hoc* grants of £50 to associations that could put them to best use seem to have been as much as the Federation in most areas could contrive. It is doubtful if any constituency association ever received anything approaching the £500 which was the maximum permitted disbursement from the Liberal Campaign Fund. The action of headquarters in insuring against the loss of candidates' deposits was evidence of weakness as much in the party's financial reserves as in its voting strength.

The 1950 election campaign thus manifested, to a degree greater than ever before, the concentration of power in the hands of the central offices and the development of a class of full-time,

* *Report of Annual Conference* 1949, p. 34.

paid, professional political workers. The battle analogies so spontaneously evoked by the contemplation of an election contest had here a precise applicability. The campaign maps studded with flags, before which each party manager was photographed in his office, did indeed indicate to an unprecedented degree troop movements controlled from a headquarters, and troops, moreover, who were regulars, in training, temperament and conditions of service. To fight without the assistance of the regulars was difficult; to defy the directions of the commander-in-chief was dangerous. To do so meant, for a constituency association, going into the battle in most cases with inadequate funds, propaganda or technical and legal advice, quite apart from the psychological discomfort that goes with being out of step with the battalion. Furthermore, this did not apply simply to the period of the election campaign proper. Increasingly, its shadow fell before it, and the peace-time organising and propaganda which were the precondition of success in battle called for a similar direction and control by the centre in the period between campaigns.

This spread in the functions of the constituency association from the mere fighting of an occasional parliamentary election to the maintenance of an all-the-year-round condition of political activity, or at the very least of political vigilance, is the concomitant, and in part the cause of the spread of the modern professional agent. Even within modern times his role has changed. His legal responsibilities under the 1883 Act still remain, but they are lightened by the expert legal assistance and advice furnished to him by his central office. With the disappearance of the limited franchise his registration duties have been reduced to a routine trickle. No longer, therefore, does he need the legal training which, even as late as the thirties, was still a desirable qualification. Such law as he needs to know he can fairly easily acquire through the party's training course, or find embodied in simple language in his election handbook; indeed, when the election itself arrives, each morning's post will bring from his central office up-to-the-minute circulars giving the " Do's " and " Don'ts " apposite to each stage of the campaign—adoption, nomination, polling day, the count. But to a degree that more than offsets this lightening of his labours there has come the increasing burden of organisation. To keep the association going

D

in dull times as well as in lively, to help the candidate or member to " nurse " his constituency, to direct the whist drives or arrange the fête, to edit the association's " news-letter ", to collect the subscriptions, to interest the press, to hire the halls and the best poster sites, to keep the canvass up to scratch, to find harmless outlets for the enthusiasms of his junior branch, to extract professional standards of performance out of volunteer assistants—all this he must learn to do—and to do it in such a way that the organisation so created can be quickly switched to the conduct of a concentrated election campaign which has to be fought on a modest, and often a tight, budget.   It is not surprising that to do this he has become a professional, and that he needs and welcomes all the assistance a central office can give him.   Moreover, with his professionalisation has come some of the detachment of the technician.   Along with his political devotion to his party's cause goes a craftsman's interest in his work, such as will enable him in the heat and fury of a campaign to admire dispassionately the smoothness of his opponent's machine, or to argue disinterestedly the relative merits of the " marked register " and the " card index " systems of canvassing.   Between him and his opposite numbers there will often develop the *camaraderie* of the experts, the respect—and sometimes even the indulgence—which grows up between men who use a common technique although for opposite ends.   To only one can it be given to be the organiser of victory, but in the kingdom of means there can be any number of kings.

In case it should seem to any reader that what has been described above marks a new era in British politics, in which electoral victory is henceforth guaranteed to the side with the better machine, perhaps a final word of caution may be in order. Just as in business advertising will not always sell, so in politics organisation cannot always deliver.   To illustrate this one simple example from the 1950 election will suffice.   In Birmingham, an old Conservative stronghold, the Conservative machine for months, even years, before the election was as I have earlier described it—fully manned, smoothly oiled, adequately fueled. All was done that organisation could contrive.   The result was the recapture of only one of the ten seats which Labour wrenched from Conservatives in 1945.   In Liverpool, on the other hand, for reasons rooted in habits of local politics, Conservative organisation was notably weak: in only one constituency was there a professional agent, and he was fighting a forlorn hope, the Exchange division. In the old Parliament (before redistribution) there were 11 Liverpool seats, and 8 of them were held by Labour. For the 1950 election the number to be contested was reduced to 9. Yet of these 9 the Conservatives carried 5 and left Labour with only 4. The moral is not, of course, that organisation is unimportant. But it would seem to be that organisation is not everything.

CHAPTER III

THE CANDIDATES

ONE THOUSAND EIGHT HUNDRED AND SIXTY-EIGHT candidates
offered themselves to the British electorate in February 1950,*
thus surpassing the previous record of 1929, when 1,730 candidates
fought for 615 seats. The Conservatives put the largest number
into the field, contesting every constituency save Huddersfield
West, Carmarthen, Greenock and Western Isles (in each of these
local support was given to Liberal candidates), while Colonel
Clifton Brown at Hexham stood as the Speaker and not in any party
interest. Labour fought 617 constituencies, abstaining from the
contest in 7 constituencies in Northern Ireland, but fighting every
seat in Great Britain save Hexham. The Liberals put 475
candidates into the field. These were variously distributed.
Every one of the 43 London Borough and of the 55 suburban
constituencies was contested; of the remaining 144 seats in
Southern England, Liberal candidates contested 131. In the
Midlands there was a marked falling off, only 66 candidates
standing out of a possible 94; this was particularly marked in the
West Midlands. In Lancashire about three-quarters of the seats
were contested, and in the West Riding of Yorkshire and the
industrial belt between Tyne and Tees little more than one half.
Liberal combativeness rose in Cheshire, the North and East
Ridings and the Border to almost 100% of the theoretical potential. In Scotland the weakest area was Clydeside, with barely
half of its 27 seats contested by Liberals, the strongest the Highlands and Islands, where 6 of the 8 seats had Liberal candidates.
In Ulster there were no Liberal candidates.

The Communist Party in 1950 for the first time attempted to
fight on a national scale, by putting up 100 candidates in constituencies all over the country (compared with a total of 21 in
1945). The distribution of these candidatures, though no doubt
owing something to the accident of local enterprise, bears for the
most part evidence of careful central direction. Thus in the

* Squadron-Leader E. L. Fleming, who was nominated for Manchester,
Moss Side (Conservative), but died between nomination day and February 23,
is included in this total and in the analysis that follows.

London area, where the heaviest concentration occurred, every borough in which a Labour Minister was standing was also contested by a Communist—Mr. Attlee's alone excepted, and there Mr. H. L. Hutchinson, a " Labour Independent ", may be presumed to have been an acceptable substitute. Elsewhere prominent members of the Ministry or of the Executive of the party had Communist opponents—Sir Stafford Cripps, Mr. Ede, Mr. Harold Wilson, Mr. Marquand, Miss Alice Bacon, Mr. Barnes and Mr. Tom Williams. Figures associated with the direction of foreign or colonial affairs were especially singled out for combat—Mr. Bevin and Mr. McNeil, Mr. Creech-Jones and Mr. Rees-Williams. Of the leading Opposition figures, Mr. Churchill was alone in being so honoured. It would appear as if care was taken to secure Communist candidates in at least one constituency in each big town, as well as in most areas of the country. Naturally the remote rural areas, such as North Wales, the Border and the Highlands, were omitted, though it is also interesting to note that the Durham coalfield had no Communist candidates. Concentration was greatest in the London area, with 36; Lancashire, with 11, and Clydeside, with 9. In all areas marginal seats were naturally preferred ; at least a quarter of the seats contested by Communists could be so regarded, though in only four instances did the Communist vote in fact exceed the majority of the successful Labour candidate.

Of the various minor parties which nominated candidates none contested more than 7 seats (the figure reached by the Welsh Nationalist Party). Treatment of these candidatures is therefore deferred to the chapter on " The Minor Parties and Independents ".

In all, only 126 of the candidates nominated were women. Of these 45 were Liberals, 42 Labour, 28 Conservative, 9 Communist and 2 Independent. Only 21 were successful (compared with 24 out of 87 in 1945), of whom 14 were Labour, 6 Conservative and 1 Liberal.

In respect of age there was an interesting difference of emphasis between the parties. As the following figures show, the Conservative candidates were on the whole appreciably younger than their Labour counterparts, though both parties had their greatest concentration in the 40–49 group. The Liberals, so far as the available evidence goes, were younger than either, while the

Communists could claim that more than half their candidates were under 40.

COMPARATIVE AGES

(expressed as percentages of total nominations)

	20–29	30–39	40–49	50–59	60–69	70 and over	Un-known
Lab. . .	5	17	33	23	16	2	4
Cons. . .	6	25	36	22	7	2	2
Lib. . .	13	29	22	13	4	1	18
Com. . .	5	47	31	7	1	—	9

There were a few interesting regional variations within the parties. Thus the Conservatives who stood in Scotland were appreciably older than those in England and Wales—out of 68 whose ages could be ascertained 35 were over 50—while Ulster holds the record for Conservative longevity, 5 out of its 12 candidates being over 60 years of age. At the other extreme was Wales, where, out of 35 known Conservative candidates, 30 were under 50 and 15 were under 40. The contrast no doubt reflects the difference between seats so safe that incumbency is probably for life and those so hopeless that they attract mainly those who have their spurs to win. A similar, though less marked, contrast exists in the ranks of Labour. Thus in the Scottish and Welsh boroughs, which include some of Labour's firmest strongholds, only 3 candidates were under 40, while 10 were over 60.* In between lay the high plateau of the forties and fifties, which accounted for a total of 25. There was no concentration of youth comparable to that displayed by the Conservatives, but, in the main, Labour candidates who contested rural constituencies were appreciably younger than their urban counterparts.

The educational attainments of candidates proved somewhat more elusive than their ages. This was a topic on which 23 Labour, 47 Conservative, 109 Liberal and 52 Communist candidates were sufficiently secretive to elude our inquiries. In the majority of instances, one suspects, silence on this subject may be taken as indicative of modest attainments—particularly where

---

* This may reflect the high incidence of trade union candidatures. *The Times* pointed out (February 8th, 1950) that the average age for the 140 trade union candidates is 52½: and for the National Union of Mine-workers candidates 58, while the average for all Labour candidates was between 45 and 50.

Labour or Conservative candidates are concerned, for official biographies usually mention anything worthy of record. The silence of the Liberals, whose official biographies are briefer, may be less significant. I doubt if our figure of Liberals educated at universities falls far short of the mark, but what proportion of the 109 unknowns had secondary schooling, and what elementary, remains a mystery. Of the 70 Labour and Conservative, I think a sizeable majority may be said to have had their formal schooling confined to the elementary stage. The same is undoubtedly true of nearly all the 52 Communists.

Apart from these uncertainties, the picture is clear enough. Labour, as might be expected, has the largest number of candidates whose education stopped at the elementary grade—184 (though 97 of these had some form of further part-time education), and although the party as a whole regards the educational attainments of its candidates as a matter for justifiable pride, there are still constituencies where " left school at 12 " is a badge of honour. The comparable known Conservative and Liberal figures are 21 (4 further part-time) and 15 (5 further part-time) respectively.

A further 145 Labour candidates attended secondary schools without going on to universities. About one-third of these did, however, have further technical or vocational training. There were 26 public-school men who did not proceed to a university. In all, 286 Labour candidates passed through the State secondary schools and 108 attended public schools. There were also a further 20 who in one way or another (e.g. abroad) were privately educated. For Conservatives and Liberals this category accounts for 13 and 14 respectively. Of Conservatives, 84 stopped at the secondary stage (14 with further part-time training), and 132 on leaving their public schools. There were in all 172 Conservative secondary-school men, compared with 364 public-school men. Of Liberals, 80 stopped at the secondary stage (13 with further technical training), and 46 after leaving their public schools. The total of Liberal secondary-school men was 200, and of public-school men 133.

255 Labour candidates attended a university in this country or abroad. For Conservatives the figure was 326, for Liberals 213. But these figures might prove misleading unless one allows for various other forms of adult education. The historic importance

of adult education to the Labour movement is brought out in the figures of 16 Labour candidates who make mention of their W.E.A. tuition, 20 who refer to the National Council of Labour Colleges, 32 who mention " evening " or " night school " and 14 who attended Ruskin College, Oxford. Neither the Conservatives nor the Liberals offer anything to parallel this, though this may perhaps be the point at which to mention the 49 Conservatives and 5 Liberals who attended Sandhurst or other military academies. The comparable figure for Labour is 3.

The distinctive role of the public schools in British life may justify a closer examination of their contributions to the hustings. Undoubtedly the most striking feature is the dominance of Eton in the Conservative Party. Including the Speaker, 107 old Etonians stood as Conservative candidates and 79 were returned. In one region—Devon and Somerset—they were particularly predominant. In 18 seats 12 stood and 10 were returned.* Old Etonians who espoused Labour were successful in a similar proportion, but in disproportionate strength ; out of 5 who stood, 4 were elected. There were also 5 Liberals, but only 1 was returned, while amongst the Communists the solitary old Etonian went down with the rest. Of the other leading public schools, Harrow came next, contributing 26 Conservative, 2 Labour and 2 Liberal candidates. Then Winchester—15 Conservative, 5 Labour and 3 Liberal. Westminster—8 Liberal, 7 Conservative and 6 Labour. Rugby—12 Conservative, 3 Labour and 4 Liberal. Haileybury—8 Conservative and 6 Labour. Charterhouse—10 Conservative, 3 Liberal and 1 Labour. In all, of the 364 Conservative public-school men who stood, 223 were successful, of the 108 Labour 61, of the 133 Liberals 5, and of the 5 Communists none. This suggests that in both major parties a public-school education may be a useful stepping-stone to a political career, since, of men so educated, a higher proportion were successful than of the rest of their colleagues.

Whether a would-be candidate is as well advised to invest in a university education as in a public school would appear to depend largely on the party (and university) of his choice.

The distribution of candidates and members between the colleges of a university is in the main of only academic interest,

---

* In the remaining six seats three of the Conservative candidates (all successful) were Harrovians.

UNIVERSITY-EDUCATED CANDIDATES [1]

	Total	Oxford	Cambridge	London
Conservative .	326 (185)	140 (92)	107 (64)	24 (8)
Labour . .	255 (129)	66 (38) [2]	32 (17)	61 (21)
Liberal . .	213 (7)	53 (1)	52 (4)	46 (1)
Communist .	17 (0)	5 (0) [3]	3 (0)	5 (0)
Independent .	21 (0)	3 (0)	2 (0)	3 (0)
	832 (321)	267 (131)	197 (85)	139 (30)

[1] Figures in brackets indicate successful candidates.
[2] These figures include 14 members of Ruskin College, of whom 9 were successful.
[3] Including 1 member of Ruskin College.

but one or two items are worth mentioning. Trinity College, Cambridge, leads, both in candidates and members, with 59 of the first and 34 of the second. Next comes Christ Church, Oxford, with 40 candidates and 29 M.P.s. Only Balliol, with 22 successes out of 36, and New College, with 19 out of 28, are otherwise remarkable. In London University, the role of the London School of Economics is of particular interest, though its electoral successes would appear to be slighter than is sometimes assumed. Of the 22 Labour candidates who numbered themselves amongst its *alumni*, only 4 were returned, of 3 Conservatives only 1, of 12 Liberals none, while the solitary Communist fared no better than his comrades elsewhere.

The occupations of candidates cannot so readily be subjected to reliable and statistically precise analysis as their education. There are several reasons for this. The first is the paucity of information. Often one knows only what the candidate wishes to tell, and what he wishes to tell is closely related to the impression he wishes to make, not on the academic enquirer, but on the average voter. There are times when the information candidates provide to the public closely resembles that vouchsafed by Mr. Dowler to Mr. Pickwick and his colleagues: " that his name was Dowler; that he was going to Bath on pleasure; that he was formerly in the army; that he had now set up in business as a gentleman; that he lived upon the profits ". The second difficulty follows from the obvious fact that people who stand for Parliament are *ex hypothesi* people with a disposition to change jobs; if they were not they would not stand for Parliament. There is something about the political calling which attracts persons with a high degree of occupational mobility. The candidate who " worked as a farm labourer and circus hand . . . and later became a horticulturist and author ", who then was " engaged on secret service work " and " worked in P.I.D." and finally was " employed in the coal industry " is exceptional not so much in the number as in the range of his occupations. What, for purposes of classification, is the " occupation group " of such a candidate ? Again, candidates vary in what one might call their " remoteness " from their occupational roots ; this is particularly true of sitting members. Obviously the label " miner " has one meaning when applied to a candidate on a month's leave from his colliery to stand for Parliament for the first time, and another when applied to an M.P. twenty years distant from the coal-face. So evident is this with certain individuals that, even in this country of amateur practitioners, we have become accustomed to thinking of them exclusively as " politicians ".

To cope with such intractabilities I have adopted certain rule-of-thumb procedures which can claim to be rooted in no more scientific basis than common-sense judgment. I have tried to find the " formative " occupation wherever possible—the occupation most likely to have moulded a man's mind and habits before he went into politics ; generally, though not always, a man's first job. Secondly, I have looked to see what occupation a sitting member keeps by him, so to speak, in Parliament—whether as a supplement to his Parliamentary earnings or, in the event of defeat, as a substitute for them. That this might sometimes result in a duplication of entries has not seemed to me an objection, but the reader of the figures that follow should bear in mind that just as a man may have two jobs, so the total of occupations may often exceed the total of candidates. Lastly, I have made no attempt to construct a " scale of intensity " to show how near or far politicians may be from their pre-parliamentary roots. Instead, in all cases I have tried to ascertain what those roots were, and have left myself only an irreducible minimum of not otherwise classifiable " politicians "—persons whose entire life has been so soaked in politics that no other label would have meaning for them. It will, I think, cause little surprise that the names of Mr. Winston Churchill, Mr. Herbert Morrison and Lady Megan Lloyd George fall into this restricted category.

Closely related to a man's occupation is his economic or professional " interest ". The claims of a full-blooded economic determinism would no doubt require a complete analysis of candidates from this point of view. Not subscribing to such a philosophy, I have not felt obliged to undertake so arduous an operation. There are, none the less, certain historic " interests " in British politics, such as the land, the Church or the trade unions. These are closely, and sometimes inextricably, bound up with certain occupations, but where their supporters are not thereby identifiable and where their importance warrants I have singled them out for separate mention.

One word of warning, however, must be given. The inadequacy of one's information and the necessarily subjective nature of the judgments that must be passed upon it make the margin of error in the figures that follow appreciably larger than in any other section of this enquiry. Thus while every care has been taken to secure accuracy, it is important for the reader to resist the hypnosis of apparent statistical precision, and to remember that the figures are better regarded as indicative of certain tendencies than as embodying quantitative finality. In the flux of politics they indicate only the shoals and the currents; they are not the contour lines of a *terra firma*.

It is natural to ask of a Labour party what percentage of its candidates are drawn from the ranks of the manual workers, and it is no uncommon thing for Labour candidates to stress any such connection which they may have. The number of instances, however, in which a man moves directly from manual work to a parliamentary candidature is not large, and only 92 of the candidates could fairly be described as predominantly manual workers. Within these, skilled workers were overwhelmingly in the majority; only about half a dozen were unskilled. The 37 miners constituted by far the largest group. A long way behind came the engineering workers, 13 strong. The rest were distributed over a variety of occupations in which railway, electrical, steel and printing workers were the most notable.

However, to stop here would be misleading. If one applies the test of the " formative " occupation, one may legitimately add to the figure for manual workers a further figure of at least 91 drawn from the ranks of existing white-collar workers who began at the manual level. Of these the great majority are trade union officials. This would give a total of 183, which, if not precisely accurate, is certainly a more reasonable index of the strength of this group within the party.

The trade union officials, indeed, constitute a kind of overlap or bridge between the manual workers and the lower-paid white-collar workers. In the total of 134 which I obtained for this group of what might as reasonably be called the upper working class as the lower middle class, trade union officials, numbering 86, greatly predominated. Other groups were railway clerks (18) and insurance agents (11).

A small but recognisable category is what might be called the quasi-professional class—the rather lower-paid and imperfectly organised group of skilled salaried workers. 16 of these offered themselves as Labour candidates, including, most notably, 6 social workers.

If one asks how well business is represented, it is probably meaningful to divide the answer into two categories: one for those fairly directly engaged at the profit-making level, and one for those who serve on a salaried basis. For the first the total is 92, but this ranges over a wide diversity of jobs and incomes. A total of 40 company directors could be identified, of shopkeepers a mere 5, of farmers, horticulturists, etc., 24. The managerial revolution has so far no proportionate investment in the ranks of Labour. Of this type of salaried industrialist or business man I could discover at most only 21.

It is the professions which contribute to Labour (as to the other major parties) the highest proportion of candidates. The total figure is 258 (though in 25 of these the professional occupation was subordinate to some other, usually private business). Law looms large. There are 51 candidates qualified to practise at the Bar and 27 solicitors. But the dominant profession is education, which numbers 90 among its full-time adherents, not including at least another 21 who in varying degrees claim to have practised it at some time or another. These 90 are divided as follows: school-teachers 51, adult teachers 15, university teachers 16, educational officials 3, research workers, etc., 5. Perhaps a further 7 might be added under this category to represent those at the receiving end of the educational process, students who stood for Parliament while still at the university. The boundaries of journalism as an occupation are hard to define, since it may engage as much or as little of a man's time as he chooses to devote to it, but 32 candidates appeared to have made it their main occupation, and at least 8 a subsidiary one. There were 16 engineers and industrial chemists, 13 persons engaged in one branch or other of medicine, 7 ministers of religion, 6 chartered accountants and 6 members of the regular army or navy (apart from a further two young men who had gone straight out of the forces into Parliament in 1945). I do not know if housewifery is a profession, but there were 5 women candidates who defied classification under any other heading.

Since Parliament is a talking-shop, it seemed to me relevant to inquire how far would-be Parliamentarians had prepared themselves for it by training in any one of the occupations concerned with the arts of persuasion or publicity. This is a group which cuts across the previous categories; it obviously should include journalists, and some would say teachers as well; including the first, but excluding the second, I arrived at a figure of 61, made up as follows :

Journalists	32
Paid Party officials	10 *
Advertising executives	4
Publicity and Public Relations Officials .	3
Film producer	1
Film actor	1
Publisher	1
Playwright	1
Politician	1
Authors	2
Social Survey workers	3
Auctioneer	1
Lecturer	1

There was another " cross category " which was interesting in the light of one of the issues of the campaign—namely, that of persons occupied in insurance. There were 3 insurance brokers, 9 insurance agents, and 1 indefinable " insurance official ", which gives a total of 13. There were at least 9 candidates who had been public servants, of either a central or a local authority (excluding, of course, those who had merely a war-time experience

* This includes 3 ex-agents.

as temporary civil servants). There were 3 candidates who were on the boards of public corporations. Finally, there were 3 whose occupations were so obscure or so vague as to elude analysis.

Of the 621 Conservative candidates, 7 could properly be described as manual workers. They included 2 miners, 1 railway-man, 1 steel-worker and 3 building employees. At the non-manual upper-working or lower-middle-class level, there was a similarly modest total, 4. In the " quasi-professional " group there were 8, amongst whom " organising secretaries " and " welfare officers " were predominant. As might be expected, business and industry, in one form or another, bulked large. 168 candidates had as their major occupation the direction or control of business firms, either as proprietors or as co-proprietors, in the form of being company directors. In one form or another they might be said to be at the employing end of a private, profit-making concern. A further 39 had this as a subsidiary occupation (mainly in the form of a company directorship). It would also appear as if in the majority of these 207 instances the business unit which the candidate directed was appreciably larger than those with which similar Labour candidates were associated. At the level of what one might call " business finance " there were 12 bankers, 7 stock-brokers, 6 insurance brokers and 5 underwriters, making a further total of 25. At the other extreme of *entrepreneur*-ship there were 4 shopkeepers, 2 builders and 6 of what one might call " sub-managerial business employees ". In what might be called the " agricultural industry " there is always the difficulty of dis-tinguishing between those who make their land keep them and those who keep their land, the distinction which popular parlance preserves in the terms " farmer " and " gentleman farmer ". So far as could be ascertained, there were, however, 12 candidates who had in farming their major occupation, and a further 16 whose acres, though not their major concern, were yet sufficiently seriously farmed by them to justify their secondary occupation being regarded as " farming ". Finally, allied to business is the salaried, managerial group, of whom there are 30.

However, despite the high incidence of business occupations, it is the professions which account for the majority of Conserva-tive, as of Labour, candidates. They total 308. The law accounts for 121, including 84 barristers and 30 solicitors. Next come the armed services, notably high : 46 from the army, 14 from the navy, and 2 from the R.A.F. (of whom 1 was a national serviceman who had had no other previous employment). Journalism, though not as large as in the Labour Party, was sizeable, numbering 27 on the writing or editorial side, as apart from those candidates who would be more appropriately listed on the proprietorial or managerial side. Education was lower than for Labour ; 18, made up of 12 school-teachers, 4 university teachers, 1 adult education teacher and 5 students. Engineers and industrial chemists number 22, slightly more than for Labour, while architects and surveyors total 13 (against a solitary Labour 1). Doctors and chartered accountants were represented by 11 candidates each. The only other considerable group consisted of ex-members of one branch or another of the public service ; there were 17 of these, divided fairly evenly between the Home Civil, the Diplomatic and the Colonial Services. There was also a sometime international civil servant, in the person of an UNRRA official. Clergymen numbered 2, and the arts were represented by an actor and a sculptress (not to mention Mr. Churchill, painter and historian).

When all other possibilities had been considered and found wanting, there remained a few groups of " irreducibles "— categories representative at least as much of the author's ignorance as of the candidates' occupation. There were, in the first place, the 7 " housewives ". Then there were the 39 candidates whom it was not possible to allocate to any category more meaningful than " private means ". No doubt the denomination " gentleman " would have had a certain appropriateness here, were it not that 5 such candidates were women. Moreover, the term " private means " has certainly lost something of its pristine significance in an age of supertax. Nevertheless, perhaps the banner and its 39 bearers may serve as not unjustifiable reminders of the party's historic associations with rank and wealth. Their numbers might even be swollen, on some computations, by adding to them a further 21 for whom I have in fact reserved the label of " land-owners ", on the basis of their having no visible means of support other than that derived from the ownership of land. Alternatively, many of the 39 might, with fuller information, well turn out to derive their income predominantly from landed property.

Perhaps only the Inland Revenue officials are in a position to supply definitive totals.

The " cross-groups " which were investigated for Labour all have their Conservative counterparts. Conservative candidates engaged, extra-parliamentarily, in the " persuasive " or " publishing " trades total 73, excluding teachers and clergymen. The principal components are as follows :

Journalists	27
Directors of newspaper companies . . .	5
Newspaper executives	2
Directors of other companies concerned with printing, publishing, etc.	7
Directors of advertising companies . . .	4
Advertising executives	3
Public Relations officer	1
Paid party officials	19 [1]

Insurance workers of every kind totalled 19, a figure not significantly different from Labour's, though drawn mainly from executive levels and containing no one at the agent level. Land, at any rate measured by occupational addiction, does not give as high a figure as might be expected. Landowners (as above), 21, and farmers (as above), 28, give a total of 49. But no doubt if one were to include in this category every candidate " with a stake in the country ", whether mercenary or recreational, the figure could be considerably inflated.

The Liberal headquarters included in their " Who's Who " of candidates an analysis of their occupations. Unfortunately, though helpful, it is neither complete nor at all points adequate, and the figures which follow are the result of an attempt to push enquiry one stage farther, on the same basis as has been employed for Labour and Conservatives.

Into the category of manual workers (almost all skilled artisans) there can be put 13 Liberal candidates ; no particular trade predominates, and they are not concentrated in any particular region of the country.[2] At the white-collar, lower-middle-class

---

[1] This includes 1 ex-agent.

[2] It is probable, if full information were available, that this figure could be doubled by adding candidates who, beginning as manual workers, have since climbed into the upper ranks of business on industry.

level there is a total of 16, divided for the most part between commercial travellers and clerical workers, though it is interesting to note the presence of one trade union organiser. The " quasi-professional " group is 27 strong, ranging from an " average adjuster " to a test pilot. Business is a considerable category, numbering in all 188. Of persons owning their own small businesses, small retailers, etc. (a category hardly worthy of separate mention amongst Conservatives or Labour), there can be listed 23. At the managerial, salaried level there are 39—also a rather higher figure than for the other two parties. At the lower wage-earning level of business employment there appeared to be 12. In estimating the numbers of candidates who were " business men " at the employing, ownership level, some difficulties arose from the all-too-vague terms in which a good many individuals described themselves. I did, however, identify 114 candidates as being in this group, of whom 85 could be described as company directors. There were also 5 stockbrokers and 3 insurance brokers. It should, however, be pointed out that the companies concerned were in most instances of modest size, what in the U.S.A. would be called " small business ". Moreover, the emphasis throughout the business group fell on the export, transport or retail trades, often in the form of family concerns or private companies run by their owners. Frequently a candidate emphasises his Samuel Smiles experience in having risen to his present business eminence by working up from humble beginnings, and many company directors stress the fact that they practice the co-partnership they preach.

Once again it is the professions which form the largest single group. Indeed, considering that the total number of Liberal candidates was only 475, the percentage represented by the 252 professional candidates is the highest for any party. The law retains its pre-eminence, with 71, including 49 barristers and 21 solicitors, but it is almost equalled by education, which, swollen by an unusually large number of students (16), totals 68. (Its other components are school-teachers 31, adult education workers 13, and university teachers 8.) Next come the 26 engineers and industrial chemists, and after them the unusually high figure of 22 chartered accountants, the inheritors perhaps of the Gladstonian tradition of scrupulous public and private book-keeping. The armed forces number 16 (army 12, navy 3, and 1 R.A.F.

E

national serviceman). Public servants total 14, of whom 7 are drawn from the Home Civil Service and 4 from the service of local authorities. There are 14 journalists, 12 architects and surveyors, 7 doctors and 2 clergymen.

Liberal " housewives " numbered 6, and " private means " accounted for 4 not otherwise definable candidates. Farming was represented by 15 who made it their main occupation and 11 who made it a subsidiary. There were 2 candidates whose holdings were sufficiently elusive to warrant the denomination " landowners ". Thus the total figure for " land " is 28. There were 2 candidates whose occupations eluded inquiry.

To the " publicity " cross-grouping the Liberals contributed in proportion to their numbers, if not quite in the same strength as the other two parties. The total of 40 includes the 14 journalists already mentioned, 6 public-relations officers, 4 broadcasting officials (apparently a Liberalising occupation), 4 book publishers, 2 advertising executives and 3 paid party officials. Finally, the insurance industry was represented by 13 candidates, ranging from an agent at one end to 3 brokers at the other.

Since a man's family rivals his job as a moulding influence on his public behaviour, it is as interesting to inquire into the family background of candidates as into their occupation. Unfortunately, it is much less feasible. Information is sparse and, when obtained, not always to be relied upon. As might be expected, the Conservatives, as the party historically associated with the hereditary principle, are the most forthcoming on this theme and phrases such as " tradition of parliamentary service " or " family has provided M.P.'s since the reign of Henry VII " are not uncommon in candidates' biographies. Even so, it is only a small percentage even of Conservative candidates about whom adequate information of this order is available. Consequently what follows must be treated as having only a very limited applicability.

How far is politics a hereditary calling in modern Britain? 63 Conservatives claim that one or more ancestors in the direct line were or are Members of Parliament, while, if peers are regarded as in all cases active legislators, the total is increased by another 26. (There are in all 44 Conservative candidates with hereditary connections with the Peerage, and a further 34 with connections by marriage.)* Of Labour candidates, 19 claimed descent from past or present Members of Parliament (3 from Liberal ones, 2 from Conservatives), while at least 4 were the offspring of peers. One Labour candidate among these had family connections with both Houses. The Liberal total was 17 for the House of Commons and 7 for the House of Lords, including an overlap of 3.

If one adds to the above figures all those candidates who made mention of their family's political activities, even when manifested outside the national legislature, the totals are as follows. For Conservatives 105 (including 9 with Liberal forebears and 4 with Labour). For Labour 48 (including 6 from Conservative stock and 4 from Liberal). For Liberal 45 (including 3 from Conservative and 4 from Labour).

Politics apart, the information on family backgrounds is too slight to warrant general conclusions, and only a few points of interest deserve mention. Amongst Conservatives the service connection is almost as strong hereditarily as occupationally. The parents of 32 candidates were army officers and 6 were naval officers. At the other extreme there is an occasional disposition to stress working-class parentage when available. There are 17 such instances, including 7 mining fathers and 3 described simply as " working men ". Labour, of course, has a large number of working-class parents, but the only distinctive group here which appears to confer a coveted degree of political virtue upon its offspring are the miners; 29 candidates claim to be of mining stock. In all parties the manse, the vicarage or the bishop's palace appears to be a fairly advantageous nursery for politics. 14 Conservatives have clerical parentage, 13 Liberals and 13 Labour.

The religious affiliations of politicians are not nearly as significant in British public life as they used to be or as they still remain in countries with politico-religious parties. Consequently it is no occasion for surprise that for the great majority of candidates no information on this topic is publicly available. Indeed, it is generally true to say that the chances of a candidate making public mention of his religious affiliation rise in proportion as his Church deviates from the Establishment; it is usually the members of the numerically minor sects who are consequently

---

* It is, incidentally, interesting to note that, of these 78, 54 were elected.

most easily identifiable. With this in mind, the figures that follow can be better understood. Roman Catholics are fairly evenly distributed over each party—26 amongst Conservatives, 20 amongst Labour, 11 amongst Liberals. What might be called " self-identified " members of the Church of England are to be found in the proportions of 14 amongst Conservatives, 9 in Labour and 6 amongst Liberals. The old " Lib-Lab " connections of Nonconformity seem still in evidence in the figures of 61 for Labour, 59 for Liberals and only 6 for Conservatives. The dominant denominations in each case are the Methodists (Liberals 36, Labour 20 and Conservatives 2) and the Quakers (Labour 13 and Liberal 5). There were some interesting regional concentrations observable amongst the Methodists. Out of their 58 candidates of all parties, 23 stood in Lancashire or Yorkshire and 9 in the West Country.

British election law, unlike American, knows nothing of a residence qualification. But what of British practice? The following figures show that while carpet-bagging is not at all uncommon (and silence by candidates on this point is usually presumptive evidence of carpet-bagging), residence either in, or adjacent to, the constituency is still the more normal practice.

LOCAL RESIDENCE

	Labour	Conservative	Liberal
Yes	269	288	257
Adjacent	62	67	55
No	118 (17) *	139 (19) *	148 (16) *
	448	494	460

* Figures in brackets indicate those candidates in " No " category who have connections in constituency.

Local government experience, similarly, is regarded as a good jumping-off place for Westminster, particularly in the Labour Party. Available figures show 294 Labour candidates who have held local government office, beside a further 61 who sought election without success. For Conservatives the comparable figures are 158 and 6 respectively. For Liberals 65 and 22. This is more common in borough than county candidatures, and is particularly conspicuous in the London Boroughs, where 32 of the 43 Labour candidates were councillors (including 7 mayors or ex-mayors) and 15 of the 43 Conservatives (including 1 mayor).

Even more valuable than previous local government experience is, of course, previous parliamentary (and with it, necessarily, electoral) experience. Here, too, Labour easily overtops Conservatives and Liberals.

	Labour	Conser-vative	Liberal
Candidates who have stood before .	419	327	101
Candidates who have been successful at least once before	339	242	18
Candidates who have been successful only once before	234	96	9
Candidates who have been successful only twice before	59	87	2
Candidates who have been successful only three times before . . .	16	26	—
Candidates who have been successful four or more times before . .	30	33	7

Pursued beyond this point the figures cease to be significant, but they reflect thus far pretty accurately the advantages of continuity which Labour derives from its " landslide " victory in 1945, the disadvantage (in terms of length of parliamentary experience) which is the consequence of its late emergence as a major party, and finally the liability imposed on the Liberals by the fact that less than a quarter of their candidates had any previous experience of the hustings and only 18 any experience of the inside of the House of Commons.

In 1945 the war service of the candidates was not unnaturally a good deal to the fore. This time it was less prominently advertised, and the figures that follow do not necessarily imply that it was always thrust before the elector's attention. The record for candidates of the three main parties is as follows :

	Conser-vative	Labour	Liberal
Candidates with a service record .	447	249	273
Candidates who fought only in World War I	148	94	60
Candidates who fought only in World War II	357	172	229
Candidates who fought in both wars .	58	17	16

The relatively low Labour figure reflects, no doubt, both the greater average age of the candidates and the high incidence of reserved occupations in labour and industry. It does not include the Scottish candidate who claims to be the only Briton who has served in the Red Army, nor any candidates whose military experiences were confined to the International Brigade.

Finally, there are two types of vital statistics which positively invite compilation, so frequently is allusion made to them by candidates in print or on the platform. I refer to the numbers of candidates who are married and the number who have children. The figures which follow err, if anything, on the side of understatement, at least in respect of Conservatives and Liberals :

	Labour	Conservatives	Liberals
Married	515	440	215
With Children	400	300	165

The markedly lower figure for Liberals presumably reflects the higher percentage of very young candidates in that party.

That concludes the particulars with respect to which comparison between the three major parties can usefully be made, but there remain a few points of distinctive interest in relation to some of the Labour Party candidacies. The Labour Party, unique amongst British parties in being what its constitution describes as " federal ", includes amongst its candidates a number sponsored by trade unions, and a special group of Co-operative Party members who stand as joint " Labour and Co-operative " candidates. In 1950 there were 140 of the first and 36 of the second. The importance to the Labour Party of the trade union and Co-operative movements warrants a closer examination of these candidatures in comparison with the rest. The table below sets out the essential particulars in statistical form :

Bracketed figures show number won in 1945 but lost in 1950.

Co-operative Party includes 3 candidates of the Royal Arsenal Co-operative Society (unique amongst Co-operative Societies in being directly affiliated to the Labour Party).

15 of the 36 Co-operative Party candidates were in the London area. 23 were south of a line from the Wash to the Severn.

23 of the 36 National Union of Mine-workers candidates secured majorities of 20,000. 8 more had majorities of 15,000–20,000.

The only National Union of Mine-workers majorities of less than 10,000 were 8,564 in Kirkcaldy, 7,188 in Midlothian, and 6,110 in Bothwell.

SPONSORSHIP OF LABOUR CANDIDATES

Sponsorship	No.	Result Won	Result Lost	Median %of Vote		
All	617	315	298	45·8		
Constituency Labour Party	441	186	255	42·2		
Co-operative Party . .	36	19	17 (9)	47·4		
National Union of Mine-workers . . .	37	37	—	73·0		56·0 All Union Candidates
Transport & General Workers Union . .	19	16	3 (1)	54·2	50·4 All Union Candidates except N.U.M.	
National Union of Railway-men	12	10	2	50·7		
National Union of General & Municipal Workers .	10	6	4 (3)	46·9		
Amalgamated Engineering Union	10	8	2 (1)	52·2		
Railway Clerks Association	11	7	4 (3)	48·3		
Union of Shop, Distributive & Allied Workers .	9	8	1 (1)	63·0		
Union of Textile Factory Workers Association .	3	2	1			
Amalgamated Society of Wood Workers .	3	3	—			
Electrical Trades Union .	2	1	1 (1)			
National Union of Boot & Shoe Operatives . .	2	1	1 (1)			
Amalgamated Society of Locomotive Engineers & Firemen . . .	2	2	—			
National Union of Agricul-tural Workers .	2	1	1			
Typographical Association .	2	1	1			
British Iron, Steel & Kin-dred Trades Association .	2	2	—			
Union of Post Office Workers	3	1	2 (2)			
Association of Engineering & Shipbuilding Draughts-men	2	—	2	47·5		
Clerical & Administrative Workers' Union . .	2	1	1 (1)			
National Union of Seamen .	1	—	1 (1)			
National Society of Opera-tive Printers & Assistants	1	1	—			
National Union of Public Employees . .	1	1	—			
Scottish Bakers Union .	1	—	1			
Amalgamated Union of Building Trades Workers of Great Britain & Ireland	1	—	1			
Amalgamated Union of Foundry Workers . .	1	—	1			
National Amalgamated Union of Life Assurance Workers . . .	1	1	—			
(Total of all smaller Unions	32	18	14 (6))			

See notes on facing page.

The figures amply confirm the popular impression about the greater " security " of trade-union-held seats in general, and the notable impregnability of candidatures sponsored by the National Union of Mine-workers. While the figure of 111 successful candidates out of 140 aspirants marks a falling off, absolutely and proportionately, from the 120-out-of-125 figure of 1945, it compares favourably with the fate of the constituency party candidatures, and leaves the union members proportionately stronger on the Labour benches in the new House of Commons. In the 1945 Parliament they represented 30% of the whole Labour Party membership. In 1950 they represented slightly more than 35%. By contrast Co-operative Party candidatures were relatively unsuccessful and sustained an approximately even share of the casualties of battle.

One other Labour organisation, the Fabian Society, true to its tradition of permeation (not to mention the modesty of its finances), does not itself sponsor candidates, but relies upon its leaven working its way throughout the party lump. Politically, however, membership of the Society might appear to be something of a doubtful asset, since of the 146 candidates who so described themselves only 57 were successful.

From most of the foregoing comparisons the Communist Party candidates have been omitted because the Party's distinctive character places it in a peculiar, not to say unique, category, and entitles it to treatment on its own. The information on the education of the 100 Communist candidates is, as I have indicated, sparse. Set out in tabular form it is as follows :

> 52 no information.
> 21 elementary schooling only.
> 3 elementary + other part-time education.*
> 4 secondary.
> 4 secondary + some form of adult education.
> 11 secondary and university.
> 5 public school and university.

Occupationally the party's candidates were notable for the high incidence of manual workers and full-time party workers. On the basis of the information in the official biographies (which may be

* Including 1 Ruskin student.

presumed, for publicity purposes, not to have under-emphasised such connections), between 45 and 52 of the candidates may be said to have been manual workers, while to these should probably be added, as in the Labour Party, 3 who had been more directly occupied as trade union officials. Of this total about half were engineering or factory workers. Miners numbered perhaps 6 and seamen 5. At the white-collar level there were 3 shop assistants and 2 clerical workers. The *petite bourgeoisie* was thus, perhaps understandably, poorly represented, unless one includes in this category the full-time party workers. These were an elusive group to pin down to a precise total owing to an occasional vagueness in the available published material, but they numbered at least 20, and perhaps as many as 30. Mr. Gallacher, the party's parliamentary septuagenarian, seemed reasonably entitled to distinctive denomination as " Politician ". The professional group totalled 22, of whom school-teachers (11) were the most numerous, journalists (6) came next and engineers and industrial scientists numbered 5. There was one doctor and one statistician. The land was represented by one candidate, a farmer or landowner.

In line with the class appeal of the party, much emphasis was laid on the working-class background of these candidates. Not many equalled the remarkable performance of the candidate for Birkenhead, who " was literally born in the Labour Movement ", but allusions to family and hereditary connections were common— e.g. " his family associations go back to the Chartist and early Trade Union struggles in the area, and since his schooldays he has been active in the Labour Movement ". Of the 21 candidates whose parentage could be established, 18 could claim that their fathers were manual workers. Of the remaining 3, 1 was a solicitor, 1 a don and 1 a peer.

Trade union membership was apparently the rule, wherever possible, the Amalgamated Engineering Union naturally claiming the largest number of adherents. There were 18 candidates who were, or had been, shop stewards. There were a good many case histories of conversion to Communism from some rival, or less dogmatic faith—e.g. " in 1940 he resigned from the Labour Party because of lies being told about Russia, and joined the Communist Party "—but unfortunately these are not susceptible of statistical analysis. 27 candidates were, however, previously members of the Labour Party, 4 of the I.L.P. and one of the Liberal Party.   In the remaining cases the date of admittance to the Communist Party was often given without indication of previous allegiance.

In accordance with the party's general line, there was a good deal of emphasis on local residence and local connections or activities.   Of the 81 candidates for whom this information was available, 59 were local residents, 18 lived near their constituency and only 4 were from a distance.   These figures should be read in the light of the presumption that the silence of the remaining 19 is equivalent to non-residence and that " London " for this purpose is treated as one locality (there were 19 Communist candidates in the London Boroughs).   Even so, the percentage of local residents is relatively high.   36 had contested local government elections, 13 with success.   14 had previously stood for Parliament, only 2 with success.

The majority (63) were married, and 51 were the fathers (or mothers) of families.   33 made mention of having travelled overseas, usually to the U.S.S.R. or Spain.   4 candidates have served gaol sentences and several have been expelled from their unions. There is a considerable record of candidates' war service—7 in World War I and a further 37 in World War II.   Finally, 9 candidates fought in the International Brigade in Spain.

Consideration of this analysis of candidates prompts two reflections.   The first is the extent to which each major party, in varying degrees and, of course, with its own variations of emphasis, presents itself to the electorate as offering a cross section of the population.   None can claim a monopoly of representativeness ; none apparently wishes to pose as the exclusive vehicle of one group.   The second is that, taking the three major parties together, they jointly present (even without Communist or Independent supplementation) a range of choice which covers pretty well every occupation, every interest and each estate.   Only those who hold the mistaken view that Parliament ought to be a microcosm of the nation can cavil at the natural predominance of the professional, administrative and " talking " classes.   And even within the bounds set by that predominance there is considerable opportunity, for those who wish to avail themselves of it, to elect to Westminster the spokesmen for almost every other group.

CHAPTER IV

THE NATIONAL CAMPAIGN:
PRELIMINARY MANŒUVRES

WHEN does an election begin? This question, always a poser for the electoral historian, presents itself with peculiar force in relation to the general election of 1950. The view was often advanced, before and after the events of February, that " people had already made up their minds " or that " the election was settled before the campaign began ", a judgment which presupposed that the actions and propaganda of the Government and the Opposition over an unspecified period between 1945 and 1950 had really determined the outcome on February 23rd before ever Parliament had been dissolved or the orators had taken to the hustings. Owing something to this thesis, but distinct from it, was the " concealed major premise " of Mr. Herbert Morrison's warning of November 26th—the reminder that, for purposes of the law, election expenditure might well be judged to commence well in advance of the dissolution of Parliament. The premise behind his semi-political, semi-legal pronouncement was that some, at least, of the Opposition's supporters had already begun their electioneering, and that the effects of it were already beginning to be discernible on the electorate.

Certainly few British general elections—none, indeed, since the passage of the 1911 Parliament Act—have cast their shadows so long before. The immunity from a snap defeat, conferred by the Government's large majority, and the internal solidarity which the Labour Party succeeded in preserving were a public guarantee that, barring some quite unforeseen event, the Government could run out the whole of its legal five-year span. The only justification for a surrender of power and an earlier appeal to the country appeared to be the tactical advantages that might accrue from skilful timing of the dissolution. Consequently at least as early as 1948 the British public began to develop the habit, normally regarded as an infirmity associated with the transatlantic system of quadrennial presidential tourneys, of looking forward to 1950 as a *terminus post quem non*. To this they even added speculations, of an ever-mounting intensity, on the prospects of a dissolution before that date.

Thus already in 1948 the annual conferences of the parties were suffused by an awareness of the electoral struggle that lay ahead. The Liberals, meeting in April, took the far-reaching decision to fight on a broad front and to put up a full quota of candidates. The Labour Party Conference, meeting in May, gave a good deal of its time to discussing problems of policy and organisation arising out of the Executive's preparation for what Mr. Morrison described as " the greatest fight of our lives ". Finally the Conservatives, at their annual Conference in October, devoted the bulk of their six sessions to a consideration of the finance, organisation, propaganda and policy which they would require to frustrate their opponents' endeavours.

As 1949 unrolled, the Labour Party's plans matured. Towards the end of February a special conference of the party was held at Shanklin, Isle of Wight, consisting of members of the National Executive and a number of Ministers of the Government. This " house party ", which met in highly publicised secrecy, devoted itself to the preparation of a draft statement of Labour policy such as had been promised by Mr. Morrison in his address to the Labour Party Conference the previous May. The product of these deliberations was generally thought to represent a victory for those elements within the party which favoured an immediate policy of consolidation rather than an aggressive programme of further nationalisation. On March 23rd, in the form of *Labour Believes in Britain*, it was issued to the constituency parties, for their consideration before the Annual Conference of the party due to meet in June. On April 11th it was released to the press. The most notable features of the proposals were the nationalisation of industrial assurance, the cement industry, sugar-refining and manufacturing, the machinery for meat distribution and water supplies. There were proposals couched in somewhat vaguer terms for " examining " the chemical industry and setting up a development council for shipping. For the rest, the most distinctive feature of the pamphlet was its acceptance of a continuing role for private enterprise, though envisaging the need of " competitive public enterprise " to keep it up to maximum efficiency.

The nationalisation proposals promoted, as might be expected, immediate protests from the interests affected, who denied the allegations of inefficiency or monopoly, or both, brought against them in the manifesto.

At the Labour Party Conference at Blackpool in the first week of June, *Labour Believes in Britain* was recommended to the delegates by Mr. Herbert Morrison with the assurance that their views would be fully considered when in due course another document more of the size and nature of *Let Us Face The Future* was prepared for the next election. He admitted that agreement with the Co-operative Movement had not been reached on all matters, but implied that further consultation would iron out remaining differences. In the course of a two-day debate only relatively minor objections to the programme were registered, some by a C.W.S. director who criticised the industrial assurance proposals, and although there were no votes taken and many important proposals were not debated, there could be little dispute that the programme was acceptable to the overwhelming majority of the delegates. The Conference was, indeed, dominated by its awareness of the election ahead, willing to close its ranks in the interests of victory, and prepared to give its leaders generous elbow-room for tactical manœuvre.

These mounting signs of Labour preparedness increased the general expectation that an election was likely in the autumn, and Conservatives who contemplated their success in the Borough Council elections of May 13th looked forward with a good deal of expectancy to such an event. Meanwhile the publicity attracted by *Labour Believes in Britain* provoked an intensified demand for a Conservative retort, and a lively controversy broke out in the columns of *The Times* and elsewhere on the desirability or otherwise of the issuance of a comparable statement of Conservative intentions. On March 18th, at the annual meeting of the Central Council of the National Union, Mr. R. A. Butler, replying to criticisms of a lack of information about policy, said that a " restatement " would be published soon, possibly in the early summer. Finally, on July 23rd, at an open air rally of some 40,000 people at Wolverhampton, Mr. Churchill delivered a long-awaited pronouncement on Conservative intentions. This was designed to coincide with the issue of *The Right Road for Britain*, a draft policy statement representing a Conservative answer to the Labour Party's earlier pamphlet. The aspect of the Conservative document which struck most readers without strong partisan leanings was the overlap between it and its Labour forerunner, even if one did not accept the *Manchester Guardian's* description of it as " Tory Socialism ".   This overlap was most marked in the section in which it welcomed the Welfare State, endorsed full employment and admitted even the possible necessity of retaining temporarily such controls as rationing and price regulation.   Even its rejection of nationalisation was confined to decentralising existing public corporations and preventing further invasions of the " private sector ".   The statement was most vulnerable in its efforts to combine higher social benefits with reduced public expenditure.   To Mr. Attlee, reviewing it at a speech in Durham on the day of its appearance, this made it " one of the most dishonest documents " that he had ever read. Elsewhere it produced a demand for a more specific Conservative remedy for the economic crisis which, in Mr. Churchill's own words, was " rapidly approaching ".

With the publication of these rival battle cries, the ideological rearmament of the principal contestants was for most practical purposes complete, and from now on it was recognised that any further refinements of policy would depend upon the exact circumstances surrounding the dissolution.   However, expectations that this would occur in the autumn received a rebuff when the House of Lords persisted in its determination not to pass the Steel Bill save with its own amendment postponing the date of the Bill's coming into operation until October 1st, 1950—well after the latest possible date for an appeal to the country.   The Government would have none of this, and re-introduced the Parliament Act, which had been specially devised to cope with this contingency.   Since the Parliament Act itself could not possibly become law before December 11th, this was taken as a sure indication that the Government had abandoned all idea of an autumn election, and on this note Parliament adjourned for the summer.

The sudden onset of Devaluation on September 18th injected a new element into the situation, although when the parties had recovered from the initial shock they were alike in agreeing that it left their economic remedies as valid as before, only more urgent and imperative.   The atmosphere of electioneering pervaded the Devaluation debates ; Mr. Churchill began his attack on the Government by virtually throwing down the gauntlet : " It is high time for another Parliament . . . and an appeal to the

ELECTION ENQUIRIES

By arrangement with the "Evening Standard"

[To face p. 69.

nation is due and overdue ". On September 30th this challenge was unexpectedly answered from what appeared to be an influential and semi-official quarter. The *Tribune*, a weekly journal of opinion, devoted its main editorial article to the theme " Let's Have an Election Now ", arguing, in dogmatic terms, the advantages of an immediate appeal to the country and the dangers of procrastination. The appearance of such a demand in a journal part-edited by Mr. Michael Foot, a member of the National Executive of the Labour Party, and part-controlled by Miss Jennie Lee, wife of Mr. Aneurin Bevan, lent colour to the surmise that there was a group associated with the Minister of Health who favoured a forward policy. For the next fortnight controversy and speculation raged fiercely. Almost every organ of opinion, save those explicitly devoted to the Government's point of view, advocated an early appeal to the country. The *Economist* said, " The sooner the General Election is held, the better ". The *Manchester Guardian*, which initially suspended judgment, was won round by October 10th to the desirability of an immediate dissolution, and even *The Times* was soon saying " frankly " that " if Ministers cannot make up their minds now on what must be done, the electors should be asked to choose for themselves as soon as possible ". On October 9th, Mr. Bevan delivered a speech at Byker-on-Tyne of which one sentence, " In a very short time, on a date I don't propose to mention, the country will be asked to give its verdict on what has been done ", provided the headlines for the following morning's London newspapers. On one front, however, there was silence—a silence which most political commentators thought to be significant. Since before Devaluation, Mr. Ernest Bevin had been absent in the United States and Canada, remote in place and spirit from the domestic controversies of his colleagues, and it was not until October 12th that he returned to the United Kingdom. On the following day a Cabinet meeting was held, and the same evening a statement was issued from No. 10 in the following terms :

> " Having regard to the disturbing effects on trade and industry and on the national effort by the continuance of speculation as to an early General Election, the Prime Minister thinks it right to inform the country of his decision not to advise his Majesty to dissolve Parliament this year."

Disappointment at this postponement was widespread, and probably few of the advocates of an immediate election were converted from their previous point of view. Nevertheless, it was felt to be a good thing that an end had been put to uncertainty, and there were many exhortations to politicians to put their electioneering thoughts on one side and buckle down to the common task of making the most of the breathing space provided by Devaluation. At the Conservative Party Conference which was meeting at Earl's Court the Prime Minister's statement was received with a somewhat more partisan scepticism. " There has undoubtedly been disturbance of trade and industry," said Mr. Churchill. " But whose fault is that ? It is the fault of one man, the Prime Minister, Mr. Attlee, who could, at any time in the last month by a nod or a gesture, have dispersed the rumours that he intended to spring a snap election."

The Conference itself was universally regarded, by observers and participants, as the last assembling of the Conservative Party before it joined battle on the hustings. Opening when expectation of an early election was at its peak, its deliberations had about them all the fervour of an eve-of-battle rally, and although the Prime Minister's statement, coming on the penultimate day of the Conference, punctured something of its " zero hour " expectancy, Mr. Churchill sent the delegates away with scorn for the " twittering calculations " of a government afraid to appeal to the country, and a warning to live the next few weeks " on the alert, ready for any blow that may be struck ". To the demand, frequently made from the floor, that the Conference should specify what the Conservative election programme would be, the leaders returned somewhat dusty answers. Mr. Eden firmly but politely refused : until the Opposition had access to the secrets of Government they could not say what their plans would be. Mr. R. A. Butler, moving the acceptance of *The Right Road for Britain* (carried with only eight dissentients), insisted that the issuance of a " vigorous and detailed election programme " must wait until the Government were willing to face the country. Mr. Churchill in his closing speech (headlined by the *Daily Herald*, " Give Me Blank Cheque ", " Still No Tory Policy ") referred to *The Right Road for Britain* as " this little book " setting out " in much detail the mood and temper " of Toryism, but contended that his party, while in opposition, had " neither the power nor the responsibility to decide the policy and shape the fortunes of the state ".

If it had been supposed that the effect of the Prime Minister's statement would really be to put an end either to electioneering or to speculation about the date of dissolution, the supposition was soon falsified. Hardly had October run its course before the political correspondents and the public men of all parties and of none were devoting their space and ingenuity to considerations of the likely date for the postponed event. On November 2nd, Lord Calverley, a Labour peer, attracted some notoriety by forecasting the date of July 6th. On November 12th the Liberal Party, " owing to the possibility of an early election ", postponed their Annual Assembly until after the general election and called a " special emergency meeting " for January 27th and 28th. Then on November 14th the compromise settlement of the dispute between Lords and Commons over the Parliament Act and the Iron and Steel Bill was announced, a settlement clearly designed to free the Government's hands for an election as early in 1950 as they might desire. With this out of the way, the real work of the session was concluded and the flood-gates of speculation were open once more. Mr. Churchill on November 16th appealed to the Prime Minister to " end uncertainty ". The *Manchester Guardian* of the same date thought it " a good thing " to have an early election.

Meanwhile debate had been warming up in another quarter. The interests threatened with nationalisation had been vigorously organising their defence. Iron and Steel, of course, had been fighting for some time, and the public had long been accustomed to read, on the hoardings and in the advertisement columns of the newspapers, figures and slogans designed to show the efficiency of the industry under its present ownership and the inadvisability of tampering with it. Soon the prospective victims of *Labour Believes in Britain* followed suit. Two of them in particular, sugar and industrial assurance, enjoyed a tactical advantage denied to the rest, in that their products were sold direct to the consumer and their consumers were in the one case probably a majority and in the other case almost a totality of the electorate. They fought back with vigour. Lord Lyle and his fellow-directors of Tate and Lyle, Ltd., the sugar concern most affected, secured from over 80% of their shareholders at an extra-ordinary

F

meeting on September 15th, authority to fight nationalisation with every weapon at their command. The most potent weapon turned out to be an ingenious publicity man's conceit, the figure of " Mr. Cube ". On every packet of sugar was printed this lively creation, accompanied by some such pungent slogan as TATE NOT STATE. With less inventiveness, but no less energy, the insurance interests put their case before the public. By September 23rd they had set up 400 anti-nationalisation committees up and down the country on which about 4,000 employees were working after office hours to publicise their objections to the Labour Party's proposals. Insurance agents also constituted a ready-made army of canvassers, the great majority of them in favour of the preservation of the *status quo*.

The first official Labour reaction to this propaganda was announced by Mr. Griffiths, the Minister of National Insurance, in a speech on November 5th, when he stated :

> " These big business campaigns raise very important issues. Parliament has recently passed more stringent laws governing the expenses of elections. Every candidate and party has to account in the candidate's return of election expenses for all the money spent from a certain date. If these insurance and sugar campaigns extend into that period, then a ruling will have to be sought as to whether the money thus spent should not be added to the election expenses of the Tory candidates."

No particular stir, however, was occasioned until Mr. Herbert Morrison in a speech at Birmingham on November 26th, carried the argument a stage further :

> " Nobody objects to these concerns putting forward a reasoned statement of their views on nationalisation or other matters affecting them," he said, " but when vested interests throw the full weight of their financial resources into political controversies . . . and do it, not by reasoned and objective statements of fact to M.P.s and candidates or by speeches, but by expensively publicised vote-catching slogans and wholly tendentious propaganda, grave questions arise. . . . It would be a very dangerous thing if it were allowed to become a feature of our political life that big business could intervene in elections both by secret subscriptions to political

funds and by direct large-scale propaganda campaigns calculated to influence the result.   It must not be thought that
the law as to permitted expenditure relates only to a period
after the issue of the writs for an election.   When the time
comes for the returns of election expenses to be rendered we
must see whether all this vast expenditure is included and
how these matters are dealt with."

To both these criticisms the answers of the interests concerned
were virtually identical—namely, that they were not attacking
the Labour Party, but the threat of nationalisation as such;
furthermore, that they had an elementary right to state the case
for their own defence.

Read now, after the returns of election expenses have been
duly rendered—returns in which no party's agents have so much
as alluded to these items—Mr. Morrison's statement wears an
appearance of pure scarecrow-ism.   There is none the less good
reason to suppose that it was seriously meant, and that it was the
expression of a deep-rooted conviction on the part of its author
as to the potency of pressure groups in swaying the voter's opinion.
Nor can it be doubted that it attained some success, not merely in
arresting the propaganda of which it complained (for much of
that might have ceased in response to any routine interpretation
of the law, as the election campaign proper got under weigh), but
in putting his political opponents on the defensive just on the eve
of the electoral fight.   Its danger, from the Labour Party's point
of view, lay in the enhanced publicity which these attacks undoubtedly gave to the interests concerned and the extent to which
they invested such figures as Mr. Cube with the sympathy always
reserved for the *méchant animal* defending himself against a
bullying Leviathan.

Mr. Morrison's opponents were not slow to reply.   Sir David
Maxwell Fyfe, as both a King's Counsel and a Conservative
leader, laid down the main counter-proposition for the defence—
that the interests affected were only exercising their constitutional
rights of free speech and self-defence, that their activities did not
aim at the return of any particular candidate (nor of Conservatives
more than Liberals) and that the Labour Party, with its contributions from trade unions and Co-operatives, was in no position
to cast the first stone.   The weaknesses of two of these lines of

rebuttal were pointed out by the Attorney-General in statements in the House of Commons on December 5th and 7th, in the course of which he emphasised that, to violate the law, expenditure need not be directed towards the return of a *particular* candidate, and also that it was not the sources of contributions which, in this connection, might make them illegal, but the circumstances surrounding their expenditure. It was, however, also admitted by the Attorney-General that the question of whether the anti-nationalisation propaganda at present appearing was illegal depended upon " questions of fact and degrees to be determined by the court on the facts of each particular case ".[1] This gave rise to demands for a test case, and indeed the by-election held in South Bradford on December 9th provided a convenient opportunity, had the Labour Party so desired, for bringing the matter to the courts—an opportunity only impaired by the fact that the pro-nationalisation candidate was successful. As it was, no test case was brought, and the Attorney-General contented himself with announcing that he had given " instructions to the Director of Public Prosecutions that should occasion arise he should institute such proceedings as he thought proper " [2] without further reference to him.

From that point the debate wandered off into even less profitable channels, Mr. Morrison complaining that shareholders in these firms had not been consulted,[3] that their employees had willy-nilly to " handle political propaganda " and their consumers " to pay for it in part ". Before Parliament rose time was found by the Government for debate on a motion tabled by Mr. Geoffrey Bing advocating the publication by political parties and para-political organisations of an annual statement of their accounts. The debate from start to finish was suffused by an aroma of electioneering, and cannot be said to have contributed much either in the way of accurate information or constructive suggestion. The Opposition were mainly concerned to emphasise the extent of the Labour Party's trade union and Co-operative support, and the Labour speakers to hint at the " secret " vested interests financing the Conservative Party.

With the adjournment the controversy subsided, and with the

---

[1] House of Commons Debates, December 7th, 1949, c. 1892.
[2] *Ibid.*, c. 1890.
[3] Lord Lyle pointed out that his shareholders had been consulted and had endorsed his action.

resumption of full-scale political warfare in the New Year it was drowned out by the more resounding themes of electoral debate. Throughout the argument one curious feature had been discernible : each side assumed, and no one contradicted it, that in the battle for votes there was a real correlation between money expended and votes won, that if only enough propaganda could be deployed the worse could be successfully presented as the better reason. In the Conservatives, who had never known what it was to build a party from obscure beginnings, this credulity might be pardonable. In a Labour Party just about to celebrate the jubilee of its foundation it exceeded the bounds of permissible *naïveté*.

On the eve of the Christmas prorogation observers of the political omens noted that the Parliamentary Labour Party had re-elected its officers and its liaison committee " until the new Parliament meets ". From the nature and timing of this announcement it was surmised that the party were anticipating a dissolution of Parliament before they met again at Westminster. The New Year's Honours List, with its elevation of five Labour M.P.'s to the Peerage practically coincident with the appointment of Mr. J. J. Lawson to be Vice-Chairman of the National Parks Commission, was regarded as another pointer to an early election, since otherwise the Government would hardly precipitate so large a crop of by-elections so late in its life. Soon reports spread that halls in many parts of the country were being booked by Labour agents for meetings on February 22nd, supposedly on the eve of the poll.

On January 5th the Prime Minister had a talk with Mr. Morrison, just returned from a Yorkshire holiday, and afterwards met those of his Ministers who formed the economic affairs committee of the Cabinet. On January 7th the Liberal Party issued a warning to their supporters to be ready for an election " any time after February 15th ". On Sunday, January 8th, Mr. Attlee drove over to Sandringham for an audience with the King. On the 10th there was a meeting of the full Cabinet, followed by a subsequent meeting of all other members of the Government at which Mr. Attlee announced his intentions. Shortly after midnight the following announcement was issued from No. 10 :

" The King has been pleased to signify his acceptance of the Prime Minister's recommendation that his Majesty should proclaim the dissolution of Parliament on Friday, February 3. In accordance with the provisions of the Representation of the People Acts, polling day will fall on Thursday, February 23. The new Parliament will be summoned to meet on Wednesday, March 1, when the first business will be the formal election of the Speaker and the swearing-in of members ; and his Majesty has graciously announced his intention formally to open Parliament on Monday, March 6. His Majesty has also been pleased to signify his intention to make a Proclamation having the effect of postponing until after the dissolution the date (now January 24) on which the present Parliament is summoned to meet.''

The *Daily Herald* Political Correspondent, who in such a context may be presumed to be an authoritative spokesman, gave two reasons for Mr. Attlee's selection of February rather than late spring for the appeal to the country. The first was that Parliament had completed the legislative programme expounded by Labour in the *Let Us Face The Future* of five years before— and indeed, had Parliament re-assembled after the Christmas recess, there would certainly have been difficulty in devising profitable employment for it. Secondly, " widespread speculation about the election date was slowing down trade and industry and causing uncertainty abroad ". The second argument had, in many persons' view, been valid for some considerable time before, but it was certainly true that any longer postponement would have had even graver effects. Mr. Attlee's announcement was consequently universally welcomed as terminating a state of suspense which was in danger of becoming intolerable, and if, as even the *Daily Herald* admitted, there were those amongst his colleagues " who favoured an election in June ", the ranks closed behind him and the voice of the critics was loyally silent.

Some speculation, however, persisted on the reasons behind the unusually long notice of dissolution which Mr. Attlee's announcement provided. The precedent of 1945 was not wholly apposite, because then Parliament was in session, and a care-taker government had to be installed to tide the country over the campaign. One of the main reasons for Mr. Attlee's action was said to be an awareness of the printing difficulties which would harass all parties faced with a rush campaign. Conservative critics added a reason of their own—that it was timed to embarrass all the private champions of industries threatened with nationalisation, who might no longer be able to plead that their propaganda was "outside" the election. Whether or not that was the intention, it was certainly in part a result. The Industrial Life Offices Association announced that they would "modify the scope" of their anti-nationalisation campaign, and forthwith proceeded to withdraw their posters. The chairman of Associated Portland Cement Manufacturers, Ltd., took similar action, though he added that this did not mean that they were "abandoning the campaign". The British Iron and Steel Federation, however, denied that the election would make any difference to their campaign, which was "purely factual",* while the Joint Action Committee of the meat trade said that they would continue to distribute leaflets and posters. The most wholly uncompromising industrialist was, however, Lord Lyle, who announced that "Mr. Cube" would continue to appear, and, further, selected January 11th for launching an anti-nationalisation petition. Only his poster campaign was "automatically coming to an end".

Whether similar considerations motivated the Labour Party itself in deciding to cancel its own jubilee celebrations, fixed for February 2nd–5th, is not certain. It could at least be argued that the expenses incurred might have been adjudged a form of election propaganda such as would have to be distributed amongst all the Labour candidates likely to bask in its reflected glory. The party's official reason was the effort and inconvenience it would impose on candidates to take them away from their constituencies at the opening of their campaign, and no doubt this was a cogent objection. None the less, the cancellation rang a little strangely on the ears of a rank and file, which had been encouraged to look forward to the jubilee, if not as the send-off for a victorious campaign, at least as a celebration of unusual significance.

The Conservative Party also undertook a modification of its publicity in response to the need for watching the legal limit of its expenses. Hoardings all over the country, which for months

---

* Cf. Attorney-General in House of Commons debate, December 7th " . . . It should not be impossible for them to present their case in a *reasoned* way . . ."

past had been enlivened by red, white and blue posters asserting, " The Conservatives would let you build a house now ", or " Socialism has failed ", began to present an odd, piebald appearance as they were " whitened out " by the simple device of pasting further posters face downward over the possible offenders. This was to tide over, in innocent, non-chargeable silence, the period until Dissolution or thereabouts, when the Central Office would fire off in three intensive weeks the poster propaganda which would necessarily have to be charged up to the expenses of Conservative candidates in whose constituency it appeared.

It was a curious accident of timing that, on the day after the dissolution announcement and on the morning of the conference of trade union executives at which the Trades Union Congress General Council was trying to win endorsement for the " wage freeze ", a pamphlet by a group of Labour back-benchers appeared that criticised to some extent the leadership of both the party and the Trades Union Congress. This was *Keeping Left*, produced by a team of authors whose membership overlapped generously with that of the " Keep Left " group of three years before. The *Daily Herald* described it as " not an alternative programme to *Labour Believes in Britain* " but " an agenda for the 1950–55 Parliament ". However that might be, its recommendations of a capital levy, tighter controls, cuts in defence and a most infelicitous scheme of " socialist wage fixing " went far beyond, even where they did not cut across, existing pronouncements of party policy. On the trade union discussions their novel proposals do not appear to have impinged ; at any rate, the General Council's proposals carried the day by a majority which, by its very narrowness, gave the impression both of trade union loyalty and restraint and at the same time implied that the continuance of that restraint depended on the perpetuation of a government in which they could trust. That *Keeping Left* was not more damaging to the Labour Party's general campaigning is perhaps more surprising, since it provided generous ammunition for Tory propagandists ; for some reason by no means clear, however, not much was heard of it in the six weeks that followed.

Events had thus far taken their course with Mr. Churchill, the Conservative Party Leader, out of the country. He was on holiday at Madeira when Mr. Attlee announced the Dissolution.

TO THE RESCUE OF MEAT

NO NATIONALISATI... OF CEMEN...

SAVE COLD STORAGE

NATIONALISATION OF WATER SUPPLY IS ALL WET

NATIONALISATION OF CHEMICALS WILL DO YOU IN

Mr POISON

"COVER UP, BLOKES! HERE'S A COP!"

LOW

By arrangement with the "Evening Standard"

[To face p. 78.

But on the evening of January 12th his flying-boat touched down at Southampton. " I heard there was going to be a general election," he said, " so I thought I had better come back in case I was wanted." But if it was anticipated that his return would provide the signal for a warming up of the electoral war, the expectation was mistaken. The considerations of caution occasioned by the expenses " scare " remained as compulsive as before. To the private interests opposing nationalisation Lord Woolton issued a delicate reminder.

> " Throughout these industrial campaigns Conservatives have been completely dissociated from them. . . . The only thing I do suggest to these gentlemen is that to avoid confusion they should desist as soon as Parliament is dissolved. . . . At the General Election we shall fight nationalisation tooth and nail and we want the ring clear for the politicians to fight."

Mr. Morrison, speaking at Lewisham two days later, followed up his earlier pronouncements by a lively warning to " the Lord who rules over Mr. Cube " and to " everybody " else " to be specially careful ", and if the law were in doubt to " err on the side of keeping it ". It was emphasised that the costs of Mr. Morrison's own meeting were being charged to his election expenses, thereby, by implication, imposing a further padlock of silence on opponents whose election budgets had not been so precisely and confidently planned to cover the whole of a six weeks' campaign. Only the Liberals, whose very poverty perhaps made them bold, were urged by their Central Association " to go all out " and open their campaign once they had made certain that they would not be exceeding the permitted total. But the acceptance, by now common to all parties, of the thesis that, for accounting purposes, January 10th marked the " beginning of the election " served to make other parties husband their ammunition. A paradoxical situation ensued, in which an election which was on every ordinary man's lips positively receded from public view, disappeared from the hoardings, was less debated on the hustings than three months before, and soon went off the front pages even of the newspapers. A " phoney war " had supervened.

Two loopholes for polemics remained—the B.B.C. and the

press release—the first being controlled by the inter-party agreement, and the second being exempt from the expenses limitation. All the parties had saved up from 1949 some of their permitted quota of " party political " broadcasts. Thus, although the election broadcasts proper were not due to begin until February 4th, the public was once a week regaled with what were in effect the first shots in the aerial campaign. Mr. J. B. Priestley, the author and playwright, opened for Labour on January 14th with a " non-party ", " unpaid ", " reasonable man " appeal to the middle-classes to " grumble with " him, but at the same time to remember the benefits of Labour rule and vote for another five years of it. If a political broadcast may be judged by the offence it gives to opponents, Mr. Priestley's exhortation to *l'homme moyen intellectuel* was a very successful curtain-raiser for Labour. On January 18th the Labour Party secured headlines in the national press by the publication of their election manifesto, *Let Us Win Through Together*, friendly comment emphasising its full-employment pledges, while critics played up its proposals for nationalisation, particularly where they seemed to touch on land ownership or retail trade. Labour naturally made much of its own fearlessness and frankness in issuing its own manifesto first. Whether in fact it secured any electoral advantage by so doing is, of course, an insoluble mystery.

The manifesto represented, for most purposes, a boiling down of *Labour Believes in Britain*, but there were a few significant differences in content and in emphasis, and these reflect both the changed circumstances of its issue and the process by which it was prepared. The preparation of an election programme was left by the Party Conference in June 1949 in the hands of the Executive. The Executive in turn handed it over to a policy committee. On this committee were represented most of the elements and most of the opinions comprised within the Labour Movement, with a membership including Mr. Attlee, Mr. Bevan, Mr. Dalton, Mr. Shinwell, Mr. Michael Foot, Mr. Reeves (representing the Co-operative Movement), and spokesmen for the Transport and General Workers Union and other trade unions with representation on the National Executive. The main business of the committee had been to harmonise the original programme with the views and interests of the Co-operative Movement. Of these private deliberations no published record exists, but the upshot was clear in the concessions obtained by the Co-operatives in the final programme. The influence of the trade unions was mainly manifested in the silence of the programme on the burning question of wages policy and the comparative playing down of the nationalisation proposals (though the substance of these remained unchanged), for which the trade unions felt no very great enthusiasm. Full employment—a theme appealing to all sections of the movement—was given pride of place. The Co-operative Movement secured two valuable concessions: the avoidance of any major interference with the retail trade, and the change from nationalisation of industrial insurance to what was mysteriously entitled " Mutualisation ". This was expounded in greater detail in a supplementary statement issued two days later (and headlined by the *Daily Express* " The Mu Swallows the Pru "). The plan substituted ownership by policy-holders for the existing proprietary companies, but left companies already " mutually owned ", such as the Co-operative and Liverpool Victoria, unaffected. There was also much emphasis upon the assurance that the interests of existing agents would be safeguarded.

Meanwhile a short-tempered controversy was being waged between the high commands of the Conservative and Liberal Parties. Soon after his installation as Chairman of the Conservative Party, in May 1947, Lord Woolton had concluded an agreement with the National Liberal Party, represented by Lord Teviot, recommending each to his own flock that Conservatives and Liberals should combine to form united constituency associations. The merits of this arrangement were frequently advertised by the authors throughout 1947 and 1948, and as frequently denied by the spokesmen for the Liberal Party proper. With the onset of 1949 and the apparent Liberal determination to run hundreds of candidates of their own, these exchanges became increasingly tart, whether on the platforms or, as more often happened, in the correspondence columns of the newspapers, notably of the *Daily Telegraph*. The issues of principle dividing the controversialists were simple. The Conservatives said there was no longer any real difference between Conservatism and Liberalism, as their harmonious and intimate relations with the National Liberals proved, and in any event the paramount necessity was to defeat Socialism. The Liberals replied that the differences between

Liberalism and Conservatism were fundamental, and that the intimacy between the National Liberals and the Conservatives was the intimacy of the Lady of Riga with the tiger that swallowed her; furthermore, that Socialism could only be beaten by a " progressive " alternative—i.e. Liberalism. Then the argument moved to tactics and organisation. The Conservatives said that the Liberals, while unable to win themselves, were splitting the anti-Socialist vote by running hopeless candidates; instead they should combine with Conservatives on the basis of the Woolton–Teviot Agreement. The Liberals said that the Conservative failures at such by-elections as South Hammersmith and Batley and Morley, where they had straight fights with Labour, proved that they had failed to regain the confidence of the electorate; if they wanted to demonstrate the sincerity of their anti-Socialism, let them stand down in constituencies where Liberals would have a better chance. By May 1949 Lord Woolton was claiming that there were 60 constituencies in which the Woolton–Teviot Agreement had worked and in which a joint Conservative–Liberal Association would sponsor a joint Liberal–Conservative candidate. Liberal spokesmen denied that these combinations were anything but shams, and expatiated upon what they described as Tory tricks and subterfuges to erect a Liberal façade before what were, in effect, purely Conservative bodies.

These altercations provided an unpropitious prelude to any form of election pact between the two anti-Socialist headquarters. Nevertheless, for one brief, fitful moment the flame of speculation burnt bright in a good many breasts that something might be arranged at the constituency level. This was on January 13th, when the news came from Huddersfield of a local agreement by which, in effect, the Conservatives agreed not to fight the West Division of the town, and the Liberals not to intervene in the East. This was effected by the Conservatives asking the Liberal candidate, Mr. Wade, for an undertaking that if the Liberals held the balance of power in Parliament he would " vote against a vote of confidence in a Socialist Administration ". Mr. Wade said he would enter into no bargain, but had no objection to stating publicly that he certainly " would not vote in such a way as to give a vote of confidence to an Administration committed to further Socialist measures ". The Conservatives said that in their view " Mr. Wade has given the undertaking for which we asked ", and accordingly withdrew their candidate. Immediately the Liberal headquarters in London gave " the Huddersfield formula " their endorsement, and expressed the hope that " Conservative Associations planning to oppose our present M.P.'s will withdraw their candidates, instead of creating a situation from which the Socialists might benefit. The same applies to many constituencies, such as Bethnal Green, where only Sir Percy Harris can recapture the seat from Socialism ". A few days later, on January 16th, the Deputy-Chairman of the Liberal Central Association said that he had been told that there were indications that seven or eight other Conservative Associations had been so impressed by the " formula " that they might withdraw their candidates " in order to get the Socialists out ". These hopes were short-lived. Conservative headquarters gave them no encouragement, and it soon became apparent that Lord Woolton was not going to be a party to any more local concessions. Nor indeed were there many constituencies in which the peculiar circumstances of Huddersfield—a National-Liberal tradition, a city divided into one predominantly Liberal and one predominantly Conservative division, and two sitting Labour members—could be paralleled. When Conservatives in Middlesbrough, a city offering perhaps the closest counterpart, announced their refusal to give Mr. Fothergill, President-elect of the Liberal Party, a free run in the West Division of the town, the " Huddersfield formula " was seen to be a plant too tender for other soils. Nowhere else in England, and only in Carmarthen in Wales, did Liberal candidates escape three-cornered fights.*

The incident over, headquarters warfare was resumed with all the added sharpness that frustrated alliance brings. It was long ago remarked by Thucydides that in civil war names lose their accustomed meaning and are adapted to the requirements of action. So it was between the Liberals and the Conservatives. On January 12th, Lord Moynihan, Chairman of the Liberal Party Organisation, wrote to Lord Woolton, his opposite number, suggesting that, to avoid creating confusion in the public mind, " Conservative candidates should fight the election as Conservatives and that the name ' Liberal ' should not be used by them in order to confuse the issue ". On the 21st, Lord Woolton

---

* In Greenock the Conservatives gave support to the Liberal candidate in a five-cornered fight, and in the Western Isles in a three-cornered fight.

replied, expressing his agreement with Lord Moynihan's objective, but disagreeing as to the best way of realising it.

> " I shall indeed be glad to do anything that would assist in clarifying the position with which the voters of this country are faced. I do not think that your object would be achieved by your suggestion that the use of the word ' Liberal ' should be confined to those whose candidatures are sponsored by your organisation. In fact this would have the opposite effect of misleading the public. The National Liberals are at least as entitled to the label ' Liberal ' as those others on whose behalf you write. In the House of Commons the National Liberals are numerically stronger than the Liberals led by Mr. Clement Davies. There is also in the country a large body of electors who have sacrificed nothing of their Liberal principles by endorsing the policy of co-operation with the Conservative party against Socialism. This policy has found expression in the adoption, in more than sixty constituencies, of candidates who combine the support and the names of both parties. Advice will be given to such candidates to ensure that there is no confusion between them and the candidates of your organisation."

At the same time the National Liberals produced their manifesto, emphasising their " open and honourable co-operation with the Conservatives " and the harmony between their policy and that set forth in *The Right Road for Britain*, and claiming that they were " interested " in 65 candidates, under the Woolton–Teviot Agreement. This was followed, on January 22nd, by a joint statement from Mr. Churchill and Lord Rosebery, President of the National-Liberal Council, announcing that " although local conditions may occasionally dictate a different course, we would urge such (i.e. Liberal-Conservative) candidates to stand as Liberal-Conservatives, or Liberal-Unionists, prefixing the word ' National ' where a Left-wing Liberal candidate has appeared in the field ". This provoked the Liberals to protest that this was a dishonest device for passing off the National-Liberals as a separate entity, though " they were not regarded as such by anyone for the purpose of the general election broadcasts ". They further denied that these joint associations had any significant Liberal membership or that (with one exception since liquidated) any of them had adopted a candidate who was at the time of adoption a member of the Liberal Party; they were all " controlled by the Conservative Party ", though they might indeed contain " one or two ex-Liberals such as Mr. Winston Churchill himself ".

So seriously, moreover, did the Liberals exercise themselves over the risk of losing their trade-mark, that Mr. Clement Davies addressed himself personally to Mr. Churchill on the matter, asking him " in the interests of fair play " to investigate certain examples of bogus Liberal-Conservative Associations, feeling certain he would wish to dissociate himself from such " devices ", and finally demanding that the Conservative Party should fight under its own name, or at least " under a name which does not clash with that of another party which is recognised throughout the world ". At the same time, Liberal headquarters let it be known that they were considering taking legal action and possibly seeking an injunction against a candidate misusing the label " Liberal ". These moves produced from Mr. Churchill on January 25th a debating reply which was masterly in its combination of cool insolence and persiflage.

> " MY DEAR DAVIES,
> I thank you for your kindness in writing to me amid your many cares.
> As you were yourself for 11 years a National Liberal, and in that capacity supported the Governments of Mr. Baldwin and Mr. Neville Chamberlain, I should not presume to correct your knowledge of the moral, intellectual and legal aspects of adding a prefix or a suffix to the honoured name of Liberal. It has certainly often been done before by honourable and distinguished men."

Mr. Churchill then argued that the local associations of the Conservative Party were independent and free to co-operate with any like-minded anti-Socialists, in order to " give effect to their most sincere convictions ". But Mr. Davies had been through all this himself and " I do not need to dwell upon it further ". He added :

> " Since, however, you have been good enough to address me, I will venture to draw your attention to the fact that you

and your friends do not seem to have any difficulty on the question of nomenclature with the Socialist Party. I have not heard, for instance, of any candidate who is standing as a Liberal-Socialist. The reason is, no doubt, that the two terms are fundamentally incompatible. No one can be at once a Socialist and a Liberal. . . .

Why, then, should you and your friends and your four hundred candidates always blame the Conservative Party, and do all in your power to help the Socialists ? . . . It is strange political conduct to scheme for the return of minority candidates with whom you disagree, be they Tories or Socialists, at the risk of bringing about a stalemate or deadlock at this anxious juncture. We hope that responsible and serious-minded Liberals will not waste their votes on this occasion, and that the solid strength of the Conservatives and National-Liberals will save the country from this danger. But if such a misfortune were to happen, the six or seven members you may have in the new Parliament, even if they agreed, would be quite unable to cope with the consequences.

There is a real measure of agreement between modern Tory democracy and the mass of Liberals who see in Socialism all that their most famous thinkers and leaders have fought against in the past. An intense passion of duty unites us in this fateful hour in an honourable freedom in which the undying flame of Liberalism burns.

I hope you and your friends will ponder carefully upon what I have set down, and do not hesitate to write to me again if you think I can be of further service.

Yours sincerely,

WINSTON S. CHURCHILL."

This, said Mr. Clement Davies, was " facetious and evasive ", but his adversary had still not said his last word. In his adoption speech at Woodford on Saturday, January 28th, Mr. Churchill returned to the theme of " the very small and select group of Liberal leaders who conceived themselves the sole heirs of the principles and traditions of Liberalism, and believed themselves to have the exclusive copyright of the word ' Liberal '. This super select attitude," he went on to say, " finds an example in the exclusion of Lady Violet Bonham-Carter and, I may add, of

"WHAT LIBERALS COULD RESIST US NOW?"

By arrangement with the " Daily Herald "

Sir Archibald Sinclair from the four broadcasts the Liberals are making between now and the Poll. In Lady Violet Bonham-Carter we have not only a Liberal of unimpeachable loyalty to the party, but one of the finest speakers in the country. Her speech against Socialism, which was so widely read two months ago, recalled the style of old and famous days. But her voice must not be heard on the air on this occasion." The lance was deftly aimed at a point in the Liberal armour which, on an optimistic view, represented the joint between the Asquithian breastplate and the Lloyd George gorget, or, if one was to credit less favourable rumours, marked a persistent gap between these two vital sections of the party. For some days this sprightly allegation went unrebutted, and Mr. Churchill followed it up on February 1st with a characteristic elaboration (apropos of a Liberal charge that the Conservatives had tried to whittle down their share of broadcasts):

> " When I saw how the Liberal group had distributed their broadcasts, I offered, with the full consent of my colleagues, one of the Conservative twenty-minute broadcasts to Lady Violet Bonham-Carter. This offer was made, of course, without any conditions whatever. Lady Violet was perfectly free to say whatever she pleased. She was dissuaded from accepting this not ungenerous offer by the Clement Davies group.
>
> The public will not, therefore, hear on the broadcast any clear exposition of the view held by the majority of Liberals, who, while remaining loyal to the Liberal Party, are strongly opposed to Socialism."

To this Lady Violet Bonham-Carter responded, " Mr. Churchill's account of his very generous offer was completely accurate."

Meanwhile the Conservatives had published their manifesto and, through the lips of Mr. Churchill, had fired their first salvo in the battle of the broadcasts. *This Is The Road* was published on January 25th, in the form of a pamphlet one-third the length of *The Right Road for Britain* (apart from an even briefer popular version in four pages). Thought by many to bear the marks of Mr. Churchill's vigorous pen, it was, for the most part, a tauter, more pungent condensation of the earlier document. There were, however, a few differences of substance.

G

The treatment of food subsidies was more precise—no reduction without compensating increases to those most affected. The proposal in the earlier programme to supply health service drugs free to private patients was dropped, as was the promise to continue university grants on their present scale. The dollar gap was given a high priority amongst the commitments of a new Conservative Government. So was the maintenance of full employment. The manifesto was accorded a polite reception ; even its foes attacked more the record and capabilities of its authors than the specific proposals which they advanced.

The Liberals were alone amongst the parties in arranging a party conference to synchronise with the election. This was their emergency two-day Assembly held in London on January 27th and 28th. There are always risks for a party holding a public conference on the eve of an election ; if the party's policy is settled there is not much to confer about, if it is not settled the airing of public differences may give an outward appearance of dissension. The Liberals did not wholly escape this dilemma, especially when unrepentant believers in *laisser-faire* demurred at a policy of guaranteed prices for agriculture. But in the main the party contrived to reaffirm their earlier policy statements without undue repetitiousness and without opening up old disagreements (not even on compulsory co-ownership), and undoubtedly to a party concerned to impress the electorate with its scale and determination the conference was justified by its news value alone, wholly apart from its revivalist value to the party workers.

This period also saw the mobilisation of the various pressure groups to whom an election is at once a challenge and an opportunity. Apart from the commercial interests threatened by nationalisation, probably the most vocal were the Roman Catholics. They were concerned to secure a modification of the religious settlement embodied in the 1944 Education Act, so as to lighten the burdens imposed on them for the maintenance of their Church schools. A large rally at the Albert Hall on January 30th and a Trafalgar Square demonstration on February 5th were the national starting-points for a campaign which, though not explicitly related to the election at its inception, soon displayed itself in the constituencies in the form of questionnaires and deputations to candidates.

Meanwhile the trade unions, as an open and active component of the Labour Party, issued on February 1st a " call to the workers " to remember the benefits brought to them and to their unions by Labour rule and to " vote Labour at this most crucial election ". In previous years it had been the practice for the T.U.C. itself to distribute its manifesto on behalf of the Labour Party, but fear of infringing the untried law relating to election expenses led them this time to leave it to newspapers, trade union journals and the Labour Party itself to give it publicity.

But the impact of these manifestoes, demonstrations and high-level altercations on the ordinary voter was so far still very slight. Probably more people had heard the broadcasts of the party leaders than any other outward or audible sign of the election—from Mr. Churchill's " Queuetopia " curtain-raiser of January 21st to the Chancellor of the Exchequer's defence of Labour economics on February 2nd. Even so, the listening audiences for these overtures were not, with the exception of Mr. Churchill's, at all impressive, and at the beginning of February there was still astonishingly little to show, in people's talk or in the outward appearance of either London or the provinces, that a great struggle was impending. There was activity, of course, but it was activity under wraps. It was the activity of silent preparation, in party headquarters, in committee rooms, not the activity of public persuasion, of open meetings, of printed exhortations. All central offices and most constituency associations were holding their fire for fear of expending their ammunition too soon.

CHAPTER V

THE NATIONAL CAMPAIGN:
FROM DISSOLUTION TO THE POLL

ON Thursday, February 2nd, the leaders of the three major parties, with their wives and many of their colleagues, attended " a service of prayer and dedication before the general election " at St. Paul's Cathedral. The service, the first of its kind in British political history, was organised as the result of a suggestion by Christian Action, and similar services were held in a number of cities outside London. The Archbishop of Canterbury, in his sermon, reminded his audience that " It is the proper business of politicians in a general election to urge their views upon the people with confidence, with vigour, even with passion, out of the sincerity of their own honest thinking and convictions, and yet never to forget that God is greater than us all in truth, in righteousness, in purpose and in love." He went on to set the amicable conflict of the election in the shadow of the deeper world conflict of Christianity and materialism, and to exhort his hearers to " be ready to learn from one another even in opposing one another ".

The following day Parliament was dissolved by royal proclamation in the traditional form : " We, being desirous and resolved, as soon as may be, to meet Our People, and to have their Advice in Parliament, do hereby make known to all Our loving subjects Our Royal Will and Pleasure to call a new Parliament." That evening the writs were posted to returning officers in Great Britain and to the Governor of Northern Ireland, and the campaign proper began.

At this stage the parties disclosed so much of their plans as was involved in the movements of their principal spokesmen. An extensive tour was announced for Mr. Attlee, to last from February 8th to 16th, " involving ", as the *Daily Herald* put it, " seven towns a day ", save for a break of two days in the middle. The route of his tour gave some hints of what Labour judged their crucial areas to be. He started in the South Midlands, from Watford to Birmingham, thence through the Black Country, the Potteries, Cheshire, Manchester and Liverpool to Preston. Resuming again on Clydeside, he was to cross to Falkirk and Edinburgh, then south to York, Doncaster and Sheffield, then via Lincoln to Nottingham and Leicester, and so back through the Home Counties to London. Mr. Churchill did not plan any single oratorical progress as extensive as his tour in 1945. By some this was attributed to the probable inclemency of February weather, but Mr. Churchill is hardly the type of campaigner to be deterred by weather, however foul. It is more likely that it was part of a fully planned Conservative strategy which sought to avoid the appearance, as in 1945, of an appeal built exclusively around one man, even when—or perhaps especially when—that man was Mr. Churchill. Although, as the campaign unfolded, it became apparent that in total Mr. Churchill's travels would not be inconsiderable, yet to a far greater degree than in 1945 he shared the burden of public meetings up and down the country with his principal colleagues.

Each party, well before dissolution, held a meeting in London to brief its candidates. Of the Conservative meeting, addressed by Mr. R. A. Butler on January 23rd, not much appeared in the press other than that it was devoted to an exposition of *This Is The Road*. But of the Labour candidates' meeting, held the following day, fuller particulars were available. Mr. Attlee reviewed the record of the Government, and advised them to rely on that for their main theme, making an ethical and spiritual appeal to the electorate whose past and future efforts could alone make the Welfare State possible. Mr. Morrison advised on tactics, warning against apathy and over-optimism and reminding candidates that Labour had a good case to put to the middle classes. The Liberals used the opportunity provided by their Emergency Assembly to brief their volunteers. Both Mr. Clement Davies and Mr. Byers warned them against vote-catching promises, both stressed that the scale of their candidatures now enabled them to offer the voters a Liberal Government " if they want one ". Mr. Martell urged on them the importance of publicity—" The press are our best friends even when they are our worst enemies. We must keep in the news."

Candidates were thus a great deal better briefed and prepared than in 1945. Only the Liberals, with their high percentage of late, and sometimes last-minute, adoptions, suffered from having to rely very often on candidates who were not thoroughly steeped in their party's policy and tactics.   But the other parties, even without last-minute briefing, would have been able to put 90% of their candidates into the field well equipped.   Conferences, pamphlets, communications from headquarters—these had been doing their work for twelve months or more.   The Labour Party's *Speakers' Handbook*, a solid volume of almost 500 pages, was available in November.   The Conservative equivalent *Campaign Guide*, an even more comprehensive tome of over 700 pages, appeared in December.   The Liberal *Handbook* appeared at the turn of the year.   There was thus no excuse for speakers on all sides not knowing all the facts as well as most of the tactical fictions.

One result of this long and careful preparation was that the campaigns, of all parties, followed an unusually predetermined course. The ambushes and feints were few.   Most of the time, as between Conservative and Labour, the contest was like an 18th-century battle-piece, with each side drawn up in formal array and then advancing across open country to overbear, by sheer weight of fire and sword, the masses that opposed them.   Thus it was striking to observe how the principles laid down openly by Mr. Morrison in his first election speech at Lewisham on January 16th were adhered to by other Labour speakers throughout the campaign.   Labour appealed, he said, as the " party of the nation ", and therefore " to everyone with a progressive mind and with public spirit among the middle, technical and professional classes, the agriculturalists and the forward-looking managers of industry ". He addressed a special word of sympathy and exhortation to housewives, and condemned Conservative attempts to " browbeat " Liberals.   Labour candidates should stick to the party manifesto, and not seek to rival their opponents in making " doubtful promises ".   Conservatives did not so early or so openly avow their intentions, but they were just as recognisable and often, indeed, identical—the appeal to the middle class, the housewife and the agriculturalist and the tireless effort to win over the Liberal vote.

The platform oratory of the campaign proper may be said to have begun with Mr. Churchill's appearance at Leeds on Saturday, February 4th.   Here, in an old Liberal area, within echoing distance, one might say, of the " Huddersfield formula ", he rebuked the Liberals for their refusal to co-operate.   " Here and there a sensible arrangement may be made, but in the main the die is cast." He attacked, too, the Liberal opposition to conscription, though he thought " the burden of national service could be sensibly reduced ". But the main burden of the speech was British Socialist folly, extravagance and wanton nationalisation, contrasting with the rejection of such remedies elsewhere, even in Germany. " Thus some peoples learn wisdom in defeat, while others are led into folly by victory." Meanwhile Lord Woolton at Birmingham defended his leader against personal attacks, " miserable gibes " (an allusion to Mr. Maurice Webb's broadcast), and a whispering campaign " that his return to power would bring war ". A more characteristic Labour criticism of Mr. Churchill was expounded the following day by Sir Hartley Shawcross at Newark, who deplored his belittling of Britain's post-war achievements and his picture of us as a country of " weary Willies and tired Tims ". The same day Mr. Morrison counter-attacked in the West Riding, gently at Wakefield, appealing to Liberals to make their first principle the avoidance of any risk of returning the Tories to power, while at Huddersfield his tone took on more of anger than of sorrow as he denounced the " formula " as " politically immoral ".

At the same week-end the Liberals spoke for themselves by issuing—the last of the parties to do so—their election manifesto, *No Easy Way*. It contained little that was surprising to anyone who had followed the evolution of Liberal policy, but it was notable for its emphasis on the dollar crisis, its strongly worded opposition to further nationalisation, its outright advocacy of separate Parliaments for Wales and Scotland and its promise of equal pay for men and women. Conservatives commented on its overlap with *This Is The Road*. Labour newspapers and politicians mainly let it go by in silence.

Mr. Attlee's first speech of the campaign was delivered in his own constituency of West Walthamstow on February 6th. It was not a major policy utterance and was chiefly notable for his defence of a February dissolution. But on Wednesday, February 8th, he set off on his 1000-mile tour. Whether the setting owed anything to the astuteness of party managers, or whether it was, as it seemed to be, merely the natural expression of the Prime Minister's habits and personality, there can be no doubt that it was a *tour de force* of unassuming advertisement. The family car, pre-war and far from *de luxe*, Mrs. Attlee at the wheel, no entourage beyond the indispensable detective, the roadside stops when, ahead of schedule, Mrs. Attlee would catch up on her knitting and Mr. Attlee would do a crossword puzzle—this was the very stuff of honest, uninvidious, unpretentious, non-queue-jumping, post-war Britain. It was as devoid of drama as Queen Victoria's *Leaves* from her *Highland Journal*, and almost as appealing. However worked upon by hostile critics, it could not be presented as part of a picture of Socialist folly and extrava-gance, nor as a curtain-raiser to the class war which would proceed via the liquidation of the middle class to the eventual establishment of a Communist State.

On the same day Mr. Churchill went west to Cardiff, pausing in Paddington to be photographed exchanging greetings with Freddie Mills, the recently defeated British contestant for the light-heavyweight boxing championship. He spoke in cold and wet weather to a crowd of 20,000 in Ninian Park, taking as his dominant theme the rebuttal of the Labour charge that Conserva-tives were not averse to a return to unemployment. But what caught the fancy of his audience and the newspapers was his mockery of the jargon of bureaucracy when, protesting against the term " accommodation units ", he added, " I don't know how we are to sing our old song ' Home, Sweet Home ', and broke into the chant

> " Accommodation unit,
> Sweet accommodation unit,
> There's no place like our accommodation unit."

Less felicitous, and dangerously evocative of old and bitter memories, was his reply to a reported rumour that, as Home Secretary forty years ago, he had sent troops to shoot down Welsh miners in the Tonypandy riots. To this there succeeded over the next week an exchange of charges and denials between him and Mr. Ness Edwards, a junior Minister and a Welsh M.P., which, from a strictly electioneering point of view, can have done Con-servatism in Wales little but harm.

A day later Mr. Churchill's appearance in Plymouth focused public attention on a constituency which afforded one of the more " newsworthy " campaigns of the election—Devonport, where Mr. Randolph Churchill was opposing Mr. Michael Foot. These two made a pair of fighters whose political cutlass-work was notable, if not for finesse, at least for vigour and determination. The arrival of Mr. Randolph Churchill's distinguished father did nothing to diminish the liveliness of the engagement. His speech was mainly an attack on Labour rationing, shortages and taxation, in the course of which he said :

> " We realise the deprivation, and often hardship, involved in the strict rationing of petrol which the Socialist Government have enforced, and we are determined to put an end to it at the earliest possible moment.
> " We cannot make any definite promises at this stage because we do not know all the facts. We have been kept in the dark to such an extent that it is impossible for us to measure the difficulties and repercussions which freeing the sale of petrol at this moment might involve. . . . We believe that by skilful management . . . and re-adjustment of the exports of sterling petrol, even if it may not be possible to abolish petrol rationing altogether, it may soon be all right for a Government concerned with the interests of owners of motor-cars and motor-cycles at any rate to increase greatly the basic ration."

Later that same day, hot on Mr. Churchill's heels, came Mr. Aneurin Bevan, to whom Mr. Churchill had scornfully and anonymously referred at Cardiff by saying, apropos of a tribute to Lloyd George, " There can be no greater insult to his memory than to suggest that to-day Wales has a second Lloyd George." To Mr. Bevan Mr. Churchill stood revealed as " a short-term merchant concerned only with election results and not the future of Great Britain ", and " trying to bribe the British people by promising an increase in the basic petrol ration ". Despite this quick fielding, Mr. Churchill's carefully worded statement enabled the London press of that evening and the next morning to score some very slick runs, in both their headlines and their news stories (see pp. 189–194), and immediately the first election " red herring " had been born.

The next day Mr. Attlee added his censures to Mr. Bevan's. He twice rebuked his opponent, saying at Liverpool :

> " No one denies that Lord Woolton is a very good window-dresser. I noticed the latest example in to-day's papers,

consisting of a happy thought of Mr. Churchill's about petrol. A lot of people would like to have more petrol, but petrol costs dollars, and if you have only a limited amount of dollars, more petrol means less food or less raw materials. Petrol is a problem which we have studied with the greatest care with experts. I cannot believe, on Mr. Churchill's statement, that he has given it one minute's consideration. It is just another little bit of window-dressing."

But Mr. Gaitskell, Mr. Attlee's own Minister of Fuel and Power, was engaged at the same time, at Harrogate, in holding out hopes not very different from Mr. Churchill's. " Can we increase the ration ? Obviously, it all depends how the dollar position goes. If, as I hope, it improves steadily, then the prospects are not bad. At this very moment discussions are going on in Washington with the Americans to see if we can find some way of getting extra petrol without spending dollars." It did not need a further " expert " exposition from Mr. Geoffrey Lloyd, Mr. Churchill's own war-time chairman of the Oil Control Board, to demonstrate that this was a victory on points for Mr. Churchill. The " motorists' vote " might not be very large, and it might not be for sale in return for an increased petrol ration, but critics who questioned Mr. Churchill's tactics on this score were in danger of misunderstanding his objective. This was to present the Government in the role of the niggardly, unimaginative upholder of austerity for austerity's sake, concerned always to find reasons for withholding plenty rather than for producing it. And in this he achieved some success, even at the risk of being himself branded as a " stunt-monger ".

Mr. Attlee on tour caused no such exhilarating diversions as these. Had he done so it would have been out of character. His function was to personify the quiet reasonableness of Labour, while the wild man of Conservatism went beyond the control even of his own party. " I am not going to enter into a slanging match with Mr. Churchill," he told a meeting at West Bromwich on February 9th, " because the issues that face us are important and should not be settled by mere heat and temper." He went on :

" The Conservative Party talks a great deal about controls and they want some controls taken off. But I believe the control they would like to keep on is control over Mr.

Churchill, and they certainly got it on the broadcast of his, in contrast with the broadcast of the other election. The Conservative Party put him on the leash in ' The Right Road for Britain ', but it is quite clear he slipped the collar. There are wild whirling words, wild accusations of extravagance and wanton waste. The Conservatives have failed to prove their case."

These delicate but well-pointed tilts went down well with the large audience which listened almost without interruption to his report on what, with a characteristic precision verging on understatement, he called his " four and a half years " stewardship. He was, said the *Manchester Guardian*, writing of his tour in the Manchester area, a " Horatio of the Hustings ", a " master of non-gesture ".

The week-end of February 11th–12th, which immediately preceded the closing date for nominations, saw the end of what might be called the first phase of the campaign, in which each side had tried out its programme on the electorate, and was able to make some estimate of which items were attracting and which were repelling the voters. Nationalisation's pros and cons, it was generally agreed, did not arouse strong responses anywhere. Housing, cost of living, red tape and rationing seemed to be evocative themes. Full employment and unemployment were a sunshine and shadow pair that Labour put in the forefront of their morality play. Conservatives had given much time in this first week to demonstrating that they loved the one and loathed the other no less than Labour did, and, furthermore, that the conflict of Good and Evil was not accurately portrayed if the angel Marshall Aid was omitted from the cast. But it remained doubtful whether they had yet been successful in getting their version accepted by the public.

These exchanges, though conducted with vigour, had not yet raised the temperature of the campaign very noticeably above its starting point. (Nor, for that matter, had the broadcasts. Mr. Griffiths' evocation of the dole-ridden thirties was perhaps the sole exception.) Mr. Bevan, reporting back to his constituents at Ebbw Vale on February 12th, claimed to have gathered an impression from his meetings in the country that the election campaign was " hotting up " and that it was being conducted more vigorously than in 1945, but his colleague Dr. Dalton, speaking at Sunderland the same evening, found the comparative quietness of the campaign so far a matter of surprise. Preferring Dr. Dalton's version, one might explain Mr. Bevan's as possibly a reflection of his own experiences in the West country, particularly at Bristol, where, on February 10th, he had considerable difficulty in obtaining a hearing. Moreover, quite apart from the prevailing orderliness of the big party rallies, the constituency campaigns were still running only at half throttle in a good many instances. In county constituencies candidates were still in the main working their way through the outlying villages, reserving the main centres of population for the closing days, while in the boroughs there was still a disposition, especially on the part of Labour, to hold fire, not to weary the electorate too early, not to expend doubtfully funds that might be needed later on.

It was during this period, when the campaign had moved out into the provinces but had not yet fully seeped through to the constituencies, that the Liberals found themselves, in some senses, most at a disadvantage. With the speeches of rival leaders providing the main news and interest, the Liberals, deficient in names of headline value, were hard put to it to keep their case before the public. Moreover, their best-known leaders were mostly the prisoners of their constituencies. With the memories of 1945 defeats in mind, and the knowledge that they were being harder pressed in 1950 than ever before, the party sensibly agreed that figures like Sir Archibald Sinclair, Mr. Clement Davies, Lady Megan Lloyd-George and Mr. Frank Byers should stick close to their rural acres. Moreover, since those rural areas were in most cases located in the remote and weather-beaten fastnesses of Wales and Scotland, they were ill-placed for winging their words to the ears of a predominantly urban populace. This left the burden of Liberal advocacy on the national plane largely to peers like Lord Beveridge, who had been somewhat withdrawn from politics since 1945, or Lord Samuel, who was approaching a green, but still onerous 80, or to Lady Violet Bonham-Carter, who, with one or two exceptions, devoted herself to constituencies north of Inverness, or to Lord Milverton, a recent recruit to Liberalism and politics from Labour and the Colonial Service.

None the less, around the week-end of February 11th a few

incidents occurred to keep the Liberal Party in the news, though not always in a very favourable light. First, there was the curious incident of Mr. Junor at Dundee. Mr. Junor, who had been adopted as Liberal candidate for Dundee West, in which his Labour opponent would have been Mr. Strachey, the Minister of Food, suddenly withdrew his candidature on February 10th, to leave a straight fight to the Conservative candidate, Mr. Scrymgeour-Wedderburn. A written agreement provided that Dundee Liberals would run no candidate in either Dundee West or East in this election, but that Dundee Unionists would stand down next time in whichever constituency they failed now. However, any possibility that this might provide a Scottish variant to the " Huddersfield formula " was shattered two days later, when the Scottish Liberal Federation refused to endorse the agreement and nominated an outside candidate of their own, Mr. Canning, whom the local Liberal Association refused to support. While this tangled skein was being woven, *The Times* published in their news column a letter from Lady Rhys Williams, formerly Chairman of the Publication and Publicity Committee of the Liberal Party, confirming Mr. Churchill's statement at Leeds that in 1947 he made a " generous offer " to " a number of leading Liberals " of " support in a certain number of constituencies ". Lord Moynihan and Mr. Martell immediately denied that anyone had approached them, and deplored any " hole-in-the-corner arrangements with any party ". But perhaps their only effective reply to such researches into the past was to put a bold face on the future. This they did with the announcement, when nominations closed on February 13th, that over 470 Liberal candidates would take the field,[1] and the further warning that, partly in the form of a leaflet already circulated for last-minute distribution, entitled *A Word to Liberals*, the Conservatives were preparing a final assault on the virtue of the Liberal rank and file.

The Liberal total apart, there was little that was surprising in the nomination figures. The major parties had made it clear from the outset that they would fight on the broadest possible front, and the result was the largest nomination list in British electoral history. Whereas in 1945 there had been 274 straight fights, this time there were only 112.[2] The main surprise of the

---

[1] The exact figure was 475, but owing to errors in computation this was variously given out at the time as 472 and 474.
[2] Of which 9 were in Northern Ireland.

nomination was the last-minute emergence of an Independent at Hexham, where the Speaker would otherwise have been un-opposed, all parties having agreed to respect his neutrality. The intruder was Mr. Hancock, who in 1945 created a comparable diversion by opposing Mr. Churchill. Leaders of all parties sent to the Speaker messages expressing regret and assuring him of the support of their own followers. A notable omission from the list of candidates nominated was Mr. Lewis Silkin, the Minister of Town and Country Planning, whose constituency had been abolished under re-distribution, and who had not been successful in finding another. Only two candidates were returned un-opposed, Sir Hugh O'Neill (Antrim North), and Major Harden (Armagh), representing the tradionally rock-ribbed Ulster, the Maine of British Conservatism.

The Liberal and Communist candidates apart, the most notable difference between the nomination lists of 1945 and 1950 was the Labour determination to fight every constituency (save Hexham) in the English counties. This was expressive, amongst other things, of the party's conviction that it could and should win the rural vote. Thus, despite the difficulties of February campaigning in the rural areas, Mr. Tom Williams, the Minister of Agriculture, did an intensive tour of East Anglia, and followed it up with an extensive tour of the rural areas of Northern England. As part of a similar strategy, Mr. Morrison followed up his tour of Yorkshire by a three-day trip throughout the South and South-west, beginning at Bournemouth on February 10th and ending at Plymouth on the 12th. In the course of his excursion he found it desirable to refute Conservative allegations that Labour was aiming at the nationalisation of the land (based on the reference in the manifesto to " public ownership " for " good food-producing land not fully used ".)

On this same tour, speaking at Exeter on February 12th, Mr. Morrison gave voice to some speculations which, to anyone familiar with his skill as an electoral tactician, bore all the marks of coat-trailing :

" There is a gentleman in journalism who is a very capable journalist, and who was a colleague of mine in the war Government—Lord Beaverbrook—who has just returned to this island. I have reason to believe that the Tory leaders were very apprehensive about it, because he was coming back to support them, and they were embarrassed by his support last time. . . .

"He is a great boy for the Empire and Commonwealth—very enthusiastic. So are we. The interesting thing is that yesterday Mr. Churchill made a statement flourishing the Commonwealth and Empire with great vigour, and Lord Woolton in his broadcast last night did the same. Even Sir David Maxwell Fyfe joined in the chorus. They are all splashed in the Beaverbrook Sunday newspaper today. It looks to me as if the noble lord has either been intimating to them that they ought to do something about this, or it may be they thought they would jump in first and see if they could please his lordship. I am only just theorising, but it may be that they are trying either to tame Lord Beaverbrook or it may be he is taming them."

The invitation was clear; it was an incitement to Lord Beaverbrook to break the silence which indeed sat so strangely on his puckish lips, and to repeat in 1950 the doubtful service he had rendered to Conservatism in 1945. But enlivenment of the election was not to come from that quarter. Someone had very effectively laid an ox upon Lord Beaverbrook's tongue. Instead it was Mr. Churchill who once again provided the major thrill of the campaign.

On Monday, February 13th, in a not very widely noted speech at Radford in Warwickshire, Mr. Eden said that an obligation rested on us to check the "momentum of international distrust" rising with "every new discovery of destructive scientific power". He added:

"There is no figure anywhere who compares in stature and in authority with Mr. Churchill. No one can more forcibly recall to harassed and perplexed humanity the choice that now confronts it, between real collaboration with its rich rewards and mounting rivalries, and hatred ending in destruction."

Two days later, on Wednesday, February 15th, Mr. Churchill, conducting a lightning foray into Scotland, spoke at Edinburgh. The next morning the newspapers of the world were carrying excerpts from his speech, which at one stroke made the British election world news and at the same time made foreign policy an issue at home.   The election had hitherto been remarkable for the absence of all argument about foreign affairs, a silence which had been attributed by all observers to the deep-seated agreement between the contestants on all the essentials of policy, but which had none the less fallen a little strangely upon a world agitated by the fateful American decision to proceed with the construction of the hydrogen bomb.   By a synchronisation which was not perhaps a coincidence, the Foreign Office had released on the very day—February 10th—that the American news appeared, an exchange of letters between the Prime Minister and a group of leading Quakers.   They had appealed for a fresh British initiative for an atomic settlement, including the possibility of a direct conference with the leaders of the great Powers.   Mr. Attlee's reply, which had about it a strong tang of departmental drafting, confined itself to a justification of British policy, and concluded that " it would be presumptuous to suppose that personal contact . . . would do anything but raise hopes unduly ". This was the background to Mr. Churchill's words.

" When all is said and done, it is my belief that the superiority in the atom bomb, if not indeed almost the monopoly of this frightful weapon in American hands, is the surest guarantee of world peace to-night.   But for that we should not be talking about all these burning domestic questions that fill our minds, our mouths, and our newspapers to-day.   It is my earnest hope that we may find our way to some more exalted and august foundation for our safety than this grim and sombre balancing power of the bomb.   We must not, however, cast away our only shield of safety unless we can find something better and surer, and more likely to last. . . .

" When we are spending such enormous sums upon our Army, Navy and Air Force, it is very odd that we should not have been able to make the atomic bomb for ourselves by now.   It seems to me one of the most extraordinary administrative lapses that have ever taken place. . . .

" I have not, of course, access to the secret information of the Government, nor am I fully informed about the attitude of the United States ; still, I cannot help coming back to this idea of another talk with Soviet Russia upon the highest level. The idea appeals to me of a supreme effort to bridge the gulf between the two worlds, so that each can live their life, if not in friendship, at least without the hatreds and manœuvres of the cold war. I am grateful to you for marking my words in these matters, because I have not always been proved wrong. It is not easy to see how things could be worsened by a parley at the summit if such a thing were possible. But that I cannot tell. At least I feel that Christian men and women should not close the door upon any hope of finding a new foundation for the life of the self-tormented human race."

Within twenty-four hours Mr. Churchill's speech brought replies from the Prime Minister and Mr. Bevin. Mr. Attlee, speaking at Nottingham on the return leg of his tour, described the speech as " full of mis-statements and misrepresentations " by " a great master of words " who had become " a slave of words ". Of his reference to Britain's tardiness with the atomic bomb he said :

" Mr. Churchill . . . knows perfectly well that the agreement was that atomic energy should be developed in America and Canada. He knows perfectly well why it takes longer here. He knows perfectly well the long time it takes anywhere. That kind of thing ought not to be thrown recklessly by a man who is a statesman into the very difficult question of that kind, accompanied by what I can only describe as gross misrepresentation of what the actual position was."

Earlier at Lincoln, on the question of an approach to Russia, Mr. Attlee remarked :

" This matter is in the hands of the United Nations. I took action almost as soon as I became Prime Minister on this topic. I went across and saw the Americans and the Canadians on it. Thereafter we have been unceasingly endeavouring to bring the whole thing under the control of the United Nations. Whether there would be any use in making another approach is a matter for consideration. I do not rule out the suggestion which has been made by Mr. Churchill, but at the present moment it rests with the United Nations. It is all

H

a very difficult subject, and I cannot make any further pronouncement on it until I have talked the matter over with the
Foreign Secretary."

Mr. Bevin, on the same evening, made his scheduled appearance
in the sequence of election broadcasts, and the three hours' hold-up
in the press release of his text led the newspapers to anticipate a
full comment on Mr. Churchill's remarks. But after recapitulating
the unhappy story of previous negotiations with Russia, Mr. Bevin
contented himself with an indirect allusion to Mr. Churchill's
suggestion : " I think it is clear from what I have said that this
is not a problem which can be solved by any stunt proposals."

In the United States Mr. Churchill's great esteem and popularity gave his words almost as startling an effect as in this country.
" It had been feared ", said *The Times* Washington correspondent,
" that some chance or calculated remark by an American politician
might become a bone of contention in the British election.   It had
not been expected that a remark made during the campaign would
start a political controversy here."   But although Mr. Churchill's
suggestion won the most widespread and sympathetic consideration in the United States, no one more highly placed than Senator
Tydings, Chairman of the Armed Services Committee of the
Senate, was actually prepared to give it his outright endorsement.
Mr. Truman refused to comment, and confined himself to repeating his oft-expressed willingness to see Marshal Stalin or the head
of any State who wished to come to Washington.   The Kremlin
remained wrapt in a characteristically enigmatic silence.

Two days after Mr. Churchill's speech Mr. Morrison followed
in his wake, in a speech in his own constituency of South Lewisham.   After alluding to the " petrol stunt which misfired " he
continued :

> " This is hardly a time for soap-box diplomacy.   I do not
> rule out high-level talks between nations who are taking
> different views about the affairs of the world if and when it is
> clear that such talks would be advantageous.   In the light of
> what our Foreign Secretary said on the wireless last night it
> is clearly his view, as it is certainly mine, that such an effort
> in the spirit of electoral stunting would be anything but
> useful. . . .
>
> " It seems to me that the most unwise and injudicious

way of launching such a proposal is by the Leader of the Opposition during the heat and excitement of a General Election. Moreover, these things would need careful preparation between us and the Soviet Union. The United States would be involved and it could cause unnecessary friction if we suddenly took the issue out of the hands of the United Nations, for delicate discussions are taking place."

He concluded by advising his hearers, even if high-level talks were instituted, not to appoint to them anyone so " flamboyant " as Mr. Churchill.

Was it a " stunt " ? On Friday, February 17th, in the last Conservative broadcast of the election series, Mr. Churchill concluded by defending himself against Mr. Bevin's use of this " scornful word ", which " only showed how far his mind dwells below the true level of events ".

" Why should it be wrong for the British nation to think about these supreme questions of life and death, perhaps for the whole world, at a time when there is a General Election ? Is that not the one time of all others when they should think about them ? What a reflection it would be upon our national dignity and moral elevation, and indeed upon the whole status of British democracy, if at this time of choice, this turning point in world history, we found nothing to talk about but material issues and nice calculations about personal gain or loss. . . .

" The only time when the people really have a chance to influence and, in fact, decide events is at a General Election. Why should they be restricted to the vote catching or vote snatching game ? Why should they be told that it is a ' stunt ' or ' soap box ' diplomacy to speak to them of the great world issues upon which our survival and salvation may well depend ? "

Into this eloquent justification there are woven, one may observe, two rather different questions. The first is the moral and educative benefit to be derived by the nation from having its attention directed to " the great world issues " upon which its survival depends. This is certainly indisputable, though the further question might well be put to Mr. Churchill, the great

Parliamentarian, whether the House of Commons does not constitute a more suitable forum for such a debate than the windy and confusing atmosphere of the hustings.   The second is the desirability and feasibility of submitting such an issue to the direct arbitrament of the electorate.   Even if it could be isolated, which it could not be, from all the very different issues which went to make up the whole electoral debate, is it the sort of issue on which the voter should properly be expected to pronounce ?   Is there a real difference of principle here between the parties, or is it only an issue of diplomatic tactics and timing, albeit an important one ?   If the latter, is it not so intimately bound up in the whole intricate web of diplomatic commitments and inter-allied consultations as to defy the simplified presentation which Mr. Churchill so masterfully imposed on it ?

Yet if Mr. Churchill thus cannot be entirely acquitted from the charge, not indeed of " stunting ", but of introducing into the election issues ill-suited for electoral decision, the significance of the incident does not end here.   It served to light up, more in the manner of its handling than in the content of the arguments deployed, a contrast between the Government and Opposition which was of the most direct relevance to the whole conduct of affairs of state, and was perfectly suited to the judgment of an adult electorate.   The contrast presented was between a challenging, eager Opposition, convinced that, despite the gravity of the situation, it is not incapable of being shaped more nearly to their hearts' desire—flexible, pragmatic, perhaps more than a little impatient, but at the same time freighted with practical experience and scarred with the wounds of many a painful, though always eventually victorious, campaign.   On the other side are the incumbents of office, more than a little weary under their load, conscious—a little too conscious—of having tried their hardest and done their best, concerned not to promise more than they can perform, preferring perhaps the nearer safety to the further chance, trusting to honest work and careful diligence, reasonable, faithful, unimaginative.   It is Ulysses and Telemachus, the one " the grey spirit yearning in desire ", the other " most blameless . . . centred in the sphere Of common duties ".   It is no part of this study to estimate which of these pictures most truly approximated to the reality of either the Government or the Opposition parties, but that these were the roles into which they cast themselves by their attitude to Mr. Churchill's proposal it is hardly possible to deny.

It would be a mistake, however, to assume that Mr. Churchill's initiative in introducing foreign policy into the election provoked a proportionate diversion of interest on the part of the average voter. Extensive inquiries in the constituencies in the week between Mr. Churchill's Edinburgh speech and polling day revealed very few instances in which the content of constituency oratory, or the topics of audiences' questions, or the response of householders to canvassers reflected any newly awakened interest in the conduct of our relations with the U.S.S.R. or in the control of atomic weapons. It is never possible to say how many voters are swayed by any single issue, but if one may judge by outward signs, Mr. Churchill's suggestion would seem neither to have won votes nor to have lost them.

Outward signs tell a different story about another address delivered on the same evening as Mr. Churchill's oration at Edinburgh. This was the broadcast of Dr. Charles Hill, the last but one of the Conservative team of election broadcasters. As the Secretary of the British Medical Association, Dr. Hill had figured prominently in the stormy negotiations between the doctors and Mr. Bevan over the establishment and operation of the National Health Service. As " the Radio Doctor " of the B.B.C., he had distilled the wisdom of his profession into early morning capsules of popular therapy which had caught the imagination and alleviated the ailments of millions of listeners. Now as a " Liberal and Conservative " * candidate for Luton, he directed his familiar broadcasting technique to persuading the electorate to vote for Mr. Churchill and Conservatism. For the content of his address the reader is referred to the analysis on page 137, but probably even more effective than what he said was his manner of saying it. Here was expressed, in popular phraseology, in an occasional pungent phrase and in a continuously " folksy " delivery, the politics of the unpolitical, the plain

---

* Dr. Hill's selection of this somewhat unusually arranged combination of labels made it necessary for him, two days before the poll, to issue a statement clarifying his position still further :

" There is absolutely no truth in the story being put out by canvassers in the division that I am an Independent Liberal. I am, in fact, being opposed by an Independent Liberal. I am a United Liberal-Conservative candidate, representing both Liberal and Conservative opinion. I would also like to make it clear that I am not a National Liberal."

man's grouse against the unco' guid, the unco' wise and the unco' powerful. It was a twenty-minutes' narrative of the adventures of *l'homme moyen sensuel* in Queuetopia. It was the Conservative answer to Mr. Priestley, the more effective because the more delayed, winged straight at the discontents and prejudices of the lower middle class, full of the changeless wisdom of common-sense and constructed according to the most sophisticated formulas of applied psychology.

In the next morning's newspapers Dr. Hill featured prominently despite the unequal competition of Mr. Churchill, the hydrogen bomb and the normal reluctance on the part of the press to reprint what had already been heard by so many. On the platform he evoked the indignant counter-attacks of his old rival, Mr. Bevan (at Portsmouth on February 15th and at Ebbw Vale on February 17th), and on the air the compliment of a passing allusion from Mr. Attlee (" a small-minded politician " who " occupied a key position " in the doctors' professional organisation). The Conservative Party headquarters singled out his broadcast for the unique distinction of being recorded and distributed to the constituencies for use on loud-speaker vans. During the remainder of the campaign mention of his name was good for an immediate round of applause or booing (or both), and phrases such as " Ask your Dad " or " Chuck it, Priestley " became the common currency of hecklers and enthusiasts. If the success of an election speech is the extent to which it becomes a point of departure for opponents' arguments, or the speed with which it becomes part of the cultural currency of a campaign, Dr. Hill's broadcast was the most successful speech of the election.

One result of these exchanges was a sensible rise in the temperature of the campaign. In his Edinburgh speech Mr. Churchill had also included a powerful attack upon the whole range of the Government's domestic policy, and although in the news columns this was swamped by his incursion into foreign affairs, it rankled in many a Labour bosom. He had spoken of " wild extravagance ", " class hatred ", " muddle " and " mismanagement ", and next to Mr. Bevin he had singled out Sir Stafford Cripps for criticism—a man whose " brilliant intellect " was " so precariously poised that his public life has been disfigured by lamentable and spasmodic utterances, to which he falls a victim in moods of excitement or moments of strain ". It was not wholly surprising that such language should have evoked from Sir Stafford, also at Edinburgh on the following day, a retort in comparable terms, protesting against " this sort of blustering and irresponsible vulgarity ", and alleging that Mr. Churchill's charges amounted to " accusations of personal corruption " such as could only be explained as the outcome of " great fear and frustration "—fear of electoral defeat and " frustration because that means the last chance for him ever to enjoy power. I do nevertheless regret that a person whom I have admired for his wartime leadership and indeed friendship should sink to quite this level of guttersnipe politics."

On the fever chart of the campaign this probably marked the highest point, but the campaign remained on what might be described as a rather feverish plateau for the next couple of days, while the sting of Mr. Churchill's " talks-with-Russia stunt " remained fresh. Mr. Churchill's last election broadcast was marked by a solemn, almost grave tone, but even here he could not resist extracting from a somewhat out-of-date version of an interview given by Mr. Attlee to an American journalist evidence that the Prime Minister was aiming at a socialist State which owned everything and employed everybody. Mr. Attlee denied that he had been correctly quoted, and deplored such a lapse from the " standards which one would expect from a statesman of Mr. Churchill's distinction". To high-light his opponent's flippancy still further, he placed it in juxtaposition to a characteristic reference to " the thoughtful atmosphere " he had observed everywhere in the course of his election tour, and warned his audience that if any new issue were " developed " between now and polling day, it would be " neither honest nor genuine. It will be a mere election stunt."

It was pointed out in *McCallum and Readman* * how successfully in 1945 Labour spokesmen had inoculated the electorate against any Conservative " stunt propaganda ". The " propaganda against propaganda " which worked so well in 1945 was invoked to full effect in 1950. Mr. Attlee's final broadcast warning was only one of a series which were launched with mounting intensity as polling day grew nearer. Even from the outset of the campaign the theme of ingenious and stick-at-nothing Tories producing a last-minute devil *ex machina* to overset Labour's happy

* P. 149.

ending was hinted at in most Labour speeches.   Then on February 17th Mr. Morrison gave to a press conference a fully orchestrated version of his favourite *motif*.   He referred to " rumours " that a " scare " was being prepared suggesting that the " mutualisation " of insurance was a Labour trick to grab " the savings of the people ".   Then, by the familiar device of *credo quia impossibile*, he went on to deplore the " scare " at the same time as he denied it could happen.

> " I find it difficult to imagine that a ' Red Letter ' could be done in 1950 : I think the electorate would not have it.   But the electoral tactics of stunts and scares is very much ingrained in the Tory party machine.   I don't like these things myself from the point of view of political morals.   It is the duty of political parties to put the issues clearly before the electorate.   Stunts and scares are a form of cheating."

Finally he refuted in advance, as a " deliberate untruth ", the particular " mutualisation " scare with which his homily began.

Within the next few days almost every other Labour Minister took up the " stunt warning " cry.   It was featured prominently in *Reynolds' News* of Sunday, February 19th, and in the *Daily Herald* of February 20th.   It was even taken up, as one man tries another's patent medicine, by the Liberals, who also warned the public " to be on their guard " and their candidates " to keep in touch with headquarters ".   Finally, by a rotation which Mr. Morrison would probably have regarded as the acme of the double bluff, it was found on the lips of Conservatives themselves.

In fact, whether because it was non-existent or because it was thus exorcised, no last-minute " stunt " made its appearance. The only issue absent from the beginning of the campaign but still doing service at the end was the " atomic talks " theme.   Mr. Attlee did not, as had been anticipated, use his advantage of the last word on the air to deal directly with Mr. Churchill's now famous proposal.   He contented himself with yet another description and justification of what had been done to secure agreement with the U.S.S.R. in the past.   Not even Monday morning's headline writers could make a counter-challenge out of the Prime Minister's oblique reproof : " The difficulty doesn't lie in the choice of persons to discuss these high matters.   All that is required is the will."   Lord Beaverbrook, however, with another

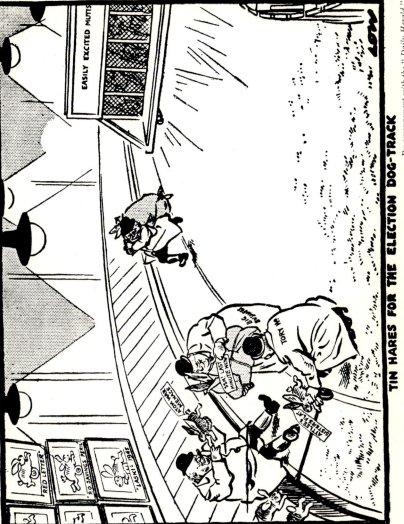

TIN HARES FOR THE ELECTION DOG-TRACK

By arrangement with the " Daily Herald "

brand of obliquity, all his own, chose this moment to break the unnatural silence which, save for mutterings about a £6 minimum weekly wage, he had maintained so long. Sunday's *Sunday Express* contained a centre page article on " What Stalin Thinks of Churchill " from Lord Beaverbrook's own pen and based on his own war-time encounters in the Kremlin. Unfortunately, the familiar Beaverbrook diapason of " Union Now in the British Empire " intruded so forcibly upon the delicate theme of " Churchill and Stalin at the Council Table " that the effectiveness of the reminiscences was a good deal impaired. For Labour Mr. Morrison and Sir Stafford Cripps continued to deplore Mr. Churchill's proposal. To Mr. Morrison at Dover on February 19th it was " badly thought out " and " it was a pity to drop this proposition into an election campaign ". Sir Stafford, speaking at Birmingham the same day, called it " stunting irresponsibility ", and could " not see salvation coming to the world by the man who made the broadcast of Friday night talking to Mr. Stalin ". Mr. Bevin, reflecting further on the idea at Eltham a day later, said he was not enamoured of " the individual business. . . . After all, it was tried at Yalta and did not work very well. I think it is better to keep Cabinet responsibility."

Mr. Churchill, however, was determined to have the last word. On the Monday before the poll he made the last of his provincial forays, to speak at Manchester and Oldham, and in the former city, in a speech which the *Manchester Guardian* described as " one of the best of his campaign ", he once more embroidered his Edinburgh theme, giving it the fresh twists and variations of a master.

> " The Socialist politicians and party managers take a poor view of democracy. They have vehemently protested against my raising at Edinburgh the great question of the atomic bomb and our relations with Soviet Russia, on which the future peace of the world depends. Such subjects, they hold, should not be mentioned at election times.
>
> " They are above the heads of the working classes. To mention them is a stunt. One after another they repeat this word with disciplined repetition. Their eyes are fixed on the past, rather than the future. They seem to think that material and domestic matters are all that the British demo-

cracy should talk about at the General Election and that the extra half-ounce of tea or half-ounce of sweets which Mr. Strachey has been good enough to give us ought to be sufficient to occupy the minds of the electorate. . . .

" It is not the Socialist politicians who shed their blood, and I cannot see why they should be given a monopoly of debating and deciding these supreme issues. I do not take the Socialist or Communist view that all should be reserved for the commissars. . . .

" The words I spoke at Edinburgh about closing no door in a sincere attempt to reach an enduring settlement with Soviet Russia have not only dominated the election in Great Britain, they have rolled round the world and may have created a new situation which, whatever happens, cannot make things worse and may possibly bring us the nearer to our hearts' desire. It is clear to most people that more vision than Mr. Bevin possesses is required in the handling of our foreign affairs. I do not, therefore, withdraw a word that I said at Edinburgh or at Woodford or on the broadcast, and I repeat that Christian men should not close the door upon any hope of finding a better foundation than the atomic bomb for the life of the self-tormented human race."

In this speech all that was to be said on this—or indeed on any other electoral theme—had been said. From overseas two voices were still to be heard. Mr. Truman delayed what was in effect his reply to Mr. Churchill until all was over in the British election save the polling. On Wednesday, February 22nd, at a speech in Virginia, he reviewed the threat presented by atomic weapons, and implicitly but unmistakably indicated his preference for the views of Mr. Attlee over those of Mr. Churchill. On the same day the Moscow radio broke its long silence, but its interpretation of Mr. Churchill's move as the product of British fear and exhaustion, could not be convincingly depicted as accepting overtures of peace.

Even if they had been more encouraging, these statements, no doubt designedly, came too late to affect the outcome. Not many political Damascus Road scenes occur on polling day. In the last twenty-four hours before the 23rd candidates and leaders confined themselves to reiterating the already oft-expressed, frequently with that exact verbal repetition which represents not the triumph of memory, but the defeat of invention.   Even the most confidential and " safely-seated " of incumbents now restricted his perambulations to his home territory, and only peers ranged abroad without a care for their own skins.   The party managers devoted themselves to the phrasing of " final messages " designed to inspire confidence without arousing apathy.   And, of course, each side had a last word for the Liberals, generally in the form of the argument that had done such good service in 1945, that a vote for the Liberals was a vote wasted.

One of the complaints that had been most frequently aired, by friend and foe alike, against Mr. Attlee's decision to hold a February election was that the weather would affect not only the campaigning, but also the vote.   Campaigning had not always been pleasant, but to the determined and the devoted the moist severities of February had not proved as serious an obstacle as had been feared.   But would the *voters* prove equally determined and devoted in face of a comparable inclemency ?   All parties scanned anxiously the Air Ministry's weather forecast for February 23rd.   It ran :

> " Mainly fair in Eastern districts, with ground frost and a few fog patches in the early morning.   There will be occasional slight rain in South-west England, Wales, and West Scotland, and this will spread slowly eastwards across Central and Southern England, and may reach the London area towards midnight."

The forecast was correct, and over much of Britain, including London, the early part of February 23rd was marked by a sunny and inviting mildness which might embolden even the most delicate of voters to venture to the poll.   Over most parts of the country the result was a steady stream of early voters, flowing at a rate which confirmed most observers in their expectation of a heavy vote.   But, true to the forecast, " rain spread slowly eastwards " as the day wore on, and by evening it was enveloping the whole country in a steady, unrelenting downpour.   Would this mean that Labour, as the party of wage-earners and late voters, would suffer from a light vote in the crucial few hours before the close of the polls ?   It was soon apparent that this was not going to happen.   The rate of polling increased as the hours drew on, and the weather got worse, until queues were forming in the rain outside town halls and schoolrooms all over Britain. When the polling-stations closed at 9 p.m. and the weary, wet tellers outside pocketed their pencils and their note-books, it was already apparent that this had been a phenomenally heavy poll. But for the best part of another twenty-four hours it was still to be anyone's guess how these moist, orderly and, for the most part, curiously silent files of citizenry had inclined the balance of their collective will.

CHAPTER VI

THE MANIFESTOES AND THE BROADCASTS

In a modern election campaign the party manifesto may be likened to an arsenal and the party broadcasts to the engagements in which the armaments drawn from it are deployed. It is true that the manifestoes are not the only sources from which the party leaders draw their debating weapons; in the heat of the fray they will often pick up any argument that comes to hand. It is even more true that the broadcasts are not the only occasions upon which these armaments are put to use; they are the standby of every orator on every platform throughout the campaign. But the manifestoes remain the fullest, the most considered and the most generally accepted statement of party doctrines. And, whatever the continuing importance of platform speeches, it is increasingly through the broadcasts, with their vast audiences and intimate appeal, that the major battles for the votes of the electorate are fought. Only two issues emerged in the course of the 1950 campaign which were not already developed in the party manifestoes; the first was the increase in the petrol ration (and that was already adumbrated in the Conservative Manifesto), and the second was the " talks with Russia " suggestion advanced by Mr. Churchill in his speech at Edinburgh on February 14th. Of these, the second was as fully developed in the election broadcasts as on the platforms of public meetings; only the first was entirely kept off the air. Conversely, there were no other issues aired in the broadcasts which had not already been presented in the manifestoes. No doubt this testified to a certain lack of inventiveness (or, in more honourable terms, a commendable consistency) on the part of the contestants. It also testified to the fact that the circumstances, political and economic, in which the election was fought left very little room for manœuvre by any party. While to the sophisticated observer this made the election rather a tame spectacle, there can be no doubt that this thorough and repeated debating of a limited number of issues gave the electorate full opportunity to explore and comprehend the differences between the parties; it may well have been a factor in producing the phenomenal poll of February 23rd.

The first party manifesto to appear was Labour's *Let Us Win Through Together*. It was principally notable for its emphasis on the contrast between full employment under the Labour Government and pre-war unemployment under Conservative Governments. In a few vivid sentences the Labour " myth " of the thirties was presented, of dole queues and means tests. The first main section of the manifesto was entitled " Work For All ". To this was linked the need for increased production, at lower costs. Here was found the justification for planning and controls; also, more by implication than by argument, for the socialised industries. Emphasis was laid on the need for enterprise both in public and private industry. Private monopolisation in the sugar and cement industries was given as the reason for their proposed nationalisation. A special section (about one-eighth of the whole manifesto) was devoted to " Agriculture and the Countryside ", pledging a continuance and development of Labour's policies of guaranteed prices, higher production and " rural amenities ", such as better housing, electrification and piped water supplies. In a reference to the need for utilising marginal land it was said, " Where the job is too big for individual farmers to tackle, public ownership will be used as the means of bringing into sound cultivation good food-producing land not fully used."

A rather defensive section dealt with the cost of living, making some admission of its increase, but claiming credit for rationing, price controls and food subsidies as devices for preventing its further rise. Further Government control of purchasing and distributive processes would, it claimed, yield even better results in the future. More than one-sixth of the manifesto dwelt on the benefits already conferred by the social services, with emphasis on Labour achievement and Tory opposition. To this was related the scheme for " mutualising " industrial assurance and a brief paragraph on housing.

A final section, " One World of Peace and Plenty ", reviewed Labour's record in foreign and Commonwealth affairs, with little reference to future policy save in the field of colonial development.

Incidental references occurred in the manifesto to " the proud record " of the trade unions and to " the great Co-operative Movement ", but sectional appeals were not dominant. A final section, " Put the Nation First ", claimed that Labour's appeal was to " all useful men and women "—Mr. Herbert Morrison's new concept of classless utilitarianism. "The fundamental question " was put in terms of " forward with ordered progress " or " back to the bleak years ". Thus the appeal to history with which the manifesto opened was also the note on which it closed.

Critics of the manifesto speedily pointed out certain omissions. There was no reference to Marshall Aid, no mention of the Atom Bomb and no treatment of defence or conscription. On foreign affairs the manifesto remained true to the conviction of *Labour Believes in Britain* that " no programme of action or legislation can be adopted in advance ". In economic affairs the dollar crisis was very far from occupying the centre of the argument, and there was some criticism of the virtual omission of the problems accompanying devaluation. Steel nationalisation was dismissed in a single sentence, but it could reasonably be claimed that this was a mere " left-over " from Labour's first five-year plan (though not an issue which had been argued in full in *Let Us Face The Future*).

The Conservative manifesto, *This Is The Road*, appeared a week later. In its full form it was a longer document than *Let Us Win Through Together*, but it was also somewhat more wordy. Whereas its rival began with a reference to past troubles, it led off with a warning of present dangers. Socialist mismanagement and false optimism were blamed for the country's failure to prepare for the crisis of 1952, when Marshall Aid would end. It then turned to denunciation of Socialist failures—the groundnuts scheme, the low rate of housing development, the decline in the purchasing power of the pound, the " crushing burden of taxation ". "A complete change in the spirit of administration is needed." An Imperial Economic Conference should be called to consider the common problem of closing the dollar gap. By releasing enterprise " larger and more efficient production " could be attained. Government spending must be cut, and a hypothetical figure of £3,300 million a year was mentioned. The end of bulk purchasing would reduce the cost of food and of food subsidies, though these would not be reduced " without compensating increases to those most affected ". Much bureaucratic waste could be eliminated. As a result of such economies, taxation could be cut, making a start on " indirect taxation and particularly purchase tax on necessities and semi-necessities ".

The manifesto addressed itself repeatedly to the issue of unemployment, went back over the history of the inter-war years, claimed that without Marshall Aid the present volume of unemployed would be between one and a half and two million, and affirmed that " the maintenance of full employment " would be " the first aim of a Conservative Government ".

In industry and business it attacked the growing and centralising power of the State and particularly " the State monopolies created by nationalisation ". It pledged the Conservatives to " bring nationalisation to a full stop here and now ", to repeal the Iron and Steel Act, to halt the nationalisation of road transport, and where possible to return it to private owners. The administration of coal and the railways would be as much decentralised as possible. On controls it spoke feelingly, but also cautiously. They " must be reduced to the minimum necessary as the supply situation improves ". " As soon as we have been able to ensure that the prime necessities of life are within the reach of every family and each individual, we shall abolish the existing rationing system."

For the trade unions it professed a desire to see them regain the free bargaining position from which the Labour Government had ousted them. Direction of labour would be abolished and " a friendly and final settlement of the question of contracting out and compulsory unionism " reached. A " workers' charter ", not legally binding, but serving as a code of fair employment practices, would encourage co-partnership and profit sharing.

On agriculture the Conservative policy closely paralleled Labour's—higher production, guaranteed prices and markets, priority in housing, electricity, water supplies and 'bus services. For the farmers of marginal land " appropriate incentives " would be provided. The Ministries of Food and Agriculture would be amalgamated.

The social services were set in the context of the principle, " Britain can only enjoy the social services for which she is prepared to work ", and the concept of a minimum below which none should be allowed to fall. Nonetheless, the promises made, though generally couched in some qualifying phrase, such as " if possible " or " we hope ", breathed an air of generosity—more houses, more schooling, a maintained and improved Health Service, equal pay in Government service for men and women, an increase in pensions rates and a new category of " working pensioners ".

The section " Britain and the World " differed little in substance from Labour's, and was only mildly critical of Labour's performance in foreign affairs. As far as defence was concerned, it stood by conscription, but believed that " by wise arrangements its burden might be sensibly reduced ".

Unlike Labour, the Conservatives made concessions to Home Rule sentiment in Scotland and Wales—" a new Minister of State with Cabinet rank " for the first, and " a member of the Cabinet with special responsibility " for the second. They also promised to appoint a Royal Commission on Anglo-Scottish relations. They looked forward to the long-awaited " reform of the House of Lords " and pledged themselves to the restoration of the university vote.

The manifesto concluded, like Labour's, by claiming that its authors would act " not for a section but for the nation ", and also by a comparable evocation of its own " myth " of the past. Labour, it said, had " tried to make out that before they got a majority the whole history of Great Britain . . . was dark and dismal ". To Conservatives by contrast the past offered a norm to be " restored ". " We shall make Britain once again a place in which hard work, thrift, honesty and neighbourliness are honoured and win their true reward in freedom and underneath the law."

Perhaps the most striking feature of *This Is The Road* was its overlap in substance, though not in form, with *Let Us Go Forward Together*. The acceptance by both of the Welfare State led sometimes to a competition in the conferring of favours on the electorate. Each emphasised the need for greater and cheaper production. Though Labour dwelt on the dangers of private ownership, and Conservatives on those of public ownership, they agreed that both forms were here to stay and that the problem was to make them as efficient as possible. Each, for reasons both of state and of campaigning, sought to foster the domestic food producer. Abroad, they had little to say of the future and did not seriously differ about the past. Their differences were in fact often differences only in attitude and emphasis, though they were none the less real enough to make the ensuing battle keen and close.

The Liberal manifesto, *No Easy Way*, was the last of the

I

major three to appear.   It began with a paragraph indicative of a peculiar difficulty the party had to overcome—that of convincing the electorate of its *raison d'être* :

> " The Liberal Party offers the electorate the opportunity of returning a Liberal Government to office.   We believe that our Party is more likely to unite the nation than either the Conservatives or the Socialists—locked as they are in what is really a class struggle."

After this prelude it addressed itself directly to a consideration of Britain's economic crisis.   Taxation was too high, but the manifesto warned against the inflationary effect of any cuts which ran ahead of, or did not directly stimulate increased production and increased exports.

Like Conservatives, Liberals demanded drastic cuts in Government expenditure and, like them, proposed increased social security benefits to offset progressive cuts in food subsidies. Bulk buying would be reduced and the Government taken out of business which private traders could handle better.   " Every control not imposed by the need for fair shares or scarcity must go."   To increase production much reliance was placed on incentives—joint   consultation,   co-partnership   and   profit-sharing (whether compusory or not was left uncertain), and, immediately, the removal of the tax on undistributed profits used to replace capital equipment.

" Nationalisation for the sake of nationalisation is nonsense." It should be considered only where no other means exist of introducing competition or control.   In any case, there should be no more of it for five years.   Liberals would repeal the Iron and Steel Act, " free road transport " and decentralise |existing nationalised undertakings.   Emphasis was laid on breaking monopolies, ending restrictive practices, abandoning protection for inefficiency and stopping the direction of labour.   It was admitted that free trade with Iron Curtain countries was not practicable, but for trade elsewhere tariffs should be reduced by stages " until all are abolished ".

Conscription was attacked as inefficient and costly, and the American success with " the voluntary principle " was invoked as the appropriate alternative.

No less than its predecessors, the Liberal manifesto promised

the farmer assured markets and guaranteed prices. It also proposed the establishment of a " Land Bank " to provide cheap
credit. There was the usual emphasis on rural amenities, including a proposal for the creation of a national water system. The
Government's housing record was attacked and proposals were
made for speeding up a wider range of house-building.

" A programme for women " included equal pay for equal work
and an improvement in pay and conditions of work for women
teachers and nurses. As for social security, the party pledged
itself to extend the family allowance to the first child and, in terms
rather similar to those of the Conservatives, to improve the
administration of the Health Service and to lighten the lot of
pensioners.

There were two distinctively Liberal sections ; the first, constitutional, advocated proportional representation, reform of the
House of Lords and separate Parliaments for Scotland and Wales ;
the second, dealing with the liberty of the individual, urged a new
Bill of Rights to operate both at home and in the colonies and a
reversion to the contracting-in principle for Trade Unionists.

In its final section, on imperial and foreign affairs, the manifesto
laid great stress on support of the United Nations. " The
Security Council . . . offers the only machinery through which the
development of the hydrogen bomb and other horrors of science
can be brought under control." More than any other manifesto
it dwelt on the need for quicker development of the Council of
Europe, advocating convertible currencies and the removal of
trade barriers within the year.

The manifesto as a whole had two drawbacks, viewed as an
instrument for electioneering. Many of its proposals seemed
insufficiently distinctive, and it was hard to find a single, easily
comprehensible theme dominating and uniting them. In one
respect, however, it stood out in marked contrast to both its
rivals : it devoted no space to the past. It was perhaps a corollary
of this that unemployment was mentioned only once—in a warning
of what would befall the country when American aid ended,
unless thrift and full production were realised first.

The Communist Party manifesto, from its title-page—*The
Socialist Road for Britain*—to its final paragraph, emphasised its
" Labour " and " democratic " character. The weight of its
attack fell against the Labour Government for its " betrayal of

the interests of the working class ". It began by what was, in effect, a rebuttal of Labour's main claim: to have cured unemployment. " The impending slump ", it claimed, was the result of the Government's economic policies, and would bring " mass unemployment " unless they were checked. To check them the first necessity was to put an end to the " wage freeze "; on this the manifesto laid great stress. Instead there should be an all-round increase along with equal pay for equal work, and a universal forty-hour, five-day working week. Compulsory arbitration and the Control of Engagement Order should be abolished. The party also favoured lower prices. Purchase tax on all but luxuries (in which category beer, tobacco and entertainment were not included) should be abolished; a capital levy and higher taxation for the rich should take their place. All " capitalist elements " should be " purged " from the nationalised industries. At the same time nationalisation should be extended to include steel, shipbuilding, building, the land, chemicals, engineering, food processing, the banks and the insurance companies. In foreign trade we should abandon the " cut-throat export drive aimed at the dollar markets ", and switch our attention to the Soviet Union and Eastern Europe.

Much stress was laid on peace, to be secured by supporting the U.S.S.R., repudiating the Brussels and Atlantic Pacts, ending the military occupation of Britain by American troops, reducing armaments, banning the atom bomb, " bringing the troops home " from Greece, Malaya and the Middle East, and " giving freedom to Colonial Peoples ".

The social services should be extended in every direction—more houses, more schools, more education, more hospitals and higher benefits, family allowances and pensions. Scottish and Welsh Parliaments should be set up at the earliest possible moments and Irish partition should be ended. Votes at 18, proportional representation, the waiving of the £150 deposit and the abolition of the House of Lords provided final constitutional embellishments.

Two other manifestoes deserve a passing mention, as expressions of parties which, though not independent forces in the election, yet represented, the one a distinctive interest, the other a distinctive appeal. The Co-operative Party, whose candidates all stood as " Labour and Co-operative " candidates, issued a brief

manifesto entitled *Forward With The People*. It bore obvious
resemblances to the official Labour thesis—sections on "The
Old Order" (unemployment and poverty), "A Proud Record"
(the results of Labour rule) and "Fair Shares". But in reference
to Labour's nationalisation proposals it added, "Even where it is
necessary to establish public direction of an industry it is desirable
that non-profit making enterprises [i.e. co-operatives] should be
encouraged to develop side by side with the public sector."
It welcomed the Labour Party's proposals to end price-fixing
rings, and wound up with a rousing refutation of Conservative
claims to be the friends and protectors of the Co-operative
Movement.

The National Liberal Party entitled its manifesto *Making
Britain Great Again*. It began with the claim that it had "remained consistently loyal to the Liberal faith", and insisted that
"as Liberals, our first immediate duty is to secure the defeat of
Socialism". "In existing circumstances this cannot be done
by Liberals alone", since even if "united within one party
organisation", they could not possibly win the necessary minimum
of three hundred seats. Hence the need for "open and honourable co-operation with the Conservatives". "At present no
contemporary difference of principle or aim between Liberals
and Conservatives stands in the way of the full co-operation
which the national situation demands." Then followed nineteen
points of National Liberal doctrine in content not easily distin-
guishable from the policies embodied in *This Is The Road*.

None of these manifestoes was much more readable *in extenso*
than in the précis of them given above. The Conservative was
perhaps the best from this point of view, but its greater reada-
bility was probably offset by the fact that there was more of it to
read. Thus, although copies of these documents were circulated
in their hundreds of thousands, it is doubtful whether one in ten
of them was read from cover to cover. No true index of their
usefulness, however, can be derived from that. Their function
was to serve as quarries from which the political architects could
select material for erection into the more pleasing edifices of
articles, speeches and broadcasts. Their distinctive value was to
be found in the area of agreement that each represented—the
highest common factor, as it were, of the different groups within
each party ; or, viewed in another aspect, the farthest inroad made

by the ideal upon the possible, where the ideal represents the popular wish and the possible represents the hard facts of habit and circumstance.   In the battle of wits which ensued upon their publication one of the main objects of each party was to probe and penetrate the weak points in these paper defences.   For this purpose no weapon was so effective as the broadcast.

The success—and also the failures—of the broadcasts of the 1945 campaign had impressed each party deeply, and there was no aspect of their electoral tactics in 1950 to which they gave more thought and care.   The services of a retired B.B.C. official were sought for advice, instruction and rehearsal and every broad-cast (with the lamentable exception of Mr. Bevin's) betrayed evidence that consideration had been given to the medium which was being employed.   Some broadcasters were obviously chosen more for their command of the ether than their eminence in party counsels, such as Mr. J. B. Priestley and Dr. Charles Hill.   Con-versely, it was reported that Mr. Aneurin Bevan's absence from Labour's rota was due in part at least to his discomfort at the microphone.   There is a risk, however, in assuming too Machia-vellian a plan in the parties' use of their broadcasting facilities. Other factors besides pure radio appeal entered into both the selection of the speakers and the content of their remarks.   The chief figures of the party must be heard.   There must be a woman speaker.   For Labour there must, if possible, always be a promi-nent trade unionist, for Conservatives an eminent peer.   For this diversity of voices there will be a comparable range of themes. Yet all must be accommodated within a strictly limited number of broadcasts.   The result is inevitably compromise and improvisa-tion, at least as much as planning and design.

The allocation of broadcasting time for electioneering purposes is made by agreement between the party leaders.   The B.B.C. may assist or advise, but the responsibility for arranging " fair shares for all " rests squarely on the main participants.   It was widely believed that in 1945 the public had been saturated with political broadcasts, which had continued night after night every weekday for almost a month.   Accordingly, in December 1949, before the election date was known, the parties agreed on a lighter diet for their listeners.   There were to be only fourteen election broadcasts in all, five Conservative, five Labour, three Liberal and one for any other party which had fifty or more candidates on nomination day (only the Communists qualified). The total time available (excluding repeats) was 120 minutes each for Conservative and Labour, forty minutes for Liberals and ten minutes for Communists. The proportionate advantages enjoyed by each party are not, however, adequately indicated by these figures. The timing of the broadcasts was at least as important as their frequency or their duration. The two major parties always broadcast after the nine o'clock news. The Liberals had only one such broadcast (Mr. Clement Davies's on Thursday, February 16th); their other two took place after the six o'clock news, as did the single Communist broadcast. (These Home Service broadcasts were repeated on recordings in the Light Programme at 7.15 p.m. for 6.15 broadcasts and 10.15 p.m. for 9.15 broadcasts; also on the Television sound track at the end of each evening's programme.*) Thus, although the potential listening audiences at 6.15 and 7.15 combined and 9.15 and 10.15 combined are not very different, the Liberals, by partial exclusion from the main series, were to some degree marked off as *tertium quids*. Moreover, their failure to secure a single Saturday time probably cut them off from a percentage of listeners readily available to their rivals, since Saturday evening is the peak listening night of the week. Furthermore, the duration of individual broadcasts was important. It could well be argued that just as thirty minutes is not half as good again as twenty minutes (because listeners' interest flags), so ten minutes is less than half as good as twenty (because there is a certain minimum time necessary to develop any argument). Thus it was doubtful whether the major parties gained much from stretching, each of them, two of their broadcasts to thirty minutes (the first and the last in each case), but it is certain that the Liberals lost by having to confine the first two of their three speakers to ten minutes each.

The Liberal grievance at their allocation of broadcasting time seems therefore justified. If, as the allocation to the Communist Party implied, the allotment of time on the air was linked with the number of candidates a party was nominating—and it is hard to see what other fair basis for calculation could be found—then their 475 candidatures entitled them to a better showing. Mr.

* Party leaders showed no desire to launch into the new and arduous medium of Television. There were no Television election broadcasts.

Churchill's offer of one of the Conservative times to Lady Violet Bonham-Carter (see p. 87) was no adequate remedy for this. The disclosure by Mr. Frank Byers that the two major parties originally proposed to offer the Liberals only one broadcast suggests even more strongly that the present system of allocating election broadcasts on a basis of party haggling does not represent the ultimate in political distributive justice.

The Communists also protested against their allocation of one ten-minute broadcast.   Certainly in 1945, when both they and the Common Wealth Party ran only slightly over twenty candidates, they each had as much.   But that was out of almost twice as many election broadcasts in all.   Moreover, a further ten-minute period (the smallest conceivable additional unit) would have been more than their strength entitled them to.   There was, indeed, a certain amount of vehement protest against their being allowed on the air at all.   So long, however, as they were a legally constituted and law-abiding party the decision to allow them to be heard was incontestable.

The election broadcasts proper do not exhaust the whole story of radio and the election.   The parties still had, at the beginning of 1950, a few broadcasting times left over from their agreed allotment for the year 1949–50, and any full analysis of the employment of broadcasting in the election ought to allow for these, since they were no less devoted to electioneering than those which came later.   There were seven such " party political " broadcasts between Mr. Attlee's announcement of January 10th and the dissolution on February 3rd, which ushered in the " election broadcasts " proper.   Labour and Conservatives had three each, and the Liberals one.

These party broadcasts apart, the B.B.C. kept as aloof from the election as if it had been occurring on another planet.   Every programme was scrutinised in search of any item, jocular or serious, which might give aid or comfort to any of the contestants, and after February 3rd virtually all mention of election politics disappeared from the British air.   Undoubtedly in view of the enormous power wielded by such a monopolistic instrument the decision to carry neutrality to the lengths of castration was the only right one.   At the same time it produced extraordinary results—as when the B.B.C. and the broadcasting system of the U.S.S.R. were alone amongst the radio services of the world in passing over in silence the headline news of Mr. Churchill's " atom talks " proposal at Edinburgh. More than this, the vast potentialities for education and discussion inherent in radio were, in relation to this great event in the nation's life, deliberately and completely suppressed. No one who has seen the perversion of these potentialities in pre-war Germany or Italy will lightly criticise the B.B.C.'s decision. At the same time it can hardly stand as the last word in the collective wisdom and courage of a mature democracy.

The B.B.C.'s Audience Research service conducted inquiries, by the familiar technique of sampling, into the proportion of the adult population which heard each broadcast, and the results are published below, by kind permission of the B.B.C.

A. *Party Political Broadcasts 9.15 p.m.* (These were not repeated).

Sat.	14 Jan.	J. B. Priestley	Labour	26%
Sat.	21 Jan.	W. Churchill	Conservative	40%
Fri.	27 Jan.	Lord Salisbury	Conservative	13%
Sat.	28 Jan.	M. Webb	Labour	27%
Mon.	30 Jan.	Sir D. Maxwell Fyfe	Conservative	17%
Tues.	31 Jan.	F. Byers	Liberal	18%
Thur.	2 Feb.	Sir S. Cripps	Labour	21%

B. *Election Broadcasts 6.15 p.m. and 7.15 p.m.*

Tues.	7 Feb.	Lord Samuel	Liberal	27%
Fri.	10 Feb.	Lady M. Lloyd-George	Liberal	29%
Thur.	16 Feb.	H. Pollitt	Communist	26%

C. *Election Broadcasts 9.15 p.m. and 10.15 p.m.*

Sat.	4 Feb.	H. Morrison	Labour	33%
Mon.	6 Feb.	A. Eden	Conservative	39%
Wed.	8 Feb.	J. Griffiths	Labour	31%
Thur.	9 Feb.	F. Horsbrugh	Conservative	33%
Sat.	11 Feb.	Lord Woolton	Conservative	39%
Mon.	13 Feb.	M. Herbison	Labour	33%
Tues.	14 Feb.	C. Hill	Conservative	42%
Wed.	15 Feb.	E. Bevin	Labour	40%
Thur.	16 Feb.	Clement Davies	Liberal	34%
Fri.	17 Feb.	W. Churchill	Conservative	51%
Sat.	18 Feb.	C. R. Attlee	Labour	44%

The figures represent the gross audience for each speaker, obtained by adding the figures for the original " live " broadcast to those for the recorded and ignoring, as insignificant, any over-lap between the two.

The party broadcasts did not draw quite as large audiences as in 1945. Whereas the audiences for the 6.15–7.15 broadcasts were not substantially different, considerably fewer people listened in 1950 to the 9.15–10.15 series. For the four weeks broad-casting of 1945 the average figures each week were 45, 44, 47 and 44%. For the three weeks of 1950 they were 33, 37 and 39%. Only Mr. Churchill held audiences of the same order as he had in 1945, with Mr. Attlee and Mr. Eden running 4–5% behind. Other speakers who had broadcast in the previous election had 10% fewer listeners in 1950. Whatever allowances may be made for errors or improvements in sampling techniques, the drop in audiences remains considerable; it effectively dis-poses of the theory that the radio alone was responsible for the record poll. It is rather the poll which prompts the question, what happened to the radio audiences?

Several answers suggest themselves. The timing of the broad-casts in relation to the rest of the evening programmes made it harder for the " continuous listener " to evade them in 1945: in 1950, on evenings which had no early broadcast, he could evade them on the Light Programme up to 10.15 p.m. Further-more, the competition of other evening diversions, political or otherwise, was more powerful in 1950 than in the still war-ridden days of 1945. This, however, might well have been offset by the timing of the 1950 election in February—an indoor month— as opposed to June in 1945. One is therefore driven to look for reasons beyond the merely circumstantial, and it is hard to resist the supposition that more voters in 1950 had already made up their minds and were not interested to the same degree in hearing the case either for their own or for any other party. Perhaps the fact that Conservative speakers on the whole attracted larger audiences than Labour points to a disposition amongst a small majority of listeners to hear what the Opposition had to say, but it may merely be another expression of the fact that as you go up the social scale you find a higher percentage of listeners to political broadcasts.

The slight drop from 1945 in the size of radio audiences should not lead to any under-estimate of the importance of the broad-casts. The figures are still extremely impressive, markedly in excess of the figures for any ordinary non-entertainment broad-cast, and representing at least three to four times the number of voters who find their way into election meetings. The parties' cultivation of this medium was therefore in no sense mis-placed. What picture of the issues did they present to their radio audiences ?

The Labour Party in its broadcasts, as in the rest of its propa-ganda, put the full employment appeal first. There was not a single broadcast, from Mr. Priestley's to Mr. Attlee's, in which this theme did not appear, and there was one—Mr. Griffith's—which was dominated by it. Conversely, nationalisation, for all its honoured place in socialist doctrine, was even less prominent in the broadcasts than in the manifesto. It went unmentioned by Sir Stafford Cripps, in a broadcast devoted largely to an examination of the Labour Government's record, and also by Mr. Maurice Webb, speaking as the Chairman of the Labour Party. Most other Labour broadcasters gave it merely a passing mention. A good deal was made of the social services and about the merits, in general, of Labour's planning. Foreign affairs were given an inconspicuous place by almost all speakers except the Foreign Secretary and the Prime Minister.

The Conservative broadcasts had " anti-socialism " as their continuously dominant theme, defined sometimes as opposition to nationalisation, but more often in terms of a general hostility to controls, bureaucracy, expansion of State power and interference with economic liberty. Their references to full employment took the form of defensive reactions to Labour's attacks on their record, but their expositions of social policy (which were frequent and sometimes lengthy) had a more positive and unsolicited quality. Mr. Churchill's two broadcasts were distinctive in every respect, but in nothing more than in his emphasis on the world context of Britain's problems.

The Liberals, with four broadcasts in all, had less scope to develop their themes ; in addition to expounding their economic and social policies, they had to give continuous attention to pro-tecting themselves against the charges especially levelled at a third party trying to recover lost ground. They always felt obliged to convince their hearers that they had a right to be heard, a right to a vote, and the ability to form a Liberal Government.

All parties envisaged the broadcasts as a series, speaker answering preceding speaker or throwing down " challenges " for a successor. The press, in its election campaign, accepted the broadcasts as opportunities for supporting action or offensives requiring counter-attack (see *infra* p. 145). Platform speakers did not, in the main, display a similar deference, though one or two broadcasts, notably Dr. Hill's and to a lesser degree Mr. Priestley's, evoked the tribute of quotation and rebuttal at the constituency level.

Mr. Priestley's opening thrust was an ably designed appeal to the potentially malcontent 1945 Labour supporter, mainly conceived as a middle-class man of goodwill who was irked by restrictions, rather bored by Labour Aristides' and by no means proof against the wiles of Tory propagandists. The talk was designed to set his little grumbles and doubts in perspective against the great achievements and the fundamental reasonableness of Labour rule. There was little of detailed policy and nothing of socialist doctrine. " You may have doubts about collectivism. . . . If there is a middle way you've more chance of finding it under a Labour Government." The appeal to Liberals was obvious—to work for their cause within the Labour fold.

A week elapsed without further political broadcasts until Mr. Churchill took the air on January 21st with what was even more directly an electioneering speech. It was a somewhat sombre talk, designed, one felt, more to confirm the faithful than to rally recruits. It began, characteristically, by opening the windows on to the world scene. It envisaged the fundamental issue as " regimentation *v.* freedom ". It emphasised the " world peril " in which the country stood. The appeal to Liberals was underlined, though in the threatening rather than the cajoling form of sharp criticism of those who might be thinking of wasting their votes. In launching the first of many rebuttals of Labour's claim to a monopoly of credit for full employment, Mr. Churchill issued the first of many Conservative reminders of the role of Marshall Aid. There was criticism of Labour's food and housing (" Mr. Bevin's—I beg pardon, Mr. Beván's—houses "). It concluded as characteristically as it had begun, opening a Churchillian vista " down the long aisles of time ".

To this, six days later, Lord Salisbury's broadcast, better suited to the House of Lords than to the Home Service of the B.B.C., was but an indifferent sequel. It was in the main a negative attack on " the octopus " of Socialism. It offered instead only the austere remedy of " we must work and we must save ".

Labour offered livelier fare the following night in a deftly modulated performance by Mr. Maurice Webb. Its patronising references to Mr. Churchill in its opening paragraph (" I felt rather sorry for the old man ") constituted perhaps the only false touch in a " reasonable man's " justification of Labour rule. It sketched the contrasting pictures of a Tory Britain of pawnshops and slump and a Labour Britain that was " up and doing ". It rejected the Marshall Aid thesis by pointing out (in what later became stock Labour arguments) that non-socialist countries with Marshall Aid had unemployment and that Britain had passed on more aid than she had received. Instead, the explanation was to be found in " planning ", presented as fair and commonsensical, in contrast to Tory " freedom ", which meant exploitation and neglect. As for our economic problem, " it is by no means so insoluble as so many suggest "—" dollars, they're the trouble ". But Mr. Webb had little to say of how the " Labour plan " would solve it.

Sir David Maxwell Fyfe was selected by the Conservatives to deliver two days later a counter-attack to Labour's unemployment theme. This he did first by the marshalling of statistics in support of the Conservative record, and secondly by seeking to win the working man's support for Conservative trade union policy and " the Worker's Charter ". It was a factual, reasoned, sober case for a jury which the speaker presumed to be willing to listen to both sides.

Mr. Frank Byers presented the Liberal case in as deliberately challenging a form as possible. " I am a Liberal, one of those people whom Mr. Churchill has called malicious and wanton. . . ." Coming at the height of the Liberal–Conservative wrangles described on pp. 81–7, the broadcast began with a refutation of Conservative claims that Liberals were splitting the anti-socialist vote. " The real issue of the election ", he claimed, was our economic survival after 1952 ; the biggest menace to it came from class jealousies fostered by class parties. The Liberal Party was alone in not being a class party (though there followed a hint of middle-class appeal), and so alone could inspire " all the individuals in the country to give of their best ". The Conservatives " have lost the confidence of the wage-earners " and would not keep their promises. Socialists were wedded to nationalisation, whereas the real problem was production. Liberals would get this by incentives such as revised and reduced taxation, profit-sharing and higher wages. There followed brief comments on conscription and social reform. But " it's not our policy . . . our opponents criticise ; they merely say the Liberals haven't a chance ". Here Mr. Byers adduced a Gallup Poll much quoted by Liberals in the campaign to show that " 38% of the electorate . . . would vote Liberal if they thought they really could have a Liberal Government ", and concluded by claiming that if they all voted they could.

To Sir Stafford Cripps on February 2nd was apparently deputed the austere task of firing at the listening public the facts and figures of Labour's record, relieved only by an occasional evocation of the contrasting gloom of the Conservative years after the first World War. The dollar crisis ? " We have to stick hard at that job until we get through with it." Then the Chancellor passed to a scrutiny of *This Is The Road*, claiming that it made extravagant and illusory promises. Labour knew the future would be hard but it was committed to banishing poverty, unemployment and insecurity and had a faith based on " our common spiritual inheritance ".

The " election broadcasts " as distinguished from the " party political broadcasts " began on February 4th with Mr. Morrison. Here, apart from a rather routine recital about a quarter of the way through of items from Labour's programme, Mr. Morrison was heard in his most persuasive vein. The battle, he insisted, was between Conservative and Labour. The most the Liberals could hope to do would be to hold the balance—" very bad for the successful working of Parliament ". (It is, incidentally, interesting to notice that in Labour broadcasts this was the first reference to the Liberals by name and the last even by implication. This was in line with Labour campaign policy in general—to present Labour as in general a party of moderation and the middle way, but not actively to woo the Liberal vote. Better to ignore the

Liberals as insignificant interlopers, likely to harm no one very much, except perhaps the Conservatives.)

Like other Labour speakers, Mr. Morrison put full employment at his masthead. " We shall make the maintenance of full employment priority No. 1." To this was related " public ownership " as " one of the pillars of full employment ". As to Conservative pledges on this theme, Mr. Morrison's reply was, in effect, " No doubt they mean well enough but you can't teach an old dog new tricks "—and then followed the now familiar historical flashback to the lean years of Toryism and the contrast they presented with the proud quinquennium of Labour achievement. Mr. Morrison the parliamentarian revived his old jibe about the inefficiency of the Conservatives even as an Opposition and of Mr. Churchill as— "You know, between ourselves, anything concerned with economics just isn't up his street." As for the Conservative programme, it was merely a vote-catching bundle of incompatibles. He implied that Conservatives would cut food subsidies, and dwelt on the new high prices that would ensue. Labour recognised two kinds of control : " Fair Shares Control ", to be ended when—but not before—there was plenty for all, and Full Employment Control, which must stay for good.

Mr. Morrison was the first Labour speaker to give much time to housing, admitting the need, defending Labour's record and insisting that Conservative proposals simply meant an unfair distribution of the limited building resources available.

There followed a brief paragraph of ethical introspection— " Friends, an election is good for the soul of political leaders "— and a conclusion devoted to evoking the moral appeal of Socialism in terms of social justice and patriotism—" the party that believes in Britain ".

Mr. Eden, unlike most Conservative speakers, wasted no time on refuting Labour's historical " myth ". " It's the future that matters." He put first the problem presented by 1952, and asked his listeners to judge the rival programmes in relation to this. Labour was wedded to nationalisation—" though, by the way, I haven't heard them say anything about it since the campaign started "—and he expatiated on the failures and follies of nationalised industry. Then followed a depiction of the need and feasibility of reducing taxation, cutting government spending and freeing industry from controls. However, like Mr. Morrison, he claimed to distinguish different kinds of controls. " Of course when we talk about controls we don't mean, as our opponents suggest, the food rationing system." The cost of living must be brought down, but " it is utterly untrue . . . that we would abolish the food subsidies ". Labour had already put up the cost of some foods. By scrapping bulk buying Conservatives could reduce prices and " if it's necessary to reduce the food subsidies . . . then we shall make no such reduction without making compensating payments to those most affected ". Thus the line of Conservative appeal, responding to contact with the sensitive antennae of millions of voting consumers, was repaired at its weakest points, those against which Labour pressure had borne most hardly.

Finally, Mr. Eden reverted to the role in which he was still most familiar to the average voter—that of expositor of the international scene. He stressed its gravity, from " the threat of the hydrogen bomb " to the " nightmare of Communism " in Asia. While eschewing party politics in foreign affairs, he outlined a policy of the three unities—the Empire, Western Europe and the Atlantic area. Socialism would rob Britain of the strength necessary to participate in these, because it " runs against the grain of the British character ".

For their second speaker (though first in the election broadcasts proper) the Liberal chose their elder statesman, Lord Samuel. On February 8th he gave a ten-minute capsule of Liberal philosophy. Like Mr. Byers, he gave space to rebutting the Conservative case for a common anti-socialist front. " Amongst the mass of the people there is an intense hostility to Toryism." While many who voted Labour in 1945 do not wish to do so again, " from Socialism to Conservatism would be out of the frying-pan into the refrigerator ". If no party wins a majority " the Liberals might be called on to form a government ". They could, if enough Liberal supporters voted Liberal. Finally, Liberals, who stand outside the class struggle of Conservatives and Socialists, would best be able to unite the nation.

In Mr. James Griffiths, who broadcast on February 8th, the Labour Party had a speaker of great emotional appeal, with the flavour of Welsh speech and the warmth of Welsh oratory. They used him to full effect to incarnate the great " myth " of the interwar years, to tell in human terms the story of the Rhondda Valley

THE TWENTY-THIRD MAN

By arrangement with the " Daily Mail "

To face p. 134.

which animated so much of Labour's full employment appeal. By quotation and allusion he depicted the Tory Pharaohs plying the incentive of empty bellies to make the people of Britain work. In place of the lash of fear a Labour Britain would invoke a new sense of partnership. To this sense of partnership Labour's social security proposals, and in particular, the " mutualisation " of insurance, would make a great contribution.

In view of its over-riding importance in Labour propaganda, this is perhaps as good a place as any in which to note Labour's general treatment of the unemployment *v.* full employment issue. In an exchange of letters with Mr. Attlee after the election,* Lord Balfour of Burleigh complained that certain remarks of his on the degree of unemployment necessary for adequate labour mobility had been widely misquoted by the Labour Party. He referred in particular to a widely distributed pamphlet *To All Women*, to the party's *Speaker's Handbook* (from which countless platform speeches were drawn) and to an " eve-of-poll " leaflet devoted exclusively to a warning of what Conservatives would do to full employment if they were returned. Without accepting Lord Balfour's economic theories as sound, Mr. Attlee did admit that " in seeking graphically to present a part of your views, the point made in *To All Women* " was an " over-simplification " and said that he had been assured that in any future reference " a fuller quotation would be given ".

Mr. Attlee's admission reflected the fact that, to buttress their deep conviction that a return to Conservative government would mean a return to unemployment, Labour propagandists combed the speeches of every Conservative spokesman, however humble or remote, for phrases which could be presented as evidence of dark Tory designs. Translated, like Lord Balfour's, into " graphic " forms these took on an even sharper edge. Pictures of dole queues, of the Jarrow marchers, of a mounted police charge in Hyde Park and the like were widely employed to etch in, with all the incisive bitterness of the visual image, the moral of what awaited a working class which deserted the Mosaic leadership before it had put the Red Sea between itself and the armies of the Egyptians. There was constructed a complex of quotation, suggestion, picture and phrase that constituted an appeal to a class memory which might be shot by argument as full of holes

* See *The Times*, April 1st, 1950.

as a sponge and still prove, for at least one generation of voters, unsinkable. For an analysis of the success of these tactics the reader is referred to pp. 297–8 below.

As their woman speaker the Conservatives chose Miss Florence Horsbrugh. With her broadcast the attack on housing was, for the first time, given pride of place. There followed an extended defence of the Conservative record on social services, partly designed to rebut some of the charges levelled by Mr. Griffiths the night before. The appeal to the housewife ran throughout it all, and with this was linked a reminder of the secrecy of the ballot—an expression of the Conservative belief that there existed a Conservative housewives' "underground" which would do its duty in the polling booth provided it could feel secure from husbandly reprisals on the hearth.

Lady Megan Lloyd-George was Miss Horsbrugh's Liberal counterpart. Beginning, like Lord Samuel, with a defence of Liberal intervention, she went on to stress the imminence of the problem of 1952. On nationalisation, Lady Megan spoke less passionately than some of her colleagues; it seemed to be mainly "inefficient nationalised industries" that she objected to. She also evoked the Labour "myth" of the thirties—but to draw from it a Liberal moral. It was, however, a moral couched in terms of the radical Liberalism of full-blooded "social security" and "social justice".

Lord Woolton on February 11th spoke with the reassuring accents of the reasonable, paternal, common-sensical business man. He began with the cost of living, and was soon expatiating on food subsidies. "If we restore competition in food buying, we'll be able to reduce the food subsidies without increasing the cost to you." "We'll keep both rationing and price control until we are sure that the necessities of life are within the reach of everybody." Next in scale of treatment came his attack on Labour's housing and his promise of more: "Housing will be our No. 1 priority". "A very few words about employment. . . . You need have no fear. I assure you that the maintenance of a high and stable level of employment is at the very foundation of Conservative policy." Like Miss Horsbrugh, he concluded with a reference to the secrecy of the ballot.

Miss Margaret Herbison brought a Scottish brogue and a manner of homely reasonableness to her exposition of Labour's domestic and social policy.   She defended conditions in Labour Britain against comparison with the less happily governed economies of the Continent.   She emphasised the threat to prices latent in Conservative talk of cutting food subsidies, and deftly linked the prosperity of British agriculture to the markets guaranteed by food subsidies.   She applied the " thirties versus the forties " contrast to health (the first Labour speaker to do this at any length) and finally gave a fair slice of her time to familiar, but effective, treatment of the well-worn issues of housing and employment.   The broadcasters were beginning to show signs of exhausting their invention.

Then came Dr. Charles Hill, speaking as a " Liberal and a Conservative ".   The tone and technique of his broadcast have been described on pp. 107–8.   The content of it was less important than its phrasing and its delivery.   It was the first effective Conservative retort *in kind* to Labour's " ghost stories of the inter-war years ", the first to evoke convincingly a popular counter-myth of cheap and abundant cakes and ale—applied to all the departments of health, employment, child welfare, food and housing.   Again, in what it said about the dollar crisis or nationalisation or trade unionism its significance lay mainly in its debunking of Labour claims, its reduction of " planning " to the level of an organised racket and its evocation of the spectre of the Socialist super-state.   In its final round it packed an anti-Liberal punch—against those who " threw away some of their votes on candidates who haven't an earthly chance of getting in " and " played the Socialist game ".

Mr. Ernest Bevin's was the first Labour broadcast after Mr. Churchill's Edinburgh speech of two nights earlier.   Nevertheless, his talk gave the impression of having been written well in advance of this development and only adjusted to the absolute minimum necessary to take account of it. (See p. 104 above.)   It was the first Labour broadcast to deal at length with foreign affairs, but it had little to say beyond narrating the record of Mr. Bevin's Secretaryship and promising to " continue the policy pursued during the last five years ".   In the last five minutes Mr. Bevin the trade unionist appealed to his old mates in the movement, sang his version of the full-employment theme, gave voice once again to his old battle-cry of the Trades Disputes Act and paid a passing compliment to nationalisation.

Mr. Pollitt, as Chairman of the Communist Party, presented their case in the allotted ten minutes on February 16th. He began with an implied contrast between his own and all other parties, and went on to denounce high profits and the wage-freeze. Then followed a précis of the party's domestic policies. An attack on the current rate of military expenditure provided the opening wedge for an exposition of the Communist world view— America in the grip of insane war-mongers and grasping business men, Russia offering a plan to control the atom bomb only to have it spurned by the West and Mr. Churchill, Mr. Attlee and Mr. Bevin all alike advocating a " war policy ".   Only Communists fought against war, slump and mass unemployment.

Mr. Clement Davies gave the last and only twenty-minute Liberal broadcast on February 16th.   The case against Socialism was presented mainly in terms of the threat to personal liberty, and the blame for Socialism laid largely at the door of the Conservatives, whose mismanagement in the thirties had alienated the working people for good and all.   Hence " class antagonism ", against which only the Liberal Party could be a bulwark.   But a vote for them would be a vote wasted ?   No, because a Liberal Government was possible for the first time since 1929 (the Gallup Poll was here cited once again), and those who were dissatisfied with Labour would not have confidence in Conservatism.   Then followed a portrayal of Liberalism as the friend of the trade unionist, of the farmer, and of " the small man ".   Nevertheless, it was in the economic field that the Liberals could do " the most effective work today ".   So far the broadcast followed the familiar lines of Liberal exposition.   But for its last few minutes Mr. Davies did what few Liberal speakers had done—evoked the memory of Britain's Liberal past.   Beside the Labour and Conservative images of the twenties and thirties he set the memories of the pre-1914 Liberal heyday, and urged his hearers once again to make Britain " the moral and spiritual leader of a distressed world ".

In 1945 Mr. Churchill had delivered four out of the ten broadcasts allotted to his party.   In 1950, his party political broadcast excepted, he confined himself to one, and that the last, on February 18th.   He began with yet another Conservative affirmation of the secrecy of the ballot, but hastened to add that this implied a responsibility for using the vote wisely.   " Above all, do not abstain . . .

or throw your votes away on candidates who have no chance of becoming Members of Parliament." Thus, to the last the Conservative pressure on the Liberal voter was maintained. (Nor indeed, when the radio was stilled, did the pressure abate. There were few Conservative candidates who did not address by leaflet or otherwise " a last word to the Liberals " to remind them of the vanity of their endeavours or the true location of their real sympathies. The Liberal supposition that this insistence on the " split " or " wasted " vote cost them heavily at the polls is not, of course, susceptible of proof, but probability is on its side.)

By carefully culled quotations from Mr. Attlee and Sir Stafford Cripps, Mr. Churchill then sought to show that " since the election fight began, the issues at stake have become more serious "—that in fact Labour was aiming at nothing less than the creation of a monster State monopoly and " a levelling down of British society to a degree not hitherto presented by any responsible person ". If we took another plunge into Socialism " we should be alone in a world fast engaged in moving the other way "—notably and recently New Zealand and Australia. But on Thursday Britain could " shake herself free " and return to the forefront of the nations who now regard us with pity and bewilderment * (the Conservative obverse to the Labour portrayal of Britain as a country which enjoyed the moral leadership of Europe—an obverse which looked odd on the platform of a party accustomed to regard pride of country as a distinctive perquisite of Conservatism).

Then followed a rebuttal of " false statements " about Conservative policy on unemployment, food subsidies and family allowances, and the frank admission : " All parties are equally desirous to maintain the social services and where necessary improve them." But how would a Socialist Government, losing money on nationalisation and wrecking national credit, find the money to pay for them ? Then followed the now familiar lines of Conservative policy on taxation (" reduce the rates of both direct and indirect taxation. . . . I will repeat that. . . .") and

* It is perhaps worth noting that Conservative allegations, such as these, about Britain having fallen upon evil days, evoked from Labour propagandists one of the few 1950 parallels to the emotionally-overcharged " Guilty Men " theme of 1945. Thus in a widely circulated " Election News " leaflet Ian Mackay wrote of ' Tory Traitors ', " bursting with good food and so full of whisky and wine that they would squirt if you squeezed them ", who slandered Britain " in every hotel lounge . . . from Shanghai to San Francisco ".

housing (" make an intense effort to recover . . . all the energy that has been spent in bitter politics ").

Mr. Churchill's subsequent repetition of his Edinburgh proposal and his replies to the critics of " talks with Russia at the highest level " are dealt with elsewhere. This was followed by the claim that if successful the Conservatives would put the nation above class or party. Last of all came a personal *coda* which to any listener with a sense of the history and achievement behind the speaker's seventy-five years could not fail to have a moving appeal irrespective of party or politics :

> " Of course, I am—as I am reminded—an old man. It is true that all the daydreams of my youth have been accomplished. I have no personal advantage to gain by undertaking once more the hard and grim duty of leading Britain and her Empire through and out of her new and formidable crisis. But while God gives me the strength, and the people show me their good will, it is my duty to try, and try I will."

Mr. Attlee reserved his one appearance in the Labour broadcasts for the last, on Saturday, February 18th. It was a sober, dignified, humane and honest talk, but the most ardent supporter of its sentiments would be hard put to find either in its wording or in its delivery much that was absorbing or inspiring. It began with that warning against a last-minute stunt which at this stage of the campaign was *de rigueur* for every Labour speaker. Mr. Attlee went on to speak as one who had " held the responsible position of Prime Minister for four and a half years ", and from such an eminence could afford to overlook " the ordinary interchange of party scores on little points ". Nevertheless, he was patently stung by the charges in Mr. Churchill's last broadcast. He claimed that the quotation Mr. Churchill attributed to him was garbled, and was " sorry that Mr. Churchill should fall so far below the standards which one would expect from a statesman of his distinction ". His charges were described as " sweeping " and " without any basis of fact ".

Modestly, and yet with a restrained pride in his Government's achievement, Mr. Attlee then reviewed the record of the Labour Government, and contrasted Mr. Churchill's picture of a " dispirited and broken people " with the energy, industry and confidence he and his wife had seen on their last ten days' motor tour of nearly 1,300 miles. It was in Milton's description of the " puissant nation " that Mr. Attlee recognised the Britain he had seen.

In his review of foreign and empire relations Mr. Attlee followed well-trodden paths, but found in them the opportunity to praise Mr. Bevin and to narrate the history of his atomic energy proposals in final reply to Mr. Churchill. His depiction of our domestic recovery gave the credit to " the people " and to " careful planning ". " It is true that we have had generous help from the Commonwealth and the United States, but that doesn't detract from your peace-time effort any more than Lend-Lease deprives Britain of its credit for its share in winning the war." This was a graceful coping-stone to the Marshall Aid controversy—more graceful than many which had been flung about in the course of the campaign. Once Marshall Aid was interjected into the election it was too much to hope that politicians, in the heat of their scrimmages, would always respect the veracities—not to mention the international civilities—and echoes of our controversy overheard across the Atlantic must often have rung strangely on American ears. But one thing the argument in its crude way certainly effected. It made the ordinary British elector conscious, as never before, of the fact of Marshall Aid and its significance to our economy.

Mr. Attlee then turned to the record of fair shares and social security, praising all participants, save " sections of the medical profession " who opposed the Health Service. He did not propose to go into " detail " about Labour's future policy, but it was interesting to notice that his resumé said of future nationalisation only : " We shall continue the development in the national interest of our great basic industries and where it is desirable we shall transform private monopoly into public service." As for the Conservative programme it had " no policy but vote-catching ". The choice was clear—" incompetence " or " ordered planning ".

" The road for Britain " was not easy, but " great progress " had been made, and our problems could be solved. It was everyone's duty to vote. " I ask you all, whatever your political views, to go to the poll." From Labour workers and supporters in particular he asked no slackening in their efforts now. " I ask you to go forward along the road with us. We shall not fail you. Let us win through together. Good night."

With these words the battle of the broadcasts ended.   Although there were four days still to go to the poll, a wise tradition kept them clear of last-minute broadcast appeals.   Although public interest had mounted as the series went on, it could hardly be pretended that anything could have been gained by extending it up to the eve of the poll.   The issues had all been canvassed. Some which had been fairly prominent in the manifestoes had dropped out as argument and counter-argument developed. Others had swollen in importance as the debate went on.   But the listener who by February 18th was not familiar with the main differences (and resemblances) between the parties had no one but himself to blame.

CHAPTER VII

THE PRESS

ANY appreciation of the performance of the British Press in the General Election must take into account certain considerations which affected almost all newspapers in their presentation of news and handling of comment. No less than in 1945 the British Press was suffering from a stringest rationing of newsprint; an increased allowance was granted for the election period, but even that only permitted *The Times* to run to twelve pages, the *Manchester Guardian* to ten, the *Daily Telegraph* to eight, and the penny dailies to range between six and eight. The restricted space thus made available had to contain, not indeed the exciting war and diplomatic news of 1945, but a fair range of home and foreign news, sport and features, which had nothing necessarily to do with the election itself. Most British national dailies were, and always are, avowedly partisan in politics, and their election reporting, like their parliamentary and political reporting in " peace-time ", was frankly coloured by their political sympathies; these were rarely concealed, and any intelligent reader knew what to expect from the paper of his choice. At the same time, irrespective of their politics, the election news that came to them was dominated by the personality of Mr. Churchill, who, as news alone, was the outstanding figure of the campaign, and by the fact that Labour was on the defensive and the Opposition parties were attacking. Finally, however rigorously they kept their feelings under control, both the Labour politicians and the great majority of pressmen could not but be conscious that the election came at the end of a four-and-a-half-year period of strained relations between Government and press, years marked by the investigations of the Royal Press Commission, several cases involving issues of parliamentary privilege and many very sharp exchanges between Ministers of the Crown and newspapermen.

Since rather misleading statements are sometimes made about the weight of newspaper circulation which the main political parties can command, it seemed worthwhile to collect and tabulate London morning newspapers' own estimates, where available, of their circulation during the election period.   Grouped under party headings, they are as follows :

Conservative :
Daily Telegraph, " net sale figure for February "	.	.	983,645
Daily Express, " net output, February 15th "	.	.	4,099,069
Daily Mail, " for February, in the region of "	.	.	2,215,000
Daily, Graphic *	.	.	772,380
			8,079,094

Liberal :
News Chronicle, " daily average net sale for February "	.		1,525,128
Manchester Guardian, " net sale on February 15th "	.		141,250
			1,666,378

Labour :
Daily Herald, " circulation for February 15th "	.	.	2,030,401
Daily Mirror, " circulation for February 15th "	.	.	4,603,123
			6,633,524

* Circulation figures were not made available by this newspaper. I have therefore employed the figures quoted in the Report of the Royal Commission on the Press, which are based upon the pegged circulations of 1947–8.

From this it will be apparent that the Conservatives command the largest volume of circulation, that the Labour figure is nevertheless considerable and that the Liberals, in proportion to the votes cast in their favour, are well served. *The Times* has been omitted from these groupings, in view of its own claim to be independent, but in terms merely of circulation (257,803 on February 15th) its addition to any of these columns would not significantly affect the balance of forces.

It is, of course, true that this is not the whole picture.   It omits, in the first place, the Sunday press.   The difficulty here is that the political attachments of many Sunday papers are a good deal less explicit and, since they are mostly organs primarily of entertainment, their political " pull " at election times is much less powerful.   Nonetheless, so far as the figures are obtainable and meaningful, they tell a story not so very different (though rather more favourable to Conservatism), as may be seen on page 182.

The second omission is the provincial and evening press. Here certain great chains, most notably Kemsley Newspapers, Associated Newspapers and the Westminster Group, form potentially powerful political forces, the first two Conservative, the second Liberal.   But although their influence is often strong, particularly in areas where there is no evening competitor or no provincial morning competitor (there is always a national morning competitor), and although their quasi-monopolistic position is sometimes abused, it is virtually impossible to reduce their circulation figures to politically meaningful totals. They differ so much in the intensity of their partisanship, even within the same chain, owing to diversities of local conditions and of local editorial policies, that they defy statistical treatment. This, however, may be said: with very few exceptions (such as the *Manchester Evening News*), the editorial sympathies of provincial papers, morning or evening, are Conservative or right-wing Liberal. There are virtually no Labour provincial mornings or evenings. Moreover, in London both the *Evening Standard* and the *Evening News* are Conservative; the *Star* might be classified as *Lib-Lab*.

The main vehicles for carrying news of the election campaign to the ordinary voter were essentially the London dailies. Although in any single town or city a local or chain paper might well have more readers than its London rivals, yet over the country as a whole the London press was the dominating influence. Owing to the B.B.C.'s abstention from all political news reporting during the election period, that influence was even more pronounced than at normal times. For that reason attention in what follows is particularly concentrated on the London press and the *Manchester Guardian*, which, though published in a provincial city, may properly be counted as a national daily.

The Newspaper Campaign

The treatment of the 1950 General Election campaign by the national daily press was overwhelmingly partisan, relatively demure, and, so far as can be judged, politically ineffective. There is no evidence that any portion of the press succeeded in gaining the attention and control of public opinion to anything like the extent that certain newspapers did in the 1924, 1931 or even 1945 elections. With few exceptions, the individual journals reflected closely the views of the leaders of their party preference and followed carefully the lines of the party manifestoes. To a surprising degree the party political and election broadcasts gave the cues for newspaper activity, whether defensive or offensive, in every type of newspaper.

These tendencies were especially noticeable in the period

between Mr. Attlee's announcement on January 10th and the dissolution on February 3rd. This period contained no out-standing newspaper controversies. It was used by the various parties principally for introducing their major campaign themes through party manifestoes or radio talks. All these themes were publicised in the news columns and praised or attacked in the editorial and special feature sections, but no special development of them by the press was evident. The Labour Party's election manifesto was thus presented on January 18th and the plans for the "mutualisation" of insurance were similarly treated on January 20th. The Conservative manifesto held the political attention of the press on January 25th and for the next couple of days, with the tax cuts and housing proposals most often featuring in the headlines. Mr. J. B. Priestley's broadcast on January 14th also stirred a good deal of press comment, as did Mr. Churchill's on January 21st.

There were two major press controversies on strictly election subjects which took place during the early part of the campaign. One was the flurry over election expenses ("First Election Wobble. 'Anti' posters taken down." *Daily Herald*, January 12th). The other was the skirmish between Liberal and Con-servative Party leaders over the use of the name "Liberal" and over the effect of the Liberal candidatures on the "anti-Socialist" vote.

In addition to these strictly election issues, there were several incidents during this period which were related, either naturally or if necessary by good propaganda technique, to the coming election. Amongst these were the allegedly partisan letting of flats in Wandsworth by the Labour-controlled Borough Council, the attempt to end petrol rationing in the western zones of Germany, and the wage claims of certain unions before the T.U.C.

The Times in its main story on the parties' campaign plans printed on January 12th observed that all political parties were going to reserve their main efforts until after February 3rd. The newspaper itself seemed to be guided by this in its own election coverage; until the campaign formally opened it paid relatively little attention to the political skirmishing. Most of *The Times*' space relating to the coming election was filled with strictly factual articles providing information on such topics as the release dates of the party manifestoes, the law on election expenses, and the adoption of candidates by constituency associations. The controversies over election expenses and the use of the label "Liberal" were reported as objectively as possible, mainly in the words of the party leaders. In its leading articles *The Times* was not quite so neutral. It was critical of the Labour Party's plan for the "mutualisation" of industrial insurance, and its sharply worded leader on the Labour election manifesto often gave the impression of being an extremely well-informed piece of anti-socialist "debunking". A few days later Mr. Churchill's first broadcast was treated more indulgently; although final judgment on Conservative claims was suspended, the judge left the defendant in little doubt that his case would be given sympathetic consideration. The leader on the Conservative Party manifesto on January 25th was noticeably less critical and more exultant than the editorial on the Labour document. The first few lines give the tone :

> " The Conservative statement of policy for the election, which is published this morning, is an able and thorough piece of work. It is longer than the Labour manifesto because it covers more ground in more detail. The purpose of a party manifesto is to win votes. The purpose of this morning's manifesto is to persuade all electors that they have nothing to lose and much to gain by a change of Government."

This may be contrasted with the opening lines of the editorial on the Labour manifesto :

> " Labour's election banner bears two devices : full employment and ' fair shares '. They are shrewdly chosen. Work for all and equal rations are to many millions the consolations of a threadbare peace-time. They have brought much credit to the Government, however limited in size each fair share may still be, and whatever the economic cost of some of the policies pursued to secure these objectives. With the benefits brought by the national health service, whatever its shortcomings and expense, they are Labour's greatest assets."

Both are documents with their way to make in an imperfect world. But whereas *Let Us Win Through Together* is " something

of a caricature " and has to be rebuked with the reminder that
" there are limits even to electioneering ", *This Is The Road* is
" an honest enough attempt, at election time, to put promises on
a basis of fact ".

The *Manchester Guardian* began even during this period an
extensive coverage of the election from all angles, including constituency surveys, special features on the election machinery,
stories on minor speeches and profiles of candidates. For instance, in the week from January 30th to February 4th, special
election material, apart from straight news and leaders in the
Guardian, measured nearly twenty-seven columns of print, in
contrast to *The Times'* sixteen columns. The *Guardian* left no
doubt that it favoured the Liberal Party in this special coverage,
paying great attention to details of the preparations of Liberal
candidates. However, the Liberals' chances were never over-
estimated. The news columns proper were scrupulously neutral,
though the by-lined " Political " or " Labour " correspondents
allowed themselves some latitude in comment. In its editorials
the *Guardian* maintained a fairly independent balance. It
opposed Labour on the issue of nationalisation, observing " experience of public ownership so far is not encouraging ", and that
the plans for further nationalisation were " fussy and irrelevant ".
While it welcomed the " moderation " and absence of " lavish
promises " in the Labour programme, it nevertheless found it " a
remarkably evasive document " which, in " dodging " the really
unpleasant aspects of the economic situation, had " nothing to
learn from the pre-war Tories ". The *Guardian* was particularly
suspicious of Labour's attitude towards traditional " liberties " ;
the following comment on a speech of Mr. Morrison's is fairly
revealing of one line of *Guardian* thinking.

> " It is strange that so good a democrat cannot see that a
> real point of principle lies behind the right to protest against
> nationalisation of one's property."

The Conservative manifesto itself was very politely received,
criticism concentrating on the suggestions for cutting taxes while
improving services. There was " much that is good in the rest
of the programme ". " The Conservatives have never in their
history produced so enlightened a statement of social policy . . .
a reasonable body of doctrine." But would " their friends in the

press " sweep them off their feet ? And what about Mr. Church-ill's " romantic " economic policies and his " capacity to play with facts as he pleases " ? But the major battle between Mr. Churchill and the *Guardian* is covered as a separate incident elsewhere.

The *Daily Telegraph* during the early period of the campaign adopted the pace of the professional politicians, and husbanded its major efforts for the final three weeks. As the most nearly recognisable press mouthpiece for the Conservative Central Office, the *Telegraph* began, however, laying the groundwork for its later efforts, and well-informed and quite extensive analyses were made of Labour Party election statements and programmes. The Conservative leanings of the newspaper were more obvious in the headlines than in the articles to which they were affixed. While a good deal of material appeared that obviously presented Conservative viewpoints, alongside this would appear other dispatches whose subjects were related to the election, but which the *Telegraph* presented in an absolutely neutral manner. German de-rationing, and even the Wandsworth housing controversy, were described with care. Editorially most indignation and con-tempt were directed towards the " dissident " Liberals who, in the *Telegraph's* opinion, destroyed the anti-Socialist front. This issue during this period ran a close second to the *Telegraph's* other main theme, the essential dishonesty of Labour's election cam-paign. The letter columns of the paper were used extensively to present the undying anti-Government sentiments of as wide a section of the population as possible. Finally, the appearance of a further instalment of Mr. Churchill's War Memoirs on January 26th served as an indirect though powerful reminder of the stature of the Conservative leader. Incidentally, the *Daily Telegraph* posters advertising the serialisation under a portrait of Mr. Churchill opportunely relieved the drabness of hoardings from which Conservative Party posters were being " blacked out " in response to the " expenses scare ".

The *Daily Herald*, as the official organ of the Labour Party, got into its campaign stride almost immediately, and in the fifteen issues following January 12th averaged eight columns a day on election stories. On eight of these days the main space on the front page was given to election matter, while all but one editorial in the fifteen issues was directly related to the election.

This was in the face of such major news events, dear to the popular press, as the *Truculent* disaster, the Mills–Maxim Fight, the Hume Trial, and the engagement of Miss Gussie Moran. All dispatches were presented so as to place the Government in the most agreeable light, although their essentially defensive character rather prevented them from seeming so obviously pointed. Small excerpts from Opposition speeches were abstracted for dissection, usually in the editorial column. An example is the elaborate ridicule poured upon a single paragraph of Mr. L. S. Amery's speech at Newcastle in the leader of January 28th. The issue of election expenses was pressed heartily, but in respect of the Conservative–Liberal altercations the *Herald* adopted the pose of a bystander—though of a bystander who was not above casting a sympathetic word to Liberals resisting the embraces of the Tory boa-constrictor. It even mustered up some righteous indignation over the shameful Tory denial of the Liberals' democratic right to run as many candidates as they pleased. The brief flurry over German de-rationing was promptly labelled a " Tory Election Stunt "—an early example of an " anti-stunt " complex which was to become much more marked presently.

The *Daily Mail's* January pace was somewhat slower than the *Herald's* and *Guardian's*, but its treatment of election stories of the lively and partisan type created a feeling of slightly more urgency than *The Times* and *Telegraph* gave. As an undoubted supporter of the Conservative case, the *Mail* both pointed its stories to carry a Conservative moral and also apportioned space so that Conservatives received the lion's share. At the same time, in spite of its undoubted bias towards Conservatism, the *Mail* did not hesitate at this stage to criticise the Central Office's performance. On January 12th, for instance, a special article by Robert Orme complained of the lack of " spark " in Conservative electioneering. On the other hand, the *Mail* made a prominent feature of its election " forum " begun on the same day, January 16th, as the *News Chronicle's*, but not persisting, in the *Daily Mail*, beyond January 31st. Certain other stories on political opponents were also well presented at various times. The editorials, without being abusive, were ably and pugnaciously written attacks on the Labour Party. The " Socialist " Party manifesto was said to " stink of hypocrisy ", while the Conservative proposals were termed " a Winner ". Perhaps the most remarkable instance of leader-writers' ingenuity appeared at the end of the Hume trial (January 27th), when the " underworld " figures of the trial were related to " an environment in which honest men are penalised but the crooked and the shifty reap rich rewards ". Generous space in news columns was accorded to de-rationing of food in Germany, the Food Ministry's argument with the butchers over wholesale prices, and the Electricity Board's 1949 surplus (" A State Industry Shows a Profit "). The general impression over this period was of a publication skilfully combining propaganda with pungent reasonableness.

The *News Chronicle* opened its election activity early, both in respect of straight election news and special feature material. The reports of the British Institute of Public Opinion polls and " The Great Debate " series, in which political figures of all parties participated, were prominent parts of the *News Chronicle's* election coverage throughout. Naturally, as a Liberal organ, the *News Chronicle*, more than any other national daily, gave prominence to the Moynihan–Woolton, Churchill–Davies exchanges. Indeed, the impression given at this time was that the *News Chronicle* regarded the Conservative Party as the major enemy, and considerable sympathy was displayed towards the Government. Lord Woolton was a favourite individual target of the editorial writers. Though the Wandsworth flat lettings were displayed prominently on the front page, as much space was given to refutation of the charges as to presenting them. From its Liberal vantage-point the *News Chronicle* was not afraid to confer compliments as well as kicks upon its political rivals, and articles both pro-Tory and pro-Labour made their appearance at various times. The heavy presentation of Liberal Party views and news started more slowly than one might expect, and was not particularly noticeable during the first two weeks after the announcement of the election. By the end of the month, however, the Liberal point of view was being more and more forcibly expressed in the editorial columns and special feature parts of the newspaper. Both Liberal and Labour speakers seemed to be quoted more often than Conservatives in January, though this might well be explained by the fact that they started campaigning earlier.

The *Daily Express* found in the election during January a welcome subject for flippant headlines, mostly on topics which were designed to embarrass the Labour Party, but were still far-

L

fetched enough to be outside the election news-track followed by the rest of the press.   Examples are " Land Take-over Feared ", the banner with which the *Express* greeted the Labour Party manifesto on January 18th, and " Rebel Bosses Warned " on January 19th, characterising a speech by Sir Stafford Cripps criticising certain types of industrialists.   The *Express* preferred human interest in election material as well as in ordinary news, and gave front-page prominence to the action of the Govan Divisional Labour Party in turning out " in tears " Mr. Neil Maclean, their sitting member.   The *Express* also gave special notice to such stories as the de-rationing of food and petrol in Germany, the Wandsworth flats, Mr. Strachey's difficulties with the butchers, conditions in British Honduras and other items showing alleged Government incompetence in the " Empire ". But even with this activity the *Express* left a feeling that its campaign had not yet warmed up.

The *Daily Mirror's* first serious response to the election began on Monday, January 23rd, when a front-page reply to Mr. Churchill's first broadcast, headed " The Insult ", lambasted him and " The Tory Party " in vigorous *Mirror* style.   Probably more important, however, was the fact that on page 2 that same day " the Ruggles family ", the *Daily Mirror's* strip cartoon " discussion group ", began their man-to-man and woman-to-woman exploration of the constituencies and the issues.   On the same page every day the *Daily Mirror* ran an " election postbag ".

With the opening of the election campaign proper on February 3rd the national press swung into its full stride.   Newspapers which had appeared to mark time during the early period after January 10th began to run increasing amounts of election material. This was true of news columns, feature articles and leaders. Despite this, their efforts seldom seemed to strike fire with either the public or the party orators, so that to the end the press strife retained a highly artificial character.   Newspapers differed, of course, in the methods they employed.   The " quality press " endeavoured to bring its efforts to a climax on the editorial page. The popular press concentrated its efforts on the use of front-page space and on the often indiscriminate intermingling of news and views.

Two notable Fleet Street events during the period were the

transfer of David Low's cartoons on February 1st from the *Evening Standard* and the *Manchester Guardian* to the *Daily Herald*, and the return of Lord Beaverbrook to England on February 9th. Both produced a change of balance in the publications concerned. In addition, this period saw the independent newspapers moving to their positions. *The Times* inclined more and more to the side of Conservatism as the campaign progressed, although never formally declaring itself. The *Daily Mirror*, which had been *piano* throughout January, long maintained nominal doubt as to how far it would incline to the left, while generally aiding Labour throughout the month. Not until the last week did it come out resoundingly for Labour.

The events most widely played during February were the release of the Liberal manifesto on February 6th, Mr. Churchill's speech at Cardiff and the issues raised there, the petrol-rationing theme, the " atom talks ", and the " Radio Doctor's " broadcast. There were one or two special themes played by special sections of the press. These included the *Daily Express's* £6-a-week minimum wage, and the *Daily Herald's* discoveries of Tory advocates of unemployment. In the last week of the campaign the Conservative popular newspapers produced stories maintaining that " overtime pay would continue to be taxed under a Labour Government " or featuring the unemployment caused in an aircraft firm by the cancellation of Government orders. The " atom talks " theme and the petrol-rationing issue are treated more extensively in the latter part of this chapter.

Mr. Churchill remained the popular newspaper figure in newspapers of all political opinions, with each side holding him up either for admiration or blame. Mr. Attlee, on the other hand, slipped quietly away on his extensive tour by car and attracted a remarkably small quantity of space and oddly little prominence even at first in the *Daily Herald*. Mr. Aneurin Bevan was the chief Government target for the Conservative press, along with Mr. Strachey and Dr. Edith Summerskill. After his February 14th broadcast, Dr. Hill received handsome treatment throughout the Conservative press.

The newspaper week from Monday, February 6th to Saturday, February 11th might well be entitled the " Petrol Week " of the campaign. The week started with the news centred around the Liberal election manifesto, which had only indifferent success in getting space in the press. The Conservative popular press tended to play it down, though of course the *Guardian* and *News Chronicle* gave it prominence. The *Daily Herald* produced the revealing headline, " Liberals, Don't Be Tricked ". There followed a couple of days of desultory party sniping, after which Mr. Churchill travelled to the West and to a major place in the headlines. At Cardiff he made his pugnacious speech denying that conditions in Britain before the war were as bad as Labour depicted them. This was heralded in the *Graphic* with " Churchill Exposes Lies on Years of Tory Hell " and the *Telegraph's* " Mr. Churchill on Socialist Lies ". The speech also furnished the *Herald* with two or three days of argument and rebuttal arising from Mr. Churchill's explanation of the famous Tonypandy incident. The next day Mr. Churchill was in Plymouth and the petrol-rationing argument broke into its short-lived glory on Friday and Saturday.

The Times during this week blossomed into full election coverage, expanding to twelve pages, of which two pages at least were always devoted to regular election news. It carried adequate and careful news reports of the major election stories of the week, in effect playing down the petrol issue, although carrying Mr. Churchill's exact words. An interesting series of leading articles appeared during the week fairly well illustrating *The Times'* position. The Monday leader opened with a few remarks on the Liberal manifesto in tones which were eloquent of *The Times'* impatience with small battalions : " The Liberals, whose purpose seems to be to amass as large a popular vote as possible up and down the country, with only distant regard to their chances of winning seats, at last (and even then with second thoughts) put out their programme yesterday." This served to introduce not, as with the other party programmes, a reasoned consideration of its proposals, but an analysis of the course of the campaign thus far, almost exclusively in Labour *v.* Conservative terms. On Tuesday the editorial emphasised the need for more attention to foreign affairs in the campaign. On Thursday the election leader's subject was the " Welfare State ", which it said both major parties agreed on, although the words had a fundamentally different implication for each—" equalitarianism " for Labour, a " satisfactory minimum " for Conservatives. On Saturday the editorial was on the constitutional issues of the election. It said : " The problem presented by the present state of constitutional evolution is the old one of reconciling popular control and civil freedom with the efficiency of the executive. The modern tendency to vest immense powers in an unwieldy administration should attract much wider attention than it does." Other leader comments during this time were critical of nationalisation.

For very understandable reasons, the *Manchester Guardian's* news coverage differed somewhat in emphasis from that of the London dailies during the week of February 6th to 11th. The main news articles of the week were the description of the Liberal Party programme and the continued strife between Conservative and Liberal Party leaders. Of course Mr. Churchill's westward tour took a prominent place, but it had to share the headline limelight with Mr. Bevan's and Mr. Attlee's invasions of the *Guardian's* own Lancashire hinterland. The total coverage for the week left one in little doubt that even at this stage the *Guardian* had more belief in the Liberal Party's election policies than in its election prospects. Editorially it followed an independent course. On February 10th it took both Labour and Conservatives to task for their use of the official production index. The leader observed " a stranger listening to the more extravagant Tory speakers might sometimes think that the Labour Government had almost stopped British industry and stifled production ". On the other hand, the Labour claim of 30% production increase was in " conflict with common sense " and could only be explained by supposing that Mr. Morrison and Sir Stafford Cripps had " innocently swallowed the statistics that someone picked out for them ". Another leader praised the Commonwealth and Colonial policy of the Government. The *Guardian's* reaction to Mr. Churchill's introduction of petrol as an election issue was fairly typical of its general position. In the first place, it reported his speech with care, generally in his own words. Secondly, it waited for twenty-four hours before it commented editorially. When it did comment it took both sides to task. It accused Mr. Churchill of " kite-flying " and " sailing rather close to the wind ", but added that in replying the Labour Ministers got themselves into a " pretty mess ". Both Mr. Churchill and Mr. Gaitskell were out of touch with the country if they imagined that there were many votes to be won with petrol. The Opposition had, in moderation, a case. But an attempt at " bribery " and " wild promises quickly to make life easier " were " quite out of keeping with the genuinely serious mood of the electorate ".

The *Daily Telegraph's* main news story of the week was the petrol-rationing outburst on Friday and Saturday. The headlines and stories began to show increasing evidence that election policy was gaining priority over strict news value. Opponents and critics continued to be fairly reported, but certain themes, such as the folly and error of " Independent " Liberal behaviour, were obviously stressed. Thus Mr. Harrod, " well known economist and a Liberal ", was awarded headline prominence as a speaker in the Conservative interest. On Thursday the publication of Mr. Churchill's War Memoirs was discontinued to make way for a series of centre-page feature articles on political and electoral topics which were, in effect, an extension of the leader columns. The editorials themselves shifted their target from Liberals to Labour. The total space allotted to the election sensibly increased.

With the opening of the formal campaign, the *Daily Herald* devoted itself even more completely to the Labour cause, and the result was almost saturation, at least in the main display portions of the paper. To illustrate this it is only necessary to give the subject of the number one story from the 6th to the 11th. In every case it will be seen that the story is related to the election. February 6th, Mr. Morrison at Wakefield; February 7th, Mr. Bevin at Diss, Norfolk; February 8th, The Budget Surplus; February 9th, Mr. Griffiths' broadcast; February 10th, January record exports; February 11th, Gaitskell, Bevan, Attlee et al. answer Churchill on petrol. Here the paper launched its offensives, while in its editorials it organised the defence. The essentially defensive nature of the editorial policy may be seen from the subject, always an individual, selected for treatment each day. They were successively Lord Woolton, Mr. Eden, Lord Samuel, Mr. Churchill at Cardiff, Mr. Churchill at Plymouth, and Mr. Churchill and the Tory Manifesto. On every day except Monday the editorial was run on the front page, and attacked some remarks made by the victim the day before.

The *Daily Mail* moved into the election campaign in earnest during this week, first with a story of Mr. Eden's broadcast in the main place on the front page, and then later in the week with petrol stories designed to drive home the moral of Mr. Churchill's remarks at Portsmouth. The editorial campaign also turned intensively to politics. In commenting on the Liberal manifesto, the leader observed that with two exceptions it had the same aims as the Conservative manifesto. These exceptions were free trade and proportional representation. Proportional representation, the *Mail* observed, was incompatible with the British temperament. The back pages of the *Mail* were this week filled with striking points from the speeches of candidates. Here there seemed to be genuine impartiality during this period, even an occasional Conservative, such as Mr. Michael Astor, being made the victim of the headliner's punch.

The *News Chronicle* during this week threw its full weight behind the Liberal Party in news columns and in editorials, at the same time as it continued the " Great Debate " series as an all-party forum. Prominence was given during the first three days of the week to the Liberal manifesto, A. J. Cummings's trip to the West Country and Wales, and Lord Samuel's broadcast. The *News Chronicle* abstained from excitement over the petrol issue ; it was at no time in the week a lead story. The editorials, longer, more restrained and more thoughtful than those in other penny dailies, continued to be devoted principally to election themes, though the *News Chronicle* continually reminded its readers, explicitly or by implication, that the General Election was not the most important issue in a world menaced by soil exhaustion, atomic warfare and Marxist materialism.

The *Daily Express* changed markedly, whether by coincidence or contagion, with the arrival of Lord Beaverbook in England. There immediately appeared the first resurrection since 1949 of the £6-a-week-minimum-wage idea. Sprightliness, however, remained the dominant note in the handling of election news, e.g. in the treatment of Mr. Churchill's Cardiff speech with the exploiting of the quip " Accommodation Unit, Sweet Accommodation Unit " in headlines. Typical election stories in the *Express* during the week were on such subjects as the allocation of petrol coupons to Mr. Strachey to travel to Dundee, the increase of rations to pigeons and the permission given to soldiers to join trade unions. The front page was increasingly used for political stories, and even the women's page and sports page began to get election notes. The major effort of the week was, of course, the petrol ration increase.

The *Daily Graphic* was perhaps the most assiduous champion of the petrol-ration increase, and eagerly devoted itself to this topic. It easily maintained during this week its record of being the most heatedly and unabashedly pro-Tory member of the nationally circulated press.   Conservative leaders had the bulk of the photographs.   Only Conservative candidates were pictured going about their campaigning.   The political situation was drawn in black and white.   Headlines from this week included " Socialists Slang Tories ", " Eden Demands—Set us Free from Frustration ", and " Churchill Exposes Lies on Years of Tory Hell ".

The *Daily Mirror*, nominally independent, but undoubtedly Labour in sympathy, still showed a calculated reserve towards the election campaign.   Only once in this week did election news reach the front page, although the brief leaders did dispose of several election topics.   The middle page spread on one day was devoted to Mr. Morrison on an election tour.   The petrol topic produced the election punch of the week in the form of a front-page lead story " The Truth About Petrol " and a back-page editorial on " The Stunt ".

The dominating topic of the week from February 13th to 18th was the " talks with the Russians " proposal made in Mr. Churchill's Edinburgh speech (see especially pp. 194–203).   Apart from this incident, the national press more or less maintained the pace set in the previous week.   The " Radio Doctor " and Mr. Churchill's second broadcast furnished the topics for many news columns and editorials.   Generally speaking, the Conservative press remained well on the offensive while the Labour press stayed on the defence.   The closing of nominations on Monday resulted in the more serious newspapers devoting a tremendous amount of space to lists of candidates and constituencies and straightforward analyses of the many statistical aspects of the election.

The Times devoted its main news columns every day to election subjects—predominantly Conservative subjects (though the choice was effectively dictated by the run of the news in a week of vigorous Conservative " offensives ").   Its special election features and regional surveys retained their share of space.   Editorially *The Times* took an independent line towards the two most heavily stressed Conservative campaign themes.   It was not until Wednesday, February 15th that the petrol issue was accorded the honour of a comment, and then only to be dismissed in a third leader as rather unimportant.   *The Times* made it clear that, while some

consideration might be shown to motorists, increasing the ration
was bound up with the dollar problem and no separate solution
was possible. The day before, a leader analysing the parties'
chances doubted morally and electorally the propriety of Labour's
heavy stress on the unemployment theme and expected " the
voter on the margin ", who was rather too obviously envisaged as
a *Times'* reader, coming down eventually on the Conservative
side, provided that the Conservatives, in the ten days remaining,
had " the courage to speak frank words as well as fair about the
future ". On the " atom talks " *The Times* observed first " at
least it will no longer be possible for historians to write that the
General Election of 1950 was concerned with every question
except the one that mattered ". This was consistent with its
previously expressed view that foreign policy needed some election airing, though, somewhat disingenuously, it seemed to think
it necessary to add : " provided that no party tries to make
political capital out of it, the change is all to the good ". However, the leader was not too enthusiastic about the prospects for
the talks and asked whether " conditions for a general settlement
yet exist ? " It concluded, " perhaps the most that could be
hoped for would be some kind of general declaration renouncing
war. Before considering such a thing, Western statesmen would
have to consider very seriously whether the temporary confidence
that might result from such a declaration would outweigh the
obvious dangers ". A guarded leader on Friday dismissed all
parties' proposals for housing as inadequate. On Saturday, after
declaring that foreign policy could not be counted as any one
party's preserve, *The Times* declared that the Conservatives'
" strongest weapon on grounds of principle . . . is still the place
of State ownership and control in the intentions of the Labour
Party." It argued that, whereas each major party accused the
other of being divided within itself, this was not true in the case
of the Conservatives. On the other hand " the question whether
the (Labour) Party will in the end be Labour or Socialist has still
to be settled ". Its editorial writer continued to have qualms
about a certain lack of economic realism in Conservative electioneering—" a myth of the good new days . . . deftly set against
the larger Labour legend of the bad old days " and admitted that
to accept Conservative claims to greater economic competence
involved an " act of faith ". But no responsive reader could be

left in any doubt that faith would be accorded in adequate proportions by polling day.

The *Manchester Guardian* during the week continued to devote space to Mr. Attlee's tour on more generous terms than most newspapers, but at the same time it left its readers in little doubt of the electorally dominating position of Mr. Churchill and his call for talks with the Russians. Although the *Guardian* made it plain that it did not generally believe that the question of another approach to Russia was a legitimate election issue, it covered the story with considerable enthusiasm and at great length. More perhaps than any other newspaper it expatiated on the reactions of the American Government, press and people to the proposal. At the same time it continued its extensive coverage of all aspects and levels of the election, with Liberal electioneering continuing to get particular attention. Editorial comment naturally dwelt on the " atom talks ". On Wednesday, February 15th, the first leader on Mr. Churchill's speech observed that all parties in Britain longed for peace just as sincerely as did Mr. Churchill. Why had Mr. Churchill introduced this issue when he did ? " Surely Mr. Churchill, who in these matters is usually so high minded, has no desire to make party capital out of peace ? " " We may recognize Mr. Churchill's earnestness and sincerity and yet wonder whether the effect of his attempt to revive the ' war trinity ' may not be to increase the distrust we are trying to dispel." The Diplomatic Correspondent on the same day also asked questions as to Mr. Churchill's intentions before stating " it is certainly a line which seems to run directly counter to that recently enunciated by Mr. Acheson ". An editorial, " Ends and Means ", on Friday, February 17th, reviewed the economic programmes of the parties and suggested that there was no considerable difference between them on the desirability of maintaining the present living standards, full employment, and the Welfare State. Even on the means of maintaining them the differences are " probably less than they seem ". Labour's record shows over-rigidity, but how would the " new, more liberal Conservatism " wear if a storm came ? " At any rate in the constituencies where there is no convincing Liberal candidate, the choice is narrow." On nationalisation the *Guardian* continued to attack Labour : " everywhere nationalisation in practice has so far been sharply disappointing ", it stated on February

18th, because the main problems connected with it had not yet been solved. It would then be " folly " to carry the programme further at this point.

The *Daily Telegraph* during the " atom week " of the campaign of course gave a large play in its news columns to Mr. Churchill's speech and reactions to it at home and abroad. In the first two days of the week it gave considerable space to Mr. Churchill's " rebuffed " offer to the Liberals and the " Liberal split " over Dundee. Other small outbursts against the Liberals, sometimes angry, sometimes contemptuous, also continued throughout the week. The front-page analyses of the political situation accepted more and more closely the viewpoint of the Conservative Central Office, but were careful to report accurately, if succinctly, the viewpoint of the enemy. The centre-page feature articles were consistently campaign pieces on the party line, but one sometimes got the impression that the paper was encountering difficulty in finding stimulating issues for its readers. The leaders in the *Telegraph* on the Edinburgh speech were strangely defensive in character, from the first defending Mr. Churchill's right to bring this foreign policy " scrutiny " into the campaign. The editorials also more and more took up the theme that the Labour Party was dishonest in covering up its Socialist character.

The *Daily Herald* succeeded in finding room for two and a half more columns of election material this week than last, thereby nearly reaching the limit for space, short of cutting down on football and racing coverage. The main article on all six days related to the election. In addition, all editorials continued to appear on the front page, with Mr. Churchill as the subject four times, Dr. Hill once, and Mr. R. A. Butler once. The ultimate in this Churchill counter-offensive was reached on Saturday, February 18th, when the banner above the main story read " What the *Herald* Says About What Churchill Said ". The initial news treatment of the Edinburgh speech was remarkable. Alone amongst that Wednesday's London dailies (except the *Daily Mirror*), the *Herald* avoided making any reference to it on its front page; that was dominated, perhaps pardonably, by reports of the North " hailing Attlee ". But whereas even the *Mirror*, in its inside treatment, picked up the " talks with Stalin " point for headlines, the *Herald* tucked it away as an obscure paragraph at the end of its report on page 2, with the sub-head, " Talks

Urged ". However, the next morning banner headlines dominated the front page, " Attlee Wades Into Winston. Bevin: Don't Stunt Atom ", the leader in the adjoining column being headed " Anything For a Vote ". From then to the end of the campaign the *Herald* gave a high priority to the exposure of the " stunt " aspect of Mr. Churchill's proposal. In its minor and back-page news columns the *Herald* made a fair attempt to report the news from the constituencies with little or no attempt to serve the kind of " human interest " sauce that the *Mail* and the *Express* thought indispensable.

The *Daily Mail* throughout the week put its spotlight on the atom bomb and the " atom talks ". They provided four days' headlines and three days' editorials. At the same time there was a sharp decline in the neutrality and seriousness of its reporting of election meetings throughout the country, with the emphasis gradually shifting from what the speakers were saying to what the hecklers said or did. With this change Labour meetings began to get more and more space, under headlines such as " Little Annie Has a Night Out " for a meeting addressed by Mr. G. R. Strauss, Minister of Supply; " The Unkindest Cut of All " for Mr. Silkin; and " No Smoking, Herbie " for Mr. Morrison. A collection of unflattering references from Conservative speeches about Mr. Strachey were published under the head " The Things They Say About Mr. Strachey ". Much was made of the " Radio Doctor ". Mr. Attlee had a seeming immunity from this rough handling, though at the price of a certain neglect in the news columns. Feature articles remained lively, well informed and, in the main, fair.

The *News Chronicle* during this week lavished its most devoted efforts on the cause of the Liberals without, however, obscuring the essential news issues. Nomination day, with its " Liberals Keep Pledge, 472 to Fight ", was a great day for the *News Chronicle*, and it made the most of it. A fourth instalment of the Gallup Poll gave little additional comfort to Liberals, but was nevertheless given pride of place on February 17th. Rather extensive coverage was also given to the " talks with Russia " theme, and the *News Chronicle* went further than any non-Conservative paper in endorsing Mr. Churchill's proposal. It eagerly recorded foreign reactions to the proposal and censured Labour for " missing its chance ". After Mr. Churchill's radio broadcast on Friday, he was editorially attacked for not being more specific in his domestic policy, and the sorrowful conclusion was reached that he had " given up to a party the qualities that once inspired mankind ".

The *Daily Express*, besides being positively ecstatic over Mr. Churchill's venture into foreign policy (banner headlines for the next four days), devoted itself under Lord Beaverbrook's personal direction (often with the aid of his own pen), to spreading the gospel of the £6 minimum wage and Empire Union. Candidates who pronounced themselves in favour of these proposals found themselves and their words carried alongside those of the nation's leaders in the columns of the *Express*. Headlines showed an effervescent quality such as " End This Wicked Wage Freeze " or " ' £6 Blatherskite ' ". The election was now the main subject for the *Express*, and its total space devoted to it began to approach the proportion achieved by the *Herald*, but it was still the election conceived as the biggest entertainment story of the week. There was no serious attempt to present the issues or to describe the strategy of the campaign.

The *Daily Graphic* during this time continued its exclusively Conservative policy, picturing only Conservative candidates at their canvassing and reporting heckling at Labour meetings. Both the petrol and the foreign issue were played to the hilt.

The *Daily Mirror*, on the other hand, held its fire and kept an iron control over the election material it admitted to its pages. The election remained on the second page and the back page, except when the most important issues, this week petrol and the " atom talks ", forced it into prominence. Often, indeed, the front page was reserved for relatively colourless and dull stories, as if the *Mirror* were prepared to go to great lengths to avoid wasteful and premature expenditure of its election ammunition. On the other hand, it was evident that considerable care was devoted to the strip cartoon on the paper's " election page ", page 2. The Ruggles family had said good-bye to its last Liberal or Conservative householder the previous Saturday. For the remainder of the series, throughout this week, they encountered no one, even in the most unlikely walks of life, who did not have the very best reasons for voting Labour. On Friday, February 17th, the *Mirror* devoted its centre page spread to a feature of " What the Parties Stand For ", a one-day forum in which

Labour, Liberals and Conservatives were all able to present their case.

The final short week of the campaign found all newspapers who had not previously reached saturation point devoting even more space to the campaign.   In spite of this the feeling persisted, as it had all along, that for journalists this was an election in which they had to go out and seek material rather than desperately endeavour to keep up with a fast moving campaign.   Probably the most striking newspaper events of the week were the calculated thunder of the *Daily Mirror's* endorsement of the Labour Party on Tuesday, February 21st, and the desperate attempt of the *Daily Mail* and *Daily Express* to present a great foreign policy success to Mr. Churchill on Polling Day.   The diversity of topics treated during the last four days indicates generally the lack of overwhelmingly important news.

The Times devoted more news space to the election than in the preceding week, giving especially long and full accounts of Mr. Attlee's final broadcast and Mr. Churchill's speech in Manchester. The remaining days full summaries were made of party activity with the space balanced scrupulously between the major parties and the same high standard of reporting as before.   Readers of the editorial page, in addition to benefiting from the acute final analyses of the parties' claims and chances, were kept on tenter-hooks of curiosity to see how far *The Times* would go in an open avowal of its political attachments.   Monday's first leader, after a slightly patronising paragraph of compliment on Mr. Attlee's broadcast, went on to express *The Times'* old concern about " the other voices behind him " and the old doubt whether Labour had an economic policy adequate to meet the end of Marshall Aid. But " the Conservative Party too has static notions about full employment ".   Set against that there is the " ransom " which Labour goes on paying to " its strictly Socialist wing "—national-isation.   " The decision of the election may well lie in the hands of those who are now disposed, compared with 1945, to turn from left to right," and *The Times* thought that nationalisation might come high on their list of reasons for doing so.   On Wednesday a second leader professed alarm at a remark of Lord Alexander's in a speech at Margate which it feared might indicate a Labour intention to reduce further the powers of the House of Lords. Finally, on Thursday, for those of its readers who were not voting too early to read their *Times* first, it gave its final advice. It hoped that the result will not be a narrow margin of success. It remembered with praise the " better programme " and " better party machine " of the Conservatives, and deplored the Labour Party's " calculated refusal to canvass the most characteristic and insidious of its proposals—those for public ownership ".

> " The Conservatives, the challengers, have had the better
> of the great debate, but their recipe for making the British
> economy more fit and flexible by restoring the sterner tests
> of true efficiency through a prudent retrenchment has itself
> been too often sadly diluted at the hustings to suggest simply
> lower taxes and cheaper prices for more goods, without
> corresponding sacrifice, abstinence or added toil."

In foreign policy there was praise for Mr. Churchill's Edinburgh proposal—" no more than a hint, but it was the hint of a statesman as well as a politician ". " Though the Labour Ministers had a sound answer, they did not give it with effect." But Conservatives showed no equivalent imagination in attacking nationalisation ; it was part of a lack on both sides of " the courage born of conviction ". As to the outcome of the election, *The Times* anticipated a swing away from the Government. " Today's proceedings will tell how wide the swing will be and whether, with new frontiers drawn to the constituencies and a mass invasion of hopeful Liberals, it can carry the Conservatives over the narrow line that divides Government from Opposition." Thus uneasily, reluctantly, but surely Conservatively, *The Times* eventually cast its vote.

The *Manchester Guardian* continued its expert analytical coverage during the week, paying particular attention to overseas and American comment on the election. Mr. Churchill's visit to Manchester brought the focus of the campaign back to their own doorstep just before the close, and it was covered with a commensurate fullness and friendly emphasis on all its features of human interest. Editorially the *Guardian* still had much to say before the polls closed. On Monday it analysed the foreign issues raised by Mr. Churchill and deplored Lord Beaverbrook's rider to " his old friend's " original proposal. It concluded that although appeasement was the very last sort of feeling Mr. Churchill would wish to stir up, " by arousing popular emotions and greatly oversimplifying and personalising complex issues this bomb electioneering may well weaken, not strengthen us ". On Tuesday the main leader was a defence of the *Guardian's* independence towards the programmes of the two major parties (for this see pp. 205–210). On Wednesday the leader employed this independence in support of the Liberals. Their survival as an independent party running 475 candidates was in itself a denial that the Labour Government had " proved itself the heir of the British radical tradition " or that " the Conservatives had taken over the title deeds ". But their Liberalism was " not merely a middle way ". " Of the three parties the Liberals have come closest to the advocacy of a really realistic policy for the economic crisis." But since there will not be enough Liberals to form a government, a vote for them is therefore wasted ? No, " a minority party usually exercises an influence immensely beyond its numbers ". " Whether the Government be Labour or Tory a Liberal Party will be its economic conscience." Nevertheless, the *Guardian* seemed still to feel that there was a second category of advice, as it were, to be given to those of its readers who, for whatever reason, were not going to vote Liberal. Certainly on polling day its leader, presenting " The Choice " largely in terms of a Labour–Conservative alternative, read strangely like the editorial of a Liberal journal in a country operating the single transferable vote. The determinant, the *Guardian* obviously considered, should be the years of economic crisis ahead. " Merely on paper assurances it might seem that, of the two largest parties, it is the Conservatives who best qualify." But " election talk is largely froth " and in fact a Labour Government " in a tight place " might " put across " a painful policy to the wage-earners better. If we could be sure that the economic crisis were only going to come on us slowly then " the Conservative programme is less unrealistic than Labour's, and the Liberal programme somewhat better than either ". " It is likely, however, that events would also move too fast for a Conservative government " and the *Guardian* rather pessimistically concludes that " we might then in any case have another election and change to-day's choice ". Neither side is giving the harsh leadership the times require, and " it is likely that the one to achieve realism and courage first will be the one which is out of office to-morrow ".

The *Daily Telegraph* in the final week wound up the " H-Bomb factor " on Monday, and afterwards devoted its main efforts to

Conservative pledges to lighten taxation, Conservative confidence
v. Labour pessimism and, over and over again, to the sinful wastefulness of a Liberal vote.   The news columns and special reports
were more than ever devoted to Tory candidates and plans.   The
Telegraph seemed to be acutely aware of the lack of fire in the last
few days, and attempted to put the blame on the " Socialists "
who had refused to bring forward the main issue of the campaign,
" more Socialism ", for the voters to hear and discuss.   More
than ever the first news story and the leaders seemed to be co-
ordinated.   But, true to its standards, the *Telegraph* attempted
no sort of last minute stunt.   On Thursday the front page was
soberly made up, and the importance of voting—and *not* voting
Liberal—was presented in decorous, restrained and, it must be
admitted, slightly campaign-weary language.

The *Daily Herald* put on a well-timed finish, driving home on
a narrow front the arguments that the Labour Party had been
seeking to stress throughout.   Its last week was clearly devoted
to exhorting the faithful rather than in arguing issues.   A good
part of the paper was devoted every day to countering the " Russian
talks " proposals of Mr. Churchill.   On Monday the editorial
effectively summed up the basis of the *Herald's* campaign. It began :

> " This is it.   General Election week is here.   On Thursday
> you vote to settle your future."

The consequences of voting for the various parties were then
presented as follows :

> " You can vote Tory.   That is rather like tearing the roof
> off your house, emptying your larder, and throwing your
> clothes away.   Then you will be properly exposed to the
> freezing blasts of Tory economics.
>
> " You can vote Liberal.   But in economics there is not
> much to choose between Liberals and Tories.   Nor is there
> any prospect of the Liberal Party getting an effective number
> of M.P's in the new Parliament.
>
> " In some constituencies you can vote Communist.   That
> would be a vote for handing over your future to a ruthless
> foreign totalitarian control.*

* The *Daily Herald* was the only national daily (except of course the *Daily
Worker*) that even envisaged as an academic possibility such behaviour on the
part of its readers.

M

" Or you can vote Labour. That means you choose fair shares for all, full employment, rising production in the national interest—social security—and a steadfast prospect of maintaining those blessings into the foreseeable future."

Wednesday's front page was a summing-up in popular journalistic form of all Labour's propaganda themes. Dominating the page, under the headline " Life in the Tory Thirties ", sub-head " Memo to Young Voters ", was a picture of cloth-capped Stepney unemployed. To the left of it was the main " news " story, " Labour Pledges Drive to Help the Housewife "—the women's vote. Below came the front-page editorial on the theme of " Labour's concern with NEEDS and Toryism's preoccupation with GREEDS ". On Thursday the final exhortation was administered under the banner " Think of Tomorrow, Vote Labour Today ". (This was the winning slogan in an election contest that attracted 188,236 entries.) This shared the front page with a Low cartoon depicting the " can't-be-bothered Labour voter " with his feet up on a couch at home while an unpleasant-looking personification of the " anti-Labour machine " contemplates him with the words " I'm depending on you to stay there, friend ". During this week the difference in tone and content between the editorial columns and the news columns became less and less until by Thursday it was practically non-existent.

The *Daily Mail*, like the *Daily Herald*, concentrated on a narrow front during the last days of the election. The *Mail's* main theme was Tax Relief. The main headlines on Monday and Tuesday, in fact, read respectively, " Overtime Tax Will Stay If Labour Win ", and " Tories Say It Again : ' We'll Lower Tax ' ". This and the H-Bomb issue were the main front-page election subjects. However, the proportion of space devoted to the election on the front page fell off a little, and other headlines began to pick up other subjects, leading one to suspect that the last week was not all that editors would want it to be from the point of view of colourful news. The inside pages dealing with the election continued their drift towards inconsequentiality and flippancy. One rose from reading them with the impression that hecklers at least were getting the fairest and most extensive coverage in history. The *Mail* did not resort to any direct personal exhortation on polling day, but summarised the issues on a front-page score-sheet. "Make up your Mind. If you want . . ., vote . . .", but only a bungler at the felicific calculus could fail to realise the superior advantages of voting Conservative. The last day's " Stalin Answers Churchill " story is treated later in the chapter.

The *News Chronicle's* treatment of the final four days entitled it to Mr. Churchill's election epithet of " demure ". The Liberal cause was given front-page display, though mainly when linked to larger world issues, e.g. the Tuesday lead story on Lord Samuel's speech, " Lord Samuel Says Ban Those Bombs ". But the *News Chronicle's* partisanship was not allowed to obscure its self-imposed duty to serve intelligent readers of all parties or none who wanted to know even at this feverish hour what was happening, in the campaign and outside it, and why. " The Great Debate " ended on Monday with articles by the Prime Minister, Mr. Eden and Mr. Clement Davies and an editorial summing up the moderation and reasonableness displayed by all sides. The Gallup Poll claimed a large portion of the front page on Wednesday, with its " Election Neck and Neck " finish. Editorially the *News Chronicle* was concerned as much to combat any attempt to " stampede " the Liberal vote—especially by Conservatives—as it was to win any last-minute " floaters " to its side. The issue of the election put by the leader on Tuesday was which party can best lead the nation now that the Welfare State has been achieved. The leader on Thursday was devoted to demonstrating that the answer was " the Liberals "—all 475 of them.

The *Daily Express* kept the " peace talks " as its main theme on the front page and continued to cast Mr. Churchill as the preserver of peace. In spite of the difficulty that other newspapers seem to have had to find election material during the final week, the *Express* carried on fairly well with such items as Mr. Attlee's stay at a private instead of a state hotel in Carlisle, Lady Astor's political efforts, and Mr. W. J. Brown's campaigning at Rugby. The *Express's* own poll continued to forecast Tory victory—right up to the dawn of Polling Day. The final editorial admonition ran as follows :

" Now is the day of decision and of destiny. When you mark your cross today you decide far more than whether the next Prime Minister will be a Tory or a Socialist. You decide instead how you and your family are going to live at all. For peace is the prime issue, this tremendous Thursday."

The concluding paragraphs were :

" Mr. Churchill today seeks neither personal power nor personal glory. He seeks instead only to give further service to this country which he has already served so well. It would be easy for him to step aside from the fray and spend his remaining years in the comfort and leisure which so long has been denied.

" But instead he fights on, not for himself but for you. For he believes that to him has fallen the supreme duty of ensuring that this, the country he loves, will go forward in peace to new heights of greatness and prosperity. For now sits Expectation in the Air."

The *Daily Graphic* maintained its steady line of Conservative effort, devoting more and more pictures and editorial material to the campaign. Nothing can better illustrate this journal's last week's effort than to quote the main headline and " over-line ", the small head run over the main banner :

Monday, " The City Hits Back : ' Stop It, Morrison ' ", and " Think and Act ! Vote for Freedom and Lower Taxes ! "

Tuesday, " Churchill : The Great Issues—Peace, Taxes ", and " Think and Act ! Vote for a Home You Can Own."

Wednesday, " Woolton Says : I Promise You Better Food ", and " Think and Act ! ' I look forward to Thursday when, with a gesture of intense wrath and contempt, the British nation will spit the Socialist trash and jargon out of their mouths for ever '—Mr. Churchill last night."

Thursday, " Rows Liven Eve-of-Poll Meetings ", and " Think and Act ! Vote today—Vote Tory ".

The *Daily Mirror* maintained the pose of thinking the election issues over until Tuesday, February 21st, when it came down on the Labour side with a suitable display. In a huge front page editorial entitled " WHERE WE STAND " the following sentiments were expressed :

" The *Daily Mirror* supports the Labour Party at the General Election. We have made this decision after full and

careful consideration of the claims of all the parties. This
has convinced us that the Labour Party's planning for
recovery is needed for the safety of Britain as a whole."

And, in an underlined passage :

" We support the Labour Party because it has kept its
promises and earned our trust. Its policy has been one of
fairness and humanity. We believe it is the only policy that
can work. We must go forward with the people because in
these days it is absolutely impossible to go forward without
them."

Mr. Ruggles on page 2, whether affected or not by this, kept *his*
voting intentions secret up to—and after—the crucial Thursday,
but his wife (and a majority of *Mirror* readers are women) made
clear her Labour attachment from the first. Nevertheless, for
all this vigorous partisanship, the *Mirror* still took care not to
overdo the election in its pages. The front-page display on
Polling Day is worth reproducing. It was set up as follows :

VOTE TODAY . . . (in red ink).
YOUR JOB
YOUR HOME
YOUR FAMILY
YOUR COUNTRY
Are at Stake
VOTE for THEM
Forward with the People.

INDIVIDUAL DAILIES

For newspapers, as well as politicians, a general election is a
testing-time. How did the individual national newspapers emerge
from it ?

In an advertisement which appeared in several periodicals early
in February, *The Times* said of itself, " At Election time, as in all
other phases of national life, *The Times* preserves its complete
political independence. Its first resolve is always to give the
news faithfully and fully and to offer responsible comment."
There can be no doubt that, everything considered, *The Times*
of the election period lived up to its claim and its resolve. There

is also no doubt that from its independent position *The Times*, after consideration, advocated the Conservative side on the majority of issues. The fact that *The Times* never declared its nominal preference should not obscure this. However, it never became a party paper, and it is noteworthy that two of the themes which the Conservative press most assiduously sought to exploit— " petrol " and " talks with Russia "—were, the first by implication and the second explicitly, dismissed by *The Times* as unsuitable campaign issues.

The main election issue, according to *The Times*, was economic —the crisis of the balance of payments—and the main anti-Labour argument was nationalisation. Again and again the other more episodic issues were summarily brushed away as trivial in comparison with this. It was presented in many forms, probably the most daring of which was *The Times'* recurrent speculation on how far towards total Socialism the more extreme elements were going to pull the Labour Party. Both parties were censured for the inadequacies of their response to the economic threats which faced the country, but, of the two, Conservatives were thought to display the greater realism. The Liberal proposals were not thought by *The Times* to merit serious consideration. For foreign affairs it gave the impression of sighing for a combination of Conservative men and Labour policies.

In news coverage *The Times* aimed not only at reliability but also at completeness and objectivity. The first it achieved to a highly creditable degree, the second within the limits of its available space, and the third whenever the intractability of the subject-matter did not prove too much for it. In relation, for example, to the conflict over nomenclature between the Liberals and the Conservatives objectivity could provide no adequate guide for correspondent or sub-editor, since the very point at issue was the existence of the object itself. It is no doubt true, as Mr. Churchill told Mr. Clement Davies, that people are free to call themselves what they like, but a newspaper cannot always solve its obligations to the facts by merely calling them what they call themselves. In effect, though admittedly with no narrowly partisan intention, *The Times* chose the Conservative horn of such dilemmas. However, in allocating space and in noting events the newspaper seemed to be entirely fair. The paper performed an invaluable service in " charting " and recording the campaign in maps, tables, lists of candidates, etc. Its regional and constituency reports, if sometimes lacking in flavour, were generally fair and informative.

The *Manchester Guardian* gave whole-hearted though not un-critical support to the Liberal Party throughout the campaign. Despite this, its news coverage was undoubtedly the most neutral in content of any of the national dailies. Its editorials were con-sistently devoted to an expression of its own frank opinions, uninhibited by any suggestion of compulsion, moral or otherwise, to give aid and comfort to the party of its choice. Indeed, its expressed belief seemed lodged more in Liberalism than in the electoral prospects of the Liberal Party. More perhaps than any other serious daily it embraced every facet of the election cam-paign with gusto, often applauding even where it could not wholly approve, and delighting in the prowess displayed even when its own interests were not engaged.

Editorially the *Guardian*, like *The Times*, felt the crucial issue to be the economic crisis facing the country. Like *The Times*, too, it admitted the paper merits of the Conservative solution (though it thought the Liberal better), but, unlike *The Times*, it mistrusted Conservative performance, if elected, and had a greater faith in the sobering effect of crisis upon Labour hotheads. It deplored further exercises in nationalisation and was doubtful of the depth of Labour's attachment to civil liberties. It did not consider foreign policy to be an election issue, and, while prepared to give Mr. Churchill the benefit of every doubt, still thought his introduction of it into the campaign a mistake. Its attitude to Mr. Churchill is discussed in more detail on pp. 205–210.

In news policy the paper played no favourites. Thus, though Mr. Churchill's personality obviously fascinated its reporting, as well as its editorial staff, it was one of the few journals that saw in Mr. Attlee an interesting personality whose newspaper stereotype as the " quiet, colourless little man " should be broken. The special election reporting of the *Guardian* was admirably executed. In freshness of observation, in fidelity to local (and human) colour, in political penetration and in vividness of writing, it had no equal. If a dash of malicious wit constitutes no disqualifica-tion, a despatch on Mr. Eden's local campaigning on February 20th probably deserves the prize for the best piece of field reporting in the campaign. Its constituency surveys (the best in any paper) spot-lighted Liberal candidates more frequently than their news value always warranted, but there were very few instances of misleading bulletins being issued on their prospects. Finally special mention should be made of the *Guardian's* coverage of foreign aspects of the election, especially in relation to the United States.

The *Daily Telegraph* was the most nearly " official " Conservative newspaper of the election. But while it devoted itself assiduously to this cause, it also made a commendable effort to keep its readers well abreast of arguments on all sides of the campaign. Whereas *The Times* seemed to conceive of itself as a newspaper for informed people whom it would like to convert gently, at any rate for this occasion, to Conservatism, the *Telegraph* apparently envisaged itself as a newspaper for Conservatives whom it would very much like to see well informed. Secondarily, of course, it hoped to bring " informed " Liberals into the same Conservative haven. As the campaign progressed the rising tempo of activity in the Conservative Central Office undoubtedly transmitted itself to the staff of the *Telegraph*, and sometimes resulted in a blurring of this delicate dual aim, but the underlying assumption remained.

The editorial object of the newspaper was to discredit " Socialism "* in all its forms. Here the legion of arguments used by Conservative leaders and candidates were put out in logical and cogent forms. The Labour-fostered " myths " of the " bad old days " before the war were demolished and the sins of the present Labour Government were exposed as pointers to Labour's future behaviour. The most prominent editorial line in the early part of the campaign was the error and futility of the Liberal Party in running a great number of candidates. The " wastefulness " of a Liberal vote was maintained as a good secondary line throughout the campaign.

The news columns were used intelligently and with good taste to carry out the basic assumption ascribed above. Genuinely objective articles were run side by side with stories undoubtedly taking the line of the Conservative Party headquarters. The Labour Party was never ignored ; its activities were carefully and

* " Labour " is always " Socialism " in the *Telegraph*.

realistically recorded from a Conservative point of view. The headlines generally conceded more to the paper's political preference than did the news accounts. Certain issues with political implications were "plugged" during the campaign, but news values were seldom seriously distorted.

The election special features and the ordinary letter columns were used especially to benefit Conservatives, seduce Liberals and rebut Labour. The special surveys were reliable if generally pro-Conservative. The *Telegraph's* nomination-day supplement was especially well executed, and for sheer technical arrangement probably the most successful venture of this type during the campaign.

Special issues which the *Telegraph* emphasised were the Conservatives' taxation relief proposals and Mr. Churchill's "talks with the Russians" suggestion. Special individual targets of the paper were in general Mr. Morrison, Mr. Bevan, Dr. Summerskill and Mr. Strachey. Of special note is the lack of political initiative of the *Telegraph*, in the sense that all of its themes and leader subjects seemed to be raised first in speeches or party declarations. This is undoubtedly the hallmark of the "official" party newspaper.

The *Daily Herald* of February 10th reported Mr. Sam Watson, the Chairman of the Labour Party, as follows :

> "'In exposing Tory Party misrepresentation the *Daily Herald* is playing a magnificent part. Its constructive political contributions, and provision of election facts to support Labour's case, make it more than a national newspaper in this important election. It is a daily tonic.'"

Mr. Watson's tribute and the *Daily Herald's* pride in such a bouquet reflect the paper's role as the official newspaper of the Labour Party. On the other hand, it competes in the popular newspaper field with at least four other London dailies. With these factors in mind, the conduct of the *Herald* was largely predictable. Its appeal throughout was to the party faithful, but it was also aware that it had to carry the main load of counter-attack against the thrusts of its rivals. It began to fight sooner and kept up the fight more intensively than any other national daily save the *Daily Worker*.

The editorial attitude of the paper was almost purely defensive, the leading article being devoted mainly to critical comments on the speeches of leading Conservatives and to reminders of the sharp contrast between the blessings of Labour Party rule and the miseries of Tory misrule between the wars. There was an almost complete absence of references to what the party would do if returned to power a second time. Much editorial care and skill were expended on inoculating *Herald* readers against the " stunts " of enemy politicians or press.

Considering the major premises of the paper, the news coverage was perhaps as fair as could be expected. The chief speakers of all parties were reported, though of course by no means fully. The most space was given to broadcasters and, amongst speakers, to Mr. Churchill, while the lead story on the front page was generally based on a speech by a prominent member of the Labour Cabinet. There were no scruples against the overflow of editorial comment into the news columns. Nor did the *Herald* hesitate to ignore news if it suspected that it would cause embarrassment to the Labour Party. Both the petrol and foreign-policy incidents were ignored or carried without emphasis for more than twenty-four hours after the event. More than any other big national daily, the *Herald* judged its news by the test of whether it would help the party. Even the announcement of B.B.C. programmes and the Olney housewives' pancake race were handled to party advantage, while there were, of course, many special election features, such as " Housewives Voice ", which were designed exclusively with that end in view.

Mr. Churchill was naturally the chief individual target of the *Herald*, with Lord Woolton, Dr. Charles Hill and Mr. Eden as subsidiaries. Mr. Morrison, Mr. Attlee and Mr. Bevin were the principal subjects of its friendly spotlight. Mr. Bevan and Mr. Shinwell, the party's *enfants terribles*, made much less frequent appearances. The issues it stressed were exclusively those which the Labour Party organisation chose to attack or defend. Even less than the *Telegraph*, had the *Herald* any political initiative of its own.

While not an official party organ, the *News Chronicle* devoted itself with fervour to the Liberal cause throughout the election, and gave less and less comfort to either Labour or Conservatives as the campaign went on. On one hand, the Liberal strife with Conservatives, both at the centre and in the constituencies, gave it the appearance of being primarily anti-Tory. On the other hand, its frequent dissatisfaction with Labour policy and its support of Mr. Churchill over the Russian " peace talks " issue put it repeatedly at odds with Labour. It was, in fact, independent. Which major party the *News Chronicle* actually benefitted in the 1950 election it is impossible to say. It certainly conceived of itself as serving a popular but intelligent readership which did not wish to be led in the blinkers of any party, which would hear all sides first (though vote Liberal in the end), and, while relishing the knockabout of the hustings, was not going to be cozened into thinking the General Election the most important issue in the world of 1950. It was in keeping with this attitude that the paper's most distinctive election features were its Gallup Polls and its " Great Debate ". In its conception and handling of the second of these the *News Chronicle* probably rendered its most valuable service to its readers and, incidentally, to popular journalism. For the first time in British election history, a whole-hearted attempt was made to bring before the readers of a single newspaper (and the enormous majority of voters are one-paper readers) the whole range of party viewpoints presented by party leaders themselves. Other journals attempted something similar, but none with the prominence and completeness of the *News Chronicle*.

Editorially the *News Chronicle* adhered to the Liberal line of attacking both main parties on both their records and their programmes. Its motto might have been " reform without socialism ". The economic crisis and foreign policy competed for first place in its judgment of what constituted crucial issues, but the right and duty of the Liberals to stand as a " Third Force " were both given prominence.

The news columns carried a great deal of outright Liberal views, not infrequently tinted with optimism, usually attributed to an individual correspondent. Straight news was not affected by the political leanings of the newspaper.

The *News Chronicle* seemed commendably free of special attitudes towards most issues and individuals. Its general opposition to nationalisation and its stress on " the woman's vote " were probably the nearest approaches to this.

The *Daily Mail* carried the unofficial banner of the Conservatives in the popular press field, although it was by no means as orthodox a party newspaper as the *Daily Telegraph*. It devoted itself to being entertaining and Conservative at the same time, and by the end of the campaign there was little news containing both these elements that did not find itself in the paper's columns. It would seem that the *Daily Mail* was not above vigorously playing special themes for political effect alone, or aiming at putting over by implication attitudes it did not state in actual words.

Its editorial policy was to attack the Government on its record. All the difficulties the country faced were by implication the fault of the Socialists. This attitude was pushed by ridicule rather than by abuse; the Ministers were not villains, but inefficient muddlers. Mr. Bevan was portrayed as the unfortunate victim of his own bitterness, while Mr. Attlee was a sincere, misguided individual of much personal merit. Only rarely was the Labour Party attacked for its allegedly Socialistic theories. The issues the *Daily Mail* pushed home were lack of food, high taxes and fear of the " H-Bomb ". Its editorials scarcely touched on the issues between the Conservative and Liberal parties.

In its news columns much the same line was expressed, helped greatly by headlines. In the last two weeks the tempo was stepped up and vote-catching slogans hit the eye at every turn. In this the emphasis fell mainly on the material benefits of Conservatism rather than its idealism, the two main themes being that the Tories would lower taxes and that only Mr. Churchill could deliver the country from the " H-Bomb " menace.

The appeal, in most of the election features as in the editorials, was to the readers' hard-headed common sense. Throughout the *Daily Mail* recognised that there was another side than its own and also, though more intermittently, that, in addition to advocacy and entertainment, there was a campaign, with strategy and tactics of its own, to be made comprehensible to its readers. But in the main it seemed to conceive its job as being to rouse the Conservative apathetics, and neither to convert nor to expound. At the same time the articles never became so strongly biased that the reader might become immunised to their appeal, and the flippancy was never carried to the extent of defeating its own purpose.

The *Daily Express* was Conservative in sentiment, but wore its Conservatism with a difference—the difference being represented by its proprietor's incalculable temperament. In one and the same month—October 1949—Lord Beaverbrook had had the Conservative whip in the House of Lords withdrawn from him, and had replied by launching his own election programme. Although his subsequent absence from Britain provided an interlude of relative calm in *Express* columns, the paper's main policy line remained unchanged. It envisaged itself, as it stated in its issue of January 6th, as appealing to the hypothetical " two million voters who do not pledge their allegiance in advance ", most of whom it asserted to be *Daily Express* readers. Its great themes to win these two million were the Empire, " freedom from controls " and the return of Mr. Churchill to power. Lord Beaverbrook's return mid-way in the campaign had the effect of re-emphasising two points in which his policy diverged from *The Right Road for Britain*—the £6-a-week minimum wage and " Empire Union Now ". A Cummings cartoon pictured a puckish Beaverbrook juggling with spanners over a Conservative " election machine " in terms almost identical with a 1945 cartoon by " Vicky ". But the anticipations of wild behaviour induced by such memories of Lord Beaverbrook's intervention in the previous general election were not to be realised. For all its individual emphasis, the paper's overlap with official Conservative policy was sufficiently extensive to leave no doubt as to which party it supported. Indeed, in the last week its own wood-notes wild were completely drowned out beneath the two great themes of " atom talks " and " Mr. Churchill ".

The *Express* is *par excellence* a paper of favourites and bogeys. Its great election favourite was, of course, Mr. Churchill. Dr. Charles Hill was a good runner-up and Mr. Brendan Bracken seldom went unreported. Its greatest bogey was Mr. Aneurin Bevan, though Mr. Strachey and Dr. Summerskill were good substitutes. A piquant detail of its election coverage was its love-match with Mr. Shinwell, whose speeches secured remarkable prominence in its columns. " Mr. Shinwell ", said the *Express*, " has made excellent speeches, poking fun at the Tories with high good humour. He emerges a better figure." " The *Daily Express* ", said Mr. Shinwell, " has been more objective in its presentation of election news than any of the newspapers opposed to the Labour Party." It would be charitable to assume that Mr. Shinwell's other election duties made his study of the national press somewhat intermittent.

The *Daily Graphic* was in some ways the most unabashedly Conservative of all the national newspapers. Its constant enthusiasm for the Conservative cause and its unvarying style of approach must eventually have caused a certain weariness amongst all but the most ardent members of the party. The pictures were almost invariably of Conservatives, while the mention of Labour candidates or Ministers was almost invariably derogatory. The newspaper seemed to conceive of itself as existing merely to furnish the faithful with pictorial evidence of their party's activities. A monastic reader trying to reconstruct the election from the *Daily Graphic's* accounts would have found it impossible to understand why so impressive a force had to be mobilised against such a puny foe.

The *Daily Mirror*, on the other hand, was the most wary of all the national papers in admitting election material to its pages. Even at the height of the campaign the proportion of election copy to other news rarely exceeded a ratio of 50 : 50. In spite (or perhaps because) of this cautious policy, the *Mirror* was probably a most valuable publication to the Labour cause. Its appeal was to the relatively a-political wage-earner, the man (and especially the woman) reader who would weary easily of sustained political news or views, whom the parties could not lure into meetings but had somehow, for victory, to lure to the ballot-box. To effect its purpose the *Mirror* was carefully organised. It centred all " feature " discussion of the election around the Ruggles Family strip cartoon on page 2. Election news proper was inserted sparsely on the back page, where the editorial often appeared also. Therefore, in the average issue, if the reader stayed away from those two pages, he could exist in a world without an election. Furthermore, even on these pages it maintained the pose of an independent until the last week, when it came down with a thump to back the Labour Party. If any one newspaper directed its policy at cornering the marginal voter, that newspaper was the *Mirror*.

The short editorials of the *Mirror* were admirable at reducing the issue to the lowest level of pungent comprehensibility. There was no time or space wasted on exploratory argument or exposition of the other side's case before knocking it down. At the same time the pro-Labour or anti-Tory statements were carefully " unattached " to any " official " or " party line ". The news columns on the front page were reserved for the most crucial political purposes, such as replying to the increased petrol proposal, declaring the " Russian peace talks " to be a stunt, announcing the *Mirror's* " decision " to back Labour, and urging its readers to vote for " the People ". Finally, towards the end of the campaign there was a most effective blending of text and photographs designed to add pictorial weight to the political arguments.

In all this there was, of course, no pretence of fair news coverage, whether as between the various party contestants or in relation to any serious estimate of what constituted important news. The principal divergent points of view found some expression at various times and places in its columns. For the rest, they had to take their chance in competition with sport, sex, the " snappy " and the sensational.

The *Daily Worker* was undoubtedly the most exclusively party paper of the campaign. Virtually no news was admitted to which a Communist twist could not be given, and none excluded, however unreliable, which might serve as grist to the party mill. No effort was spared to show that there was no essential difference between the Labour and Conservative Parties; even when the formal attack was anti-Tory, the moral was always anti-Labour. The overwhelmingly predominant themes were the " wage freeze " and the " horror bomb ". These were plugged constantly in front-page articles with banner heads. Housing was another weapon used against the Labour Party, while unemployment was used to combat the Tories. Mr. Bevin was the *Worker's bête noire*. Its heroes were, of course, the leaders of its own party, whose meetings were always reported with prominence, however minute the audience. In general, there was no difference in content or tone between the different portions of the *Daily Worker*. All were devoted with equal ardour to presenting facts picked by Communists to a readership of either the converted or the convertible.

THE NATIONAL SUNDAY NEWSPAPERS

Eleven Sunday newspapers were examined during the election period, of which two count as " quality " papers and the remainder as " popular " papers.   The rough political preferences shown by these newspapers were as follows :

Conservative supporters numbered seven : the *Sunday Times, Sunday Express, News of the World, Sunday Empire News, Sunday Chronicle, Sunday Dispatch* and *Sunday Graphic.*

Labour supporters numbered three : *Reynolds' News*, the *People* and the *Sunday Pictorial.*

The *Observer* maintained a strictly independent course.

Up to date circulation figures for all these papers were not obtainable, but totals based on the Report of the Royal Commission on the press which, in turn, was based on 1947 pegged circulations, would not be seriously misleading.   According to this, the Conservative newspapers had a total circulation of slightly more than 17 million, and the Labour of a little above 9 million.   Such changes as have taken place since have had the total effect of adjusting that balance rather more in Labour's favour.   The *Observer's* circulation in 1950 was a little over 400,000.

The *Observer* threaded its way through the political war very successfully, offering an ingenious, good-humoured and pungent commentary wherever it felt that the conduct of the contestants invited it.   The news columns were reasonably balanced between the parties, many special features of its inside pages showed considerable diversity of approach, but nearly all maintained the independent spirit of the newspaper itself.   Spokesmen of all parties were given space to state their case.   Editorially the *Observer* adhered to its announced refusal to tell its readers how to vote.   It proclaimed both early and late its advocacy of a number of unexceptionable causes, and found curates' eggs in every party's basket, but preserved to the end a sibyllic silence about its own voting intentions.

The Kemsley-owned *Sunday Times*, the other quality paper in this category, in general followed the course of its Camrose companion, the *Daily Telegraph*.   It aimed at an informed Conservatism, and pursued this line of policy in a dignified manner and with a fair news coverage.   The editorial page showed a marked tendency to present " the common case " that both

Liberals and Conservatives had against the " Socialists ", the need for a common front and the vanity of " Independent " Liberals' wishes. The foreign policy implications of the election were stressed and the suggestion of " talks with the Russians " was defended. The case against the Labour Party was made along orthodox Conservative lines. The news pages were decidedly concerned with Conservative speeches, and from January 22nd to the Sunday before the election there was not an issue in which Mr. Churchill's name was not in head type on the front page.

The *News of the World*, with its weekly sale of approximately 8 million copies, threaded its way softly through the election campaign, taking care to entertain, and not to offend, a readership not all of which could possibly be wooed to Conservatism. In fact it attempted very little wooing. Editorially it steered clear of politics almost entirely, demanding only that politicians " put first things first ", meaning the atom bomb. A much-publicised forum was run in two issues, including representatives of the three main parties. In its news display it favoured the Conservatives. A list of successive main political headlines were: January 22nd : " A Basic Standard of Life for All, Conservative Leader Foresees a Great Awakening " (Churchill). January 29th : " Mr. Churchill Gives Warning of a ' Socialist Plot ' "; February 12th : " Housing and Work Come First, Says Woolton "; and on February 19th : " Mr. Churchill Warns of Russia's Armed Might ". The election made little impression on the distinctive inside features of the paper.

The *Sunday Express*, although produced by a separate staff and having a slightly wealthier readership than the *Daily Express*, maintained most of the characteristics of its daily sister. As such it was pronouncedly more political in tone and intent than most of the other Sunday journals. The determined Conservative sentiment was never in doubt as it pushed home most of the familiar charges against the Labour Party. The issue of February 19th was noteworthy for the effort it made to make the " peace talks " a major issue (see page 198). In Mr. Nat Gubbins' analyses of " the floating vote " it contributed one of the few convincingly humorous features inspired by the election in any newspaper.

The *Sunday Dispatch* maintained a hearty Conservative line,

N

leaving no doubt as to its sympathies either in the editorial columns or in its news. It publicised alleged " women's " and " middle-class " revolts among voters, emphasising that Conservatives would procure better food and lower taxes if they came to power. In its editorial columns it summoned Liberals to vote for Conservatives. It was also noteworthy for airing the old bogey of whether the Labour Party would refuse to give up the power it won. On February 12th the leader printed some alleged excerpts from Sir Stafford Cripps' writings (unspecified), and then in one paragraph asked :

> " If they (Socialist leaders) do win and, if things go from the present bad to the future worse, will the electors be given a chance to change their rulers ? "

The *Sunday Empire News*, published in Manchester, also hewed close to the Conservative Party line, carrying each week of the election a front-page story featuring either Mr. Churchill or Lord Woolton. However, it also kept a wide variety of the usual Sunday news dispatches in its columns. The " atom bomb talks " were trumpeted heartily throughout the entire edition on February 19th, while food supplies and food prices seemed to be featured on the other Sundays. The editorials were of the same type, the one on the 19th being entitled " A Matter of Life and Death ", and hailing Mr. Churchill's foreign policy move as a stroke of high statesmanship.

The *Sunday Graphic* is to all intents and purposes the Sunday edition of the *Daily Graphic*, and gave the same unvarying support in all departments to the Conservative campaign.

The *Sunday Chronicle* follows in London very much the same formula of entertainment combined with ardent Conservatism which its Kemsley sister, the *Sunday Empire News*, employs in Manchester. Frequent front-page stories based on Mr. Churchill and Lord Woolton were mixed with attacks on the bunglers of Socialism. The inherent political sense of all women, who could be relied on to see through the folly of the Labour Government, was often referred to in special articles. For its last pre-election issue its leader concentrated its fire on what it termed the " Lib-Labs ", whom it blamed for all the ills of the past five years.

The *People* spreads over a rich variety of entertainment a very thin coating of Labour advocacy. During the campaign two or

three front-page articles each week put forward the Labour arguments as presented by the leaders of the Government. Occasional derisive dispatches were devoted to attacks on the Government by Conservative speakers. A front-page column of
comment entitled " Good Morning People " was used in the same
defensive manner as the *Daily Herald's* editorials to refute some
recent Conservative utterance, although without nearly as much
ardour. The election made no very serious inroads on the regular
Sunday features. In general, unemployment was not emphasised
by the *People*, and the policy seemed merely to refute the charges
against Labour. The attack of the Conservatives on the Liberals
was well covered.

The *Sunday Pictorial*, in essence a Sunday edition of the *Daily
Mirror*, with a somewhat greater number of features such as the
other Sunday newspapers find so popular, was another Labour
Party supporter. Like its daily counterpart, it avoided election
stories in the early part of the campaign, but the last two issues
contained features and pictorial displays which had evidently been
planned with great care. One of these was an election " quiz "
which gave the claims of the three main parties. In general, the
front-page displays in the last three Sundays of the campaign
fitted into the Labour " anti-stunt " technique. In a huge spread
in the February 19th issue Mr. Attlee was hailed as having delivered the " greatest speech of all ". The main line of attack was
to emphasise the solid achievements of the Government and to
ridicule the " gloomy " picture of Britain presented by Mr.
Churchill and other Conservative speakers. In its medium the
Sunday Pictorial undoubtedly was one of the most effective
propaganda publications of the campaign.

Reynolds' News, as an official Co-operative organ, devoted a
far greater amount of space to political subjects than any other
popular Sunday paper, with the possible exception of the *Sunday
Express*. The front page carried a number of stories with a
political bearing on every Sunday during the campaign. Most
of these were frankly partisan, either scotching the claims of a
" gloomy " Britain or launching counter-attacks against the
" petrol " and " talks-with-Russia " moves. On February 5th a
violent attack against the Liberal manifesto appeared, making the
surprising discovery that it proposed to " scrap all " food subsidies
—probably the most bitter such dispatch to appear in any Labour

newspaper throughout the campaign. In other respects *Reynolds'*
News followed the general Labour line, though without stressing
the full-employment theme to quite the full extent. Inside
columns of great variety by Labour and Co-operative politicians
also gave ardent support to Labour.

THE PROVINCIAL PRESS

The provincial press, if by that term is understood any newspaper published outside London, covers a very wide range of
journals. There are, first of all, certain newspapers which have
virtually the importance of their metropolitan opposite numbers,
and in their own area may count for even more.

In Scotland the *Glasgow Herald* and the *Scotsman* are not only
national newspapers of distinction, but also provide a service of
news and comment in every respect comparable to their London
counterparts. Both are independent, both are conservative and
both have an influence far in excess of their modest circulation.
They also resemble each other in their avoidance of sensationalism
and in the care with which they separate their news from their
comment. All these characteristics were exemplified in their
election coverage. The *Herald* was probably the more lively and
enterprising of the two. It tackled the problem of election
reporting with a certain relish, and the space it allocated to it,
especially to constituency coverage, was almost lavish. Speeches
were often reported in full, whether of the Opposition or of
Government spokesmen. They were balanced in prominence and
soberly headlined (so soberly, indeed, in one instance that no
hint of Mr. Churchill's foreign policy suggestion appeared in the
headlines of his Edinburgh speech). Editorially the *Herald* was
moderate but firm in its Conservatism. It felt nationalisation
and the problem of Britain's economic recovery to be the main
issue and, by implication, dismissed foreign policy as irrelevant.

The *Scotsman* also devoted a great deal of space each day to the
election news, and gave its readers a very fair picture of the course
of the campaign both in Scotland and England. If slightly more
space was devoted to Conservative campaigning than to Labour,
it was not in excess of what could be justified on a reasonable
estimate of pure news value. Its tours of Scottish constituencies
were well informed and fair; though its correspondents could not

always conceal their sympathy for the Conservative candidate, all sides were given a good display. It rated the " atom talks " issue higher than did the *Herald*, playing it as the lead story every day from the 15th to the 21st. In its editorials it expressed a vigorous Conservatism, attacking Labour along a broad front. More than the *Herald* it explored Labour's Scottish record, and it also surpassed its neighbour in its conception of foreign policy as an important issue in the campaign.

In England, perhaps the closest counterpart to the *Glasgow Herald* and the *Scotsman* as a paper with a wide and influential as well as high quality, regional coverage is the *Yorkshire Post*. No less than they, it acquitted itself creditably in its treatment of the election and cast its weight, similarly, into the Conservative side of the scales. Fact and opinion were generally kept in their separate compartments, though the size and make-up of the paper did not always facilitate this—e.g. a front-page " Plain Facts " column, which was virtually an additional daily editorial. The Conservatives secured the major share of space, but headlines were usually, though not always, free of party bias. Editorially it raked Labour from stem to stern, concentrating most attention on the Government's alleged economic bungling and what it called the " bread-and-butter " issues of food, housing, cost of living and the like.

Although a large number of other provincial papers were read during the election it was unfortunately not possible to subject the provincial press as a whole to anything like as close a scrutiny as the papers that have been mentioned above. Consequently the impressions that follow, though based on a fairly wide range of samples, remain personal impressions ; beneath the generalisations there is often a wide range of individual diversity.

In its ceaseless war against metropolitan or " chain " domination, the provincial press, to judge by appearances, found the election a very welcome circumstance. Here was an event which, while being of national importance, made *local* news, which they were better able to cover and expound than any of their rivals. In response they opened their headlines and their news and feature columns to it generously ; only over their editorial columns, in many cases, did they keep a close guard. If the main criticism which can be directed against the national press is the length to which it carried its partisanship, then most of the provincial press can be acquitted of serious sin on this score. Though the bulk of the larger provincial dailies and evenings were Conservative and made no secret of that fact, they were less disposed, especially in their coverage of local campaigns, to ignore the claims of the other side. For this there was a very good reason, outside the realm of journalistic ethics altogether—namely, that, in the main, they were competing for a readership which contained supporters of all parties, none of whom they wished seriously to offend. Even where a paper enjoyed a local monopoly it was seldom free from competition from outside. This consideration, in fact, drove the provincial press all too often into an opposite, though possibly more venial, sin of their own—a virtual abdication of political judgment. If readers of such papers expected to find in them editorial guidance, or even clarification, they must have been sorely disappointed. A good many papers abandoned any idea of leading local opinion, and simply converted themselves into political forums, allocating space, often on a basis of arithmetical equality, to each contestant, local, national or both—thereby securing simultaneously free copy and immunity from *ex parte* criticism.

Save in the rare instances where a newspaper was crudely " loading " its news, the main features in which bias manifested itself were reports of speeches (disproportionate length or prominence or over-emphasis on interruptions, etc.), " gossip items ", photographs or " Letters to the Editor ". Even here, however, a good many instances of what at first sight might appear to be a biased news policy turned out on closer inspection to be the result merely of the greater journalistic enterprise of one of the local party machines—generally the Conservative. Many local papers, unable to cope with the sudden strain put on their reporting staffs, took ready-made material that was offered them, and many a local party organisation with a competent press officer took advantage of this. Indeed, one instance was encountered of a rural weekly complaining to a Labour Party agent of failure to supply press reports in quantity adequate to balance those of his opponent.

In most localities, but especially in small towns and rural areas, the local evening or weekly paper is an indispensable notice-board in which to advertise political meetings as well as, sometimes, to place a brief statement of a candidate's policy. Here, too, in its allocation of space and prominence, the local press seems to have behaved impartially, though there were one or two instances of a practice which seems potentially open to abuse—the raising of advertisement rates for political notices.

The editorial tone of most provincial papers was milder, even when frankly partisan, than that of their popular London counterparts. They generally addressed themselves to issues of national or local policy, and there were very few attacks on the personalities of local candidates. Even the West Country editorial writer who always addressed the Lord President of the Council as " Our 'Erb " adopted a more respectful tone when referring to local Labour candidates.

Just as it was not the rule for provincial papers to be strongly partisan, so it was rare for them to attempt much political analysis or to go beneath the obvious surface of the campaign. The kind of speculative exploration of local campaign tactics and machinery to which the reader of even a minor provincial American newspaper is accustomed is something so rare in Britain as to cause surprise when it occurs. What the reader of the good provincial daily or local weekly could confidently look for in 1950 was plain, straightforward reports of meetings and a certain amount of readable " human interest " material on the local campaign.

PETROL IN THE PRESS

The first incident in the campaign which allowed full scope for newspapers to engage in partisan interpretation on a major scale resulted from the passage in Mr. Churchill's speech of February 9th, quoted on page 95. The press treatment of this speech and of its repercussions was sufficiently distinctive to warrant more detailed examination. The statement was most carefully worded ; it promised nothing in the letter, though a good deal in the spirit. The London evening papers that same day came out in headlines with the news that Churchill had promised an outright increase in " the basic ". The morning papers also were able to do a good deal with the passage, especially with the help of a statement that Mr. Geoffrey Lloyd, Minister of Fuel in the " Caretaker Government " of 1945, made the same evening as the Churchill speech. The *Daily Express* stretched the statement to the greatest extent with a banner declaring " The Petrol IS

There " ; it characteristically decorated the lower part of the main story with pictures of two petrol coupons.   The leading paragraph of the story stated simply :

> " Mr. Churchill set the hustings alight yesterday by chal-lenging the Socialists on three vital issues—petrol, food and sweets.   He made it clear that Britain could have more of each quickly."

Following this, Mr. Churchill's words were quoted, as well as the more forthright statement of Mr. Lloyd that " if the Conservatives are returned they will make a substantial increase in the petrol ration ".

The *Daily Graphic* was more exact, displaying a headline de-claring " Churchill Challenges Socialist on Petrol " on the first page and then beginning the story itself overleaf, with Mr. Churchill's statement, followed by Mr. Lloyd's.

The *Daily Mirror* displayed the petrol-ration story moderately on page six under a small banner reading " Tories Accused : Petrol Bribe ".   Underneath this the statements by Mr. Churchill and Mr. Lloyd were displayed, followed by a reply by Mr. Bevan on which the headline was based.   The *News Chronicle* used Mr. Bevan's reply on page two, while on page one the only references to the matter were the statements of Mr. Churchill and Mr. Bevan, reduced to one paragraph each, and run together at the foot of the page under the small head " Two Voices ".

The *Daily Mail's* reaction was a headlined " Why Not More Petrol ? " followed by a sub-head " Churchill, AA, RAC, All Demand to Know ".   The story began : " Petrol rationing promises to become one of the big issues of Britain's election—as it did in Australia."   This was followed by a cautious passage giving the exact meaning of Mr. Churchill's words, and then repeating statements by Mr. Aneurin Bevan and Mr. Lloyd.

Somewhat more cautiously, the *Daily Telegraph's* headlines announced " Mr. Churchill on Petrol Hopes ", " No Pledge, But Aim to End Rationing ", " Mr. Bevan—'He Should be Ashamed ' ".   The summary immediately below these headlines was fairly evenly apportioned between Mr. Churchill and Mr. Bevan, but the report below this was dominated by the accounts of Mr. Churchill's West-Country trip in general.

The *Manchester Guardian* carried the exact words of Mr.

Churchill under the headline " Mr. Churchill's Hope for Motorists ". *The Times'* headline ran " Prime Minister's Heavy Day in Election Campaign ", and then in a sub-head clearly emphasised the status of the petrol question : " Mr. Churchill Raises Issue of Petrol Ration ". The ensuing story, in its own words and in Mr. Churchill's also, carefully defined the exact state of the controversy.

With this opening day's range of headlines it appeared that the country was in for a fine display of journalistic fireworks. The chances of this were materially heightened on the 10th, when Mr. Gaitskell, the Fuel Minister, appeared to take a different line from his Government colleagues. His statement (quoted on page 96), hinting just about as much as Mr. Churchill did originally, fitted badly, from a party propaganda point of view, with the immediate rebuttals delivered by Mr. Bevan and Mr. Attlee. This seeming conflict between the replies of the Labour Party leaders furnished the Conservative press with their second day's headlines on February 11th.

The *Daily Graphic* treated the matter as the main story of the day, with a headline " More Petrol—Now Gaitskell Drops a Hint ". The story was a skilful blending of Mr. Gaitskell's statement with a long one by Mr. Lloyd, in which he said that but for Government muddling a refinery capable of producing enough sterling oil would have been in operation.

The *Daily Mail* on Saturday carried on its front page the banner headline " This Paltry Petrol Ration—' No Excuse ' ". Underneath this a story attributed to L. D. Williams, City Editor, began as follows :

> " Mr. Geoffrey Lloyd, war-time Minister of Petroleum, told me in an interview last night that Socialist partisanship against motorists and delay in building refineries had kept petrol on the ration in this country."

This story continued to attack the refinery building programme of the Government and also their policy in hiring and building oil-carrying ships. It exceeded a column in length, continuing on a back page of the paper. In contrast, statements on the subject by Mr. Gaitskell, Mr. Bevan and Mr. Attlee were covered in three, four and two paragraphs respectively.

The *Daily Express* chose to stress the Labour leaders' contradictions in the main story of the day, under the headline " Petrol Row Blows Up ". The first paragraph read :

> " Mr. Attlee last evening dismissed Mr. Churchill's ' happy thought about petrol ' as ' window dressing '. A little later Mr. Gaitskell, Minister of Fuel, said that petrol talks are going on in Washington, and, if the dollar position improves, prospects of a bigger ration are ' not bad '."

After this Mr. Callaghan, Parliamentary Secretary to the Ministry of Transport, was quoted as saying that abolition of the ration " would throw thousands out of work ". Extended quotations from all these speakers followed, including Mr. Geoffrey Lloyd's detailed attack on the refinery building policy of the Government.

The *Daily Telegraph* also treated the petrol controversy as the main story, under the headline " Socialists Share Petrol Hopes ". The first six paragraphs were a very able summing up of the declarations of the chief figures concerned, in which the alleged conflict between Mr. Gaitskell's statement and those made by the rest of the Labour Party leaders was apparent but not emphasised. The most significant part of the *Telegraph's* report was perhaps a paragraph, vague in itself, but evidently intended to be significant to some of the newspaper's readers. This read :

> " I understand that Mr. Churchill's declaration was made because there had been pressure on the Conservatives to state their case. It appears that there is no difference of object between the parties on this issue, but it was aired on Conservative initiative."

Following this somewhat equivocal statement the " Political Correspondent " passed on to a report on Mr. R. A. Butler's views on the general campaign prospects. From this time on, it is worth noting, the journals closest to official Conservative Party sources appeared to lose interest in the petrol issue.

The Times of the same day also made the controversy its leading story, once again emphasising its electioneering aspect with the headline " Petrol Rationing as an Election Issue ". In a summary set in bold-face type the statements of Mr. Gaitskell and Mr. Attlee were summarised in two conflicting statements, one following the other. In columns below were the contentions of Mr. Gaitskell and Mr. Lloyd *in extenso*, together with an exposition of the Conservative attitude in terms almost identical with those in the *Telegraph*. *The Times* correspondent made no reference to Labour's apparent self-contradiction.

The *Guardian* issue of February 11th subordinated the story of the petrol-rationing clash, first of all to Mr. Attlee's appearance in Manchester, and secondly to Communist activities in France. The petrol story itself consisted entirely of Mr. Gaitskell's explanation made at Harrogate. In addition, Mr. Attlee's brief Manchester reference to the subject was noted in the main story. It was in this issue that the *Guardian* editorial appeared chiding Mr. Churchill for " sailing close to the wind " of political expediency in bringing up the subject of petrol.

The *News Chronicle* also tended to play down the petrol issue in comparison with other dailies. In a front-page column with a small head it carried one after another brief statements about the subject by Messrs. Attlee, Gaitskell, Douglas Jay, Callaghan, Bevan and Geoffrey Lloyd.

The *Daily Herald*, which had virtually ignored " petrol " in its previous day's issue, on February 11th launched a big counter-attack. A front-page banner proclaimed " Petrol—or Bread, Labour Answers ' Wild Winston ', Talks Going On ". The first paragraph made the standard Labour reply to Conservative newspaper claims, namely that of " stunt " or " ramp ".

The paragraph heading the main story read as follows :

> " Mr. Churchill's more-petrol Election ramp was answered by Labour Ministers last night. They put the question squarely ; do you want more petrol, or do you want to spend the dollars on food and on goods essential to full employment ? "

Following this were the statements by Messrs. Attlee, Callaghan, Gaitskell, Douglas Jay and Bevan. However, no reference appeared to Mr. Geoffrey Lloyd's detailed statement on the refinery position that the rest of the press had found so alluring. Mr. Churchill was the one target of the *Daily Herald's* counter-offensive. In addition to the main column, a front-page editorial skilfully reconciled Gaitskell's statement with the rest of the party's speakers (indeed, no reader merely of the *Herald* would have suspected any element of contradiction).   It then went on to expose Mr. Churchill's careful statement as a stock example of Tory " double-talk ", the technique of the " half promise " in examples of which the Conservative manifesto was said to abound.

The *Daily Mirror* also counter-attacked mightily, but with even less finesse than the *Herald*.   Under a front-page head of " The Truth About Petrol " a story by Harold Hutchinson began as follows :

> " The truth about petrol is very simple.   It is this : We can have MORE petrol if we are ready to have LESS food, fewer films, less tobacco, less cotton, or less machinery."

On this " austerity " note it proceeded to dismiss the matter.

TALKS WITH THE RUSSIANS

The news theme which appeared to have received the most elaborate development and calculated treatment by the press during the campaign was the suggestion of " talks at the highest level " with the Russians, introduced by Mr. Churchill during his Edinburgh speech on February 14th.   The statement by Mr. Churchill which provoked such world-wide attention is given verbatim on pp. 102–3.   Not only was it naturally the subject of immediate headline displays in British newspapers, but in the days that followed much of the press succeeded in maintaining this theme of " peace talks " in a position of prominence which reflects a conscious editorial policy.   The press battle which ranged around it provides one of the few distinctive press contributions to the 1950 campaign.

By a fortunate coincidence, the *Daily Mail* stumbled on to the " atomic theme " the day before Mr. Churchill turned his electoral spotlight on it at Edinburgh.   On Monday, February 13th, the banner headline of the *Mail* read " Einstein : This Bomb Can End the World ".   This display was based on an interview that Mr. Einstein had given to correspondents in the United States on modern day science and peace.   This must have made *Daily Mail* readers well disposed to follow the signpost of the headline two days later " Churchill Wants H-Bomb Talk With Stalin ".

The headlines of other papers on Wednesday, February 15th, —the morning after the Churchill speech—presented the news as follows:

> *The Times*: " Mr. Churchill's Call For Approach to Russia."
> *Manchester Guardian*: " Mr. Churchill Assails Foreign Policy, Thrusts at Mr. Bevin, Calls For Talks With Russia ' At the Summit '."
> *The Daily Telegraph*: " Mr. Churchill's Plea on Russia, ' Supreme Effort ' for Talk on H-Bomb."
> The *News Chronicle*: " Let's Talk to Stalin on Peace."
> The *Daily Express*: " Winston: Let Big 3 Meet, Call For New Talks With Stalin."

Neither the *Daily Mirror* nor the *Daily Herald* mentioned the Churchill speech on their front pages.

The following day, February 16th, found all national newspapers featuring the peace-talk proposals, mostly on the basis of Mr. Bevin's off-hand reference to the matter during his election broadcast. This, together with the reaction in the United States and a rejoinder on the subject by Mr. Attlee at Lincoln, furnished the stories which again took the front place in all the major newspapers. The headlines once again indicate fairly well the attitude of each national daily. They were:

> *The Times*: " Mr. Bevin's Reply to Call for Talks with Russia."
> The *Guardian*: " American Response to Mr. Churchill—Doubts in Washington."
> The *Daily Telegraph*: " Socialist Reply to Mr. Churchill, Mr. Bevin Talks of Stunt Proposals."
> The *News Chronicle*: " Bevin and Attlee Answer Churchill."
> The *Daily Express*: " Bevin Calls It a Stunt."
> The *Daily Mail*: " Churchill Has Them Thinking."
> The *Daily Graphic*: " Big Socialist Attack; ' Stunt by Churchill '."

The *Daily Mirror* once again had no front-page reference to the story. On the other hand, the *Daily Herald* had two stories headed respectively, " Attlee Wades Into Winston " and " Bevin : Don't Stunt Atom ".

On Friday, February 17th, the " atom talks " issue dropped out of the main news position in the *Manchester Guardian, The Times*, the *News Chronicle* and the *Daily Telegraph*. The *Daily Mirror's* front page was worried over the headlined question " But Do Drunken Mice See Pink Men ? " It was only on the back page that " Now Truman Rejects the Churchill ' Plan ' " was accorded the prominence of a second lead. The headlines of the remainder of the national daily press continued on the " peace-talks " theme. The *Daily Mail's* banner proclaimed " Don't Let Churchill Talk to Stalin—Says Morrison ". The *Daily Express* with a full banner declared " Atom Peace Call in U.S., Services Boss Backs Churchill ". The *Daily Herald* carried a banner rebuttal " Morrison . . . Stop This Soap-box Diplomacy ".

The banners in the *Daily Mail* and the *Daily Herald* were based on Mr. Herbert Morrison's Lewisham speech (text on pp. 104–5). It was indicative of the mounting temperature of the press campaign that these rather routine echoes of earlier Labour pronouncements should have become the leading news story of the day in two such papers.

The headlines of the *Daily Graphic* and *Daily Express* were based on dispatches from Washington, reporting that Senator Tydings had warmly endorsed Mr. Churchill's sentiments during an attack on the foreign policy of the Secretary of State, Mr. Acheson. The misleading implications of the headline titles for the Chairman of the Senate Armed Services Committee were nowhere corrected in the ensuing dispatches. No hint was given of the fact that even the most powerful of American senators has no administrative control whatsoever over any of the American armed services. Neither was it mentioned that, although Senator Tydings was a Democrat, he had been for some time a vigorous critic of the Administration's conduct of foreign policy. His endorsement was a frail peg indeed on which to hang reports on an " Atom Peace Call in U.S.".

On Friday night Mr. Churchill made an election broadcast, in which he returned to the issue he had raised at Edinburgh and also defended himself against the " stunt " charge. This naturally received prominent treatment throughout the daily press, and two papers—the *Manchester Guardian* and the *News Chronicle*—based their main headlines on his words. The *Guardian* reported " Mr. Churchill Returns to his Theme, Approach to Russia ? ' Election Stunt ' Charge Resented ". The *News Chronicle's* banner stated " Bombs : Churchill Holds to his Plan ". The *Daily Express* also retained its devotion to this general theme, but preferred again to go to the United States for its distinctive variation. This time the headline read " UNO Boss Backs Winston ". The story beneath wove together the words of Mr. Churchill and Mr. Trygve Lie. Mr. Lie had given a written answer at a press conference, in which he stated that he welcomed talks at all levels, and in or out of the United Nations, on the subject of peace. In the hands of the *Daily Express* this became an implied endorsement of Mr. Churchill's proposal. The *Daily Express* also announced that the *Sunday Express* on the next day would tell " What Stalin Thinks of Churchill " in an article by Lord Beaverbrook. The rest of the daily press chose other subjects for their main story.

The Sunday press the next day showed a remarkable diversity in news treatment. Some carried no reference to the " atom talks " in their main stories, while others detected pointers for a " Big 3 Conference " in the most surprising quarters. Among those reporting nothing on the peace story were *Reynolds' News*, the *People*, the *Sunday Dispatch*, and the *Sunday Pictorial*. Others, including the *Observer*, the *Sunday Times*, the *News of the World*, the *Sunday Empire News*, the *Sunday Chronicle* and the *Sunday Express*, treated various aspects of the peace talks as the most important story of the day. The *Observer* noted that four leaders in Britain and the U.S. had expressed varying degrees of enthusiasm for a conference on atomic weapons : Mr. Churchill and Mr. Attlee in Britain, and Senator Connally and Mr. Stassen in the United States (although Mr. Stassen had added that he did not think a meeting with Stalin would do much good *). The *Sunday Times* based its story on Mr. Churchill's words and those of Senator Connally. The *Empire News* covered both Mr. Attlee and Mr. Churchill in their main story. The *Sunday Chronicle* ran a banner head reading : " Big Three H-Bomb Talk May be Near ". This was based on a " feeling " not further specified and

* An opinion which Mr. Stassen seems later to have revised. Cf. his letter to Stalin of October 4th, 1950.

also the remarks previously cited by Messrs. Churchill, Attlee, Stassen and Connally.

But it remained for the *Sunday Express* to make the biggest display. The following diverse information was rammed into four levels of banner headlines on the front page.

Churchill's New Declaration on Russia.
WE OUGHT TO CLOSE NO DOOR
Gigantic Soviet Offensive Power: 25,000 Planes.
U.S. Forecasts a Stalin Peace Gesture.

Underneath these headlines the dispatch itself ran as follows:

> " Late last night the British United Press in a cable from Washington said:
> " High U.S. officials are said to believe that Stalin may be considering making a spectacular ' peace ' gesture. Authoritative quarters in Washington say that Moscow press reports suggest high level conferences with the U.S. on world problems, including the control of atomic weapons. And the Associated Press cabled: Mr. Dean Acheson, U.S. Secretary of State, is considering making a major speech on Russian relations within two or three weeks."

At this point the story dwelt briefly on Senator Connally's words before switching to Mr. Churchill's speech at Loughton the night before. On the editorial page was the promised special article by Lord Beaverbrook. After describing a war-time meeting of Mr. Churchill and Stalin, the article pointed the moral:

> " His (Stalin's) words and actions showed clearly that Churchill as an ally had his admiration and respect. With that background, if we can get Churchill to a discussion with Stalin at the council table, what an opportunity opens, what a prospect of a negotiation ending in peace and tranquillity."

The diversity of judgment on the issue shown by the Sunday papers was repeated on Monday by the national dailies. The *Manchester Guardian's* main story by Alistair Cooke was headed " Mr. Churchill Wins Ear of Americans ". This summarised the partisan skirmishing that the proposal had provoked in American political circles. The *Daily Telegraph* also made the reactions to Mr. Churchill its lead story, but whereas the *Guardian's* headline

was based on the party rumblings Mr. Churchill had produced in
America, the *Telegraph's* story was based on manifestations in
England, notably a sermon delivered in St. Paul's by Canon
Gibbs-Smith. Its headlines ran as follows : " H-Bomb Factor
in Election, Initiative Which May Swing Waverers, Sermon at
St. Paul's on ' Crucial Issue '. Sir S. Cripps : ' No Salvation in
Churchill-Stalin Talk '."

The *Daily Herald* also gave the main place on its front page
to this theme, reporting hopefully, if defensively " Attlee and
Cripps Nail Tory Atom Stunt ". The *News Chronicle* put it on
the front page, but only as the third most prominent news item,
under the head " H-Bomb is the Major Issue ". The pronouncements of Canon Gibbs-Smith, Mr. Attlee and Mr. Churchill, and
in America " a wave of public opinion . . . now washing around
the White House " were all cited as evidence that this was so.

The *Daily Express* dethroned the issue from its banner headlines
to make way for its penultimate public opinion poll. The atom-
bomb talks were carried in the number three position, however,
under the head of " 1-2-3-4 Attacks on Atom Plan ". This
column recorded the rejoinders of four Labour Party leaders to
Mr. Churchill's hopes, which under the care of the *Express* had
now sprouted into a " plan ". At the bottom of the column the
Express paid its respects to Canon Gibbs-Smith, giving a paragraph
from his sermon in a series of three items which also included
quotations from Drew Pearson and Lord Beaverbrook's article of
the previous day.

The *Daily Mail* front page showed signs of flagging. Instead
of the " H-Bomb " there were stories summarised by the following
three headlines : " Overtime Tax Will Stay if Labour Win ",
" Romance With Paulette ? Rubbish, says Earl ", and " Channel
Ship Twice Rams Breakwater ". Neither did *The Times* find
cause to devote a headline to the week-end's comments, although
they were mentioned in the general election story which dominated
the centre page.

On Tuesday, February 21st, the " bomb talks " were victims
of the strange diversity of headline treatment which was com-
mented on earlier. The *News Chronicle* banner reported " Lord
Samuel Says Ban Those Bombs ", while underneath it quoted :
" Mr. Churchill : My Words Have Rolled Round the World ".
The *Daily Graphic* reported simply " Churchill : The Great

o

Issues—Peace, Taxes ". The *Daily Express* carried a reference to the foreign talks in the second most prominent front-page position, lifting a sentence from Mr. Shinwell for the purpose of headlining " H-Bomb is the Vital Issue ". The *Manchester Guardian*, in its treatment of Mr. Churchill's visit to Manchester, did not stress his passage referring to this proposal, although it was mentioned in the summary at the head of the main story. The rest of the press chose other topics for their main headlines, with the exception of the *Herald*, which used a front-page editorial to ask " What's Really Behind the Atom Ramp ? "

Wednesday, February 22nd, was, journalistically speaking, the quiet day before the final atomic thunder-clap. Only the *News Chronicle* used a prominent headline to refer to the foreign issue, this one reading " U.N. Atom Control is Only Hope for Man— Noel-Baker ".

On polling day, Thursday, February 23rd, the papers interested in the deployment of the " talks " theme had their last chance, and used it. The *Daily Express* put the issue simply in a banner head with voting crosses at each end as follows : " X PEACE WITH WINSTON X ".

The *Daily Mail* proclaimed : " STALIN ANSWERS CHURCHILL ".

These were the only two national dailies to use the foreign talks as the lead stories. The other papers behaved as follows :

> *The Times :* " Nation Goes to Poll Today " as the main head with a small head reading " Forces for World Peace ".
>
> The *Daily Telegraph* : " Record Poll Likely Today ", as the main head with " Atom Control : U.S. to Make ' Every Effort ' " in the second position.
>
> The *Daily Herald* : " Think of Tomorrow, Vote Labour Today " in the main position, and " Stalin Turns Down Winston " in the second position.
>
> The *News Chronicle* : " Today's Clues to Result of Election " first, and " Truman Hints at New Start in Atom Talks " in the second position.
>
> The *Daily Mirror* : " Vote Today " in red, with a smaller head on the front page declaring " No Sham Agreements on Atomic Control for Me, says Truman."
>
> The *Daily Graphic* : " Rows Liven Eve-of-Poll Meetings "

on the front page, and on the second page " Truman Opens Way to New Atom Talk."

The *Manchester Guardian* : " Britain Votes Today ", with no major headline reference to atom talks whatsoever on the main news page.

These were the headlines. An examination of the stories run beneath them is even more illuminating.

Under the *Daily Express*'s headline " Peace with Winston " the first few paragraphs of the story read as follows :

> " President Truman in a grave statement on atomic weapons said today : ' We shall continue to examine every avenue and every possibility of reaching a real agreement for effective control '.
>
> " The President reiterated his support for the Baruch Plan, which involves international inspection, and declared : ' The stakes are too large to let us or any nation stand on pride of authorship. We ask only for a plan that provides an effective workable system . . . anything else would be a sham agreement. We believe that the United Nations is the proper forum in which to reach such an agreement.'
>
> " (Mr. Churchill has said that if elected Prime Minister at today's poll, he will attempt top-level talks with Stalin.) "

It will be seen that the banner head has less than no relation to the actual story, since President Truman's words were, if anything, in opposition to the *Express*'s version of what Mr. Churchill had said. But by featuring as a sub-head Mr. Truman's phrase " Stakes are too large to let any nation stand on pride ", the *Express* supplied, so far as was possible, the missing middle term, thus coming as near as could be to converting a dissent into an endorsement.

The *Daily Mail* chose to feature the Moscow radio talk in its main news position, with the General Election and President Truman's statement getting secondary headlines. The complete headline with secondary bank read as follows : " Stalin Answers Churchill, ' His Atom Peace Move is More than an Election Trick ' ", It was only the small type of the ensuing text that made it clear that, in Moscow's view, the " something more " was a " confession " of the bankruptcy of the " Fulton Policy " and that, so far from " Stalin " taking Mr. Churchill seriously, a Moscow commentator was using his speech as a propaganda vehicle designed to demonstrate the British people's " war weariness ". Such sub-editing was certainly a queer way of clarifying the news.

In contrast to these interpretations, *The Times* carried unobtrusively a small two-paragraph report of the Moscow radio statement and reported President Truman's speech as a mere reiteration of the policy of the Atlantic Pact, E.R.P. and Point Four. No connection whatsoever was drawn between this speech and the election.

The *Daily Herald* used the Moscow report in the second position on its front page. The Moscow radio attack on Churchill was simply presented in an eight-paragraph dispatch as a final torpedoing of a Conservative campaign stunt.

The *Daily Telegraph* presented the Truman speech as a straight comment on world affairs, and made no effort to relate it to the election, which was the main story of the day. Underneath the story on the Truman speech, the report on the Moscow radio comment was also presented without comment, although the passage castigating Mr. Churchill was not in the portion of the dispatch which appeared on the front page.

The *News Chronicle* version of the speech by President Truman, run as the second most important article of the day, was interpreted more forcefully by the newspaper's correspondent in Washington, Robert Waithman. He appeared to be alone in the opinion that the speech was " bound to be interpreted as a gesture to the Russians on the international control of atomic energy ". He also said that it meant that the U.S. was ready to go beyond the Baruch Plan. Nowhere in the story or in the sub-editing of it was any link with Mr. Churchill's proposals hinted at.

The *Daily Mirror*, in its front-page report of the President's address, emphasised a passage in which Mr. Truman eschewed " sham agreements ", thus turning the address against Mr. Churchill's contention. Underneath this dispatch a two-paragraph report of the Moscow radio report received the prominent head of " It's a Stunt, Says Moscow ".

Diametrically opposed to the *Daily Mirror's* interpretation of the Truman speech was that of its rival, the *Daily Graphic*. In its page two article on the speech, under the head " Truman Opens

Way to New Atom Talk ", the *Daily Graphic's* Washington correspondent wrote :

> " Mr. Truman yesterday invited Russia to submit a new plan for atomic control and promised that the U.S. would examine ' every avenue and every possibility of reaching real agreement '."

After this startling beginning the article went on to describe the circumstances of the President's speech, and concluded as follows :

> " Mr. Churchill's utterance is therefore thought to have prodded Mr. Truman into giving some hope that the next suitable moment would be seized to explore the possibilities of dependable accord with Russia. His clear-cut appeal for an alternative plan that can be discussed is seen as an advance on his previous attitude that it was useless to try to deal now with the Kremlin.
> " Feeling in Washington is that, thanks to Mr. Churchill, the door to negotiations with Russia is open wider."

The *Manchester Guardian* carried the Truman speech at column length on the foreign news page. The emphasis in this dispatch, attributed to the British United Press and Reuters, was on the President's declared intention of using force if necessary to resist Communism.

What stands out from this necessarily brief analysis is the relative frequency with which news about the same event was interpreted with nearly opposite meanings by different sections of the national press. Nor was there always much agreement about what constituted significant new facts in a story which, if important at all, was important to everybody. In fact, of course, at least half the national press was not interested primarily in presenting the news as it took place, but in handling it with an eye to its effect on the party of each newspaper's choice.

The Election and Export Figures

A telling commentary on the partisan state of mind with which news editors judge national news during an election campaign when it impinges on party propaganda aims is furnished by the treatment accorded to the release, on February 10th, of the national export figures for January.   The announcement that January had set a record in total sterling value of goods exported to dollar areas might seem, in view of the long-watched battle of the dollar gap, to be a piece of news that would interest a wide public, whatever political moral they drew from it.   In fact in their presentation of it most newspapers took their cue from the President of the Board of Trade; he released it from a campaigning platform, and they accepted it purely as a piece of campaign propaganda.

As might be expected, the *Daily Herald* accorded the figures the most prominence and space, making them the chief story of the day, under an exultant banner " Exports Best Ever ".   Underneath the headlines eight-column inches of type told of the country's success in selling in the dollar market.

The *Manchester Guardian* judged the figures to be worthy of prominent display, and carried the story at the very top of the main news page, under a one-column-wide head which, with the rest of the story, took up ten-column inches of space.

The Times also apparently thought the story relatively important, and allocated a total of five and a half inches, including a medium head to the story.   The story was placed in a strong position at the very top of the main news page.

The *Daily Mirror* made a considerable display of the story, especially considering the newspaper's normal judgment of news value.   A two-column-wide " box ", two and a half inches in depth (making a total of five-column inches in all) at the bottom of the front outside page, gave the essential figures.

The *News Chronicle* similarly gave five-column inches to the figures, and placed the story near the top of the front page.

The *Daily Telegraph* gave the story a total of five inches of column space about the middle of the front page.

To the *Daily Express* the figures were worth only two inches of space, including a small head, near the middle of the front page. The *Daily Mail* also gave it two inches below the middle fold.

The *Daily Graphic*, a picture paper, carried the report on page two.   The total export figures were combined, however, with an item about the 1949 figures on car exports, also a record.   Thus the headline read: " Britain is Top Car Exporter ".   Only the last sentence of the two-and-a-half-inch item related to the January export record.   The earlier part of the item told only

how the automobile industry had exceeded Government targets
for the year.

The *Daily Worker* made no mention of the figures at all.

MR. CHURCHILL *v.* THE *MANCHESTER GUARDIAN*

Few of the minor features of the election campaign were more
piquant than the series of exchanges between Mr. Churchill and
the *Manchester Guardian*. Though of no great consequence in
relation to the larger battle of which it formed a part, the duel is
of interest for the light it throws on the personalities of a great
man and a great newspaper.

On Mr. Churchill's side it was conducted almost in the manner
and with the gusto of a Victorian politician's clashes with the
highly personal newspapers of the last century.

On the *Guardian*'s side the exchange was carried on with a
respect tinged with affection and occasionally spiced with asperity.
Although unable to follow Mr. Churchill where his Conservative
footsteps led, it was transparently devoted to him as a man and a
patriot, and equally obviously fascinated by his virtuosity as a
politician. Mr. Churchill no less obviously esteemed the *Guardian*'s good opinion as a jewel not for sale in the ordinary political
market, and admired it for its independence and for the forth-
rightness of its expression. The fact that this jewel was fast in a
Liberal setting made it none the less attractive to a Conservative
leader wooing the Liberal vote and an ex-Liberal Minister who
had never wholly renounced the political attachments of his
youth. The *Guardian* no less discerned under Mr. Churchill's
faint dis-ease in his Tory Zion the image of the great national
leader that the Liberal Party so obviously needed in its struggle
for electoral survival. Each knew the other to be a foeman worthy
of its steel, and neither sought nor gave quarter.

The opening blow was delivered by the *Guardian* in an editorial
on January 30th, taking up Mr. Churchill's " Queuetopia "
adoption speech the previous Saturday night.

" Mr. Churchill is very wise—in retrospect. One does
not remember in the earlier years of the Labour Government
that he denounced it for importing food that varied the diet
of the British people—' large quantities of foods and fruits,

which, however desirable as indulgences, were not indispensable to our recovery'. Indeed he rather agreed with the Mr. Priestley of those days that our food was too dull.''

The broadside continued to rake our most famous cigar-smoker in similar terms over tobacco. It then concluded:

" This new tale of Mr. Churchill's is, of course, typical electioneering, not meant to be taken over-seriously. If Mr. Churchill were serious we should expect the Tory manifesto to have given the people fair warning that their tobacco will be cut and their food made duller. For the dollar situation is now vastly more acute than in the years on which Mr. Churchill now looks back with all the sharpened perception of hind-sight."

The reply was not long in coming. That afternoon Mr. Churchill released a statement including the whole passage to which the *Guardian* objected and pointing out that,

" So far from having been guilty of ' hindsight ' or ' typical electioneering not meant to be taken over-seriously ', I was only repeating at Woodford the actual words I used two and a half years ago. Carelessness should not lead the *Manchester Guardian* so far from fact. It might lead them to be suspected by those who do not know their high character of bias veiled by an air of lofty impartiality and detachment."

The *Guardian* printed the statement in a box on the main news page on Tuesday and replied in the following editorial:

Mr. Churchill.

" Mr. Churchill does us the honour of contesting our comment on his speech at Woodford on Saturday. We thank him for the compliment. But he is mistaken in thinking we had forgotten his Blenheim speech, although we confess to have missed the self-plagiarism—or, rather, oratorical economy—to which he draws attention. The Blenheim speech, we are afraid, was another example of how easy it is to be wise after the event. It was made on August 4th, 1947. This was more than a month after Mr. Dalton had announced the first cuts in dollar imports (including newsprint) and only a fortnight before he suspended the convertibility of the pound. Like the rest of his party, Mr. Churchill was slow to spot the rapid widening of the dollar gap which had started seven months before. Since quotation is now in vogue we may perhaps repeat our own comment on the Blenheim speech (on August 5th, 1947). We agreed with Mr. Churchill about the Government's mistakes—'It has been too slow to face the inevitable'—but we thought it unrealistic to say that the Government should have started cutting twelve months before—that is, before the gap widened and the fuel crisis set British industry back. And on the 'indulgences' we wrote :

> 'To contend that we have frittered away a large part of the loan in " indulgences " which we could well have done without—on tobacco, films, foods and fruits—is to give the Americans quite a wrong idea of what the loan has meant to us in our painful recovery. It is a pity Mr. Churchill did not choose to give figures of these " indulgences " and say outright that had he been Prime Minister he would have cut off our imports of tobacco, of films, of petrol, of foods and fruits months ago. It does not seem long since Mr. Churchill himself was reviling the Government because it did not give us enough of such " indulgences ", and it is straying away from the facts to say that we have " wasted " a large part of the loan.'

The words are still apposite."

The next day the incident was carried farther in the letter columns of the *Guardian*, in a letter from Mr. Churchill and a note from the editor as follows :

> " Sir,—In your leading article headed ' Hind-sight ' of January 30 you criticised my speech at Woodford on January 28, specifying particularly the words ' large quantities of food and fruits which, however desirable as indulgences, were not indispensable to recovery.'
> " You complained that I had not given such a warning at an earlier period, but had reserved it for ' typical electioneering, not meant to be taken over-seriously '. I pointed out

that I was only repeating words I had used two and a half years ago. Thus you made a statement of fact which was untrue and proceeded to comment upon it with acerbity. I should have thought that you would have expressed regret for your untrue statement, which I am quite ready to believe was not intentional. I regret that you have not seen fit to do so. So much for your comments on my speech at Woodford on Saturday last.

"In your leading article of to-day you publish your comments on my speech at Blenheim two and a half years earlier. These, however interesting, have nothing to do with the point at issue between us. I am content that your readers should judge this performance on its merits.—

"Yours, etc.

"WINSTON S. CHURCHILL."

(Mr. Churchill and we seem, unfortunately, to be at cross-purposes. Since the country has been living in an atmosphere of open dollar crisis for two and a half years (since June, 1947) it would have been foolish of us to accuse him of overlooking it, as, of course, from the Blenheim speech onward, he did not. Our reference to "hind-sight" was meant to apply to the earlier period, before the convertibility crisis. That was why we recalled our comments on the Blenheim speech and our complaint that then, as now, Mr. Churchill was too vague to be helpful. If we were unclear, and Mr. Churchill gained a wrong impression, we are sorry.

(Mr. Boothby, in the letter below, also refers in the main to the summer of 1947 when the seriousness of the crisis was apparent to all—except, perhaps to Mr. Dalton and his optimistic followers. We have as little desire as Mr. Boothby to defend their short-sightedness and lack of courage.

ED. " GUARD ".)

This ended the first round of personal exchanges—a win on points, one might say, for Mr. Churchill. However, for all the admiration which the *Guardian* continued to display for Mr. Churchill's electioneering, it exercised to the full its right to scrutinise and reject his policies, and in particular devoted a

great deal of its constructive energies to stiffening the Liberal will
to resist all the blandishments of Conservative politicians trying
to seduce the Third Party vote. Out of this developed the second
clash between them. In Manchester on February 20th Mr.
Churchill went to the unusual lengths of referring directly,
though not by name, to the editor of the *Manchester Guardian*.
Towards the end of a long speech he said:

> "I will now say a word about the *Manchester Guardian*.
> It is a newspaper which in my opinion ranks with the *Christian
> Science Monitor* in Boston. During this election its reports
> of speeches have been the best. Nevertheless, I will venture
> upon a comment. What a remarkable position of superiority
> is that occupied by the editor of the *Manchester Guardian*.
> On the one hand are ten or twelve million or more of reac-
> tionary Tories. We shall know the true numbers by the end
> of the week. On the other are ten or twelve million of
> ignorant Socialists. As he sits on his editorial chair, almost
> throne, he metes out the justice of the high, the middle, and
> the low, to both these sections of his misguided fellow-
> countrymen. Meanwhile around his knees plays the little
> Liberal spaniel, to whom he gives an affectionate pat, or from
> time to time a cuff for some unfortunate indiscretion. It
> must be a wonderful position for a man to occupy, especially
> when he has no accountable responsibility for what may
> happen to our harassed native land. So long as an unending
> flow of brilliant articles are produced putting everyone in
> their place and often stating all the arguments on both sides
> of every question, his duty in the world is done. But I
> think this is a time when all true Englishmen must choose
> their side, for, believe me, the very life of the nation as a great
> Power in the world has quite needlessly been brought into
> jeopardy. Ponder, please, Mr. *Manchester Guardian*, on
> these words of a fifty years' reader, and do not forget them as
> you sometimes do after a few years have passed."

The *Guardian* published this as part of the full text of the
speech, without any headline reference or any other pointer save
a cross-head, " The ' Manchester Guardian ' ", at the appropriate
point on page eight. Its first leader, entitled " Mr. Churchill ",
contained the paper's only comment and reply. It opened with

a number of references to Mr. Churchill no less elegant than his initial compliments to them. His speech " was one of his best of his campaign ". " He closed his tour in fine form." " There were plenty of shrewd and telling hits." " The only big hall Manchester can now offer him is too small to do him justice." " No front-rank speaker in the election could have referred so affectionately to the ' Palatinate ', and few of his hearers could have forgotten that its political fortunes and his have been closely linked for just over half a century." Then followed a passage of political argument, taking issue with Mr. Churchill and the Conservatives on some features of their policy. And finally :

> " Towards the end of his speech Mr. Churchill reproved us, in that friendly spirit he always shows, for not choosing a side. He does not think much of the Liberals, so he would have us give what poor help we can to one of the others. We admit the impeachment. This election has, however, been curiously unlike most others in the recent past. It is being fought under the shadow of a grave economic crisis which, unlike past crises, threatens to depress our standards irrevocably. Yet neither of the two great parties seems to us, and to many others who are thinking on the same lines, to be facing the crisis seriously. The party remedies are inadequate. But if we grant that the Conservatives (and still more the Liberals) have a better grasp of the issues on paper, while the Labour people are wallowing too much in sheer sentiment and distorted history, there remains the question of what party would make the best crisis Government. It is hard to be convinced that the Conservatives (even led by Mr. Churchill with all his virtues) or Labour (with such an encumbrance as Mr. Aneurin Bevan) can be whole-heartedly supported. All common political instinct demands that one choose a side—it makes things wonderfully easy—but sometimes, perhaps, the wisest course is to try to tell all sides their faults—and suffer the brickbats that always afflict the candid friend."

CHAPTER VIII

THE ELECTION ADDRESSES

THE election address is one of the few literary art forms which has been thrown up by British politics. The limitations imposed on its size by the free postal facilities (which restrict the weight to 2 oz.) mean that it can seldom exceed 2,000 words.* Into this must be put a statement of the candidate's policy, as well as anything else which he thinks it essential for his constituents to know. True, free postage is not always used for election addresses. A candidate may prefer to deliver them by hand, and reserve the mails for his " last word ". But the form is little affected by this, and nine times out of ten it still remains that of a folded sheet, bearing on the outside the candidate's picture, inside the candidate's message, and on the back page any other points he wishes to drive home. There are passionately controversial schools of thought as to the timing of these missives, whether they should go out early in the campaign or be reserved for a last-minute punch, but all parties and all candidates agree that they are an essential part of a campaign.

It is, of course, important not to exaggerate the significance of the election address. It is only one part of the whole armament of propaganda. But to the student of an election it has a distinctive value. It is pervasive in that, more nearly than any other device, it reaches every voter; at the same time it is a product of the constituency organisation, and as such is one of the few reliable indices as to what is distinctive about the local campaigns. It is true that the Central Office frequently takes a hand in these productions. The Labour Party employed a certain standard model, which they recommended for use to constituencies which needed assistance. The Liberals had a centrally produced leaflet, on the front page of which the picture and name of the candidate could be " fudged "—a useful device in constituencies where there was a last-minute adoption and no strong Liberal organisation. The Conservatives do not appear

* Though a candidate at the Hartlepools brought out a twelve-page illustrated booklet, and Mr. Willey of Cleveland contented himself with 416 words.

to have issued much in the way of a common text, though they did make available recommended lay-outs. Of course, members of all parties drew heavily on the language and themes of their parties' manifestoes in preparing their statements of policy. Nevertheless, when every allowance is made for these standardising influences, there remains a substantial residue of local expression which provides the most convenient clue to the nature of constituency appeals. A good election address represents the form in which a national policy emerges when filtered through the personality of a candidate. And even a bad one tells one something about the character of a local campaign.

> " The old-fashioned sort of Election Address bores people stiff. They don't need to read it (and they DON'T read it), *they know what's in it BEFORE they open it !* The hoary patter—aren't we tired of it ! ' If elected I shall,' ' I pledge myself to,' ' If you honour me with your support at the Poll, I shall . . .' It's got a beard on it. I (W. Weir Gilmour) have tried to turn out a DIFFERENT SORT OF ELECTION MESSAGE. Something bright, readable and fully informative."

The Liberal candidate who gave voice to this frank opinion substituted for the format he despised an eight-page document in lay-out and style resembling a tabloid newspaper—with headlines, " boxes ", a cartoon and reprints of articles from other sources. However, there were very few candidates who went to such lengths of unorthodoxy. The enormous majority of the addresses were cast in the conventional letter form, " Dear Sir or Madam ", " To the Electors of Blankshire ", " Dear Friends ", and ending " Yours sincerely " or " Yours faithfully ". Sometimes the cover would be emblazoned with the invitation " Let's Talk It Over—Like Sensible People " (a favourite Labour form), or " I hope to meet you personally—meanwhile here is my policy " (often employed by Conservatives). It was very rare to find an address which did not contain a straightforward portrait of the candidate on the cover. Occasionally, however, a family appeal was stressed ; there was one Conservative address based upon the illustrated cover of the manifesto, *The Right Road for Britain*, which showed the candidate, his wife and two children striding towards his constituents. There was, indeed, a

Fox Photos, Ltd.

JARROW   MARCHERS

[To face p. 213.

good deal of family appeal.   One Labour candidate enclosed a special folder, *From Family to Family*, containing messages (and photographs) from his wife, his 16-year-old son, his 14-year-old daughter and his 81-year-old mother.   Another candidate, writing some few hours after his wife had made him " a general election gift . . . of a daughter ", went on to envisage the future into which young Jane would grow up.   Another candidate enlivened his address with a portrait of himself and his wife on their wedding day, while " A Message from the Candidate's Fiancée " helped to bolster the appeal of a Labour bachelor.   A rather different type of appeal was made by a candidate in a Norfolk division, who printed a group of photographs of himself going the rounds in his constituency, including one taken " with his favourite sow, Sue ".   It was, of course, standard practice for married candidates to append messages from their wives, appealing for the women's vote, generally in the form of " I am no politician, but . . .", but I encountered only one instance of a woman candidate including a portrait and endorsement from her husband.

A good many addresses were enlivened with pictorial material, often of a rather surprising kind, like that of the Liberal candidate in the Midlands who featured a picture of the local football team scoring one of its goals in the Third Division.   Labour made particular use of photographs of " The Bad Old Days ", to drive home the moral that a vote for the Tories would mean a return to All That.   The Jarrow marchers must have tramped through several hundred thousand copies of Labour addresses.   An equivalent number of bonny babies and smiling children bore similar testimony to the merits of five years of Labour Government.   Whether because their appeal was more restrained or because it is more difficult to photograph the future than the past, Conservatives made markedly less use of pictorial devices.   An occasional line-cut of " Homes for All " or " Children's Allowances " had to serve as a substitute.   Sometimes, however, in rebuttal of Labour's " unemployment " allegations, Conservative candidates incorporated the Central Office's unemployment graph —or else inserted it as a supplementary leaflet.

Some other novelties of presentation were noticeable.   A few candidates for rural areas printed maps of their constituencies, sometimes designed, like Mr. Dye's in Norfolk, to show how close to the heart of his constituency the candidate resided. Sometimes the arguments for and against were summarised through the medium of a parody of the B.B.C.'s popular " Twenty Questions "—almost always leading questions designed not to embarrass the most simple-minded constituent. There was one candidate who, exemplifying the schoolmaster element in his party, printed an " End-of-Term Report " on the Government's years in office. There were one or two regrettable lapses into verse.

As might be expected, a great many candidates, particularly sitting members, incorporated evidence of the labours they had undertaken for their constituents, and frequently quoted testimonials from grateful citizens and admiring colleagues, or from the local or national press. Where competition was so keen, especially amongst Labour members, it was often hard for an observer to decide which candidate could lay claim to a record performance on behalf of his constituents. Should Mr. Freeman, who had " received and answered over 40,000 letters ", claim priority over Mr. Bing, who had " written over 24,000 letters " ? It was not always easy to establish a common basis of measurement. In the matter of interviews to constituents, Mr. Rogers of North Kensington appeared to be in the lead, with 9,000. Labour candidates often quoted testimonials of a more general character endorsing the record of the party and the Government, particularly where independent foreign witnesses were available. The testimonies of Mr. Hoffman, E.C.A. Administrator, the French Professor Bonnet, who had given high praise to the health of the nation's children, and a deputation of American farmers who had admired British agriculture, were the most frequently quoted of these. Liberals often quoted American personalities, living or dead, particularly of the New Deal period, in support of Liberal arguments, and one candidate, after ascribing a large measure of British recovery to American aid, reminded his constituents that " President Truman is a Liberal ".

It was interesting to compare, whenever available, election addresses of identical candidates in similar constituencies in 1945 and 1950. As might be expected after five years of " recovery ", the paper, lay-out and printing of the 1950 addresses marked a considerable advance on 1945 for every party (though in one or two of the more remote parts of the country Gladstonian type-

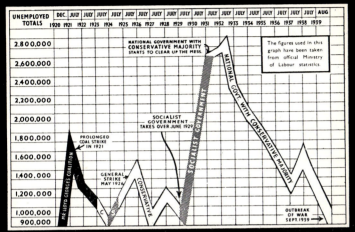

[To face p. 214.

faces appeared to be still in use). Most candidates' photographs revealed something of the ravages of the years, though there were one or two faces which were identical with those that had smiled from the same block in 1945. The service men who had been so frequent in 1945 had nearly all shed their uniforms, even dropping their military titles, save in a very few cases. The slogans had been similarly brought up to date, but there were one or two amusing instances of adaptation. Mrs. Braddock, who in 1945 presented herself as " A Woman for Westminster ", now, as the sitting member, changed into the definite article, " The Woman for Westminster ". However, her masthead, " Security and Peace ", remained unchanged. It was interesting too to notice how quickly time had passed for the candidate in a London dormitory constituency who in 1945 had described himself as " over thirty years " a resident there, and now increased the total to " over forty ".

The most distinctive difference in Conservative addresses was the reduced prominence of Mr. Churchill. In 1945 endorsements from him had been almost universal, either in the form of a letter, or a picture, or of a reference to his role as national leader. This time fully half the addresses contained no reference to him at all, only one-eighth quoted a letter of endorsement, and the references to his record which appeared in about one-third of the addresses were markedly less prominent. Of course five years had also brought a change in the content of the addresses of all parties. Readers who wish to institute a detailed comparison of these are referred to *McCallum and Readman*, Chapter V.

For the purpose of analysing the main themes of the 1950 addresses, a random sample was made of each party's productions, designed to cover, in roughly proportionate strength, each area of the country. The size of the sample was 148 Labour, 130 Conservative and 79 Liberal. In what follows I have generally expressed the figures as percentages of the whole, since that makes for ease of comparison between the different parties. It will, however, be obvious, both from the size of the sample and from the subject-matter of such an analysis, that no extravagant reliance should be placed on the precise figures or percentages. They serve only as rough indications of the frequency with which certain characteristics or appeals manifest themselves. In making the analyses a distinction was drawn between casual mention of a

P

topic and emphatic treatment of it. Where this has seemed significant I have indicated the instances of emphasis by figures enclosed in brackets.

Though there was a good deal of variety in the printing colours employed, the parties had certain marked preferences. Labour inclined to red or black, and with these achieved some effective pieces of two-colour printing. The Conservatives, whose lay-out was more uniform than that of Labour, favoured blue or black, though there were one or two instances of lively reds. The Liberals, whose addresses were in the main more inexpensively produced than their rivals', made rather less use of colour, but, where they did employ it, used buff or red or green, according in the main as the party's colours in a constituency dictated. As far as lay-out was concerned, Labour were generally liveliest, Conservatives were decorous but effective, and the Liberals, as so often, covered a very wide range of quality, from the colourful and the eye-catching to the drab and the hard to read. It was perhaps a price the Liberals paid for their elaborately reasoned appeal that the texts were sometimes too close-packed for comfort. All parties in varying degrees used their addresses for listing their meetings, as window-cards (by turning the address inside out and displaying the candidate's name and picture on one side) and also for providing advice and information about polling day. There was rather less of this last than on previous occasions because of the issuance of an official poll card. On the other hand, candidates often felt it necessary to draw attention to the changes in the law, particularly in the use of motor-cars, and to appeal to their constituents not to be deterred from voting.

The Labour addresses incorporated (as from a common model) many more standardised slogans, such as " Drive and Public Spirit ", or " Make Finance the Servant and Not the Master of Policy ", than did their opponents'. At the same time the contents and wording of individual Labour addresses showed wider variations than did those of the Conservatives. There was little evidence in Conservative posters of reliance upon a common stock of slogans, but the candidates' own expositions had about them a closer similarity. The Liberals, as might be expected, showed the widest range and the least indebtedness to a common source ; they ranged from rather jejune vote-catching appeals to very frank expositions of the country's economic crisis.

There was not much to choose between the parties in the emphasis, or absence of emphasis, that was laid upon the personal appeal of the candidate himself. Though the photograph was almost universal, biographical details were not much in evidence in more than about 50% of the addresses. A Labour candidate in East Anglia asked the constituents, " Do you vote for the candidate or the party ? " and apparently in the conviction that many of them would choose the first alternative, went on to list his record of service to the constituency, with photographs and details. There were other notable instances of what might be called the parish-pump appeal. One candidate, after listing an intensive but undistinguished record in North-Country local government, attributed to his supporters the belief that " a good Parliamentarian is made from the person who has travelled through the various forms of local government ", but this sentiment did not apparently command widespread support in other constituencies. Only 21% of Conservatives mentioned their local government record, and only 18% of Labour and 11% of Liberals. Quite a number of candidates with local government records let the matter go unmentioned in their addresses. The emphasis on " personal service " was heaviest in the Labour Party, as might be expected from a party with the highest number of sitting members. Even so, it was not remarkable. 35% (15%) of Labour addresses alluded to it, though the percentage rose to nearly 50% in Scotland, and it was also high in rural areas. Amongst Conservatives the figure was 18%, and for Liberals, who of course had few sitting members, it was only 9%. On the other hand, it was the Conservatives who laid most emphasis on their candidates' local background : 41% of their addresses made references to this, particularly in areas where they were fighting against heavy odds. " A Blankshire Man for Blankshire " was a not uncommon recommendation. And sometimes a candidate would demonstrate his local patriotism by referring to his prominence in local sports : thus Mr. Pitman's wife said that almost her first recollection of her husband was " watching him playing football for Bath when he was Captain of Bath Football Club, and I knew then his devotion for his native city ". Labour showed only 20% emphasising their local background. Liberals came highest, with nearly 50%. Labour might have been expected to lay more emphasis on candidates' trade union connections, but in fact only 20% of them did so (there may often have been instances in which this was covered by a supplementary pamphlet addressed to trade unionists). Conservatives took such opportunities of stressing this as offered themselves, though the total figure of 4 in 130 addresses is not very impressive. It is not very different from the figure of 5 out of 79 Liberals. War service, as might be expected, was a good deal less prominent than in 1945. Allusions to it occurred most frequently amongst Conservatives, of whom 37% listed it *a propos* of their biographical particulars, though in no instance was it particularly prominent. The comparable figures for Liberals and Labour were 29% and 14%.

Several candidates thought it desirable to refer to their wide experience in other fields, and sometimes to refer to their extensive travels. One or two Conservatives used this to point the contrast between Continental well-being and British austerity. Labour drew a different moral. The main result of Mr. Skeffington-Lodge's " wide travels abroad " was to enable him " to see things in proper perspective. . . . After every trip I thankfully returned to the atmosphere of fairness, decency and useful work that we have in Britain." Mrs. Xenia Field similarly always returned " satisfied that our way is the right and just way ". The addresses differed markedly in the stress they laid upon the candidate's humble or distinguished upbringing. The great majority were unselfconscious about this, but there were exceptions. Labour and Liberal candidates showed a frequent disposition to catalogue their academic distinctions. One candidate appeared to regard it as a recommendation to his constituents that he had " obtained three distinctions in Matriculation, yet was unable to afford to go to a University ". Many Labour candidates stressed their working-class background. Several Conservatives, too, generally those fighting strong Labour seats, made references to this. A Samuel Smiles note was frequently discernible in Conservative addresses. The candidate for Sevenoaks was reared in the " hard and wise Yorkshire manner ", and the candidate for Peterborough owed " nothing to influence or social background ". He was " a man of the people in the truest sense of the term ". A Liberal candidate from Eton and Oxford made mention of the fact that he was " born and brought up in a distressed area in South Wales ".

The dominant theme in Labour addresses was employment. Either in the positive form of full employment or in the negative form of the avoidance of unemployment, this was featured in virtually every Labour address—143 out of 148, with 89 which gave it special prominence. Only the social services, described as an achievement of a Labour Government, came close to this— 96% (56%). This represented the spearhead of the Labour attack, and it was driven home in a variety of ways. There were the pictorial devices already mentioned, and there were often personal reminiscences or personal pledges, like that of the candidate who stated underneath his photograph, " If you were on the dole I should not be able to look you in the face ". Much use was made of quotations from Conservative " apologists " for unemployment, in particular Mr. Higgs and Lord Balfour (quoted on Sir Stafford Cripps' address). Conservatives met this in two ways. 80% of their addresses referred to their pledge to guarantee full employment, and approximately three-quarters of these laid considerable stress on this theme. But they also, 52% of them, related the present high level of employment to the cushioning effect of Marshall Aid. Liberals made a good deal less of this. 51% promised full employment, but only a handful used Marshall Aid as a pin with which to prick the bubble of Labour claims. Social services enjoyed almost exactly the same prominence in Conservative addresses as employment, 81% (60%), generally in terms of what Conservatives had already done and what, if returned, they would do again. Liberals put social services almost as high—72% (about 50%).

The dominant Conservative interest, however, was Housing. This was featured in 93% of the sample, and was prominent in over three-quarters of these. Labour housing failures were attacked and Conservative pledges were reiterated. Labour, on the defensive here, gave the topic high prominence, mentioning it in 85% of the addresses and stressing it in slightly less than a half. The Liberal treatment was almost identical—82%.

These constituted the dominant themes common to all parties, but there was one topic which in Conservative addresses assumed comparable importance. That was the general theme of Government expenditure and the need for reducing it, which cropped up in 81% of the addresses and was prominent in two-thirds of them. Naturally there was no Labour counterpart to this, and the

Liberals mentioned it in only 39% of cases. The Liberals had four themes of almost comparable importance—namely, peace and the United Nations 77%, co-partnership and co-ownership 77%, the abolition of conscription 76% and tax reforms 75%. However, none of these is unduly prominent in the majority of addresses, and co-partnership, one of the most vaunted Liberal policies, is stressed in less than one-third of the sample.

In Labour's presentation of its case the next level of prominence is occupied, about evenly, by "Fair Shares for All" and the virtues of Labour's food policy, notably subsidies. These occur in 64% and 65% of the addresses respectively, and are stressed in about half of them. To Conservatives the debating counterpart of "fair shares" is the high cost of living, and this occurs with comparable frequency—68%. Food, in terms of Labour's promises of betterment, is mentioned in 61% of cases, and subsidies in about one-fifth of these. The Liberals feel much less strongly about food; rather less than a quarter of the addresses mention it, though they are more outspoken on the matter of subsidies, to the extent of 34%. 30% of them expatiate on the cost of living and high prices. Other Conservative themes which came within this range of frequency are the Empire, 64%; Marshall Aid (either in terms of its usefulness or the problems presented by its termination), 68%, and their aversion to nationalisation, 67%. It might have been expected that Labour would dilate with at least comparable vigour on the nationalisation theme, but in fact it is mentioned in only 56% of the addresses, and is often cloaked in the relatively unevocative phrase "Public Ownership". Liberals run Conservatives close on nationalisation, mentioning it in 62% of cases. Labour has markedly less to say about the Empire, 39%, and is relatively reticent on Marshall Aid, only 19% of candidates alluding to it (most of these election addresses were written before Labour felt the need to launch a full-scale rebuttal of the charge that Marshall Aid masked unemployment). Foreign affairs and the United Nations occupy less space in Labour and Conservative addresses than they do in Liberal; the figures for Labour are 47% and for Conservatives 32%. There are, of course, certain Labour candidates to whom they are the dominant themes, such as Mr. Mackay and Mr. Hardman, but in the main they receive only incidental mention. The same applies to the Conservatives. There is notably little said about the atom bomb. I encountered one mention of it in the Conservative sample, one mention in the Labour and seven in the Liberal. Defence is also unobtrusive. Conservatives mention it most, 28%, Liberals next, 10%, and Labour in only two addresses out of the whole.

The economic problems of the country were not tackled as directly as might have seemed desirable. 23% of Conservatives emphasised the need for greater production, 36% of Labour dwelt on the production theme, but mainly in terms of what had been accomplished.* It was Liberals who spoke most of future needs, in 43% of their addresses. The export drive as such was featured seldom—17% Conservatives, 8% Liberals. The dollar gap as such was similarly unprominent (15% Conservative, 10% Liberals), though it was often mentioned in connection with Marshall Aid. The only party to say much about monopoly were the Liberals, who singled it out for attack in 57% of their addresses. Conservatives were concerned about removing controls and releasing free enterprise, 36% making mention of this. The new note in the Labour manifesto about stimulating enterprise was seldom echoed in their addresses, and monopoly was attacked in only 9% of them.

Education was mentioned in almost half the Labour addresses, 49%, in a quarter of the Conservatives and in 39% of the Liberal. Mention of agriculture was notably dependent upon the type of constituency. Labour and Conservatives said little about it when fighting urban seats. In all, only 33% of the Conservative addresses mentioned it, to 40% of Labour and 67% of Liberals.

These constituted the main themes of policy. It was notable how few Labour members deviated from the party line. The most conspicuous of these was probably Mr. Emrys Hughes, who devoted half his address to quotations from his speeches in the House criticising the Government. Mr. R. R. Stokes also revealed himself as a sturdy individualist on such matters as the education settlement, the harsh burden of taxation on the middle classes and the objections to conscription. Conservatives, perhaps because they were more concerned with criticism, seemed to have fewer differences among themselves. At the same time it is interesting to notice that some of the principal points of

---

* There was some dispute about the extent of this, estimates ranging from " 30% increase since 1938 " to " over 50% ".

This Is The Road failed to find mention in more than a handful of Conservative addresses. Such examples are the co-ownership, equal pay, trade unions and anti-monopoly proposals. Liberals, as might be expected, are notably diverse, and in fact many of the addresses suffered from an effort to include too much detail.

There were notably few regional deviations in policy. The Conservatives gave perhaps the most conspicuous example, in reserving their proposals for Scottish devolution almost entirely to their Scottish addresses (24 out of 28). Labour, who comtemplated no concessions to the Scottish or Welsh Home Rule movements, were silent on this. The Liberals, who had made the most outright pledges on Home Rule, mentioned it throughout, in addresses in both England, Scotland and Wales, 53% in all.

Apart from positive policy themes, there are what might be termed the tactics of approach. The Conservatives lay stress on their claim to represent all classes and to embody the spirit of national unity (mentioned in 31% of the addresses). Liberals make this a dominant theme, claiming to be the only properly classless party (70% of addresses). Labour mention it relatively seldom (11%), and indeed it is interesting to notice the divergence between those Labour addresses which stress the country-before-party theme (" putting first the interests of the nation as a whole not of any section ") and those which retain the old element of appeal to class loyalty (" Vote For Your Own. Vote Labour."). Positively Marxist language is utterly at a discount. I met only one instance of it, by a candidate fighting a hopeless rural seat. The Conservatives are restrained in their counter-attacks on this theme; only 12% of their addresses make any allusion to such favourite quotations as Mr. Bevan's " vermin " and Mr. Shinwell's " two hoots ". They make more mention, however, of the argument that Socialism is a stepping-stone to something worse. 32% touched this " Beware of Communism " note; 6% of Labour replied by saying that Socialism is the best bulwark against Red Tyranny. Both Labour and Conservatives naturally woo the Liberal vote, but Conservatives predominate in the proportion of 3 : 1 (Conservatives 15%, Labour 5%). Only one Conservative candidate had the temerity to evoke Mr. Gladstone (and he was campaigning in Midlothian), but Labour often claimed to be the inheritors of the " great Liberal governments " of 1906 and 1910. Otherwise Conservatives stressed the common front against Socialism and Labour, insisting that there is "no middle way". It was, however, interesting to notice how often, even when fighting Liberal strongholds in Wales, Labour decided that silence was the best weapon. Conservatives obviously believed the reverse, and to their 15% mention in addresses there should undoubtedly be added a very much higher figure for leaflets specially addressed to Liberals which were either inserted with the addresses or sent as a "last message". The Liberal reply to this took the form of "The Liberals Can Win" or "At Last You Can Have A Liberal Government". This note was struck in 51% of their addresses, and in 28% of them they directed themselves to refute the argument that they were splitting the vote.

Was the vote secret? It was surprising how often mention was made of this theme, considering the limited space available and the publicity given to it elsewhere. Conservatives mentioned it in 18% of cases, Labour in 12% and Liberals in 8%. One candidate even went so far with his assurances as to inform his constituents that "No one may put your number on a ballot paper". He did not add that it could nevertheless be identified through the numbered counterfoil.

It was interesting to note one or two features of the election addresses of the party leaders. Mr. Attlee's closely printed, dun-coloured exposition of Labour's policy was conspicuous for its extreme personal modesty and its avoidance of any allusion to the author's own achievements. Mr. Morrison's bright and lively letter to the electors of South Lewisham was no less characteristic. The cover was dominated by a photograph of the Lord President of the Council with tousled hair, surrounded by a children's percussion band and telling them, "See who can make the most noise". A précis of Labour's programme was accompanied by a typical Morrisonian appeal to "the middle class no less than the working class", and winding up, "Herbert Morrison asks his supporters to give all his opponents a fair hearing". Mr. Churchill's address was distinguished by the emphasis laid upon the appeal to Liberals, the invocation of "men like Morley, Grey and Asquith, whom I knew so well in my youth", and the contrast presented between "individual liberty and State domination".

The Communist Party's addresses had a distinctive interest of their own. There was little in them of the professional jargon of Marxism.   The prophet was mentioned in only two, once at Totnes, where *The Communist Manifesto* was quoted as the authority for the statement " the Communists have no interests separate from those of the working class as a whole ", and once at Shipley, where the essentially British nature of Communism was expounded as follows : " The vision of men like Owen, clarified by Marx and Engels, and immortalised by the great poet William Morris, is the birthright of the British people ".   For the rest, the appeal was ably couched in exclusively non-theological terms. Even the note of " comradeship " was not stressed.   Although almost all the addresses struck a " matey " note by identifying candidates by the briefest of first names, they almost all began with a fairly orthodox style of address, such as " Dear Friend ", and usually ended " Yours sincerely ".   The candidates did, however, wherever possible, stress their working-class background and, where not possible, sought the next best : " I come of working-class parentage though a schoolmaster " (Manchester, Blackley).   There was also much emphasis on candidates' activities in Communist working-class operations, such as the squatters' movement.

Great pains were taken to employ the local appeal wherever possible : " We certainly shan't forget the rocket that fell on the ' Virginia plant ' ", or " The first signs of the slump are shown with over three thousand signing on at the Marylebone Labour Exchange ", or again, this time in the London and Westminster division, " A Yankee military H.Q. has been set up in Grosvenor Square ".   Similarly, no localised ailments of the body politic went neglected ; wherever there was a dissident or depressed group, the address appealed to it.   The candidate for North-East Leeds found space for special appeals to Jews, Catholics and Irish.   The candidate for Warrington addressed himself to the " six hundred men threatened with the sack or a 25-mile-trip to work " because of the American base at Burtonwood.   In dockyard towns they dwelt on the theme of dockside unemployment, in Scottish constituencies on home rule,* amongst Irish constituents they became anti-partitionist, and in Wales they supported a Welsh parliament.

* Except at Motherwell, where, opposing a member of the Scottish National Party, they denounced him as offering " a peculiar brand of Scottish Toryism ".

This did not mean that there were no policy themes common to these addresses. Almost every one of them contained an attack on the United States, and " Yankee financiers " or the invasion of Britain by " swaggering, arrogant Yanks " was a dominant topic. We are " selling our independence for a handful of American dollars " (West Lothian). " Even our screw threads must be changed at the American demand " (East Fulham). Mr. Clarence Cannon was especially singled out for criticism for his remark about " sending the soldiers of other nations into the holocaust ". He was variously described as " a Senator ", " a leading American official ", " one of the leading American statesmen ", and the " Chairman of the House of Representatives' Appropriation Committee ". Next to American imperialism the addresses dwelt on the benefits of peace and trade with the U.S.S.R., sometimes coupled with the new People's Republic of China. This would open up a prospect of peace instead of the certainty of war.

Domestically, the wage freeze and the increase in the cost of living were the subjects of continual attack. Much emphasis was laid on the Labour Government's indulgence of profiteers, and one of the regular features of the addresses was the inclusion of the profit figures of firms established in the constituency. Much was made of the prospects of unemployment and the continued housing shortage.

The contrast with 1945 Communist addresses was remarkable. Then they had made much of the common front between the three Great Powers, Britain, U.S.S.R. and the U.S.A., and at home they had emphasised their loyalty to the Labour movement. A constituent of Mr. Carritt's in 1945 was made to say, " There doesn't seem to be a great deal of difference between what Labour and Communists are fighting for ". But now, just as the U.S.A. is denounced as a war-monger, so Labour is attacked as having broken the pledges and disappointed the hopes of 1945. It is now " the Tory Fifth Column " which dominates the Labour leadership, and it is the " so-called Labour leaders ", " following in the footsteps of MacDonald and Thomas ", who are the principal targets of the party's wrath. Often an address would feature a row of items dominated by the heading " They Both Agree ", listing points of Labour and Conservative programmes.

Thus whereas in 1945 Communist candidates opposing Labour

had taken a defensive tone, justifying themselves on the grounds that they were first in the field or that only Labour obstinacy had prevented the formation of a United Front, now they wasted little time in justifying their intervention.   Labour had betrayed the workers, consequently the workers' interests would be safe only if they voted for a Communist candidate.   The Communist policy was the only alternative policy to the evil alliance of Toryism and Labour, consequently the more prominent the Labour leader the more important to vote Communist.

Here and there, generally amongst weaker Communist candidates, there was a recognition of the need to rebut the argument about splitting the vote.   Usually the addresses were content with a purely debating reply: " It is said that I will split the vote. That is untrue.   Those who split the working class are those who follow the same line of policy as the Tories " (Acton), or " Your vote will only be ' split ' by supporting policies against your own interests " (Coventry East).   However, occasionally the true party line was made explicit: " Unlike other parties, we do not just make promises to win your votes and tell you that all your problems can be solved by your vote at a general election. Elections are important—but the fight for a correct policy must go on all the time and you must play your part " (Portsmouth West).

CHAPTER IX

THE CAMPAIGN IN THE CONSTITUENCIES

In the constituencies Mr. Attlee's announcement of a January–February election campaign was seldom received with enthusiasm. The political objections to it came mainly from the Opposition, alleging that the Labour Government was hoping to evade the consequences of Devaluation and the Budget by getting the election out of the way first. (I even heard of one Conservative agent who, subscribing to a seasonal theory of political behaviour, believed that people tended towards Socialism in the spring.) The weaker constituency organisations, mostly the Liberals, often yielded to that most persistent of campaigners' fallacies, the illusion that if only the election had come later they would have been better prepared—overlooking the fact that this held true equally for their rivals, and that in many instances it was only the occasion which had called forth such organisation as there was. Only in one respect might this complaint have been justified. A February election meant a fight on an old register—prepared in the previous June and published in mid-October. In many areas this had become rather out-of-date, and many weaker organisations, which had put in little work on the hard grind of tracing removals and the like looked to the publication of the new register on March 15th to set them right. Indeed, although the stock criticism of the Government for " going to the country on an out-of-date register " came, as always, from the Opposition, the Conservatives probably suffered less from it than Labour, since their superior organisation had been working on the register longer.

All parties, however, were at one in disliking the purely climatic implications of a February campaign—dark nights, weather likely to range from rain to snow, fog, floods, and all the agues of winter and spring combined. Rural constituencies in particular viewed the prospect with alarm. Conservatives said that it was a blow directed especially at them, since they were *par excellence* the party of the countryside. Labour incumbents of rural seats spoke even more complainingly, though not so audibly, wondering if Mr. Attlee had forgotten how much of his 1945 majority had been won in country areas and how vital they would be to a party fighting to hold its own. Liberals, whose hard-pressed cohort of members came almost all from remote and often mountainous constituencies, with more acres than voters, thought themselves most ill-used of all. In fact, as it turned out, the weather shared in the general " demureness " of the election. The terrors of the icy spring of 1947 were not repeated. The weather was generally mild. There was some fog, a certain amount of rain, occasional but not very dramatic floods and rather less snow and ice than is normal for such a time of year. There was even a fair incidence of sunshine.

What worried experienced agents most, of course, about February weather and February nights was their possibly deterrent effect upon the voluntary worker, especially the canvasser. Here certainly Labour's feeling of inferiority had some basis in fact. Conservatives had undoubtedly put in more work on marking up their registers, often with the assistance of paid canvassers (and canvassing " tutors "), before ever the January 10th announcement was made. Moreover, they could probably draw on more voluntary canvassers, particularly women, to operate in the restricted hours of daylight than could a party predominantly composed of wage-earners. It would be dangerous, however, to try to make too much of this last point. The evenings are generally the golden hours for canvassing, when most people are at home from work, and at that time there was little to choose between the man-power—or the devotion—which each party could command. Similarly, there was a certain temptation to over-confidence inherent in the possession of a 1949-marked register. Too many light-hearted answers (particularly favourable ones) got entered up as settled votes, when quite often they were not settled at all.

Indeed, inspection of canvass returns of all parties induces a pervasive scepticism as to the reliability of most such figures and the estimates which even quite experienced organisers often based on them. The extent of the canvass is the entering-point of error. Repeatedly the claims of 90% or high 80%'s proved to have been inflated—to represent, for example, the number of houses, not the number of voters. Then, all too often the estimate of one householder as to the opinion of the rest served to mislead, even where not so intended. Finally, the canvasser's own reading of his victim's psychology was often erroneous. It is not in nature for zeal and scepticism to dwell in equal proportions in the breasts of voluntary workers. To these often-concealed sources of error one must add the admitted causes of incompleteness. The first is, of course, the disparity between the size of the task and the number and quality of the toilers. In the three or four weeks which is the maximum feasible period for an election canvass an average of about 55,000 electors should be covered by a force of volunteers which can work only within certain hours and on certain days. Even when, as in the strongest constituencies, a force of perhaps 200 is available, it is reasonably certain that such a total will include quite a large, weak "tail". Moreover, to be of much use, they must canvass in pairs. Canvassing is a wearisome, often disagreeable job—the hardest, it is generally agreed, to lure volunteers to undertake. This partly is due to the misunderstanding of its nature which still often persists amongst both party workers and the public. It is a rare canvass now which aims at winning the voter from hostility or indifference to support. Its aim is almost always to ascertain the voter's intentions: "I represent Mr. X, the such-and-such candidate. Can he count on your support?"—just that and nothing more. The object of it is the "marked register"—a complete record of the electorate, each marked according as he or she is "For", "Against" or "Doubtful". The magnitude even of this operation, if allowance is made for return visits to "Outs" (canvassers' shorthand for voters who are not at home), is sufficient of itself to explain the organisers' constant injunctions to their canvassing teams not to "waste time arguing". Invite the victim to a meeting, by all means. Promise him perhaps a visit from the candidate, if he has a question and looks like a possible convert. Offer him literature and, if friendly, a window-bill. But *Don't Argue!* Not only is time precious, but time wasted on opponents may even have the effect of arousing sleeping dogs who might otherwise lie torpid on polling day.

No doubt many canvassers fall short of this ideal of rigidly disciplined fervour. The supply of laconic evangelists is always limited. But even where volunteers are skilled and numerous it is easy for a canvass to fall behind. In February the bad weather over so much of the country during the week after Dissolution set back many a canvass, and sooner or later in the campaign there came to most honest organisers that dreadful moment when they realised that Polling Day would overtake them before they had completed their canvass returns, that here a weak ward or there an uncovered concentration of " Outs " would persist like an unmapped hinterland to mar their register at the end.

These difficulties lead the average agent to think of his canvass in terms of a " target " to be aimed at; if so many votes are needed to win, then he will aim at building up a register of " pledges " large enough to provide himself with a majority, with a wise margin to spare. This will often lead him, at any rate initially, to ignore " doubtful " or " difficult " areas in his division. He is, after all, seeking less to convert than to discover where his support lies, so that on polling day he can " get out the vote " in sufficient strength. That is not to say that there is no connection between a modern canvass and the building up of a candidate's support. There is always that essential function of " showing the flag " which enters into so much of the ritual of election campaigning—the function not indeed of arguing or persuading the voter that he ought to vote for you, but of buttering up his ego by *asking* him to vote for you. As the Labour Party's handbook on the *Conduct of Parliamentary Elections* * puts it :

> " The Election Agent must face the fact that if this calling on electors is ignored the personal touch will be lacking and the poll will not fulfill expectation. How often electors are heard to say, ' Why should I trouble ? No one has asked me for my vote ! ' The person does not mean that his vote was available for anyone who asked—he meant his vote was of value to someone—but that someone had not troubled himself about it."

No canvass, of course, can be any more reliable than the electorate wish to make it. A Labour candidate in a rural area in the West Country eventually abandoned his enterprise as worthless—so many more people were saying they were for him than obviously were. Politeness was encroaching on veracity. Elsewhere there is some evidence that timidity is the disturbing element at work. The social pressure to conform may prove irresistible. Even when generous discount has been made for

* P. 49.

the propaganda element in Labour stories about "feudal" pressure in the countryside and in Conservative stories about trade union pressure in industrial or mining districts, there remains a substratum of obvious truth.

In such a setting the canvassing system has its dangers. The voter whose sympathies diverge from the local norm may, of course, decline to answer, or take refuge in an affected uncertainty, or even—and every canvasser can quote instances of this—dissemble outright. But the first alternative constitutes in fact an admission of intention, the second and third are objectionable deceptions. It would be a doubtfully healthy development if the needs of the party organisations ever established as a kind of unwritten precept of good citizenship the obligation to co-operate in the canvass. The right to add the words " No Canvassers " to the " No Hawkers, No Circulars " injunction is the social corollary of the safeguards of the secret ballot.

Modern electioneering has developed another device potentially more objectionable than the canvass because avowedly, and not just incidentally, an instrument of mass pressure and persuasion. This is the window-card—" the most important single piece of publicity ", as a Labour organiser described it. The point of the window-card is that it constitutes an outward and visible sign of voting intention. It links the party's propaganda with concrete evidence of its success. As one circular to the party faithful put it :

> " Enclosed herewith are two window-bills which we want you to place in your windows NOT BEFORE but ON the morning of

> MONDAY, FEBRUARY 6TH.

> If you fall in with this arrangement you will be contributing to a sudden mass window display which should prove an effective encouragement to the ordinary Labour voter to follow your example, and finally produce an outstanding exhibition of first-rate publicity."

One does not need to credit partisan reports of bricks heaved through opponents' windows to realise that here is a powerful instrument not only of mass demonstration, but also of minority intimidation, especially in closely settled or socially homogeneous

Q

neighbourhoods. It was a good deal used in 1950—generally in the form of distinctive, brightly coloured, gummed cards bearing the candidate's name. It was no uncommon thing, for example in London constituencies, for a party organisation to print and distribute 20,000 of these. They were used by all parties.

Here again, however, one may notice—and perhaps derive some comfort from—the resources of ingenuity and subterfuge available to the *homo non-politicus* in his passive resistance to being organised. An experienced voluntary worker in a North London constituency wrote as follows :

> " There is without doubt considerable resistance in the early stages of the campaign on the part of the rank-and-file supporters to show window-bills. Some allow themselves to be persuaded and some are goaded into showing their colours by Opposition bills going up around them. On the other hand, there is a widespread feeling that there is something not quite ' nice ' about showing window-bills. Respectability is outraged by a double crown poster in the front parlour and posters in the bedroom are positively indecent. Strangely enough, this inhibition seemed to be more widespread amongst Labour supporters than amongst Conservatives. The latter are helped by possessing more windows and garages. Garage doors are favourite display boards ; there is something ' detached ' about them.
>
> " Right from the start of the campaign, we tried to get as many bills up as possible, believing that a good show of bills would raise morale. Objections to our efforts ranged from curt refusal (even on the part of active members) to reasoned amendments such as an offer to put up bills as soon as neighbours were to put up Tory bills ; Tory neighbours, who were in the majority, might not put up bills at all unless goaded into doing so, so on balance we would gain by members *not* putting up bills. A most disingenuous reason, which nevertheless cropped up several times, was ' All my neighbours know that I support Labour, so there is no need for me to put up window-bills '. Notwithstanding the above comments on being goaded into putting up window-bills, once there is a really good show of bills of one party, it is most difficult to get up Opposition bills. This works both

ways: in the one road in the ward which has a Labour majority, we showed 26 bills to 3 Conservatives', though the actual majority, even in this road, is nothing like it. The Liberals, being a zealous minority party, had a show of window-bills quite out of proportion to their actual voting strength."

It should be added by way of postscript to these remarks on canvassing and window-bills that, so far as could be judged, there were extremely few genuine instances of intimidation or even attempted intimidation of voters. Each side made the most of such examples as came its way—they constitute one of the few forms of election propaganda which is also news—but when the dust settled it was found that there was very little of substance behind the allegations. One of the hardest realities to disentangle from its assiduous partisan wrappings of myth was the alleged anxiety as to the secrecy of the ballot. In every election campaign there is a crop of unconvincible sceptics who regard the practice of marking the elector's number on the counterfoil, which itself bears the same serial number as the ballot-paper, as destroying the secrecy of the ballot. But in 1950 it appeared as if even more eminent barristers than usual were employed by the press to lay these fears at rest and explain the efficacy of the subsequent precautions against unauthorised disclosure. Even so, a surprising number of candidates, of every major party, thought it worthwhile devoting precious space on their election addresses to the same theme, as did Miss Horsbrugh in her election broadcast. The persistent indestructibility of scepticism was best illustrated by the examples reported from various parts of the country after the count, of ballot-papers with £1 notes wrapped in them or pinned to them—a touching evidence of the faith of honest doubt.

If the window-card achieves the maximum of display with the minimum of exposition, the election meeting, at least as usually practised, reverses the proportions. The public meeting remains, in British election practice, the most unshakeably Victorian of institutions. It still rests on the three great Victorian democratic beliefs, in the efficacy of reason, the propriety of fair play and the moral superiority of the ear over the eye. By that I do not mean that it usually affords either a feast of reason or a flow of wit, but rather that the average British election audience distrusts a speaker who addresses himself too obviously to its emotions, dislikes a chairman who won't let a heckler be heard (or hecklers who won't let a speaker be heard) and—apparently—disapproves of any attempt to relieve the drab hideousness of the ordinary public-hall by any of the arts of concealment or display. This all makes for meetings which are serious, sober, well-conducted, inquiring and rather dull—which is exactly what 90% of the election meetings were. The frequent employment, moreover, for election meeting purposes of classrooms in schools (available by law free of charge, save for a cleaner's fee) intensified still further this emphasis on the expository and the instructional. For the liveliest rallies between the hecklers and the heckled one had to go to the larger halls or the open air. But what remained absent—or one should rather say subordinate—to a degree sometimes surprising to foreign observers, was the element of the rally, the deliberate and ostentatious concentration of the converted. One meeting in every election is by common practice dedicated to this role—the adoption meeting, at which at the very outset of his campaign the candidate is formally " adopted " by his constituency association. This apart, the theory that he is on every appearance offering himself to his entire electorate and wooing all their suffrages dominates the whole of his speaking campaign.

In one particular the 1950 campaign carried this avoidance of over-demonstrativeness farther than most. There were fewer of those mass meetings addressed by great visiting national figures that the Victorians loved and that often persisted into our own time. For this there were three obvious reasons—the first the war-time destruction in so many cities of their large public-halls (cf. the *Manchester Guardian*'s regret that their city had no hall to match Mr. Churchill's powers), the second the cost of such meetings in a modest election budget, the third the substitution of the radio talk for the public appearance. Even in 1950 there were a few such great meetings—Mr. Churchill and Mr. Attlee at the Usher Hall in Edinburgh or Mr. Churchill in the open air at Ninian Park in Cardiff were examples—but the " show " meeting in the large hall remained an abnormal feature of the campaign.

The normal election meeting consisted of a couple of hundred people gathering in a schoolroom or a parish hall, assembled to hear (or question) the candidate, though they would probably have to sustain in addition some supporting speeches from prominent local politicians filling out the programme. If a candidate was fortunate in having a densely populated borough to fight he could probably cover it pretty adequately by a meeting a night—say twenty meetings to the campaign. But a rural division with scattered hamlets, every one of which expects the candidates to appear before it, imposed a much heavier speaking load. Here three or four meetings a night might be needed if the ground was to be covered, making easily a total of eighty or ninety in the campaign. This was possible only by careful planning and timing, with the candidate, like the old-style music-hall artists, moving quickly from meeting to meeting, while supporting speakers filled in the (often considerable) intervals on either side of his own thirty-minute appearance. It is this sort of campaigning that understandably makes candidates and workers prefer a summer election.

Normally a February campaign would not rely very much on open-air meetings. Their usefulness necessarily varies with the constituency, but in certain neighbourhoods they are a valuable (and inexpensive) means of advertising the candidate to a public that might never make the effort involved in attendance at a fixed place at a fixed time. Their employment in February was in fact more widespread than had been expected. The weather often proved surprisingly kind—so kind, in fact, that I know of one London constituency where the whole speaking programme was changed, cutting down indoor meetings and switching to a succession of open-air meetings adjoining a crowded shopping area. In cities the " blitzed " site was often a good location for the candidate's soap-box or else, in a Midland or North-Country town, a corner of the great market square. In Liverpool candidates posted themselves athwart the crowds debouching from the ferries, while everywhere the pitch opposite the factory gates was a strategic point for catching workers in their lunch interval or at the close of the day.

A device often employed in 1950 combined some of the advantages of the canvass, the indoor and the outdoor meeting. This was the " cottage " meeting, so called, organised by a householder with a room to spare who would invite as many of his " convertible " neighbours as possible to meet the candidate, hear his views and ask him questions. A Scottish variant (especially favoured by the Communists) was the " back-court " meeting, held in the courtyard of a tenement house whose amplifying properties would generally guarantee perfect reception by all resident within its compact limits.

It was not usual for candidates to participate in joint meetings, much less man-to-man debates. To the constituent anxious to " hear all sides " and disposed very often to view the campaign as a sporting contest, there is a great deal of attraction about such sessions. The candidates, however, and still more their organisers, view them differently. If they are in the lead they may feel that the perils outweigh the profits. " Why should I help him to get an audience ? " was a frequent rejoinder made to emissaries who came bearing " challenges " or " invitations ". Indeed, it is true to say that the dividends to be reaped from a joint meeting are seldom, if ever, evenly distributed amongst all contestants, and that consequently there may often be perfectly legitimate grounds behind an apparently churlish refusal. This, I suspect, was sometimes overlooked by well-intentioned " honest brokers " who issued invitations to " all-party meetings ". A good many of the clergy undertook this office ; a notable example was that of the Bishop of Reading, who booked the town hall at his own expense to enable all the candidates a few days before the poll to expound " the moral issue of the General Election ". Other " non-political " organisations, such as the United Nations Association, the Workers Educational Association, Rotary, the Townswomen's Guild and the like often filled a similar role. There is, indeed, in the very idea something which appeals directly to the age-old belief in trial by ordeal, and no doubt any candidate with confidence in his cause and his capacity will be prepared to subject himself to the test of debate. But the very fact that it is from the (numerically) weaker candidates—notably Liberals and Communists—that the challenges almost always come, indicates clearly who stands to gain most from such exchanges. It was a Communist fighting a rural constituency in which he polled less than 400 votes who suggested they should be made compulsory !

There was notably little attempt at any election meeting to snare the voter by the delights of the eye. The standard properties are always the chair, the table, the drinking-glass and the carafe of long-standing water. Even Mr. Churchill finds it necessary to add only the despatch box—as indispensable apparently to his oratory as the top-hat to the conjuror. If it is a Conservative meeting, it is highly probable that a Union Jack will drape the table; if a Liberal, it is less obligatory but still likely; if Labour, it will be a rare exception. In some Scottish constituencies the Liberals testified to their devotion to home rule by displaying the Scottish Lion, and in Wales sometimes similarly exhibited the Welsh Dragon. Indeed, the Liberals took more pains, as a rule, to bring colour into their meetings than did either of their major rivals. More than most they displayed portraits of their leading parliamentarians—part of a conscious campaign to present themselves as a party led by figures of national stature. At one or two Labour meetings I encountered a few rather unprominent posters of Mr. Attlee and Keir Hardie. Mr. Churchill was a conspicuous absentee from Conservative halls, where he had loomed so large in 1945 : I encountered only one English city, Nottingham, in which his portrait was consistently displayed. Apart from portraits, a hall might sometimes carry a few rosettes or window-bills or posters, while streamers advertising the *Daily Herald*, *Reynolds' News*, the *Daily Telegraph* or the *News Chronicle* might be found at meetings of the appropriate parties. Drab as this might appear, it could hardly be doubted that it expressed quite adequately the character of these public occasions. One had only to see a typical platform group set in a more theatrical décor—as on the odd occasion of a meeting held in a cinema or theatre—to realise how incongruous was the setting of even the most restrained of backdrop designers.

Such relief as was offered to the monotony of sustained oratory lay in fund-raising and in song. The Labour Party made a deliberate feature of their appeal for funds. Often there would be a special platform speaker with no other function than to loosen the audience's purse-strings. Sometimes there was the auctioneer's device of the competitive donation, more often the simple passing around of the plate. Liberals resorted to these practices almost as often. With Conservatives, I suspect, the collection is still a relatively new feature of their mass appeal; it was certainly much less regularly employed by them, and often with a certain restraint—e.g. at the exits on leaving rather than in the hall itself. In general, one sometimes got the impression that the frequency and verve of fund-raising were in inverse proportion to a party's local ascendancy. There was, for example, little of it by Labour in Durham or South Wales and little by Conservatives in the West Country.

To the average British election audience singing comes as reluctantly as the collection—if not more so. There are few musical sounds less impressive than the average meeting shuffling its feet and clearing its throat for the first bars of " God Save the King "—unless it is that same meeting simulating the revolutionary fervour of " The Red Flag ". (This seemingly unnatural conjunction did in fact occur at at least one Labour meeting in the Midlands.) Perhaps for this reason the National Anthem was not a very frequent coda to routine election meetings. Conservatives, as might be expected, employed it most; once or twice it served as device for winding up with some semblance of order a meeting virtually disrupted by opposition hecklers. " The Red Flag ", even by Communists, was not generally judged an appropriately evocative anthem for election purposes. It would be interesting to have precise figures of its employment; I suspect it would be found to be a poor second to " Jerusalem ". Occasionally, as an alternative to these efforts from the audience, the platform would itself provide some musical entertainment—the local soprano singing " The Pipes of Pan " or a loud-speaker grinding through " Land of Hope and Glory ". The tepid applause which such diversions evoked always suggested that the temperature of the meeting remained sensibly unaffected by them.

No generalisations can be entirely valid that range over so vast a field as the thousands of election meetings held all over the country during the month of February. Certainly there was much diversity in attendance; I heard Cabinet Ministers speak to half-empty halls and nondescripts with microphones hold the ear of overflow meetings. There was much diversity in the incidence of hecklers and questioners; they were seldom wholly absent, but their liveliness and pungency varied a good deal from place to place. But in general when it was a question of the behaviour of these audiences one could not but be struck by the identity of the epithets employed by observers all over the country; " serious ", " inquiring ", " thoughtful "—these terms recurred over and over again, and my own observations amply confirmed their validity. There can be no doubt that this was the massive norm against which should be set a Lord Woolton being shouted down at St. Pancras or a Miss Jennie Lee evoking passionate responses at Cannock to her reiterated question, " Do you remember the Means Test ? " Audiences might consist mainly of the converted—I suspect they mostly do—but these were the devout who wanted to be supplied with the evidences of their faith.   If they were Labour they generally wanted to hear the record of their Government, and have it set against the iniquities of the Tory 'thirties.   If they were Conservatives they wanted documented indictments of Socialist misrule and figures to refute the fables told about their own past.   If they were Liberals they would often even go to the lengths of listening to detailed schemes for income-tax reform.   Of course the appeal to emotion was never far absent from these justifications by works, but in the main it was kept to a creditable minimum.   The remarkable feature of so many audiences was their willingness to be lectured at, their apparent capacity to swallow whole slabs of unrelieved exposition.   Moreover, the subject-matter of these sermons was, nine times out of ten, economic.   Political themes, as such, seldom dominated the argument.   And here how flat-footed and jargon-loaded was the average orator—even the average Minister or his shadow Opposition counterpart.   It was impossible to listen to these outpourings of chilly, grey, economic abstractions or to watch the puzzled earnestness of so many audiences without feeling that the election oratory of 1950 was becalmed between two ages of politics.   The old fustian and rodomontade no longer go down.   The Cobden who can translate the economics of the Welfare State into comprehensible re-vitalis-ing politics has yet to appear.   Is that perhaps one reason why the electors heard so little about the true nature of Britain's economic maladies and the regimen necessary for their cure ?

Most agents are sceptical about meetings as a device for winning votes.   I suspect that, superficially at least, they are right.   Few " floaters " are landed in Town Halls.   The public meeting is indeed, in one aspect, only a part of an election ritual, a perform-ance whose omission would shock, though its execution can hardly profit.   But its significance for a campaign does not end here.   It is the candidate's projection screen ; the figure he cuts on the platform is the figure he will eventually cut before his public, something for which the calculated agencies of print and P.R.O.'s can construct no effective substitute.   Furthermore, the fact that so much of a candidate's opinions has to find expression on this public stage—spoken impromptu but before witnesses by ear and pen—imposes a form and a constraint upon electioneering whose consequences are incalculable.

Nevertheless, for the candidate with an election to win the most depressing fact probably remains that, let him orate as tirelessly as he will, he can hardly hope to reach by meetings as much as, say, one-eighth of his electorate, even if his charm wins him crowded halls every night.   What other devices can he command to advertise himself and his wares ?

In 1950, as in 1945, his most obvious secondary resource was the travelling loud-speaker.   No constituency organisation, however modest, would think nowadays of fighting an election without one.   More than any other device, it carries the candidate into the home of the voter—more even than the free election post, because literature can be thrown away unread, but no one has yet found a means of making a loud-speaker unheard.   Yet woe betide the campaigner who, rejoicing in this weapon, ignores its double-edge and forgets that the gap between persuasion and provocation is a narrow one when the instrument is a travelling megaphone.   This was recognised by many candidates of all parties who issued statements like the following, from the columns of a Dorset paper :

> " We wish it to be known that if loud-speakers are heard electioneering after 6.30 p.m., they are not acting on behalf of the Conservative Party, for we are of opinion consideration should be given to invalids, and the sleep of small children should not be disturbed after this hour."

Sometimes candidates made an all-party agreement limiting the hours of use.   Sometimes—though this was rare—a candidate would forego the use of them entirely, like the Labour candidate in Liverpool, Wavertree, a constituency with a good many shift-workers who get their sleep in the day.

This admitted element of nuisance has sometimes led people to advocate the banning of loud-speakers at elections.   This would not greatly harm well-established local party organisations, though it would increase their difficulties.   But it would load the scales still further against the small party or the poor or indepen-

Reproduced by kind permission of the Conservative and Unionist Central Office, the Labour Party and the Liberal Party Publications Dept.

[*To face p.* 241.

dent candidate. For all its tiresomeness, the loud-speaker van is almost the only sling left to an election David with which to come within striking distance of the political Goliaths. To a candidate who has not the time or resources to do an extensive door-to-door canvass or to advertise himself by print or poster, the loud-speaker is a fairly cheap short cut to publicity. Conversely, the thorough organiser regards it as a dangerous invention, prone to seduce his workers from the hard grind " on the doorsteps ". " Less loud speakers and more personal contact with the electorate ", was the penitent resolution which one Labour organiser proposed for himself after his setback at the polls. The majority of campaigners in 1950 did restrict their loud-speaker activity to announcements of meetings, an occasional " sloganeering " tour, linking the candidates' name to that of his party, and, upon occasion, announcing the candidates' presence and inviting householders to come out and meet him. Sometimes one heard recordings being played—speeches of party leaders or the popular broadcast of Dr. Charles Hill. But it was seldom in February weather that passers-by were tempted to stop and listen to canned oratory. For the same reason, the Conservative employment of mobile cinema vans was of limited value; they were hired out from headquarters to constituencies, and their success was entirely dependent on fine weather coinciding with the day of their loan.

More old-fashioned than the cinema, but vastly more useful for advertisement, was the poster. The expense restrictions coupled with the high costs of printing kept down the volume of poster publicity to a point almost certainly below that of 1945. In many constituencies they were quite late appearing, and in several there were not enough of them to make a powerful impact. Yet in general they were important—the principal outward and visible sign of a campaign otherwise mainly indoor. In most constituencies one gathered the impression that the Conservative posters, in their bright red, white and blue, were the more numerous and the more prominent, though Labour was seldom seriously behind. Liberals seemed to make rather less use of their headquarters' productions and relied upon local designs to a greater degree than their rivals. I saw no Communist posters save those printed (or drawn) for the use of an individual constituency.

A surprising feature of a campaign so centrally organised and directed was the range of local diversity in the matter of party colours. In March 1949 the Central Council of the Conservative National Union debated a proposal that there should be agreed " official " party colours—red, white and blue. This was criticised as annexing to a party colours whose symbolism properly belonged to the whole country, the flag and the Empire. In the end a majority favoured standardising the party colour as blue. However, in the election it was noticeable that the Central Office posters were almost always in red, white and blue. But while a majority of constituent associations employed either this combination or blue alone, there were areas in the North and the Midlands where red remained the party colour, while Conservatives in Westmorland claimed that yellow had been theirs " since Cromwell's time ". Labour usually regarded red as its appropriate wear, but I frequently encountered a combination of yellow and black. Liberals often favoured green or yellow, but there were many instances of them using blue or red, not to mention combinations such as purple and yellow, or blue and white. No doubt the sad explanation of such diversity is to be found in the modest part that colour plays in even the liveliest campaign; if it counted for more, the central offices would soon organise it.

Other visual devices for securing publicity were rare. The procession as an electioneering device has long since ceased to be respectable. Within the Metropolitan area processions had been banned by the Home Office to prevent Fascist-provoked disorders. But even elsewhere they were very seldom employed, except by the Communist Party, who occasionally mounted a " poster parade " or a " torch-light " procession. I met with only one instance of their employment by Labour—in Dundee. Nor was their twentieth-century equivalent—the motor " cavalcade "—much in evidence. In a period of petrol rationing it may have smacked too much of conspicuous waste.

Occasionally an enterprising constituency association might design a " float ", and tour the town exhibiting a house of the kind that Mr. Bevan wouldn't build but the Conservatives would, or otherwise turning into tableau form some theme of the campaign. Usually, however, time and money could be directed to better purpose elsewhere. More sensible, perhaps, was the

Labour Party in Glasgow, Hillhead, which put on short plays specially written for the election, performed on a mobile lorry-stage in the open air and running for about ten minutes each. One of them, with an obvious moral, was entitled " The Mug-wump ". The neighbouring constituency of Woodside was also responsible (Conservative enterprise this time) for the employ-ment of " lapel photographs "—cardboard button-holes bearing a picture of the candidate. The electric sign flashing VOTE LIBERAL from the roof of the National Liberal Club in London was, I believe, unique, though it is now a veteran of several campaigns.

In the ritual of British electioneering there are only two " festi-vals ", so to speak—occasions which provide automatic publicity for the candidate and his supporters. Those are the Nomination and the Poll. One of the most revered of press photographers' *clichés* is the picture of the candidate (often all the candidates in a group) handing in nomination papers to the Returning Officer. Generally it is the aim of a candidate to get his nomination papers " assented to " by a number of representative citizens in the division, to emphasise the breadth of his support. Sometimes zeal in such matters goes to great lengths and candidates' sup-porters may run to hundreds or thousands. The record in 1950 was claimed by Mr. Aitken, the Conservative candidate for Bury St. Edmunds, with 18,107 signatures. Where so large a total (one-third of the electorate) can be compiled there are obvious publicity benefits in so demonstrating one's strength. (Mr. Aitken polled 22,559, to win by 4,129 over his closest opponent, a Labour candidate.)

On Polling Day publicity must take second place to efficiency of operation, in the actual business of " getting out the vote ". But where the two can be combined, that constitutes an organiser's *beau ideal*. Before the 1948 Act an impressive display of motor transport flashing the party's rosettes and bunting and bearing its supporters to the polls was the most obviously effective combina-tion. The limitation on cars incited candidates in 1950 to make much semi-serious use of horse-drawn vehicles of every kind. For the rest, ubiquitous loud-speaker cars issuing " last-minute " appeals to " vote for X " are the most effective way of drumming up support. Whether the reported employment in Bristol North-East of racing greyhounds to carry messages from polling-stations to committee rooms proved as effective in execution as it was ingenious in invention is unfortunately not known.

There was no very great difference in the techniques employed by the two major parties for getting out their vote on polling day. The main contrast—but this was one which ran through parties, not between them—was between those constituency organisations which based their system on "tellers" at the polling-stations and those which relied on "street wardens". With the first system (by far the most widely employed) you post a worker at the entrance of each polling-station to collect from voters their register number, or, failing that, their name and address. (The most co-operative voters are those who yield up their poll card.) This information is then rushed back to the committee rooms, where party supporters are marked off, as they vote, on copies of the marked register. This enables "knockers-up" to concentrate their efforts on supporters who have not yet voted. The system requires a good many tellers and messengers and also committee rooms conveniently near each polling-station. Under the street-warden system there is ideally one party supporter in each street who makes himself responsible for "knocking up" the pledges in the street and hustling them to the polls. It dispenses with tellers and reduces the number of necessary committee rooms, but it presupposes a large and well-disposed team of "wardens". Sometimes an organisation would use something of each system; for example, there were several Labour associations which, at 6 p.m. on polling day, pulled all their tellers off the polling-stations and sent them to "knock up" every house in certain safe Labour wards. Constituency associations differed as much in their efficiency in such operations as in the thoroughness of their canvass. Success was a function of organising ability, the adequacy of the canvass, the numbers of available workers and, of course, the tractability of the constituency. Sometimes the advantage in this combination of elements inclined to Labour, sometimes (perhaps slightly more often?) to the Conservatives, but only rarely to the Liberals. But that the general level of organising competence was high may reasonably be regarded as a part deduction from the size of the poll.

It was interesting to compare the constituency party head-quarters from which these local operations were directed. What struck one immediately about the typical Conservative headquarters was the extent to which it resembled an H.Q. in the military sense. Here the military metaphors of electioneering became concrete. The effect was heightened by the large number of Conservative agents who were ex-military men. " *Il y avait evidemment un Colonel,*" as a French observer remarked after visiting a succession of Conservative committee rooms. Frequently the headquarters staff applied this same language to themselves—" the O/C Transport ", " O/C Loud-speakers "—and the schedules of operations and voluntary workers' instructions read not infrequently like battle orders. With this were blended the other virtues, not always military, of the well-run office. The typical Conservative headquarters was bright, clean, often freshly painted, welcoming, with an efficient switchboard and adequate telephone extensions, reasonably spacious accommodation and a nucleus of permanent staff who knew their jobs and could organise the volunteers efficiently. It generally occupied permanent premises, conveniently situated, even when it was not, as often, located in the main street of the town.

Labour headquarters were much less impressive. Their addresses, " Unity House ", " Trades Hall ", " Co-op Guild Rooms ", " Miners' Hall ", indicate how often they were housed in premises made available, sometimes only temporarily, to the political side of the movement by its industrial or Co-operative wings. They were seldom " well situated " as that term would be understood by an estate agent, but that does not necessarily mean that they were inconveniently placed for the areas they were concerned most to serve. By comparison with their opponents' they were dingy, often grubby, cramped and bare. But they had the necessary tools of their trade—the telephone, the duplicator, the filing cabinets. They were as unglamorous as tramp-steamers, and as serviceable. Moreover, though their permanent staff was smaller than the Conservatives', it might well score in its intimate connection with the other aspects of the constituents' lives—as trade union or Co-operative members. Where the Conservative organisation was often a " campaign headquarters " in the American sense, the Labour was more frequently an outcrop of a full-time, workaday activity which had a more than political reason for existence.

In headquarters' organisation, as in so much else, Liberal associations differed enormously. Sometimes they had premises of their own as competently, if not always as impressively, run as the Conservatives'. Sometimes their committee room, housed in a briefly vacated couple of rooms above a shop or office, gave an impression of desperate improvisation—a slit trench, almost, from which bands of gallant riflemen were resisting the onslaught of the enemy's mechanised armour. It was seldom that they were up to the strength even of their Labour opponents in trained staff, office space or equipment. And although their workers were often numerous and always enthusiastic, they were seldom properly steeped in an awareness of what electoral organisation involves. Too often they were talking policy when they ought to have been concentrating on tactics, arguing about navigation sometimes when the ship was going down.

About the average Communist Party committee room there always hung something of that conspiratorial aroma which the party imparts to its most routine operations. For the most part these indigent back rooms had nothing to hide—not even a marked register, like their better-established rivals, because the Communists were peculiar in using the canvass not for their own information, but as a form of propaganda. None the less, they contrived to infuse the crowded, zealous bustle of their cramped quarters with an air of furtiveness worthy of a more desperate villainy. This was Guy Fawkes trying to make his way not into the cellars but on to the back benches of the House of Commons.

To the candidate assessing his chances the officially embattled enemy were not the only foes he had to fear. There were also the skirmishers who hung about his flanks—the " pressure groups ", as American usage well calls them. To individuals or groups wanting favours or endorsement or promises of legislative support, a General Election is a natural opportunity, and although such bodies have never attained in Britain to the importunity and exuberance they sometimes display in the United States, their operations are a familiar, and indeed time-honoured, feature of the British electoral scene. The following lists, kindly supplied to me by a candidate from his own postbag, are quite typical. There were first of all the national organisations, such as: The British League for European Freedom; The British Health Freedom Society; The National Tenants' Association; The United Nations Association; The Good Templars Lodge;

The Musicians' Union; The National Federation of Housewives; The Civil Servants Clerical Association; The Civil Service Federation; The Postal Reform League; The Anti-Partition of Ireland League; The Post Office Engineers' Union; Federal Union; The National Union of Teachers; The Independent Traders Alliance; The National Association of Local Government Officers; The Royal Automobile Club; The Automobile Association; The National Farmers' Union; The Associated Portland Cement Manufacturers. Additional topics covered by similar national associations included: Land Values; Tithe Act; Police Widows' Pensions; War Damage; Chiropodists; Agricultural Contractors; Silicosis; Duties on Hydrocarbon Light Oils; Professional Women's Clubs—Educational and Sickness Benefit; Contraception; Rent Restriction Acts; Nursery Schools; Long Service Forces Pensions; Vaccination; Vivisection; International Women's Day; Leasehold Tenure; Business Tenancies; Admission of Aliens; Land Drainage Rates; Livestock on Allotments; Allotments—Security of Tenure; Town and Country Planning Act; Flying Clubs; Broadcasting.

But this was not all. These were supplemented and reinforced by local representations. In this particular constituency the best organised of these local pressure groups was the Lord's Day Observance Society, whose supporters poured in hundreds of letters. But in most constituencies in 1950 the best-organised religious group were the Roman Catholics seeking more financial aid for their denominational schools. Pledges were sought from candidates, sometimes by " Catholic Electors' Associations ", and candidates' answers to questionnaires were read from Catholic pulpits. In certain areas where the Catholic vote was strong, such as Liverpool or many parts of Lancashire, it became a dominant issue of the election, and although the national parties were at one in standing by the settlement embodied in the 1944 Education Act, many candidates of all parties in their own constituencies gave undertakings which went a good way beyond this. How far the Catholic vote was determined by this consideration—how far, indeed, there was a " Catholic vote " as such—is doubtful, but there were few constituencies in which the issue did not appear, and there may have been one or two in which it was crucial.

R

Other groups in the sample constituency mentioned included Protestants, opposing the Catholics' claims, school-teachers (seldom less than one from each school, raising such issues as salaries, equal pay, size of classes, etc.), cinemas (nearly every one in the division seeking a revision of entertainment tax), British Legion branches about pensions, etc., various societies about blood sports, garage and car-owners about roads, petrol and taxes, cyclists about road safety and publicans about taxes and licensing hours. In addition, a wide range of private individuals wrote for help—persons affected by the present state of the Marriage and Divorce Law, many women on the theme of equal pay, and spinsters seeking pensions at 55, housewives or parents complaining of the cost of living. Finally there was the " pure " protest or lunatic fringe, ranging from victims of the law's delay to advocates of spiritualism.

The total burden which this imposed on candidates was considerable. Quite apart from considerations of how their replies would affect voters, candidates found the sheer load of answering correspondence and receiving deputations a considerable addition to a heavy campaign schedule. Many adopted a rule-of-thumb principle of only replying to those communications which came from inside their constituency. The national party organisations also advised their candidates to be careful in their replies and not to go beyond the statements of party policy contained in the manifestoes. Such guiding principles reduced, but could not eliminate, the problems and frequent irritations which such pressure groups present. In many constituencies they were productive of more bad tempers than the inter-party warfare proper.

Every General Election produces (in print) its crop of " whispering campaigns ". If one were to credit the existence of all the " rumours " which party leaders think it politic to deny and denounce, Britain at election time would be more rumour-ridden than ever Britain at war. That Liberal candidates would withdraw at the last moment, that the " mutualisation " of insurance would deprive holders of their policies, that Mr. Churchill was dead—these " whispers ", and many more, were reported to be emanating from hostile rumour factories at various stages in the campaign. Resonant and indignant denials of such reports furnished material for many a flagging orator and copy for hungry news editors. But what did they really amount to? I met none of them in the campaign save in a form perfectly explicable on other grounds—as a genuine expression of opinion or probability, or as the obvious backwash of the official denial itself. I think it is very doubtful if the political grapevine transmits even half the load which politicians credit it with.

What I did encounter during the campaign was a certain crop of election stories—often repeated with the genuine conviction that the incident described had occurred within the narrator's own constituency. Often they were only suited for oral repetition, but two may serve to give the flavour of the rest. In the first the candidate is expatiating on the benefits brought by Socialism, and instances the " bonny babies " born during the years of Labour Government. A heckler interrupts, " But all under private enterprise ". The second was reported most often from rural constituencies. A farmer applies for membership of the local Conservative Club, claiming to have been a lifelong supporter of the party. The secretary asks, " But if you're a Conservative why ever haven't you joined before ? " The answer is, " Because it's only since this d——d Labour Government's been in that I've been able to afford the subscription."

Here and there feelings seem to have run a little high upon occasion under the stress of the campaign. Significantly, this was less common in constituencies where the parties were running neck and neck than in areas where one enjoyed a secure ascendancy. Thus it was the West Country which appeared to have the most exuberant " Young Conservatives ", the most animated membership of the " Vermin Clubs " (a Conservative response to Mr. Bevan's inelegant epithet) and the most vehement style of platform oratory. Similarly, it was in secure Labour mining constituencies in the Midlands or in Durham that Tory iniquities were painted in darkest dye and rumours of Labour intimidation and sharp practice were most rife. Even so these were only slight elevations rising from a plain of political good manners and public restraint which covered virtually the whole country. No doubt the embattled middle class addressing envelopes in a thousand Conservative committee rooms often spoke in harsher whispers than these. No doubt Labour canvassers often spoke on doorsteps more abusively than their counterparts on public platforms. But the atmosphere of the election was set much more by the public utterances of the politicians and by the conduct of the professional organisers ; in general, the first were restrained and the second were law-abiding. Indeed, much of the asperity of the hustings was relieved by the professional *camaraderie* of the technicians. There was much that was symbolic of the whole campaign in the friendly co-operation which existed between the " tellers " of different parties outside the polling-booths, collaborating in the collection of voters' numbers irrespective of party. Incidents could be multiplied of courtesies on the battle-field ; no party held a monopoly. But one may perhaps serve for a thousand—the occasion of Lord Woolton's visit to Worksop, a mining town in a Labour constituency. He was received by the Labour mayor, entertained, with a party of Conservative workers, to tea in the Mayor's parlour, and had the balcony of the Town Hall placed at his disposal for a speech.

That such emollients did not imply a " soft " campaign will hardly need stressing to anyone who watched or participated in it. It was a fight in which each side felt that the stakes were great, and on which they expended all the pent-up effort they could command. It was fought with many a post-war shortage and restriction still harassing the combatants, within the framework of a law in many respects novel and irksome and at a season which added climatic discomforts of its own. A young candidate, in a county constituency summed up his personal impressions as follows :

> " There is much I could talk about—the great burden your friends and supporters can be to you ; how much one prefers opponents' questions to any other kind ; the vital need for somewhere to get away from it all and relax ; the strain of being polite to people who bore you to tears ; the sense of frustration at not being able to make people see your point of view—and the quite indescribable thrill of knowing that you've made a good speech, and moved the audience to enthusiasm for what you believe in, the flash of inspiration that brings a laugh far more spontaneous than anything you get when you deliberately plan and lead for one—where does that flash come from ? "

Perhaps his experience may stand as a reminder of what, for all its relative " demureness ", the 1950 election meant to most of its participants.

CHAPTER X

THE MINOR PARTIES AND INDEPENDENTS

In one of the Church's few departures from electoral impartiality the Archbishop of York advised " the average voter " that, since in these days " the independent Member of Parliament has comparatively little influence ", he would " be wise to give his vote to the party which is most likely to promote the opinion which he holds. Occasionally, however, a candidate is so outstanding in his qualifications and so exceptionally suited for the constituency in which he is seeking election, that it is right to vote for him notwithstanding party considerations." Whether such advice had any effect or not on the voters,* certainly fewer candidates offered themselves either as Independents or as representatives of minor parties than in 1945. Compared with the 104 such candidates who stood then, there were only 56 (including the Speaker) in 1950. The abolition of university representation probably accounted for quite a few; 17 Independents fought in university contests in 1945. But, in general, as the results suggest, the reduction in candidatures reflected a certain slump in political dissent. Was it that the four national parties offered accommodation more generous than of old, or that nonconformity lacked the will or the cash to oppose them ?

Certainly the Labour Party was not latitudinarian enough for all. Five candidates, all sitting members, constituted a left-wing group of " Labour Independents ", " fellow-travellers with Labour ", as one of their number, Mr. Zilliacus, described himself, " fellow-travellers with Communism ", as most Labour men regarded them. They had all suffered expulsion from the Labour Party over foreign policy issues, Mr. Pritt (North Hammersmith) in 1940, Mr. Platts-Mills (Shoreditch and Finsbury) in 1948, Mr. Hutchinson (Walthamstow West), Mr. Solley (Thurrock) and Mr. Zilliacus (Gateshead East) in 1949. At one stage in their history, at the time of the 1949 expulsions, it seemed conceivable that this group might become the British equivalent of the American " Progressives ", with Mr. Zilliacus as the British Henry Wallace. But the movement never gathered momentum,

* It was certainly quoted in at least one Conservative election address.

and indeed Mr. Zilliacus came to resemble Mr. Wallace more in his deviations from his fellow-deviationists than in any assumption of party leadership. He was the only member of the group not to sign their election-eve manifesto " Crisis and Cure ", and from many points of view he was independent of them. The manifesto did not differ observably from the policy outlined in the Communist Party's *Socialist Road for Britain*—Friendship with the U.S.S.R., withdrawal of United States military aid, cuts in military expenditure, abolition of conscription and trade with Eastern Europe constituted a foreign policy; " freedom for colonial peoples " an imperial policy; higher wages, more social services, more nationalisation (including land) a domestic policy. The election addresses of the four London candidates were based on these same appeals, together with reminders of the candidates' own records and the " broken promises " of Labour. All had good local organisations and fought tough campaigns, but all, even Mr. Pritt, who had survived the lightnings in 1945, went down before the Labour ticket. The four London candidates polled only 20,013 votes between them, Mr. Pritt doing best with 8,457.

Mr. Zilliacus' contest at East Gateshead was somewhat different. With endorsements from Mr. Bernard Shaw and Mr. J. B. Priestley, a strong hold on local affections, a Pickwickian geniality and a record of League advocacy and " Titoism " which could be fairly convincingly presented as something more than mere " fellow-travelling ", he claimed to be still a Labour Party supporter resisting the crack of the Transport House whip. The fact that his Labour opponent, Mr. Moody, was a stranger to Gateshead and previously member for a Liverpool constituency made it easier for Mr. Zilliacus to sustain the role of the injured rather than injuring party. The contest attracted widespread national, and even international (see p. 277), attention, and was closely and bitterly fought. (Labour did not stop short of utilising the slogan " Britain for the British ".) Mr. Zilliacus nevertheless emerged bottom of the three-cornered poll, with only 5,001 votes.

The Independent Labour Party, or rather that pale shadow of its former self which had survived the secession of its principal figures to the Labour Party in 1947, put up four candidates in 1950. Two were on Clydeside, at Bridgeton and Shettleston, one at Burnley and the other at Newcastle Central. The pacifist element in the party was well to the fore in the propaganda of all these candidates. The first item in their programme was the abolition of conscription, the second, " neutrality in the event of a third world war ". Britain was to " refuse the Capitalist values of the U.S.A." equally with " the so-called Communist values of the Soviet Union ". The pacifist candidate in Newcastle advocated, " if necessary ", unilateral disarmament by Britain, but this did not appear to be official I.L.P. policy, any more than the Republicanism which he shared with Mr. Carradice of Burnley. In domestic politics a strong vein of anarcho-syndicalism provided the chief items—" workers control " and " 100 per cent. Socialism ". Despite their emphasis on peace and disarmament, the I.L.P. candidates were not given any of the Communist support enjoyed by the Labour Independent Group. Quite the reverse. At Shettleston and Burnley they were opposed by Communist candidates, both of whom polled more votes than they did. At Burnley Mr. Carradice polled 295, at Newcastle Central Mr. Barton polled 812. On Clydeside the local tradition presumably counted for more, though not much more. The figures were, at Bridgeton 1,974 and at Shettleston 1,031. In each of these constituencies successful Labour candidates were old I.L.P. men before the fusion, Mr. McGovern at Shettleston having been Chairman of the Party.

Less sullied even than the I.L.P. by the contamination of practical politics was the " S.P.G.B."—the Socialist Party of Great Britain. This was a group of non-violent Marxists, who preached an undiluted gospel of class struggle and poured an equal contempt on every other party, including Labour and the Communists. They put up two candidates, one in North Paddington (where they had previously fought in 1945 and at a 1947 by-election) and the other at East Ham South. Their propaganda had the austere purity of perfectionism, offering, as they truly said, no vote-catching promises. Their candidates had the self-effacing devotion of members of a monastic order. " One thing we must warn you about," they told their followers. " Do not trust in leaders, trust in yourselves alone. Unless you understand the cause and the solution of your miserable condition no leader can help you, no matter how honest and sincere he may be ; if you do understand, then you do not require leaders ; you will know what you want and how to instruct your delegates to get you what you want." Their 1950 intervention can hardly have much accelerated the revolution of their dreams. In East Ham South they won 256 votes. In North Paddington the 1945 figure of 472 was more than halved, and reduced to a mere 192.

In two widely separated constituencies, Glasgow Central and East Woolwich, another utopian splinter group devoted to Socialism and pacifism, the United Socialist Movement, ran candidates who were both veteran campaigners. Glasgow was the headquarters of the movement, where Mr. Aldred, its leader, fought a forlorn hope and polled 485 votes. East Woolwich was chosen for a demonstration against Mr. Bevin's foreign policy. There Mr. Hancock polled 252 votes. His policy was succinctly stated as follows: " The only thing that matters in this election is to register our determination that there shall be NO MORE WAR ! ", but his address also took exception to " old Labour comrades, such as Lord Citrine, getting £8,500 a year for a government job ".

Quite different from these groups, indeed quite in a class by himself, was the " Independent Socialist ", Mr. Cleather, who opposed Mrs. Braddock at Liverpool Exchange. His was a puzzling candidature, which not surprisingly involved the allegation that he was a " Tory stooge ". The employee of a Liverpool assurance society, he fought on a policy consisting almost entirely of opposition to nationalisation in general and the " mutualisation " proposals in particular. This he described as " the New Socialism ", " which will meet the needs of 1950, not 1850 ", but its positive aspects were considerably less clear than its negative. Its support amongst the electorate was restricted to 381 votes.

There were no splinter Conservative parties comparable to those on the left of official Labour. There were, however, a few candidates who might be described in varying degrees as Independent Conservatives. The most distinguished of these was undoubtedly Mr. D. L. Lipson,* the sitting member at Cheltenham since 1937, who had to defend his title against both official Conservative and Labour opponents. In 1945 he had been successful against similar opposition, but in 1950 it proved too much for him, and despite a vote of 10,449, he came bottom of the poll. His programme advocated " an end to party squabbles, and a National

* Who, however, described himself simply as an " Independent Candidate ".

Government ". In details his policy was not greatly different from *This Is The Road*, but he put full employment as his first priority and favoured the retention of food subsidies. He was much criticised for a voting record which had often led him into the Government lobby between 1945 and 1950, and despite endorsements from Sir Arthur Salter and Mr. Wilson Harris, he did not escape the fate which in 1950 befell every candidate who had the effrontery to cross party lines.

At Greenock the Conservatives, who gave their official backing to the Liberal candidate, were a good deal embarrassed by the emergence of an Independent who claimed Mr. Churchill as his leader and sought Conservative support. He was Mr. J. S. Thomson, a local Councillor and garage proprietor, who in 1945 had worked for Mr. Hector McNeil, but had since resigned from the Labour Party, and now fought on a platform critical of Labour's neglect of Scottish and in particular of Greenock interests. He campaigned single-handed, acting as his own agent and chairman and dispensing with any supporting speakers ; his meetings were reported to have been amongst the most crowded and the most entertaining of any in Scotland. The Conservatives claimed that he split the anti-Labour vote. Certainly his 6,458 (supposing it all to have been anti-McNeil) was quite a considerable figure in a five-cornered contest.

More freakish candidatures were those of Dr. Lyburn (Tonbridge) and Mr. Thorley (Beverley), both of whom described themselves as " Independent Conservatives ". Dr. Lyburn had stood (and lost his deposit) before in 1945. In 1950 he suffered a similar fate, polling only 739 in a four-cornered contest, in which his distinctive appeals were for a coalition government and diagnostic clinics. " In this atomic age diagnostic clinics must play their part in our survival on this earthly planet." Mr. Thorley, a petty officer in the Royal Navy, produced a set of pungent variations on Conservative themes ; " scrap the Agricultural Committees ", " Britain first, Empire second, Foreigners last ". " Food : Less Snoek, Whalemeat, etc., More Sugar, Beef and Bacon ". He added an endorsement of Roman Catholic claims for their parochial schools. He won 1,121 votes in a safe Conservative constituency.

At Halifax a curious contest developed, indicative of the complications produced by the would-be relationship of Conservatives and Liberals.   Negotiations for a local application of the " Huddersfield formula " having broken down, a Liberal and a Conservative candidate were both nominated, but a determined group of collaborators, undeterred by this, went forward with the nomination of a " Liberal-Conservative " candidate as well. This was a vice-president of the Bradford Conservative Association, Mr. R. H. Blackburn.   In a contest in which Labour, Conservative and Liberal met with success in that order Mr. Blackburn came bottom of the poll with 1,551 votes.

Besides these groups and individuals which ranged themselves in some relation to right or left of the main parties, there were a certain number of nationalist candidates whose appeal cut across all orthodox party lines.

Scottish Nationalist activities commanded a particular interest in a year which was notable for the growing power and prominence of the National Covenant movement.   The Covenant campaign for signatures to their petition for a Scottish Parliament reached the million mark while the election was still on, though the leaders of the movement were careful to dissociate it entirely from election politics.   (One suspects that the February election came a little too early for the Covenant's time-table.)   Consequently those candidates who carried the banner of Scottish Home Rule did so without the Covenant's endorsement, though in the reflected glow of its success and, no doubt, with many of its signatories amongst its supporters.

In all eight * candidates representing various branches of Scottish Nationalism offered themselves to the electorate.   Between them they represented most of the " splinter parties " of the movement.   There was relatively little difference in their electoral policies, and they fought on what was virtually a common front.   The Scottish National Party was the largest group, with four candidates (financial stringency, they explained, prevented more), amongst whom Dr. McIntyre was unique in having been successful once before—in the Motherwell by-election in 1945, which returned him to Parliament for thirty-two days before the General Election of that year unseated him.   He was the Chairman of the party.   The most successful of their candidates, however, was Mr. D. Stewart, who contested Perth and East Perthshire,

* The Anti-Partition candidate at Greenock described himself also as a " Scottish Nationalist " and was given Nationalist support.

overtopping the Liberal candidate and securing 4,118 votes.
Probably the most colourful of their campaigners was the poet
C. M. Grieve (well known under his pen-name of Hugh Mc-
Diarmid), who fought the forlorn hope of Kelvingrove, where he
polled 639 votes. He was particularly vigorous in denouncing
the Covenant's neutrality, and alleged that the movement " was
being rigged behind the scenes in favour of the Liberal Party "
(the only party to give it their support). Two Scottish Home
Rule candidates stood; the one in the Western Isles described
himself as a " Hearth and Home " candidate, refused to " fly in
the face of Providence and Common Sense by arranging meetings
far in advance ", and claimed that his election expenses amounted
only to £49. His motto was " Keep the Loom from Rusting,
the Boat from Rotting and the Beetle out of the Roof-tree ".
Another two candidates stood, one as an " Independent Scottish
Nationalist " in Edinburgh and the other as a " Scottish Self-
Government " candidate in West Lothian.

The policies of all these candidates had the same general aim—
a separate Parliament for Scotland—but they differed on the
lengths to which they wished to carry Scottish independence.
There was more stress in most of their campaigning on the ills of
the present system—the neglect of Scottish industry, agriculture,
housing (this was very prominent) and health—than detailed
elaboration of positive proposals. A note of Distributism ran
through much of their policy, and enabled them to attack Labour
and Conservatives with equal vigour, though Labour, as the
present neglectful " London " Government, naturally bore the
brunt of the onslaught. Surprisingly, in view of his unpopu-
larity with the movement and openly expressed dislike of it,
Mr. Woodburn, the Secretary of State for Scotland, was not
opposed by them in Clackmannan.

All the candidates lost their deposits. The total number of
votes polled was 12,584 * making an average per candidate of
1,573.

Irish Anti-Partition candidates stood in three constituencies in
Scotland on Clydeside and one (Bootle) in England. Their
incidence naturally coincided with the presence of voters of Irish
extraction, but a full explanation of their choice of constituencies
would have to take into account the intricate local politics of each

* Compared with the 30,595 votes won by their seven candidates in 1945.

division, since their candidatures had their rise just as often in local feelings and personalities as in any design based on voting prospects or publicity value. Thus they announced that they would put up a candidate in Govan, Glasgow, only if Mr. Neil Maclean, the sitting Labour Member, who failed to secure re-adoption by his local association, decided not to stand on his own. (In the end neither Mr. Maclean nor an Anti-Partitionist was nominated, but their statement was expressive of their tactics.) The common feature of the Anti-Partition candidatures was that all their Labour opponents had failed to vote against the " iniquitous Ireland Bill " of 1949.

Anti-Partition candidates described themselves as being, on non-Irish issues, supporters of the Labour Party—e.g. Mr. McGuinness of the Gorbals and Mr. O'Callaghan of Coatbridge and Airdrie, who used the form " The Anti-Partition Candidate and the True Labour Man ", and claimed in their addresses that it was " the Irish people more than any other " who " built the British Labour Party ". However, there was very little Labour policy in their programmes or their speeches, and on non-Irish themes their attacks on the Government differed little from those of the more fiery Conservative candidates. Emphasis fell heavily on housing (they generally stood in constituencies where this was a crying need), education (they ardently supported Catholic claims), more social benefits and opposition to conscription. They also gave vigorous support to Scottish Nationalism, and their candidate in Greenock stood under the joint auspices of both parties.

Their meetings were eloquent and indignant, spiced with personalities and highly local in their appeal. In Mr. Eoin O'Mahoney, Mr. McGuinness's agent in the Gorbals, they possessed one of the most colourful figures of the election, whose splendid brogue and beard enlivened many an otherwise drab Clydeside meeting. A resident of Southern Ireland, with Jacobite sympathies, he crossed the water to organise what must have been one of the most un-machine-like election machines of the campaign.

The two Irish Nationalist candidates in Ulster were differently circumstanced from their allies across the water. They felt themselves to be fighting, not for advertisement on the soil of another country, but for possession of the soil of their own.

Their appeal was adapted accordingly—as well as to the peculiarities of Ulster electioneering. Both had been members at Westminster before, though Mr. Healy of Fermanagh and South Tyrone had been out of Westminster since 1935, and only Mr. Mulvey of Mid-Ulster was a sitting member. Both announced that, if elected, they would abstain from taking their seats. Both were elected, by small majorities, and did abstain, at any rate initially.

Their supporters in England and Scotland were less successful. All lost their deposits and were at the bottom of the poll (even below Communist opponents). Their total vote was 5,045.

In Ulster two other parties raised the banner of Irish independence, each in their distinctive way. The Irish Labour Party put up two candidates north of the border, in Belfast West and South Down (both, in effect, industrial constituencies of Belfast). In the first Mr. Beattie ran the Ulster Unionist, Rev. J. G. MacManaway, close, but in the second Irish Labour was outnumbered two to one. The Sinn Fein, equally concerned to publicise their own brand of Irish Nationalism, put up candidates in Belfast West and Londonderry. Both fought *in absentia* from cells in Belfast Gaol, where they were serving prison sentences. In Belfast West Mr. Beattie's candidature left them with only 1,482 votes to glean, but in Londonderry, with a clear field, Mr. McAteer polled 21,880.

In Wales the nationalist appeal was in the hands of two parties, the Welsh Nationalists proper (" Plaid Cymru ") and the Welsh Republicans. Of these, the former were by far the stronger, with seven official (and one unofficial) candidates spread fairly evenly over the urban and rural constituencies, North and South. The social and cultural roots of the movement were well illustrated by the occupation of the candidates, who included (apart from two full-time party organisers) a farmer, a Baptist minister and three schoolmasters. Two poets and critics testified to the literary influences within the party. The immediate objective of the party was " a Parliament for Wales within five years ", but the driving force of the movement often seemed less political than moral, cultural and linguistic (they were the only election addresses in 1950 mainly written in a language other than English). There was frequent stress on the peace-making and internationalising influence of an independent Wales (the party has strong pacifist sympathies).   Although the economic implications of the policy were seldom fully set out, a pronounced affinity to Distributism was noticeable in most addresses.   The tone of the party's appeal was idealist and emotional, though moderate, and directed more against Welsh grievances than English oppressiveness.   A correspondent in one constituency analysed the party's support as coming from the following five elements: the Liberal-Radical chapel element, some of the Catholics, old Socialists with syndicalist memories, young intellectuals, and " the sporting vote ".   The analysis would seem to hold reasonably well for most of their candidatures.

All the candidates lost their deposits, and all save one came at the bottom of the poll.   The party derived comfort, however, from the fact that the total votes of its official candidates were a few thousand more than in 1945, when they ran the same number (though not all for the same seats).   The average vote in 1950 was a little over 2,500 per candidate.   The Independent Nationalist also polled 1,571 at Merthyr Tydfil and the Welsh Republican 631 at Ogmore.   The policy of the last-named differed from that of the Nationalist Party proper in its more thorough-going perfectionism and its wishful economics and, of course, in its explicit rejection of " the English Crown and all royalist institutions ".   Its candidate announced that he had come to Welsh Republicanism by way of the Labour Party, the I.L.P. and the Socialist League.

The only other organised party to put up an election candidate was the Social Credit Party.   Their " founder-leader ", Mr. Hargrave, fought Stoke Newington and polled 551 votes.   He added a few electoral appeals to the central economic doctrines of Social Credit; " No racial antagonism ", " No ' Left-Right ' Split: we must pull together as One Big Family ", and " More fresh home-grown food ".   In Mr. Augustus John he had perhaps the most distinguished artistic supporter of any candidate in the election.

Only one candidate presented to the electors the political principles of Fascism.   That was Mr. Symington of Market Harborough, who described himself as a supporter of Sir Oswald Mosley's policy, though in conflict with his racial views.   He was a farmer, company director and member of the local urban district council.   He secured 273 votes.

There was no specifically religious party which put up candidates of its own in 1950, but in West Ham North a Miss Dickinson stood as a self-styled " Christian Democrat ". This she explained as signifying the nucleus of a " strong centre party with a leaning towards the left ". The political applications of the candidate's Christian Democracy had about them a dominant flavour of left-wing Liberalism. She polled 503 votes.

It would have been surprising if an election taking place in the shadow of the reports of the hydrogen bomb had not produced at least one pacifist candidate, with no party affiliation at all. In the Aston division of Birmingham a " small business man ", Mr. Keatley, stood as an " Independent Peace Candidate " in opposition to " party politics ", conscription and war. For his campaign he relied almost entirely on the circulation of 25,000 copies of a brief election address. He polled 338 votes.

One of the traditional forcing beds of Independent candidatures is currency reform. Mr. Craven-Ellis won distinction in 1950 as the only non-party exponent of this, and also as the only candidate who changed his constituency for fear of over-spending. He began his campaign in Southampton (Test), but transferred to Southampton (Itchen) when he discovered that his rate of expenditure was running too high and that he might find himself exceeding the permitted limit before polling day. From 1931 to 1945 he had sat in Parliament as a " National " member, and in 1950, apart from his currency views, his general policy approximated more nearly to Conservatism than anything else. He polled 1,380 votes and his expenses amounted to £854.

The candidate with the most individual panacea was Mr. Hancock, who opposed the Speaker at Hexham. " The Hancock Plan " appeared to consist, in its less cosmic aspects, of a scheme for diverting all productive effort to the production of " necessities ", as a result of which " we need work only one day a week instead of five or six days ". Mr. Hancock, who in 1945 polled over 10,000 votes against Mr. Churchill, had less success in impressing the Northumberland electorate, only 4,154 of whom cast their votes in his favour.

Besides those already mentioned, there were three contests involving Independents which attracted national interest. At Grantham the sitting member, Mr. Kendall, stood again. He was an engineer whose " people's car " project had excited much public notice. His policy aimed at the establishment of " an economic system that combines the immense productivity of free enterprise with the social justice and stability which national planning can provide ". He claimed that the Independent in the House of Commons could be " a watchdog against policies which go too far to the Left . . . or too far to the Right ". Although unsuccessful, he polled 12,792 votes.

A somewhat different justification for Independency was advanced at Bridgwater by Commander Stephen King-Hall, who had unsuccessfully contested Ormskirk in 1945. " If you send me to Parliament I shall support the Government when it behaves in the interest of the nation as a whole and I shall attack it without mercy in speech and print if it puts class or party above the national interest." For the rest his policy bore a general resemblance to that of the Liberal Party, sufficiently close, indeed, for them to abstain from opposing him. Moreover, individual Liberals like Lord Samuel and Lord Layton gave him their endorsement, though he insisted that as an Independent he should be judged solely on his own merits. Despite a strenuous campaign, fought largely with the aid of his own family, he came bottom of the poll with only 6,708 votes.

The contest at Rugby, which centred around the candidature of Mr. W. J. Brown, may serve as a kind of epitaph to the fate of Independents everywhere in the election of 1950. A trade unionist who opposed Socialism, a Beaverbrook " columnist " who opposed Conservatism, Mr. Brown represented *in excelsis* the crusading angularity of the individualist who is unhappy if he finds himself swimming with the tide. He campaigned at Rugby virtually single-handed, touring the constituency in an aged car equipped with a loud-speaker, from which he beamed greetings and slogans upon a constituency that had returned him in 1942 and 1945.

> " Vote for Billy Brown of Rugby Town
> The Man who Never Lets You Down ".

Against this knight-errantry the Conservative and Labour candidates opposed the argument that a vote for an Independent was wasted because single-handed he could do nothing for his constituency. To a remarkable degree their propaganda concentrated its fire, from each side, on the Independent candidate. He for his part replied by pointing to his services to the constituency, to the role in Parliament of the Independent member, from Wilberforce to A. P. Herbert, and to his programme—which might in a word be described as liberal with a small " l ".   Both the Labour and Conservative candidates had strong organisations. The voting was :

Johnson (Lab.)	15,983
Dance (Conserv.)	14,947
Brown (Indep.)	8,080

Thus in every constituency in the country the party label defeated the candidate who stood in his own name alone, and the great party labels defeated all the minor ones.   Victory at every point went to the big battalions, and the political equivalent of logistics appeared to overwhelm the skill and fighting spirit of all the Joan of Arcs and Prince Ruperts of electoral warfare.   The total absence of Independents made the Parliament of 1950 unique in its generation.   That did not mean that its members were all cut to a pattern.   A Conservative Party which could range from Sir Waldron Smithers to Mr. David Eccles, a Labour Party which could still embrace Mr. Fenner Brockway and Mr. Bellenger, a Liberal Party whose modest membership could nevertheless find room for Lady Megan Lloyd George and Mr. Donald Wade—these were fairly latitudinarian parties.   But they were still parties and 1950 remained *par excellence* the year of party victories and Independents' defeats.

CHAPTER XI

WORLD REACTIONS

IT is probably true to say that the General Election of 1950 provoked more interest overseas than any other British election in history. The 1945 election had in some degree taken world opinion by surprise—by the speed of its onset and still more by its swift reversal of fortunes. In the five years that followed, the British experiment in Social Democracy was watched with widespread interest as the first example of the application of Socialist principles to a democratic and industrial great Power. The contest of 1950 was consequently viewed as affording the first inquest into the success or otherwise of such an experiment and as determining how far, or at the very least how fast, Britain would proceed along the road to State Socialism. With this was linked a solicitude, obvious amongst friends but undoubtedly also existent amongst foes, about the effect of the struggle between the parties on Britain's conduct and leadership in international affairs. Although, as was only to be expected, the issues and conduct of the election were not always fully comprehensible to foreign observers, they were in the main better placed to appreciate its nature than they had been in 1945. Then the dazzling dominance of Mr. Churchill in world politics had blinded their eyes to the forces in operation against him. Now Mr. Attlee and his Government had become, not indeed world figures of comparable appeal, but certainly figures who were known, recognisable and, to some degree, comprehensible forces. There was consequently in existence for most overseas observers who were interested in the election at all a rough frame of reference into which its developments could be fitted.

This the press and radio of the world undertook to do. For the most part, of course, they relied for their coverage upon the accustomed news channels and correspondents regularly stationed in the United Kingdom. Nevertheless to a degree not previously known they supplemented these by specially despatched or assigned correspondents of their own, some of them seasoned students of British politics, others deft but ignorant explorers who often found themselves voyaging in strange seas of thought in groups. As a result this " most observed of all elections ", as one harassed party headquarters official described it, took on at times the paradoxical appearance of a battle in which the spectators outnumbered the contestants, so privately was so much of it fought and so publicly was so much of it reported.

In the main the overseas reporting of the election followed similar lines to those taken by the British press. The foreign press was slow to warm up; it was puzzled by the prevailing " demureness ", it snatched rather at crumbs because exciting news was so scarce and it found its best " leads " and its best " stories " in the exploits of Mr. Churchill. Partly because of the need to add sauce to such plain fare, partly from yielding too ready credence to the stock denunciations of the hustings, most correspondents tended to see the lines between the parties as too clear, the colours as too sharply contrasting. Nonetheless the broad issues were fairly enough presented, on the whole, and the main story got across, generally commendably free from partisan distortion. Of course, like all correspondents in all capitals everywhere, too many of the newspapermen and broadcasters yielded to the assumption that everything could be observed from London, but it is probably true to say that in 1950 their record in braving the provincial unknown was slightly better than usual. However, had more of them devoted to the constituencies and the organisation some of the coverage they lavished on the high strategy and the outward drama, they would have avoided some of their most frequent errors—e.g. the overestimation of the electoral impact of Mr. Churchill's Edinburgh speech.

Naturally interest in the election was highest in the English-speaking countries. But proximity was not necessarily a maximising factor. This was well illustrated by the example of Eire, which maintained her assiduous provincialism, at least in her press and public comment, throughout most of the campaign.* The amount of space given in the press was generally quite small and reports were not prominent. The general attitude which lay behind this was well expressed by the *Irish Times*, which stated on February 15th that, " Ireland's interest in the British general election is remote so far as the struggle between the Socialists and

* In considering the performance of the Irish press, it should of course be remembered that British newspapers also circulate in Eire.

Conservatives is concerned ", but, it added significantly, " All Irishmen, however, have a very real interest in the six counties of Northern Ireland ". Accordingly the spotlight of election reporting was directed especially at the Ulster campaigns. Thus the foray of Mr. Macbride across the border to speak on behalf of Anti-Partition candidates was a dominant news item. Similarly the Roman Catholic campaign for their parochial schools was reported far more extensively in Eire than in Britain. There was, moreover, an initial disposition to over-estimate the role of the " Irish vote " in British constituencies * and the extent to which it could and would be organised.

Such issues apart, the election reporting was, as between the parties, fair enough, on the general principle that, from the Irish point of view, there was nothing to choose between them. The drama of the results, as a sporting event if nothing more, fully captured the heart of Irish sub-editors, and both prominence and space were accorded them in all newspapers. Finally a word of praise is due to the news coverage provided by Radio Eireann, who sent two observers into the field whose reports both in content and presentation were excellently done.

The Australians, as if to provide further proof of the irrelevance of distance to interest, showed a keen curiosity and concern. Where the Irish felt that the outcome had no significance for them, the Australians felt just the reverse. Having themselves only a month or two before defeated a Labour government in their federal elections, they were almost as interested as British Conservatives in the application of the *argumentum ex Australia*. Perhaps, too, the argument could be applied the other way round in a year which was due to see five more Australian elections at the State level. These reflections lent a certain partisan flavour to Australian reporting of the events of February, which was restrained only by a sense of Commonwealth unity over-riding party affinities. The fact that the overwhelming majority of the Australian press is Conservative meant that its partisanship was by no means evenly distributed, and this undoubtedly resulted in a certain disposition to take the estimates and interpretations of British Conservative sources at their face value. Naturally any issues which were common to both countries' electoral campaigns

* An over-optimism which had its counterpart in an undue concern over the same issue displayed by Unionists.

excited special interest. Thus petrol rationing, which the Country Party had pledged itself to end in Australia, was a British issue which was seized on by the Australian press almost as eagerly as by the British, once it had been ventilated by Mr. Churchill.

The great bulk of Australian election news was supplied through the Australian Associated Press, and had in consequence some of the inevitable two-dimensional qualities of agency reporting; where pure factualism was deserted, it was generally in the interests of " human interest stories ". For analysis or background news the papers relied on individual by-lined correspondents, where they had them, or on syndicated features. These were not in the main of a very high level, although the best papers, such as the *Melbourne Herald*, were commendably full and often informative. But the selection of British comment quoted was too often uneven and sometimes capricious. " Public opinion polls " were often quoted without identification or evaluation. The speeches or broadcasts of minor but still influential politicians were unduly under-played. The Liberal intervention was at first over-estimated and subsequently, by Conservative papers, over-blamed.

Comment, of course, varied with the politics of the journal concerned. But it was interesting to notice that even the respect and sympathy accorded to Mr. Churchill did not save his " atom talks " proposals from a general and guarded, but nonetheless adverse, criticism. As for the results, they could be and were hailed either as a defeat for Socialism, or as a victory for Labour. In the country of the compulsory vote the size of the poll occasioned little comment, but there was general regret that the outcome had not been more decisive and a general expectation that a second appeal to the country would have to be made very soon.

The New Zealand reaction to the election was broadly similar to the Australian, the resemblance being heightened by New Zealand also having rejected in November a Labour government of its own. Some party controversy in fact developed from this by reason of the defeated New Zealand Labour Party sending shortly before polling day a message to their British opposite numbers. In this they argued that New Zealand was already paying the price of her November decision, and counselled their British comrades to be warned by her example. This, contended

Mr. Holland, the Conservative Prime Minister, violated the rule he had himself observed of not interfering with another country's internal politics; furthermore, the consequences alleged were quite untrue. The result of the poll gave no general satisfaction, the enthusiasm even of Conservatives being muted.

The South African press, whether English or Afrikaans, was less inclined to take sides. While the campaign was on, in particular, it refrained from partisan comment. Its news came largely from Reuter–S.A.P.A. (South African Press Association) sources, but some papers, notably the *Johannesburg Star*, had services of their own. The *Star* was indeed notable for the fullness, fairness and political sagacity of its coverage. Despite the competition of the racial riots on the Rand which cut across the closing week of the campaign, it found space for a very full treatment of the last stages and of the results. The *Cape Times*, while less full, was reliable and circumspect. A leading article in the *Star* of February 25th is indicative of the sober way in which most of the press viewed the campaign. It pointed out how extremists had been wiped out and described the extent to which the two parties' programmes had overlapped. "The millions who voted Labour apparently preferred a bird in the hand, but at least as many millions did not vote Labour, indicating that a clear majority of the British people has yet to be converted to socialism."

In general the Nationalist and Afrikans press gave considerably less prominence both to the campaign and to the results. *Die Vaderland* said that the economic situation for Britain was more grave than any of the electoral contestants could bring themselves to disclose. *Die Burger* was, however, apparently alone in anticipating a future of great ideological bitterness, likely to grow progressively worse. The Opposition press admitted to a considerable dissatisfaction with the result, though not to serious alarm. Few went as far as the Rand *Daily Mail*, which headlined its leader "The Worst Possible Result", but the *Cape Times* thought that "the more the results are contemplated the more unsatisfactory they appear". This was the point of view expressed by General Smuts when he described the result as a "stalemate" which was "a matter of concern and anxiety to the whole world", and said it was "imperative that the British democratic machine should act promptly and efficiently and once more give the world a strong and authoritative British Government". But whereas the *Cape Times* drew from this the moral that another election should be held as soon as possible, the *Star* pointed out that it would not necessarily yield any different result ; the parties should therefore drop their ideological controversies and devise a compromise.

Indian opinion was frankly sympathetic to the Government which it felt responsible for giving her independence, and this sentiment found expression in newspapers which supported the Congress Party. Interest in the campaign was not, however, very high in these journals, and it was in the independent, English-language papers, such as the *Times of India* and the *Statesman*, that the fullest coverage, largely from Reuter sources, was to be found. In editorial opinion these papers were pro-Conservative, as their comments on the results bore out. " Labour should not consider itself empowered to proceed with so controversial a measure as further nationalisation without a fresh contest, uncomplicated by the intervention of minor parties " (*Times of India*). " Labour will return to power in chastened mood. This is assuredly no mandate for extravagances. It is healthy that more attention will need to be paid to the Opposition " (*Statesman*).

The Canadian press accorded the election a generous proportion of their extensive space. The bulk of their coverage was provided by the news agencies, the Canadian Press in particular, but the larger newspapers not only used their regular London staffs but also sent over special correspondents of their own. Without implying any disparagement of several other newspapers which gave excellent coverage, it is perhaps proper to single out the *Montreal Gazette* for the special fullness and reliability of their reporting.

The interests of the Canadian press did not diverge notably from those of the British. Mr. Churchill stole the most headlines, but Mr. Attlee was given good space, both as a speaker and as an election personality. The Edinburgh " talks with Russia " speech was unique in securing universal headline treatment (and in dominating election reporting for the days that followed), but other election events were given a prominence roughly proportionate to their treatment in Britain. The election was almost always conceived in Labour *v.* Conservative terms, but one Liberal journal, the *Winnipeg Free Press*, found British Liberalism worthy of rather more spacious treatment. Though the Canadian press was generally pro-Conservative in its sympathies, reporting was reasonably well-balanced and non-partisan. The basic issue at stake was generally thought to be the further spread of nationalisation, and it was recognised that all parties accepted the Welfare State as a permanency and mainly differed about its administration and its financing.

Canadians naturally had their ears cocked for treatment of the dollar crisis and of Marshall Aid, and any mention of these topics could count on securing full reports in the Canadian press. The most serious criticism of the campaign was levelled at the tendency to neglect the balance of payments issue, and so deprive the electorate of discussion of what was regarded as a fundamental problem. Other aspects of the election which had particular interest for Canadians were the forecasts of the public opinion polls (with especial attention to the pronouncements of the Beaverbrook press), Mr. Churchill's " Seven-point Statement ", the Liberal Party's complaints over their broadcasting times (a lively issue *mutatis mutandis* in Canadian politics) and the unusually quiet tone of the campaign itself.

The results were generally interpreted as a protest against further nationalisation, though an affirmation of belief in the Welfare State. The more Conservative papers naturally read a more positive and final repudiation of Socialism into the voting than did the rest, but even the *Toronto Daily Star* admitted that it meant that Socialism had gone far enough for the present. The same city's *Globe and Mail* found the " indecisive " result unsatisfactory, but admitted that it was probably an accurate enough reflection of British public opinion. The *Winnipeg Free Press* thought it constituted a verdict against both Socialism and the Conservative Party, but most of all it regretted that at a time when " heroic and disagreeable measures " were called for " the energies of the nation would be confused by weakness and confusion in government and parliament ". This latter sentiment, expressed in various forms, was common to most Canadian opinion everywhere.

Interest in the United States was sustained at a level quite comparable with that of Canada, and was fed by an even greater volume of reporting. Unworried by any newsprint scarcity, the most voracious press and radio in the world catered fully for a public trained by Mr. Truman's 1948 victory to anticipate the

unexpected, and by his " Fair Deal " to watch either eagerly or
anxiously for any omens of the future of " Welfare Socialism ".
Moreover, almost like an American election, this one could be
seen approaching in ample time for newspapers and broadcasting
chains to organise their staffs, prepare reinforcements and map
their coverage in advance.   What that coverage involved may be
gauged by the fact that in the last fortnight of the campaign the
New York Times bureau was cabling an average of 15,000 words a
day and the *New York Herald-Tribune* 12,000.   These were the
giants, but papers of lesser dimensions carried a wordage which
was fully proportionate.   The result was that in most of the great
centres of population, especially those on the Eastern seaboard,
the American reader had available to him almost as full a picture
of election developments as the reader of any single British penny
daily—and one which was considerably less partisan.   This did
not hold, of course, for the small-town papers or the popular
" tabloids ".   Their coverage was much more " spotty " or
sensational, and their treatment of election news was largely
dependent on the competition afforded by other items often of
local or " human " interest.

There were times, nevertheless—especially in the earlier stages
of the campaign—when the election became a trickle of newsprint
alongside the department store advertisements on the inside pages
even of the metropolitan dailies.   This reflected the halting
development of the campaign and the difficulty of maintaining
interest in an often undemonstrative contest in face of the competition of ample national and other international news.   It is
revealing to see which election " stories " the *New York Times*
judged worthy of front-page treatment.   They are, in order of
appearance, as follows: Mr. Attlee's January 8th visit to the
King and consequent talk of an early election, his dissolution
announcement of January 10th, the publication of *Let Us Win
Through Together*, Mr. Churchill's first broadcast, his speech in
Leeds and Mr. Morrison's broadcast, Mr. Churchill's Edinburgh
speech, Mr. Bevin's reply in his broadcast, Mr. Churchill's second
broadcast, Mr. Attlee's broadcast, a February 20th analysis of
party prospects, and an eve of poll forecast.   With due allowance
made for the sobriety of *Times* treatment, this was the pattern of
prominence followed by most of the press.

Mr. Churchill, of course, was the personality who most excited

American interest. But Mr. Attlee was not slighted. To correspondents habituated to the " campaign train " tours of American contests, Mr. Attlee's motor tour had the charm of a familiar custom in a novel guise, and many were the comments on the Prime Minister's " quiet swing in an antique car ", as the *New York Daily News* described it. Mr. Attlee's style of platform oratory (" more like a lecture tour than electioneering ", *New York Times*), and his personality (" the soft-spoken, mildmannered man who looks more like a schoolmaster or a bank clerk than the executive of the British Empire ", *Baltimore Sun*), fascinated correspondents and were faithfully reported in their despatches. A commendably high number of bureaus sent correspondents singly or in teams into the provinces. The *Christian Science Monitor*, a notable example, visited Cardiff, Manchester, Edinburgh, Sheffield, Glasgow and Greenwich, as well as several minor towns and rural constituencies. Even the *Wall St. Journal* ventured away from the citadels of finance to watch the fate of free enterprise in Chippenham, Bristol and the Midlands. A generous wealth of well-informed feature material on election machinery, issues, propaganda, personalities and comment accompanied the " straight " reporting of the main developments and overflowed into the great open spaces of the " Sunday supplements ".

In all this the balance of reporting was generally well held. There had been an early disposition, especially in the more popular papers, to see the election in much the same exaggerated terms as the 1948 American election had been viewed—as a dramatic clash between the black of " Socialism " and the white of " free enterprise ". But as the campaign developed and more and more journals received eyewitness reports of what was happening, a more level awareness—even if sometimes a puzzled awareness— of the real nature of the party programmes and appeals began to dawn, until by polling day even the Hearst press had provided its readers with a fairly realistic picture of the main issues. Nor was there much erroneous forecasting ; perhaps 1948 had induced caution. Some correspondents, attracted by the Liberal challenge, estimated too highly the electoral rewards of gallantry, but for the most part they were content to steer by the polls, and so were never far off course. One or two issues held particular interest for Americans, but they were also important for Britons

—the 1952 problem and the role of Marshall Aid, and, above all
of course, Mr. Churchill's proposals for talks with Russia.

The story of American official response to Mr. Churchill's
proposals is told elsewhere. The press reaction was to hail it
as the first big news " story " of the election, and to concentrate
almost disproportionate attention (in terms of the election itself)
on the relatively meagre crop of subsequent British developments
from it. Editorially it was treated with respect (though often with
generous discount for its electioneering significance), but few
papers were prepared to give the proposals positive endorsement.
Probably no journal of prominence was as much moved by Mr.
Churchill's appeal as the *Washington Post*, but the most they
could bring themselves to advocate was a kind of " citizens'
commission " to consider the problem and endeavour to formu-
late some solution. They warned that a mission to Moscow
was " not something to rush into, for failure would simply
intensify the (arms) race ".

On such an issue all organs of opinion naturally felt themselves
at liberty to comment freely, but on most other issues of the election comment was generally sparse and restrained. At the onset of
the campaign the State Department had struck a warning note
about the dangers of interfering in a neighbour's internal politics
and about the desirability of not taking quick offence if a few
British electoral brickbats should fly over the American fence.
Although one or two Americans visiting Britain—generally those
with Labour sympathies—could not entirely resist the temptation
to join in a good scrap when one was so ready to hand, there was
in fact a minimum of Anglo-American " incidents " arising out
of the election. Even Mr. Hoffman's testimony before the Senate
Foreign Relations Committee published on February 17th,
sharply criticising Labour's attitude to Western Europe, did not,
as it easily might have, become a partisan weapon in the campaign.
Of course it was not to be expected that a press which was three-
quarters Republican (and much of it vehemently Republican)
should abstain from all harsh comment on the behaviour of the
Labour Government and Labour politicians, nor that the remaining Democrats should never belabour British Conservatism and
its works. But few papers were as outspoken as the Luce weekly,
Life, which in its pre-election issue said flatly : " We hope the
Socialists lose ; their defeat would be a good thing for Britain

and a good thing for the United States." Nor were many as active as the *Nation*, which sent Mr. Churchill a cable after his Plymouth speech asking whether a Conservative Government could get along with less Marshall Aid than a Labour one.

Thus it was not until the results were known that the American press felt able to indulge in completely uninhibited comment. At first the ding-dong " battle of the gap " forced successive revisions of opinion. Beneath a large photograph of Mr. Attlee early editions of the *New York Post* carried the caption, " No wonder he can smile ". In later editions this became, " It's a wonder he can smile ". But even when they were known, the results only served to befog the path of the dogmatists and cramp the style of both Left and Right. The Right were the more jubilant, but it was a jubilee with restraint, a hallelujah with balanced clauses. The *Indianapolis News* spoke for many others : " The British voters may not have shot Santa Claus, but they have certainly bounced him about ". For most commentators it was the " stopping of Socialism in its tracks " (*San Francisco Chronicle*) that represented the best feature of the result, with the hope and implication generally present that next time would see the job carried one stage farther. Only the rout of the Communists and fellow-travellers gave universal satisfaction—that and the conduct of the election itself, including a poll so much higher than any with which the United States is familiar. The rebuff to the Liberals was often regretted, but comfort was generally found in the belief that liberalism was now accommodated in the Labour or Conservative party, or indeed in both. Overclouding the whole panorama of the results, however, was the depressing conviction—giving rise to a momentary note of alarm—that the election had not produced a stable government, one able to take decisions in foreign affairs on the basis of a sure and safe majority. It was feared that there was no single leader who could speak for the British people and that a further delay in all pending negotiations was inevitable while matters sorted themselves out— either by the formation of a coalition or by a new appeal to the country. Only by degrees did realisation dawn that the first was unlikely and the second unnecessary.

No account of American election coverage would be complete which omitted mention of the radio. All of the four major networks devoted considerable time and staff to reporting the progress of the campaign. Notable amongst these was the Columbia Broadcasting System. There were few major meetings of the election campaign which lacked the presence of a C.B.S. microphone, and one of the ironical by-products of American interest and B.B.C. neutrality is that the nearest to a complete set of recordings of Mr. Churchill's campaign speeches that exists anywhere is in the files of C.B.S. The Columbia System brought Mr. Edward Murrow from New York and seconded additional C.B.S. correspondents from Europe to provide a service of news and features which more than trebled their normal output from London during the period between February 4th and February 27th. In addition to recordings from public meetings and interviews with voters, candidates and agents, they also re-broadcast simultaneously the whole of Mr. Churchill's two radio addresses, and also Mr. Morrison's, Mr. Eden's, Mr. Bevin's and Mr. Attlee's. The notable feature of their coverage and comment, apart from its extent and reliability, was its combination of vividness and impartiality. Whether or not it brought in direct dividends as a commercial enterprise, it certainly constituted a *tour de force* of sustained radio reporting.

Between Western Europe and the general election there hung the two barriers of language and shortage of newsprint, but interest was nevertheless considerable. Over most of the Continent Socialism had seemed to be a receding tide since 1945, and this added to the curiosity generally felt about the fate of the British " experiment ". Often the predominantly Conservative sympathies of the press were fortified by the feeling that a government headed by Mr. Churchill would make Britain a " better European " than she had hitherto shown herself.

In France the election had to compete, in a press always somewhat insular, with the absorbing " *affaire des generaux* ". Nevertheless it often became front-page news, and much space was devoted to expounding the idiosyncrasies of British electoral methods, so un-bizarre, so intensive and yet so unobtrusive. The cartoonist in *Figaro* who depicted the Horse Guards sentries remaining impassive and immobile while bill-stickers covered them with election posters summed up what seemed to many Frenchmen the essential paradox of British behaviour. Naturally the greatest interest was aroused by Mr. Churchill's proposal of a " Big Three " meeting; naturally, too, French susceptibilities were hurt by the implication that France would be excluded. Opinion was divided on the idea of a direct approach to Russia as such, but in the main it was favourable. The feature of the results which gave most pleasure was undoubtedly the elimination of the Communists. Second to that came the " calm and dignity " with which the contest had been conducted. For the rest, opinion largely divided on straight party lines, though few either of Right or Left sought comfort in the paradox of M. Blum, who observed that " Labour's victory is the more significant for being so hardly won ". Many shared the fears of *Le Monde* that " Britain, in her turn, may now find herself in the situation of relative impotence and semi-paralysis that results, in France and in most western democracies, from an equal division of opinion between two opposed ideologies ".

In Italy the election was followed with even more anxiety and interest than in France. There was a widespread disposition to link the rise or fall of British parties to the fate of their counterparts on the Continent and in Italy. Correspondents admitted frankly to their difficulties in reporting the operation of a system so different from their own. The *Corriere della Sera* wrote from London: " We foreign observers find the radio speeches so radically different from anything that would have been said in similar circumstances on the continent, that we are all once again convinced of the profound difference between the people who live here and the people who live across the Channel." On polling day it commented on " the simplicity of the procedure and the almost incredible mutual trust on which it is founded ". The news of the results created widespread interest, and the easy resolution (by Italian standards) of the seeming stalemate provoked a chorus of praise ; even journalists who had hitherto been by no means friendly in their attitude to Britain yielded to a momentary enthusiasm for the " civilised " way in which Labour shouldered its burdens and Liberals and Conservatives acquiesced in the resulting situation.

The more stable democracies of the Low Countries and Scandinavia found less at which to marvel or surmise, but were equally interested and responsive. A large group of Dutch newspapers made a special study of Chislehurst, as a sample constituency. The Swedish daily, *Svenska Dagbladet*, secured the scoop of an interview with Mr. Aneurin Bevan, in which he delivered himself of the surprising opinion that this was " the most bitter election campaign " he had ever fought.

Germany was brought into the election by the controversy in its early stages about the ending of rationing there and the quality of the ensuing German diet. This gave some of the press a kind of injured interest in the contest, but in general their reporting was rather thin, poorly informed and doctrinaire. The procedure and the tone of the campaign later excited almost more interest than the issues, and the popularity of Mr. Churchill (second to Bismarck in a German public opinion poll) made him seen even more the dominant personality than in fact he was. Indeed, the majority of Germans probably found their main disappointment over the result in the fact that British foreign policy, so far from being transferred to Mr. Churchill, would still remain in the hands of Mr. Bevin.

The West European country whose press presented the most uniform line of comment on the election was, of course, Spain. There no British party could hope for very warm commendation, but the Conservatives (and Mr. Churchill amongst them) were undoubtedly the favourites. The disposition was general to describe the outcome as a Conservative " victory ", though sometimes, as by the *A.B.C.*, this was admitted to inhere in moral rather than material terms.

Yugoslav treatment of the election, as might have been expected, provided a mixture of Western and Eastern attitudes. The news reporting was reasonably straight, though sometimes odd quirks crept in, probably due as much to ignorance as to design, e.g. *Borba*, after quite a reasonable description of the role of the election agents, concluded : " It sometimes happens that these agents break into offices and steal the lists. This happened to Mr. Herbert Morrison." Mr. Zilliacus's campaign at Gateshead excited particular interest, and though his chances of success were not over-estimated, it was thought that the result of Labour's opposition would be that " Mr. Churchill's partisan may enter Parliament ". As for the Edinburgh speech, comment agreed closely with Moscow—that it was not just an electioneering stunt, but a shrewd appreciation " of the mood of the British electorate and its hidden desires " for peace.

Behind the Iron Curtain the picture presented of the election was clear, pungent, lurid and false. The ingenuity of the distortion was sometimes so extreme as to make it difficult to believe that it could possibly be the product of deliberate deception; it often seemed easier to accept it as the honest effort of a two-dimensional intelligence to comprehend a three-dimensional world. This applied particularly to the reports and comment circulated inside the U.S.S.R. In satellite countries the carpentry of conscious falsification was more obvious, in proportion as the concessions to observable actuality had to be larger. The satellite attitudes are hardly worth separate analysis. Their themes and devices are all taken from Russian models; the differences are mainly of degree, as adjustment is made for varying levels of local sophistication.

The election served two main purposes to the Communist and Cominform propaganda machine—the exposure of " bourgeois democracy " as a hollow sham and the exaltation by contrast of the " people's democracy " of the U.S.S.R., which, by a happy coincidence, was due to hold its own elections on March 12th. For the mills of the Russian press and radio no detail was too small, too irrelevant or too absurd to be ground into the fine flour of supporting evidence. The main themes were the essential identity of all three " bourgeois parties " (though Moscow did not often condescend to notice the Liberals), the particular hollowness of Labour's claim to represent the workers, and the diabolical ingenuity with which the whole electoral, political and social machinery was rigged against the only real democratic party, the Communists. The Communists were, of course, given a prominence out of all proportion to their electoral importance. Mr. Pollitt's broadcast was reprinted verbatim and extracts from the speeches and statements of Communist Party leaders were frequent. However, despite this exaggerated prominence, there was little disposition to present the party's chances as rosy. Moscow evidently had little faith in its prospects, and wisely abstained from hazarding " face " by optimistic forecasts; it preferred to dwell on the disabilities under which it so cruelly laboured.

A few quotations will serve to indicate the treatment by Soviet press and radio of these themes. This is from an article in *Trud* on the composition of the Conservative and Labour parties:

" The very make-up of the House of Commons shows that it is chiefly composed of representatives of the privileged classes. The Conservative Party is composed of industrial magnates, landowning aristocrats, dealers and professional politicians—Baldwin, Walter Fletcher, Sir Patrick Hannon, Col. Hutchison, for example—and the Labour Party is not far behind. The only difference is that in this case, together with the company directors, industrialists, corrupt bourgeois journalists and stockbrokers, a big part is also played by a substantial layer of trade union bureaucrats who have long since severed their connections with the masses."

The hollowness of Labour's proletarian pretensions was exposed in similar terms by *New Times*. Referring to a statement by Morgan Phillips that all the Labour Party's candidates were working day and night for the ordinary people of Britain, it insisted that of the 26 candidates purporting to be railwaymen, 17 were Government executives, and of the 37 so-called miners only 2 were actually working underground, the others belonging to " the higher bureaucracy " of the bourgeois State. Among these were Bevan, James Griffiths and Tom Williams. The *Sunday Express*, *New Times* continued, had not missed the opportunity to ridicule the Labour leader's boasts, and had published a book showing that many of the Labour candidates were industrialists, men of independent means and shareholders in monopolist concerns.

As for the " pseudo-democratic " election system, a commentator on the Moscow radio, replying to an inquiry by some Soviet listeners, gave an exhaustive exposure of its true nature.

> " Numerous restrictions, for example the age limit and the residence qualification, deprived many people of their right to vote. Only those who have reached the age of 21 are allowed to vote and the residence qualification provides that the electors must have lived in the same place for at least three months. Thus the vote is denied to the unemployed, who now number about 500,000, to seasonal workers and to millions of people living in slums and lodging houses."

According to British law, the commentator went on, every candidate had to pay a deposit of £150, which was forfeited if he failed to gain sufficient votes. Such expenditure could be afforded only by a party with substantial funds at its disposal.

T

" The bourgeois parties even managed to speculate in deposits. Several days ago the British Press said that the Liberal Party had insured 200 out of 400 deposits with Lloyds."

Furthermore, the bourgeois parties spent enormous sums on propaganda. They had at their disposal the press, the radio, the cinema and meeting-halls, and millions of pounds were provided by financial magnates and rich business-men. On top of that, the constituencies were so drawn as to insure the success of the bourgeois parties. Some constituencies had only 27,000 electors, and others 158,000, and each of these sent one member to Westminster, even if he only gained one more vote than his opponent. In some districts only one candidate was nominated, and he was elected automatically without any voting.

" Thus the electors are simply deprived of any opportunity to express their wishes, and whether they approve of their candidate or not he will be regarded as their representative in Parliament."

Under such an electoral system any progressive party, even if it collected a majority of votes, would only win a very small number of seats in Parliament. In any event, the many millions of people in the British colonies took no part in the elections, although Parliament dealt with their affairs.

In addition, the Communist Party was exposed to special victimisation. A *Daily Graphic* article was cited by Moscow home radio on January 20th as evidence of discrimination against them in the hiring of halls for meetings. The press (as witness statements by Mr. Morrison and Mr. Bevan) was all in the hands of monopoly capital, the *Daily Worker* alone excepted (January 25th), and of course the B.B.C. allowance of broadcasting time was grossly unfair, as witness Mr. Pollitt's own protest to the Prime Minister (January 26th).

Over all there brooded the sinister shadow of M.I.5. A Tass dispatch from London exposed the whole voting procedure. The official lists of candidates put up in each constituency did not bear the party allegiance of the candidate, and this was not even marked on the ballot form. The dispatch cited a statement in the *Daily Telegraph* that voters had expressed misgivings about the secrecy

of the ballot. The system under which the elector's registration
number was entered on the counterfoil bearing the same number
as the ballot form, said Tass, could be extremely useful for an
organisation like M.I.5, " which has extraordinary powers and
may on the basis of a study of the ballot form establish the political
convictions of any elector ". The dispatch went on to quote
instances of victimisation, and noted that the Catholic clergy had
threatened to excommunicate Catholics voting for Communist
candidates.

Despite this the bourgeois parties were in desperate straits.
Tass quoted three instances from the British press. The *Star*
had remarked on the small audiences at political meetings, and
how Mr. Bevin had addressed a gathering of " 75 women, 6 men
and 8 children ". The *Daily Mail* had reported that the Labour
Party was " engaging phone operators to vote for Labour candidates " (*sic*). The *Daily Herald* had pointed out that 10s. notes
had been circulated bearing the inscription " Vote Conservative ".

Above all—though Moscow preserved silence on this for over
a week—Mr. Churchill's Edinburgh appeal represented how hungry
the British public was for reassurance on the one issue all the
bourgeois parties had evaded—peace.

While the high command of Soviet propaganda was determining
the proper handling of Mr. Churchill's proposal, the low echelons
produced their *tour de force*. This, on the eve of the poll, was a
radio play based upon the experiences at Eatanswill of that first
of all serious election observers, Mr. Pickwick. " The novel ",
said Moscow, " portrays with great satirical force the ugly repul-
sive comedy of elections in England, the dark doings of political
bigwigs. All means are employed—bribery, corruption, intoxica-
tion of voters and newspaper calumny." Eight leading actors of
the Moscow stage went through each Eatanswill incident with
gusto, while midway through the performance an announcer
indicated the obvious moral by referring to the " swindling
manœuvres " of present-day elections in the West.

And the results of our contemporary Eatanswill? At first
Moscow confined itself to printing them briefly and without com-
ment. It was not until March 5th that *Izvestia* entrusted to
" An Observer " the task of explaining what had happened.
Labour had been " defeated ", whatever its leaders might pretend
to the contrary. The attempt to portray the defeat as unexpected

and sensational was preposterous; Labour's policies had necessarily led the voters to lose faith in it. Nor, apparently, had the Conservatives won : " the great masses of the voters have again rejected Churchill's party ". But what about the Communists ?

> " The failure of the English Communist Party . . . is explained by the fact that it has not yet become a mass party of the working class and also by the specific conditions under which the Communists had to function during the elections. It goes without saying that against the Communists were aimed all the ' charms ' of bourgeois democracy, expressed particularly in the restrictions on pre-election campaigning and propaganda (being granted extremely limited broadcasting time, being refused quarters for election meetings, etc.)."

Between the lines Cominform disappointment was clear enough. It was a fortunate relief for Soviet readers that they could turn the page and read how elections are conducted in the Union of Soviet Socialist Republics, where only a few days later 99% of the voters cast their ballots for the Communist Party and its great Leader, Marshal Stalin.

CHAPTER XII

THE FORECASTS AND THE RESULTS

Long awaited and closely fought, the 1950 General Election was made the subject of more eager and anxious forecasts than any within recent memory. It was almost true, as one wit remarked, that the voters were more polled against than polling. Certainly the institution of the public opinion poll established itself to a degree hitherto unknown in British politics. In 1945 it had been, electorally speaking, still something of a novelty. The 1948 elections in the United States had damaged its prestige, without apparently impairing its appeal. Consequently the 1950 election had a certain cruciality for the polls ; they could count on an audience, but it would be a critical one before whom they must not fail.

The parties also had an interest in the public opinion polls. All parties employed them, though not all made public their findings. Allusion has already been made to the use made by the Liberal Party of a figure of 38% of the electorate " who would vote Liberal if they thought they really could have a Liberal Government ". An identical figure, curiously enough, had earlier been employed by the Conservatives; it represented the percentage of trade unionists disclosed " by a Gallup poll " as being members of the Conservative Party in March 1949. These were the only poll figures which the parties were observed to publish, but for their own guidance they all took soundings of public opinion through sampling agencies, as well as taking due note of the polls made public in the newspapers. They did not abandon their older practice of testing the progress of their fortunes through canvass returns from the constituencies, but in 1950 for the first time polling analysis became one of the recognised adjuncts of political planning.

As far as the public were concerned there were two main series of public opinion polls relating to the election. The first was that conducted by the British Institute of Public Opinion (B.I.P.O.), popularly known as the Gallup Poll, and published by the *News Chronicle*. The second was the *Daily Express Poll of Public Opinion* published in the newspaper of that name. Of these, the oldest, the most regular and the most reliable was the first. In the broad picture of public opinion movements which both presented they did not differ. Both agreed that as late as November 1949 a majority of voters favoured the Conservatives, but that thereafter Conservative popularity shrank, until it was not possible to be confident which way victory would incline on polling day. Nevertheless the differences between them, and especially in their presentation by the press, are instructive to observe.

A B.I.P.O. survey taken in October 1949 showed the following percentages : * Conservatives 50, Labour 39, Liberals 8, Others 1. This marked the pre-election high tide of Conservatism. By November the figures were Conservatives 48, Labour 38, Liberals 11, Others 1. No further results were released until January 20th; representing a poll conducted several days earlier, they indicated, in effect, the state of the public mind at the outset of the campaign. They revealed, as the *News Chronicle* headline put it, that the Tory lead had " dramatically narrowed ". The figures were in fact Conservatives 44, Labour 41½, Liberals 12½, Others 2 ; there was a particularly notable drop in the ' Don't Knows ' from 14 to 8, reflecting, no doubt, the crystallising effect of the Dissolution announcement itself. By January 30th, the next publication date, Labour had moved into the lead, but only, as the *News Chronicle* pointed out, " by a hair's-breadth ". The figures were Labour 45½, Conservatives 44, Liberals 10, Others ½. February 10th showed little change : Labour 45½, Conservatives 43, Liberals 12, Others ½. Hardly surprisingly, the *News Chronicle* accompanied this presentation with a warning that the margin of error in a sample poll might easily be greater than the 1½% shown between Conservatives and Labour—and also that " there was an immense amount of chance " in the relation of seats to votes. By February 17th the Labour lead had slightly increased—Labour 45, Conservatives 42½, Liberals 12, Others ½—but still not enough to make it possible, as the *News Chronicle* said, " to predict which party will, in fact, lead in the popular vote on February 23rd ". Finally, on February 22nd, under the headline " Election Neck and Neck ", the *News Chronicle* published the last pre-election poll : Labour 45, Conservatives 43½, Liberals 10½, Others 1. " Support for the two main parties", it commented, "is so evenly matched that it is impossible to say which will lead in the voting on Thursday."

The first *Daily Express* election poll was published on January

* Eliminating (as in subsequently quoted polls) the ' Don't Knows '.

23rd. The figures were slightly kinder to Conservatives than B.I.P.O.'s had been: Conservatives 48, Labour 42, Liberals 9, Others 1. There were only 10% of Don't Knows. January 30th (contrast with B.I.P.O.) showed the smallest conceivable movement of Conservatives and Labour—respectively 47½ and 42½; Liberals 8½, Others 1½. February 6th, headlined " Tories Keep the Lead ", gave the figures as Conservatives 45, Labour 44, Liberals 10, Others 1. ' Don't Knows ' had risen, surprisingly, to 11. February 13th (" They're Neck and Neck ") made Conservative and Labour equal at 45 each. Liberals had 9½, Others ½. However, by the next publication date, February 20th, the trend had been reversed (" Tories Back in the Lead "): Conservatives 46, Labour 44½, Liberals 9, Others ½. ' Don't Knows ' had dropped to 10. The last poll results appeared on February 23rd, under the heading " Tories keep the lead ", and ran Conservatives 44½, Labour 44, Liberals 11, Others ½.

Since the percentages of the actual vote were Labour 46·1, Conservatives 43·4, Liberals 9·2, Others 1·3, it will be seen that neither poll was very wide of the mark, though the *Daily Express* was seriously misleading in putting the Conservatives at the top. (It was, however, surprising that in its post-election issue of February 27th it quoted, not its last poll, but its last poll but one for comparison with the actual results.) The B.I.P.O.'s estimate was strikingly accurate, being only 1·1% out in respect of Labour, 0·1% for the Conservatives, 1·3% for the Liberals and 0·3% for Others. Such close approximation to the actual result entitles it to be regarded as also providing the more accurate chart of the movement of opinion over the period of the campaign. It also more than restores to the public opinion poll any credit which it may have lost by the performance of its various practitioners in the United States presidential election in 1948.

The public that had voted so heavily on February 23rd had to wait longer than usual for its results. It was just before 11 p.m. when the Borough of Salford, true to its tradition, announced the first result in Salford West—a Labour victory. Crowds gathered in Piccadilly Circus and Trafalgar Square, where the returns were flashed on screens, which in turn were photographed by television cameras for inclusion in the first televised commentary on election results to be seen in Britain. Though it was a rainy evening,

London was *en fête* to a degree seldom seen since 1945, and West End hotels and restaurants were full of convivial and optimistic ' election night parties '. Though excitement was keen amongst the crowds outside, a holiday mood of good humour prevailed as cheer and counter-cheer greeted successive results. However, when results were known from the 266 constituencies who were conducting the count that night the outcome was still very uncertain. The figures then showed Labour well in the lead with 163 to the Conservatives' 102 and the Liberals' 1 (Mr. Donald Wade). This was sufficient to cause Labour elation, with Mr. Morgan Phillips confidently predicting a Labour victory, and Conservative depression, demonstrated in a marked reluctance to make further prophecies at all. In fact, however, the only thing conclusive about the first night's results was the disaster to the Liberals ; though there could not now be any sweeping victory for the Conservatives, it should have been more generally realised that later returns from the less urban constituencies were likely to right the balance in their favour.

This was what happened when the count continued on the following day. Whenever a fresh result was released the B.B.C. interrupted their programme to announce it, and many wireless sets were not turned off all day, as people watched with mounting excitement what the evening papers well called ' the battle of the gap ', the Conservative struggle to eliminate the margin that separated them from Labour. To anyone who experienced it, a bare time-table of some stages in the announcement of the results will serve to revive the suspense and thrill of the occasion.

	Labour	Conservative	Liberal
11.45 a.m.	163	105	1
12.45 p.m.	172	114	1
1.45	196	152	1
2.45	219	194	1
3.55	255	241	5
4.44	266	259	6
4.46	266	260	6
5.44	299	277	7
6.44	310	281	7
7.44	311	286	7
8.30	313	289	7

From this it will be apparent that shortly before five o'clock there was a spell—it lasted about ten minutes—when the combined

totals of Conservatives and Liberals drew level with Labour.
This was the most exciting sequence of the race, something that
few sporting events could rival. Four times Labour's lead was
wiped out, but each time the Labour total edged forward by one
seat, until in the following hour the strangely delayed returns
from the Scottish urban and colliery constituencies came in.
Even so, it was not until 6.20 p.m. that Labour won the assurance
that it would be the biggest single party in the new House of
Commons, and not for two hours afterwards that it picked up the
three additional seats needed to give it an absolute majority; this
was accorded by Mrs. Mann's victory at Coatbridge. At the end
of the day the totals were Labour 314, Conservative 295, Liberal 7
and Irish Nationalist 1. The narrow majority thus afforded
invested the outstanding returns with an interest not normally
attaching to contests in such constituencies as the Western Isles
or Ross and Cromarty. It was, in fact, not until Monday,
February 27th, that news of these last outlying constituencies was
all to hand, and revealed that Labour could count on an absolute
majority of 7. Even then one result was still to come—Manchester (Moss Side), where the death of the Conservative candidate
before polling day caused postponement of the election until
March 9th. The vacant candidacy was filled by Miss Florence
Horsbrugh, the unsuccessful Conservative contestant at Midlothian and Peebles. Her victory at Moss Side brought the final
electoral figures up to Labour 315, Conservative 298, Liberal 9,
Irish Nationalist 2.

The near-stalemate of these results had a profoundly inhibiting
effect upon party officials and leaders, as the consciousness dawned
that another not far distant election was implicit in them, and that
any comment on the last might become material for the next.
Conservative headquarters, for all the restrained gratification they
felt at their gains, issued on Friday evening the 24th a statement
from Lord Woolton that " in the grave situation that has arisen
the Conservative Party do not propose to make any comment at
present upon the result ". Mr. Churchill at Woodford earlier in
the day similarly contented himself with the oracular utterance,
" Of all the memorable occasions when I have stood here this, in
my view, exceeds in importance all others. We cannot tell, and
I am certainly not going to pronounce, what is going to happen."

Labour had even less to say on Friday, but the following night,

in the somewhat muted celebrations of the party's jubilee, postponed from February 2nd, Mr. Morgan Phillips surveyed the
ragged path to victory. " This party of ours ", he said, " polled
the highest vote of any single political party in the history of
British politics. We are the only political party in this campaign
to survive without losing a deposit." Many seats had been lost
by very narrow majorities, some through intervention of the
Communists ; in other cases he believed that the intervention of
the Liberals took a number of votes from the Labour candidate.
He described how the Labour Government's " vigour and
determination " had created " discontent among certain sections ",
how " the big industrial interests " had subscribed to the Tory
Party funds, and how " new organisations financed by business
interests " had been carrying on an anti-Labour campaign for
three years—at an average rate on the hoardings alone, he claimed,
of £20,000 a month.

The first prominent Liberal comment on their *débâcle* came
from Lady Megan Lloyd George, who blamed it on what she
described as the " crazy " electoral system. Had there been a
true reflection of their vote, there would have been a strong body
of Liberals in the House. On Saturday evening the Liberal
headquarters in their first official statement had less to say about
their downfall than about their intentions :—

> " The Liberal Party carries on. Let there be no doubt
> about that. Backed by more than two and a half million
> people in all parts of the country, Liberals feel more than
> ever that in the end only Liberalism can solve the deadlock
> between the opposing Right and Left ideologies, which the
> election has thrown into such startling relief. Now that the
> party machines have crushed the Independent, protection of
> the rights of minorities rests solely in the hands of Liberal
> Members of Parliament, and Liberals everywhere will back
> them to a man."

Politicians can bide their time ; editors have to go to press.
Newspaper comment was not similarly delayed. The Labour
press found no cause for enthusiasm in the results. The *Daily
Herald* headline to its February 24th issue was expressive of
Labour's suspense and anxiety : ' So Far—The Line Holds '.
Its leader on the 25th admitted " the extreme narrowness of the

majority is a disappointment to us ".   True to the defensive tone
which it had adopted from the first, it attributed this to a Tory
" campaign of detraction " in which " Ministers have been abused
and derided with savage violence ".   The Tories had " been
conducting a war of nerves against the electorate " as well as trying
to " seduce them by bribes ".   Comfort was found in the " in-
finitely greater disappointment " which the result implied for the
Tories and the " big increase in the Labour vote ".   The election
" marks, not the end of our exertions, but a new beginning ",
leading to " a substantial majority " next time.   The tone of the
leader was bitter and apologetic, suited to defeat rather than to
victory.   The *Daily Mirror* of February 24th emphasised the
' Record Polls ' and on 25th regarded the country as facing a
" New Election to End Stalemate ".   Its leader regretted the
lack of " a more clear-cut result ", but thought the size of the
poll soared " above the gains and losses of party warfare ".
The note of chagrin was surprisingly absent.

On Sunday *Reynolds' News* was mainly looking forward to
" the next battle ".   It had only a few editorial comments to
make on the last.   The election had proved beyond any doubt
that the country had " no use for splinter parties—the Liberals
and the Communists ".   As for the performance of the Labour
organisation, it had demonstrably exaggerated the progress it had
made in the countryside.   " In too many constituencies the
Labour Party only came to life on the eve of the election."   The
" reverse should be a tonic to the Movement ".   *The People* took
a surprising line of its own.   Finding its leading news in an
alleged Liberal " Offer to do a Deal ", it gave up its centre-page
editorial to a scheme for a two-party agreement.   The British
people's ' verdict ' was that they were " neither for more nationalisation and controls nor for going back to free enterprise ".   Mr.
Attlee and Mr. Churchill should therefore " get together and
decide on a compromise programme ".   Labour should drop all
nationalisation proposals, including iron and steel.   " In turn,
Mr. Churchill should concede that he has no mandate to tinker
with the food subsidies."

The headlines of the *Daily Express* early in the morning of
February 24th gave an impressionistic view of first Conservative
reactions—" A Huge Poll—few changes—but the Radio Doctor
is *IN*—Socialists Holding On ".   The *Express's* more considered

reaction came on the 25th, " New Election Soon. Britain Votes
Out Nationalisation ", and its editorial went on ebulliently to
argue that Mr. Attlee had " lost the confidence of the country "
and should resign ; the King would then send for Mr. Churchill,
who " would probably resolve to go to the country ". The
Liberals, " farcically " disenfranchised under the electoral system,
would split and the majority would go Tory. Even if Mr. Attlee
" postponed the hour of testing ", " a new election is inevitable
at an early date ".

A more nearly official Conservative reaction was supplied by
the *Daily Telegraph* of the same date. It admitted that " victory,
if that is the name for it ", had gone to Labour, but with it " no
moral authority ", " not a vestige of a ' mandate ' ". It blamed
their " success, such as it is " upon " the reckless intrusion of the
Liberal Party ". The Conservatives could console themselves
with having " all but wiped out a two-to-one majority " and given
" an abrupt check " to " progress towards the Socialist Commonwealth ". The *Telegraph* still seemed, however, to find its main
consolation in " the final and total eclipse of the Liberal Party ",
whose intervention had been an " irrelevancy ", which was
obsessed " with old, unhappy, far-off things " and ought now to
pronounce its own dissolution. The slaughter of Communists
and fellow-travellers was " gratifying ". As for Mr. Attlee's
Government, it could hardly hope to govern effectively for long,
" and the possibility of another election, perhaps not later than
the autumn ", could not be excluded.

A point of view midway between those of the *Telegraph* and
the *Express* was voiced by the *Daily Mail*. The Government's
small majority " makes another election virtually certain, perhaps
in a few months ". Like the *Telegraph*, it blamed this " government on a razor's edge " largely on " Liberal intervention at the
polls ". " Their effort chiefly served a wrecking purpose " yet,
the *Mail* generously conceded, " they were entitled to make it ".
Let them now realise that " the game is up " and join the Tories.
The Tories have done well and should be encouraged by the
result which shows the tide is running in their favour. Finally,
the result " vindicates the two-party system ", and by the total
rejection of Communists and the record poll proves the maturity
of British democracy.

The *News Chronicle*, for the Liberals, shared in the general expectation that, as Mr. A. J. Cummings put it, " Government by one party cannot last ". Its cure for this, however, was not a fresh election, for it was not likely that that would alter anything. Instead, it asked Labour to recognise that the result deprived it of any mandate for nationalisation. But equally " the country has refused to give an unequivocal mandate to the Conservative Party ". The Liberals, " more than any other party, stand for the common ground which now exists between the Conservatives and the Socialists ". Let the leaders of all three parties meet and agree on a common programme for carrying on the government. Elsewhere the paper admitted to " the dashing of high Liberal hopes ", but said the party's effort would " remain as a memorable and enduring protest against the insufferable tyranny of the sleek, soulless party machines that seek to dominate the country ". " It was a brave effort, well worth making—and well worth making again ", and Liberals must not rest until they have a fairer voting system. It denounced as " black shame " " the insolence of those who would deny to Liberals the right to run their own candidates and the right to vote for their own party ". The fight must go on.

The *Manchester Guardian* (February 25th) viewed the situation as a stalemate. A coalition was probably impracticable, so, since the Government had to be carried on, the most sensible course would probably be for Mr. Attlee to put through an agreed Budget " and after a decent interval go to the country again ". In an analysis of the returns it found the strength of the Liberal vote " disappointing ", and felt it to be " a matter for deep discussion whether a thinly scattered vote of this kind can become the basis for a political party on national lines ". " The whole future of the Liberal Party " might be at stake in the strange political situation which now existed. In a leader on the same theme on the 27th it emphasised the smallness of the Government's majority and the fact that with only 46% of the vote it had no mandate for its full programme. This should lead it to seek a period of " mildness and conciliation " with, if possible, an agreed Budget. A further leader on " the Liberal vote " defended it against the Conservative attempt to use it as a scapegoat for defeat.

The Times of February 25th was unhappy at " the national dilemma " which the election result had produced. It would be, it felt, " to misconstrue the people's wishes to suppose that, in producing deadlock, they have voted for a coalition ". It did not favour " recourse to an indefinite period of rule by compromise ". An election " not many months from now " was, it thought, inevitable. Meanwhile *The Times* joined in favouring a working agreement between the parties, especially on the Budget. It thought that for the future Thursday's vote would " at least compel the Labour Party to make a working agreement with common sense ".

> " The programme of public ownership has almost surely been brought to a halt. The Labour leaders would do well to seize this chance of asking how much their dogged adherence to irrelevant doctrine has been a factor in their own near-downfall—and in bringing the country to this situation in which two electoral camps gaze at each other with suspicion and alarm, while the policies needed to meet the wider needs of the nation remain almost unconsidered."

But it was for the Liberals that *The Times* reserved its heaviest thunders. In its first leader on Monday, February 27th, it attacked them in defeat with a vehemence and prominence which it had never accorded them while the election was in progress. " The controllers of the Liberal organisation " had rendered a " national disservice " by preventing the electorate passing on the fundamental issue of whether they wished " the policy of Socialism to proceed " or not. Nothing could excuse " the irresponsible spattering of the electoral map with hundreds of candidatures for which there never was the remotest chance of substantial support ". When the £150 deposit rule had been introduced " it was never foreseen that a great and historic party would use its considerable financial resources to evade the spirit of the rule ". Fortunately, not many Lloyds' underwriters would be likely a second time to assume a risk that would strike with consternation the comparative realists of the turf. The Liberal Party in future could best serve Liberalism " by leaving, or helping, its supporters to judge for themselves which of the two larger parties can do most to put the Liberal spirit into practice ".

The *Daily Worker*, obliged to laugh off the greatest cataclysm of all, buried the news of Communist defeats deep in the body of its news dispatches, where it was attributed to the strength of " the two-party feeling ". The vote for Labour (which had been high in every Communist-contested seat) was now interpreted as " quite obviously a heavy vote against the Tories " (Mr. Gallacher), and, " not so much a vote of confidence so much as it was a vote opposing the Tories " (Mr. Piratin). Mr. Pollitt explained that the workers had not " understood " what they had done (although he also affirmed that " the main body of the working class has stood firm against the offensive of Toryism "). Now, however, " the great issues will be settled, not in the arena of this reactionary Parliament, but by the workers' mass struggle in the factories and the streets ".

The Conservative Sunday press added little to this range of opinion. The *Express* and the *Dispatch* had a new interest in speculating on Mr. Aneurin Bevan as the Labour Achilles sulking in his tent—this on account of his non-attendance at the Cabinet which met to consider the problems of victory. But on their editorial page both agreed in denouncing the Liberals: their behaviour was "shameful folly" to the *Express* and "selfish" to the *Dispatch*.

The popular Kemsley Sundays, the *Chronicle* and the *Empire News*, were less harsh on the Liberals than might have been expected. For Labour they advised a policy of moderation, based on the largest possible area of agreement between the parties. The *Sunday Times*, however, their ' quality ' neighbour, felt more strongly. Mr. R. C. K. Ensor, himself once a Liberal editor, mocked the " topsy-turvy satisfaction " which an ' anti-Socialist ' party achieved by returning a Socialist Government to power. The leader-writer expatiated on their " frustration and ignominy " and berated " the fatal corporate conceit of Liberal leaders " and still more " the independent newspapers which encouraged them in their folly ". For the rest, the *Sunday Times* interpreted the result as a defeat for Socialism, if not for the Labour Party, and said that Mr. Attlee had " no mandate ", and ought therefore to strive to govern " in the spirit not of party faction but of national service ". These sentiments were set against a background of conviction, in the news columns, that another election was soon inevitable and that no party contemplated entering a coalition.

The *Observer*, true to its ' independence ', abstained from both grief and joy over the outcome of the election. Mr. R. B. McCallum found the Liberal losses an unsurprising consequence of the electoral system and their struggle " a remarkable example of political fortitude ".   The accompanying leader column assessed the probabilities of the situation, advised against a coalition, prophesied accurately that the Government might well " survive for a considerable time ", and trusted the parties would both abstain from extremism.   But in retrospect it found the election unsatisfactory despite its moderation and high poll : it had looked backwards too much to the past, and fear had been a too dominant motive amongst the electorate.

The week-end passed without any more politicians' post-mortems.   But on Monday 27th Mr. Herbert Morrison gave his version of what had occurred.   The Conservatives had " over the months " past " done their very best to make this an election of an acute class character ".   Then, after an analysis of their financial backing in terms almost identical with Mr. Morgan Phillips's, he added : " Well, they have not won the election, in spite of all their varied labels and aliases, the support of large numbers of newspapers, and an unscrupulous campaign ".   Then followed a description of the fate which had befallen " the stooges and converts ", who had been beaten by Labour.   As for the Liberals, they had " made a brave effort " and Lloyds had " lost a lot of money " by ensuring their deposits.   " The gentlemen of the City really should be more careful about politics, because they are not too well informed."   Were the Liberals " a party of progress or of vacillation or of reaction " ?   Mr. Morrison remained puzzled, and thought that they had been damaged " partly because they had no clear, independent policy, and partly because they were injured by the Tory-like speeches of some of their leaders, and the partially pro-Conservative leading articles of some of the Liberal newspapers ".   Mr. Morrison hazarded no further speculation about what had damaged the Labour Party.

Mr. Churchill reserved his post-election comments for the debate on the address in the House of Commons on March 7th. He quoted with approval the comment of *The Times* on the Liberal candidatures, and added some familiar criticisms of his own, though using the constitutional injustice done to 2,600,000 voters as an argument for a Select Committee on electoral reform.   As for the main issue of the election, that consisted, of course, in the clash between the conception of the Socialist State and individual freedom :

> " It is a significant and serious fact which should not escape the attention of thoughtful men that the differences which separate us have become more pronounced by the voting, because each of the main parties has very often increased its strength in those very parts of the country where it was already the stronger. We shall certainly not survive by splitting into two nations. Yet that is the road we are travelling now, and there is no sign of our reaching or even approaching our journey's end.
>
> " The basic fact before us is that the electors by a majority of 1,750,000 have voted against the advance to a Socialist State, and, in particular, against the nationalisation of steel and other industries which were threatened. The Government, therefore, have no mandate, as is recognised in the Gracious Speech, to proceed in this Parliament with their main policy." *

The source and the setting of these post-election analyses reflect the political sympathies of the speakers ; they were also, as a result of the peculiar events of February 23rd, all made with one eye on the second general election, which, as *The Times* Parliamentary Correspondent put it, was " increasingly likely " to come within three or four months. This was particularly obvious in the references to the Liberals, whose vote each party hoped to secure next time. Is there anything that can be said from a more detached point of view about the causes and the significance of the results ? A close analysis of the figures themselves points to various conclusions. These are set out in the Appendix by Mr. David Butler on pp. 316–327. What follows here must necessarily be of a more speculative character.

In many ways the most remarkable feature of the results was the high turnout. The Coventry divisions which ran out of ballot papers symbolised, in an unhappy form, the unprecedented interest of the voters. The thesis that this could be attributed to the effect of the broadcasts has been discussed and rejected on p. 128. But it must also be admitted that attendance at

* House of Commons Debates, March 7th, 1950, c. 154–5.

U

meetings, though mainly good, was not especially notable. In
fact, as everyone agreed, the election campaign had borne few
outward testimonies to the widespread awareness revealed on
polling day.   It is more reasonable to believe that the interest of
the voting public had been built up and maintained long before
the campaign started.   Improved literacy and education no doubt
deserve their share of the credit; the greatly increased sale of
newspapers per head of population may point in the same direction.   But perhaps more important was the growing pressure,
agreeable or disagreeable, of the activities of government upon the
individual, so that even the least political of citizens had been
made aware of what he owed, for good or bad, to those who controlled the machinery of State.   Working on this awareness, and
preparing for an election long foreseeable, were party organisations
more extensive and effective than ever before, whose canvassing
and knocking-up on polling day turned interest, and often even
indifference, into votes.

To ask why this poll divided amongst the parties in the way it
did is to take another step into the conjectural.   The figures of
swing indicate how small a change in terms of percentages of those
voting is represented by the sweeping parliamentary contrasts of
1945 and 1950—a mere 3%.   Why did Labour lose this small
percentage of the votes which meant so much to it in Parliament ?
The lack of any statistical unit in British election results smaller
than the constituency makes any neat correlation of voting behaviour with occupation, income or class virtually impossible.
Fortunately for the health of our society, there are no socially
monochrome constituencies.   Consequently the shifts of Labour's
strength depicted on the electoral map of Britain give only broad
hints, not precise answers to our question.   The clearest of such
pointers is to be found in the fact that Labour's losses were
heaviest in the dormitory areas of the big towns, particularly of
London.   These are the residential areas *par excellence* of the
middle and lower-middle class, the office worker, or the professional man.   Every hint gained from other sources * confirms
the impression that these were the groups for whom Labour's
gospel had lost most of its appeal.

* Notably the B.I.P.O. analysis which showed that whereas in 1945 54% of
those rated as middle class would vote Conservative, 21% Labour and 11%
Liberal, by 1950 the figures had moved to 63% Conservative, 16% Labour,
13% Liberal.

Much was said before, during and after the election of the allegiance of the rural vote. But here, too, the unit of comparison was too large. In the strict sense of an area in which all the voters are directly connected with the soil there are no rural constituencies in Britain. Every so-called rural constituency contains towns and industries, large or small, and a wide diversity of occupation. When the *Daily Mirror* sent their " Mr. Ruggles " around the country to conduct their electoral post-mortem, there was one discovery which that perspicacious observer made that had often eluded other eyes—namely, that even in country areas farm workers are in a minority. Even supposing therefore, what is by no means certain, that Labour in rural constituencies in 1945 commanded the support of the agricultural workers, its losses in those same territories in 1950 would not necessarily reflect a change in their opinions. In fact, Labour losses in the rural areas were below their national average—under 2% in the West Country, the South-West and East Anglia, compared with 3% for the country as a whole and 8½% in highly-urbanised Middlesex. But, of course, even in 1945 these were areas of Labour weakness; all that the 1950 results show is that they were not the main sources of Labour's decline.

If it is hard to be sure whose support Labour lost, it is even harder to say why they lost it. Only one of the main issues canvassed can be given a territorial attachment strong enough to warrant an attempt to link it to constituency returns. That is unemployment. Even for this such an operation is most hazardous, so numerous are the variables which defy elimination. Nevertheless, in view of the importance which Labour attached to this appeal, it seemed worth juxtaposing some figures for unemployment incidence in the 1930's with the figures for the Labour vote in the same areas in 1950. (See table on next page.)

Of course the areas grouped together under " A " have more in common than experience of high unemployment; they are industrial and/or working class in composition; rural Wales excepted, they have a Labour tradition which antedates the thirties. Conversely, areas " B " are mainly those dormitory or quasi-residential areas whose normal allegiance has always been Conservative. For all these reasons the figures must not be pushed too far. But at the same time the fidelity to Labour of the areas with high unemployment, and the marked swing away of areas

Unemployment in the 1930's and the Labour vote in 1950

Area	% of nat. average	Lab. % 1950	Swing since 1945
London and Suburbs .	Less than 60%	47·2	6·4
Rest of Southern England	Less than 80%	38·2	3·3
Midlands . . .	About average	50·9	2·2
Scotland . . .	More than 120%	46·2	3·1
Northern England .	More than 130%	49·6	3·2
Wales	More than 160%	58·1	0·3
Whole country .	100%	46·8	3·4
"A"			
Industrial Wales . .	More than 170%	66·5	0·3
N.E. England . .	More than 160%	59·4	0·9
Clydeside . . .	More than 160%	51·2	2·8
Rural Wales . . .	More than 130%	41·9	+0·6
"B"			
Sussex . . .	Less than 50%	28·7	1·9
South-Central . .	Less than 50%	39·5	2·8
Middlesex . . .	Less than 50%	43·2	8·8
County of London .	Less than 50%	51·0	4·8
Surrey . . .	Less than 50%	34·4	5·9

(The unemployment figures for the various areas are reproduced, by kind permission, from *Prospects of the Industrial Areas of Great Britain*, by M. P. Fogarty, and are designed to show variations from the national average of unemployment in the period 1931–36.)

where it was relatively low, is certainly suggestive. It confirms to some degree the impression gathered from constituency inquiries—that the employment theme held the faithful and the older voters, but meant less to a younger generation voting for the first time in an environment where memories were less powerful and less painful. In short, where the employment argument meant anything it meant a great deal, but as an appeal to the past it necessarily lost in effectiveness with every year that went by.

The same was not true of nationalisation. Here there was no tradition, no folk-memory (save perhaps in the coalfields), only a half-hearted appeal to a not very widely or deeply held dogma. A canvasser in the London area put it well: "The Labour Party attitude to nationalisation resembles the British attitude to religion. It is regarded as something beyond dispute and rather wholesome, but at the same time rather inconvenient and without the ability to rouse fervour." It is hard to believe that it could have won a single vote for Labour, whereas the hard-pressed argument against it may well have seduced many of the otherwise faithful. No evidence exists to support the thesis advanced, in the first disappointment of victory, by certain Labour publicists, that more emphasis on nationalisation would have won Labour more votes.

For the other main issues, the differences between the two major parties were so much matters of degree, emphasis, attitude and (real or supposed) party record, that they defy separate analysis. On the social services, for example, how can it be said which of the two programmes, so largely similar, or which of the two records, neither discreditable, exercised the greater appeal for the electorate? These are mysteries which even the public opinion poll is as yet too blunt an instrument to uncover.

The debate on the Liberal vote which broke out with such vigour the moment the results were announced continued without abatement afterwards. To the Liberals the result was profoundly disappointing; it remained to be seen whether it was also disastrous. To win only 9 seats with 475 candidates, and to lose 319 deposits—this was defeat on a scale which it would be hard to parallel. The voice of the B.B.C. announcer repeating like a refrain at the end of each constituency return, " The Liberal candidate forfeited his deposit ", constituted a commentary more mocking in its objectivity than any that the harshest critic could have devised. The failure, moreover, of their sometime leader, Sir Archibald Sinclair, to recover the seat lost by so narrow a margin in 1945 was matched only by the comparable misfortune of their Chief Whip, Mr. Frank Byers, who lost his seat in North Dorset by 97 votes. Any, or indeed all of these defeats might, however, have been anticipated by the strategists of the party— and indeed to some extent probably were. What can hardly have been expected was the small number of votes that the party's candidates were able to muster between them. While the figure of 2,621,489 was an absolute advance on the 2,239,668 of 1945, per candidate it represented a decline, since in 1945 only 307 candidates had been standing. The impressive demonstration of popular support with which the party hoped to buttress its demand for a revised electoral system had been only half achieved.

Where the analysable evidence is so limited it is of little avail to ask what deficiencies, if any, in the Liberal policy accounted for their failure to attract more voters. Their deficiencies in candidates and organisation have already been discussed. Their tactical disability as a third party, attempting to recover a lost position, needs no amplification. The argument of the wasted vote, always powerful, told with particular force in a year in which every sign from public opinion polls to the man in the street's own experience demonstrated that the Liberal potential was small and the balance between Labour and Conservative was fine indeed. That over two and a half million voters could be found in these circumstances still determined to vote Liberal is rather what invites explanation. But only in the most general terms can any such explanation be offered.

If regard is had only to the seats that Liberals won, it is true that, West Huddersfield and Suffolk, Eye, apart, they are revealed as still a party of the Celtic fringe. It is also true, as the Appendix points out, that the majority of their other " good " areas fall in the same regions. But what is most significant about the Liberal vote is nevertheless its even spread. Of its 2,621,489, English counties and boroughs accounted for over a million each, 2,104,871 in all, distributed over 369 constituencies of every kind. The typical Liberal vote was a figure of five to six thousand, not varying greatly in borough or county, North or South. It was, of course, precisely the evenness of this spread which most worked against the party under the existing system of representation, and made it, parliamentarily speaking, the almost impotent organ of a ubiquitous minority. It also seems to have been a remarkably diversified minority. Analyses of the composition of Liberal voters, as revealed in B.I.P.O. polls, show that to a greater degree than any other party the Liberal Party seems to have drawn its support evenly from both sexes, all ages, all classes and all occupations.

In the heat of the ' stalemate ' one theory which was energetically canvassed was the view that the Liberal vote was made up of persons who, if no Liberal candidate had existed, would have given their votes to the Conservative, and so simultaneously broken the deadlock and installed a Conservative Government. A good deal of hypothetical arithmetic was heatedly deployed in an endeavour to put this conviction upon a statistical basis, but in fact there is little in the election results from which any certain conclusions can be drawn. A B.I.P.O. poll conducted shortly before polling day showed that 33% of Liberals said that if they had no candidate they would vote Conservative. 26% said they would vote Labour. 20% said " don't know " and 20% said " wouldn't vote ". The " don't know " and the " wouldn't vote " categories must have been deceptively swelled by Liberals who, having a flesh-and-blood candidate to whom they were committed, loyally refused to entertain a hypothetical question. In the statistical appendix figures are given which suggest that abstention by frustrated Liberals was in fact on a very small scale. But the B.I.P.O. figures do confirm the impression gained by some of the more dispassionate observers during the election that Liberal intervention drew votes from both sides fairly equally over the country as a whole, although there may have been considerable regional differences. An examination of the results in some of the constituencies whose boundaries were unchanged gives further confirmation to this impression. In 1950 there were 26 seats fought by all three leading parties which in 1945 had been contested solely by Conservative and Labour. On balance, the swing in these constituencies averaged almost 1% more than the swing in the areas surrounding them. This would suggest that as a result of Liberal intervention Labour fared slightly worse than they would otherwise have done. It should be pointed out, however, that 19 of these 26 seats were in the London area, and even apart from this geographic bias, the sample is too small and the argument too tenuous for confident national conclusions to be drawn from them. But they do offer some evidence to set against the supposition held by many partisans that Liberal intervention hurt the Conservatives much more than Labour.

Many equally extravagant claims were made about the responsibility of the Liberals for producing ' the parliamentary stalemate '. If all who voted Liberal had supported the Conservatives, that party would have won 69 seats which in the event went to Labour. But such a hypothesis is obviously absurd. Opinion may differ on how the Liberals would have divided in their choice of second-best, but few would suggest that either side would secure as much as a 30% majority amongst them. A 30% majority implies a 65–35% split, or perhaps a 50–20% split, with 30% abstaining. If 30% of the net Liberal vote had been transferred to the Conservatives, 17 Labour seats would have fallen to them. A 20% transfer would have produced a turnover of 12 seats, and a 10% transfer a turnover of 5. On the less likely assumption that the absence of Liberal candidates would have benefited Labour, a

10% transfer of votes would have given Labour an additional 11 seats. In fact no likely division of the Liberal vote would have produced what is normally regarded as a decisive parliamentary majority.

Whatever the country's reasons for rejecting Liberals and liberal-minded Independents, they did not include an addiction to extremism either of the Left or the Right. That is proved by the moderation of the Labour and Conservative programmes and, still more, by the fate of the Communists and the fellow-travellers. Whichever way the Communist vote is viewed, whether as a percentage of the national whole, or as a percentage of the poll wherever they stood, or in terms of candidates successful, or by numbers of deposits lost, it remains a record of sheer, unmitigated disaster. By comparison their 1945 performance—two seats instead of none and 10% more votes with less than one quarter the number of candidates standing—was a triumphant victory.

Whichever way the election results are regarded, it seems impossible to deny that they constituted a mandate for moderation. The parties anticipated as much in the presentation of their programmes, the voters implied as much by their behaviour during the campaign. The votes, when counted, made it clear that no party could claim to have swept the field. This was so obvious that it is hard to see how the opinion could have originated, to which Mr. Churchill lent his support,* that the result revealed a country split into two nations. Only an obsession with those most misleading visual representations of the results—maps of Britain shaded to indicate constituency victories—could excuse so erroneous an interpretation. It was true that Labour continued to hold those urban and industrial areas which have always been its mainstay and that Conservatism continued to find its greatest strength in the counties. But the most superficial examination of constituency returns will reveal that there was no part of the country in which the two major parties did not have sizeable bodies of supporters—as the figures for lost deposits further testify. If this is true territorially, it is scarcely less true socially. For the social composition of the British parties there is the clear evidence of the public opinion polls. The following is a breakdown of the B.I.P.O. polls taken during the election :

* See *supra* p. 295.

	Con.	Lab.	Lib.	Other	Don't know
Upper class . .	77	8·5	11·5	1	2
Middle class . .	63	16	13	1	7
Working class .	29	48	9	1	13
Men . . .	38	42	10	1	9
Women . .	38·5	37	10	0·5	14
Aged 21–29 . .	36	45	10	1	13
Aged 30–49 . .	39	41	10	1	9
Aged 50–64 . .	45	33	10	1	11
Aged 65 and over .	33	40	11	—	7

This table makes clear beyond dispute that while there were several interesting and significant differences in the composition of the parties, each of them embraced a sizeable proportion of every group. Even the disparity between Conservatives and Labour in respect of social class (defined as a combination of social standing and income) is less pronounced than at first sight it appears ; if the Conservatives had a markedly stronger hold on the affections of the upper and middle classes, the working classes (three-quarters of the electorate) divided roughly in the proportion of 3 : 5. Indeed, if no such division occurred, no election could ever be won by the Conservative Party. But that does not imply the reverse proposition, that when an election is not won by the Conservatives a dangerous fissure has developed in the country.

A British general election is generally expected to do three things : return a government, provide a ' mandate ', and educate the electorate by the processes of public debate. The General Election of 1950, though it had many admirable features, failed to perform any of these functions satisfactorily. It did indeed return the Labour Government of Mr. Attlee, but by a margin of seats so small that defeat in the division lobbies was a constant possibility, and the parliamentary burden thereby laid upon Ministers and Members was the heaviest in a century. As to the Government's ' mandate ', opinions naturally differed on each side of the House, but the omission of fresh nationalisation proposals from the King's Speech suggested that even the Government agreed that these features of its programme had received no endorsement from the electorate. However, at that point clarity ceased. As to Iron

and Steel, the Government adhered to their position that it had
not properly been an election issue at all, though to the extent that
it had been their majority constituted an endorsement of the
action already taken. The Opposition contended that it had
been a principal issue (they had frequently tried to make it so)
and that the Government's narrow majority laid on them an
obligation to halt the operation of the 1949 Act. For the rest,
since the principal issues of the election had not been legislative,
but administrative—employment, housing, controls, taxation and
expenditure, etc.—there was an even wider scope than usual for
disagreement over their implications, the permissible limits of
action by Government and Opposition, and—so similar had the
parties' programmes often been—over the relationship of election
pledges to motions and votes in the House of Commons.

Were the fuzziness of its ' mandate ' the worst feature of the
February result, the 1950 Election would not, however, have
differed very seriously from the general run of such contests. The
most serious criticism which can be made of it lies elsewhere. It
is that for all its admirable reasonableness and sobriety, its high
poll and its low tempers, the election did not bring squarely before
the public the crucial issues of the time. No one, even amongst
the contestants, denied that diplomatically and militarily the
country was in the gravest peril; only an occasional political
Pangloss could regard our economic position as anything but
critical. Yet foreign affairs was virtually excluded from election
print and speech until Mr. Churchill spoke at Edinburgh, and the
problems of our balance of payments were seldom put in the forefront of discussion even at the beginning; as the campaign
continued they counted for less and less. There were many
reasons for these omissions, not all discreditable. Foreign affairs
does not easily lend itself to electoral debate, least of all when
there is substantial agreement between the major parties. As Mr.
Churchill's speech showed, there are dangers as well as benefits in
injecting certain issues into a campaign. Economics, once it gets
away from the pay packet and the grocer's bill, is a difficult topic
to distil into the liquor of electioneering. Moreover, politicians
in the main showed a very proper reluctance to win power by
promises which they could not keep. Then, too, the Britain of
1950 had had a rich diet of ' crises ' ever since the thirties; the
politician who put such a dish in front of the electorate ran the

risk of surfeiting his public. Above all, perhaps, no party could honestly propound any guaranteed remedy for our national ills, so much did their cure transcend the powers of Parliament and the boundaries of national sovereignty.

Nonetheless, the fact remained that at a moment when our national survival was at stake the fundamental issues were most of the time buried beneath other considerations which, important enough in themselves, were by comparison almost grotesquely trivial and irrelevant. Nothing, for example, could have been less related to the problems of the fifties than the constant harping on the memories and legends of the thirties. Such assiduous " myth-making " was a form of escapism for which there was no legitimate excuse. A harsh critic might even say that most of the election was an exercise in escapism, that, shutting out the intractable bogeys of the atom and hydrogen bombs, of Russian aggression and the end of Marshall Aid, the nation forgot its cares for a few brief weeks in the cosy and familiar operations of democratic electioneering, the manœuvres, the poses, the clichés, the personalities, the arithmetic, the hard fight bounded by the rigid rules, like a moving picture set in a dark frame. To say this would be to say too much. The election was by no means all escapism, and the cosy ritual of electioneering is not separable from the gymnastic exercises which keep the muscles of democracy from getting flabby and the rump of government from waxing over-fat. Nevertheless, these indispensable functions have often been combined—and are best performed when combined—with a frank and intelligible exposition to the electorate of all the problems of State. In 1950 that exposition was all too seldom attempted and only very rarely achieved.

APPENDIX

AN EXAMINATION OF THE RESULTS
By D. E. BUTLER

I. The National Result

(a) *Votes*

Elector-ate	Votes cast	Conser-vative	Labour	Liberal	Com-munist	Other
34,269,770	28,772,671	12,502,567	13,266,592	2,621,548	91,684	290,218

(b) *Candidates*

Total	Cons.	Lab.	Lib.	Com.	Other
1,868	620	617	475	100	56

(c) *Members Elected*

Total	Cons.	Lab.	Lib.	Com.	Other
625	298	315	9	—	3

II. The Result Tabulated

(a) THE WHOLE COUNTRY	Electorate (in '000s)	% Voting	Members Elected					Votes (as % of votes cast in constituencies where the party concerned put up candidates)[1]					Swing since 1945 (average of Con. % gain and Lab. % loss)
			Total	Con.	Lab.	Lib.	Other	Con.	Lab.	Lib.	Com.	Other	
UNITED KINGDOM .	34,141	84·0	625	298	315	9	3	620† 43·7	617 46·7	475 11·8	100 2·0	56 12·6	3·3
GREAT BRITAIN													
England .	28,373	84·4	506	252	251	2	1	504 44·0	505 46·2	413 11·4	80 1·4	26 9·2	3·6
Wales . .	1,802	84·9	36	4	27	5	—	35 28·3	36 58·1	21 21·2	4 5·2	9 5·3	0·3
Scotland .	3,370	80·9	71	32	37	2	—	69 46·2	71 46·2	41 11·5	16 4·1	15 5·2	3·1
Total .	33,545	84·1	613	288	315	9	1	608 43·3	612 46·8	475 11·8	100 2·0	50 7·5	3·4

For notes see pages 313–316.

(b) AREAS OF ENGLAND	Electorate (in '000s)	% Voting	Members Elected					Votes (as % of votes cast in constituencies where the party concerned put up candidates)[1]					Swing since 1945 (average of Con. % gain and Lab. % loss)
			Total	Con.	Lab.	Lib.	Other	Con.	Lab.	Lib.	Com.	Other	
ENGLAND													
London Area	5,764	82·6	98	45	53	—	—	98 / 43·2	98 / 47·2	98 / 8·6	36 / 1·9	8 / 5·5	6·4
South and East	7,900	84·2	144	111	32	1	—	144 / 49·2	144 / 38·2	131 / 13·5	12 / 0·8	5 / 9·9	3·3
Midlands	5,321	85·0	94	35	59	—	—	94 / 41·0	94 / 50·9	66 / 10·7	9 / 0·9	4 / 11·4	2·2
North	9,387	85·4	170	61	107	1	1	168 / 41·8	169 / 49·6	118 / 12·1	23 / 1·3	9 / 11·2	3·2
Total	28,373	84·4	506	252	251	2	1	504 / 44·0	505 / 46·2	413 / 11·4	80 / 1·4	26 / 9·2	3·6
LONDON AREA													
A. County of London	2,436	79·3	43	12	31	—	—	43 / 39·7	43 / 51·0	43 / 7·4	19 / 2·3	5 / 7·9	4·8
B. Suburban Boroughs	3,328	85·0	55	33	22	—	—	55 / 45·5	55 / 44·6	55 / 9·3	17 / 1·4	3 / 1·2	7·2
Total	5,764	82·6	98	45	53	—	—	98 / 43·2	98 / 47·2	98 / 8·6	36 / 1·9	8 / 5·5	6·4
SOUTH AND EAST													
C. South-east	2,015	83·6	35	32	3	—	—	35 / 55·1	35 / 34·4	33 / 11·0	1 / 0·7	1 / 1·3	4·1
D. Wessex	1,144	83·2	20	18	2	—	—	20 / 52·4	20 / 37·1	14 / 15·2	1 / 0·5	1 / 2·5	4·4
E. West of England	794	84·6	15	12	3	—	—	15 / 48·4	15 / 32·7	14 / 20·2	1 / 0·8	—	1·1
F. Severn	1,173	85·3	22	14	8	—	—	22 / 42·5	22 / 43·5	20 / 13·3	3 / 0·9	2 / 20·0	1·5
G. South-Central	1,333	85·1	25	18	7	—	—	25 / 47·3	25 / 39·5	25 / 13·1	5 / 0·8	—	2·8
H. Essex	558	84·0	10	8	2	—	—	10 / 48·5	10 / 41·1	9 / 10·7	—	1 / 9·8	8·1
I. East Anglia	882	84·0	17	9	7	1	—	17 / 44·4	17 / 42·3	16 / 13·9	1 / 0·6	—	1·7
Total	7,900	84·2	144	111	32	1	—	144 / 49·2	144 / 38·2	131 / 13·5	12 / 0·8	5 / 9·9	3·3
MIDLANDS													
J. West Midlands	2,976	84·1	52	20	32	—	—	52 / 42·7	52 / 51·2	31 / 9·6	4 / 0·9	2 / 9·7	2·6
K. North-east Midlands	1,866	86·8	33	9	24	—	—	33 / 37·2	33 / 52·4	29 / 11·5	5 / 0·9	1 / 0·5	1·7
L. Lincolnshire	479	83·6	9	6	3	—	—	9 / 45·9	9 / 42·8	6 / 12·2	—	1 / 27·5	0·9
Total	5,321	85·0	94	35	59	—	—	94 / 41·0	94 / 50·9	66 / 10·7	9 / 0·9	4 / 11·4	2·2
NORTH OF ENGLAND													
M. Cheshire	877	86·9	15	12	3	—	—	15 / 50·6	15 / 37·3	14 / 12·9	2 / 1·3	—	3·1
N. Lancashire	3,551	85·0	64	25	39	—	—	64 / 45·2	64 / 46·9	47 / 9·7	11 / 1·3	3 / 1·3	3·8
O. West Riding	2,429	86·0	45	11	33	1	—	44 / 37·1	45 / 55·6	26 / 13·3	7 / 1·6	1 / 2·6	3·7
P. East and North Riding	644	83·3	11	8	3	—	—	11 / 47·4	11 / 38·2	11 / 14·2	—	1 / 2·3	4·2
Q. North-east	1,560	85·7	28	2	26	—	—	28 / 33·9	28 / 59·4	15 / 10·8	3 / 0·8	2 / 7·9	0·9
R. Border	326	82·6	7	3	3	—	1	6 / 42·1	6 / 39·5	5 / 21·8	—	2 / 100·0	1·6
Total	9,387	85·4	170	61	107	1	1	168 / 41·8	169 / 49·6	118 / 12·1	23 / 1·3	9 / 11·2	3·2

For notes and explanation of areas see pages 313–316.

(c) Sub-Areas of England	Electorate (in '000s)	% Voting	Members Elected — Total	Con.	Lab.	Lib.	Other	Votes (as % of votes cast in constituencies where the party concerned put up candidates)[1] — Con.	Lab.	Lib.	Com.	Other	Swing since 1945 (average of Con. % gain and Lab. % loss)
County of London													
South of Thames	1,133	81·9	20	6	14	—	—	^{20}39·9	^{20}53·1	^{20}6·4	^{8}1·4	^{1}0·6	5·4
East End	369	76·4	6	—	6	—	—	^{6}20·0	^{6}62·7	^{6}11·1	^{4}5·2	^{2}7·9	2·2
Business and Residential	464	75·3	8	6	2	—	—	^{8}56·6	^{8}33·3	^{8}9·0	^{4}1·8	^{1}0·5	5·2
Remainder	470	79·1	9	—	9	—	—	^{9}38·1	^{9}53·6	^{9}5·6	^{3}1·6	^{1}25·2	3·7 §
Total	2,436	79·3	43	12	31	—	—	^{43}39·7	^{43}51·0	^{43}7·4	^{19}2·3	^{5}7·9	4·8
Suburban Boroughs													
Middlesex	1,631	85·2	28	17	11	—	—	^{28}46·3	^{28}43·2	^{28}10·0	^{10}1·5	—	7·1
Kent and Surrey	845	86·2	13	12	1	—	—	^{13}52·8	^{13}38·6	^{13}8·5	^{2}0·8	—	8·8 *
Essex	851	83·5	14	4	10	—	—	^{14}36·7	^{14}53·7	^{14}8·9	^{5}1·4	^{3}1·2	8·2
Total	3,328	85·0	55	33	22	—	—	^{55}45·5	^{55}44·6	^{55}9·3	^{17}1·4	^{3}1·2	7·2
South-East England													
Kent	804	84·5	14	11	3	—	—	^{14}50·9	^{14}40·8	^{12}9·3	^{1}0·7	^{1}1·3	5·1 *
Surrey	543	85·1	10	10	—	—	—	^{10}57·1	^{10}31·5	^{10}11·4	—	—	4·0
Sussex	668	81·5	11	11	—	—	—	^{11}58·7	^{11}28·7	^{11}12·5	—	—	1·9
Total	2,015	83·6	35	32	3	—	—	^{35}55·1	^{35}34·4	^{33}11·0	^{1}0·7	^{1}1·3	4·1
Wessex													
Hampshire Ports	367	83·7	6	4	2	—	—	^{6}53·0	^{6}43·2	^{3}6·5	^{1}0·5	^{1}2·5	7·6
Remainder	777	83·0	14	14	—	—	—	^{14}52·2	^{14}34·2	^{11}17·9	—	—	3·0
Total	1,144	83·2	20	18	2	—	—	^{20}52·4	^{20}37·1	^{14}15·2	^{1}0·5	^{1}2·5	4·4
West of England													
Cornwall	241	83·5	5	4	1	—	—	^{5}44·2	^{5}29·6	^{5}26·2	—	—	2·2 ‖
Devon (exc. Plymouth)	417	84·5	8	8	—	—	—	^{8}51·9	^{8}29·0	^{7}21·9	^{1}0·8	—	0·5
Plymouth	136	86·8	2	—	2	—	—	^{2}45·5	^{2}49·2	^{2}5·3	—	—	3·4 *
Total	794	84·6	15	12	3	—	—	^{15}48·4	^{15}32·7	^{14}20·2	^{1}0·8	—	1·1

For notes and explanation of areas see pages 313–316.

(c) Sub-Areas of England (cont.)	Electorate (in '000s)	% Voting	Members Elected					Votes (as % of votes cast in constituencies where the party concerned put up candidates)[1]					Swing since 1945 (average of Con. % gain and Lab. % loss)
			Total	Con.	Lab.	Lib.	Other	Con.	Lab.	Lib.	Com.	Other	
SEVERN													
Somerset	387	86·8	7	7	—	—	—	[7] 47·0	[7] 38·3	[6] 14·7	—	[1] 15·1	1·6
Glos. and N. Wilts. (exc. Bristol)	474	84·5	9	5	4	—	—	[9] 40·8	[9] 43·2	[8] 14·7	[2] 0·8	[1] 25·2	1·4
Bristol	312	84·4	6	2	4	—	—	[6] 39·3	[6] 50·6	[6] 9·9	[1] 1·1	—	2·9 *
Total	1,173	85·3	22	14	8	—	—	[22] 42·5	[22] 43·5	[20] 13·3	[3] 0·9	[2] 20·0	1·5
SOUTH-CENTRAL													
Oxon, Berks., Bucks.	711	84·1	14	9	5	—	—	[14] 47·3	[14] 38·9	[14] 13·5	[4] 0·9	—	1·9
Beds., and Herts.	622	86·1	11	9	2	—	—	[11] 47·3	[11] 40·1	[11] 12·6	[1] 0·5	—	3·9
Total	1,333	85·1	25	18	7	—	—	[25] 47·3	[25] 39·5	[25] 13·1	[5] 0·8	—	2·8
ESSEX	558	84·0	10	8	2	—	—	[10] 48·5	[10] 41·1	[9] 10·7	—	[1] 9·8	8·1
EAST ANGLIA													
Norfolk	365	84·3	8	3	5	—	—	[8] 44·2	[8] 46·9	[7] 10·0	—	—	2·3
Suffolk, Ely, Hunts., Cambs.	517	83·8	9	6	2	1	—	[9] 44·5	[9] 39·0	[9] 16·4	[1] 0·6	—	1·2
Total	882	84·0	17	9	7	1	—	[17] 44·4	[17] 42·3	[16] 13·9	[1] 0·6	—	1·7
WEST MIDLANDS													
Birmingham	765	81·9	13	4	9	—	—	[13] 42·7	[13] 51·8	[10] 6·6	[3] 0·9	[1] 0·7	2·4
Coventry	176	87·7	3	—	3	—	—	[3] 36·7	[3] 56·6	[3] 6·4	[1] 1·0	—	4·3
Black Country	618	85·2	10	1	9	—	—	[10] 34·9	[10] 57·4	[6] 12·9	—	—	2·7 *
Potteries	247	85·2	4	—	4	—	—	[4] 33·2	[4] 64·8	[1] 8·1	—	—	3·1 *
Staffs. and Warwick Counties	680	85·6	12	6	6	—	—	[12] 47·6	[12] 47·1	[5] 9·7	—	[1] 20·7	3·0 *
Salop, Hereford, Worcs.	490	82·3	10	9	1	—	—	[10] 52·9	[10] 39·0	[6] 13·2	—	—	3·0‖
Total	2,976	84·1	52	20	32	—	—	[52] 42·7	[52] 51·2	[31] 9·6	[4] 0·9	[2] 9·7	2·6

For notes and explanation of areas see pages 313–316.

(c) Sub-Areas of England (cont.)	Electorate (in '000s)	% Voting	Members Elected					Votes (as % of votes cast in constituencies where the party concerned put up candidates)[1]					Swing since 1945 (average of Con. % gain and Lab. % loss)
			Total	Con.	Lab.	Lib.	Other	Con.	Lab.	Lib.	Com.	Other	
North-East Midlands													
Nottingham	205	84·7	4	—	4	—	—	4 / 37·8	4 / 51·0	4 / 10·8	1 / 1·5	—	2·4 *
Leicester	203	85·4	4	1	3	—	—	4 / 38·5	4 / 50·3	4 / 11·0	1 / 0·8	—	2·3 *
Leics., Notts., Northants.	888	87·5	15	6	9	—	—	15 / 38·9	15 / 50·4	13 / 11·9	2 / 0·8	1 / 0·5	1·3
Derbyshire	569	87·1	10	2	8	—	—	10 / 33·8	10 / 56·8	8 / 11·4	1 / 1·0	—	1·3
Total	1,865	86·8	33	9	24	—	—	33 / 37·2	33 / 52·4	29 / 11·5	5 / 0·9	1 / 0·5	1·7
Lincolnshire	479	83·6	9	6	3	—	—	9 / 45·9	9 / 42·8	6 / 12·2	—	1 / 27·5	0·9
Cheshire	877	86·9	15	12	3	—	—	15 / 50·6	15 / 37·3	14 / 12·9	2 / 1·3	—	3·1
Lancashire													
Liverpool	518	80·1	9	5	4	—	—	9 / 48·0	9 / 46·1	6 / 8·2	1 / 1·4	1 / 1·1	2·5 *
Manchester	480	82·2	9	3	6	—	—	9 / 42·9	9 / 48·1	8 / 9·4	3 / 1·4	—	4·4 *
South Lancs.	2,027	87·0	36	9	27	—	—	36 / 42·6	36 / 49·2	25 / 11·2	6 / 1·2	2 / 1·3	3·8
North Lancs.	527	84·7	10	8	2	—	—	10 / 54·7	10 / 37·6	8 / 9·6	1 / 0·8	—	8·8
Total	3,551	85·0	64	25	39	—	—	64 / 45·2	64 / 46·9	47 / 9·7	11 / 1·3	3 / 1·3	3·8
West Riding													
Sheffield	368	86·0	7	2	5	—	—	7 / 39·4	7 / 57·7	7 / 7·1	3 / 2·0	—	3·2 *§
Leeds	358	83·8	7	2	5	—	—	7 / 42·2	7 / 50·1	7 / 7·4	1 / 1·6	—	7·6 *
Bradford	208	85·8	4	1	3	—	—	4 / 35·0	4 / 51·7	4 / 13·0	1 / 1·2	—	0·6 §
Remainder	1,495	87·1	27	6	20	1	—	26 / 35·7	27 / 56·9	13 / 16·9	2 / 1·3	1 / 2·6	3·2 *
Total	2,429	86·4	45	11	33	1	—	44 / 37·1	45 / 55·6	26 / 13·3	7 / 1·6	1 / 2·6	3·7
North and East Riding County Divisions and York	421	83·2	7	6	1	—	—	7 / 51·9	7 / 32·6	7 / 15·2	—	1 / 2·3	4·3 *||
Hull	223	83·5	4	2	2	—	—	4 / 38·9	4 / 48·7	4 / 12·4	—	—	8·6 *
Total	644	83·3	11	8	3	—	—	11 / 47·4	11 / 38·2	11 / 14·2	—	1 / 2·3	4·2

For notes and explanation of areas see pages 313–316.

(c) SUB-AREAS OF ENGLAND (cont.)

	Electorate (in '000s)	% Voting	Members Elected					Votes (as % of votes cast in constituencies where the party concerned put up candidates)[1]					Swing since 1945 (average of Con. % gain and Lab. % loss)
			Total	Con.	Lab.	Lib.	Other	Con.	Lab.	Lib.	Com.	Other	
NORTH-EAST ENGLAND													
Newcastle .	223	84·3	4	1	3	—	—	[4] 42·3	[4] 52·0	[2] 9·8	[1] 0·9	[1] 2·1	2·2 *
Boroughs .	791	85·5	14	1	13	—	—	[14] 35·5	[14] 54·6	[10] 11·8	[2] 0·7	[1] 14·8	0·9 *
Durham County Divisions .	545	86·6	10	—	10	—	—	[10] 28·2	[10] 69·2	[3] 8·2	—	—	-0·9 *
Total .	1,560	85·7	28	2	26	—	—	[28] 33·9	[28] 59·4	[15] 10·8	[3] 0·8	[2] 7·9	0·9
BORDER .	326	82·6	7	3	3	—	1	[6] 42·1	[6] 39·5	[5] 21·8	—	[2] 100·0	1·6

(d) AREAS OF WALES

	Electorate (in '000s)	% Voting	Members Elected					Votes (as % of votes cast in constituencies where the party concerned put up candidates)[1]					Swing since 1945 (average of Con. % gain and Lab. % loss)
			Total	Con.	Lab.	Lib.	Other	Con.	Lab.	Lib.	Com.	Other	
WALES													
S. Rural Wales .	616	84·8	13	2	6	5	—	[35] 32·4	[36] 41·9	[21] 30·0	—	[9] 7·3 §	-0·6
T. Industrial Wales .	1,186	84·9	23	2	21	—	—	[12] 26·4	[13] 66·5	[12] 11·8	[4] 5·2	[3] 4·4	0·3
Total .	1,802	84·9	36	4	27	5	—	[35] 28·3	[36] 58·1	[21] 21·2	[4] 5·2	[9] 5·3	0·3
INDUSTRIAL WALES													
Cardiff, Swansea, Newport .	365	84·1	6	1	5	—	—	[6] 39·9	[6] 53·9	[3] 11·5	—	—	3·7 *
Remainder .	821	85·2	17	1	16	—	—	[17] 20·4	[17] 72·0	[6] 11·9	[4] 5·2	[6] 4·4	-2·3 *
Total .	1,186	84·9	23	2	21	—	—	[12] 26·4	[13] 66·5	[12] 11·8	[4] 5·2	[3] 4·4	0·3

For notes and explanation of areas see pages 313–316.

X

(e) AREAS OF SCOTLAND	Electorate (in '000s)	% Voting	Members Elected					Votes (as % of votes cast in constituencies where the party concerned put up candidates)[1]					Swing since 1945 (average of Con. % gain and Lab. % loss)
			Total	Con.	Lab.	Lib.	Other	Con.	Lab.	Lib.	Com.	Other	
SCOTLAND													
U. Highlands	291	71·7	8	6	1	1	—	(7) 51·7	(8) 29·8	(6) 25·7	—	(3) 5·7	2·3 ‖
V. North-East	472	82·1	10	7	3	—	—	(10) 50·0	(10) 40·6	(7) 12·3	(2) 2·5	—	4·5
W. Clyde	1,337	81·6	27	9	18	—	—	(26) 44·1	(27) 51·2	(14) 6·6	(9) 3·5	(9) 6·2	2·8 §
X. Forth	741	82·2	15	5	10	—	—	(15) 44·7	(15) 47·5	(9) 9·3	(4) 6·8	(3) 2·4	2·4
Y. Lowlands	528	81·3	11	5	5	1	—	(11) 47·4	(11) 45·5	(5) 16·2	(1) 2·2	—	4·2 ‖
Total	3,370	80·9	71	32	37	2	—	(69) 46·2	(71) 46·2	(41) 11·5	(16) 4·1	(15) 5·2	3·1
CLYDE													
Glasgow	719	80·0	15	7	8	—	—	(15) 44·4	(15) 49·8	(9) 5·2	(6) 3·9	(5) 3·5	1·1 §
Lanark, Dumbarton, Renfrew	618	83·5	12	2	10	—	—	(11) 43·8	(12) 52·8	(5) 9·0	(3) 2·8	(4) 10·0	3·9
Total	1,337	81·6	27	9	18	—	—	(26) 44·1	(27) 51·2	(14) 6·6	(9) 3·5	(9) 6·2	2·8 §
FORTH													
Edinburgh	344	80·7	7	4	3	—	—	(7) 49·7	(7) 40·9	(7) 9·1	(1) 1·9	(1) 1·1	5·4 *
Fife, Stirling, W. Lothian	397	83·5	8	1	7	—	—	(8) 40·5	(8) 53·1	(2) 9·9	(3) 8·1	(2) 3·0	0·0 §
Total	741	82·2	15	5	10	—	—	(15) 44·7	(15) 47·5	(9) 9·3	(4) 6·8	(3) 2·4	24

(f) NORTHERN IRELAND	Electorate (in '000s)	% Voting	Members Elected					Votes (as % of votes cast in constituencies where the party concerned put up candidates)[1]					Swing since 1945 (average of Con. % gain and Lab. % loss)
			Total	Con.	Lab.	Lib.	Other	Con.	Lab.	Lib.	Com.	Other	
Z. Northern Ireland	725	77·5	12	10	—	—	2	(12†) 62·8	(5) 27·0	—	—	(6) 45·6	**

For notes and explanation of areas see pages 313–316.

(g) LARGE CITIES	Electorate (in '000s)	% Voting	Members Elected					Votes (as % of votes cast in constituencies where the party concerned put up candidates)[1]					Swing since 1945 (average of Con. % gain and Lab. % loss)
			Total	Con.	Lab.	Lib.	Other	Con.	Lab.	Lib.	Com.	Other	
County of London . .	2,436	79·3	43	12	31	—	—	[43] 39·7	[43] 51·0	[43] 7·4	[19] 2·3	[5] 7·9	4·8
Glasgow .	719	80·0	15	7	8	—	—	[15] 44·4	[15] 49·8	[9] 5·2	[6] 3·9	[5] 3·5	1·1 *§
Birmingham .	765	81·9	13	4	9	—	—	[13] 42·7	[13] 51·8	[10] 6·6	[3] 0·9	[1] 0·7	2·4
Liverpool .	518	80·1	9	5	4	—	—	[9] 48·0	[9] 46·1	[8] 8·2	[1] 1·4	[1] 1·1	2·5 *
Manchester .	480	82·2	9	3	6	—	—	[9] 42·9	[9] 48·1	[8] 9·4	[3] 1·4	—	4·4 *
Sheffield .	368	86·0	7	2	5	—	—	[7] 39·4	[7] 57·7	[7] 7·1	[2] 2·0	—	3·2 *§
Leeds . .	358	83·8	7	2	5	—	—	[7] 42·2	[7] 50·1	[7] 7·4	[1] 1·6	—	7·6 *
Edinburgh .	344	80·7	7	4	3	—	—	[7] 49·7	[7] 40·9	[7] 9·1	[1] 1·9	[1] 0·8	5·4 *
Bristol .	312	84·4	6	2	4	—	—	[6] 39·3	[6] 50·6	[6] 9·9	[1] 1·1	—	2·9 *
Newcastle .	223	84·3	4	1	3	—	—	[4] 42·3	[4] 52·0	[2] 9·8	[1] 0·9	[1] 2·1	2·2 *
Hull . .	223	83·5	4	2	2	—	—	[4] 38·9	[4] 48·7	[4] 12·4	—	—	8·6 *
Bradford .	208	85·8	4	1	3	—	—	[4] 35·0	[4] 51·7	[4] 13·0	[1] 1·2	—	0·6 §
Nottingham .	205	84·7	4	—	4	—	—	[4] 37·8	[4] 51·0	[4] 10·8	[1] 1·5	—	2·4 *
Leicester .	203	85·4	4	1	3	—	—	[4] 38·5	[4] 50·3	[4] 11·0	[1] 0·8	—	2·3 *
Belfast . .	282	76·4	4	4	—	—	—	[4] 62·5	[3] 32·7	—	—	[2] 48·6	—**

[1] The small figures above the percentages indicate the number of seats where the party concerned put up candidates.

† Two candidates were returned unopposed in Northern Ireland.

* Owing to the redistribution of seats which took place in 1948 the boundaries of many areas have changed sufficiently to limit the value of a comparison between the results in 1945 and 1950. Where it seems possible that the difference between the areas compared may have distorted the figure for swing by 1% or more, the latter has been marked thus : *

§ ‖ In some cases the figure for swing may be distorted because some seats were uncontested by one party or other in 1945 or because their vote was seriously split by a breakaway candidate. Where it appears that the figure for swing might on this account be an appreciable underestimate of the movement of opinion from right to left, a § has been placed. In no case does the underestimate seem as much as 2%; all cases where it seems more than 1% have been marked. Against cases when an overestimate of more than 1% seems probable a ‖ has been placed; only in the Lowlands and in the Salop, Hereford, Worcs., sub-area does it seem likely that the overestimate is as much as 2%.

** Owing to the number of seats left uncontested by the Labour Party it is not possible to give any figure for swing in Northern Ireland or in Belfast. A pointer to the movement of opinion may be found in the swing in the two Belfast constituencies which were fought simply by Conservative and Labour in both 1945 and 1950. These constituencies were unaffected by the redistribution. The swing in them averaged 8·1%.

Most of the areas are self-explanatory. There is no overlapping between sub-areas and no overlapping between the areas into which the sub-areas are grouped. The following sub-areas seem, however, to require further definition :

Area	Sub-Area	Constituencies included
County of London	Business and Residential	Chelsea, Westminster, Hampstead, Kensington, Paddington, St. Marylebone.
	East End	Bethnal Green, N. Hackney and Stoke Newington, S. Hackney, Poplar, Shoreditch and Finsbury, Stepney.
	Remainder	Fulham, Hammersmith, Islington, Holborn and St. Pancras S., St. Pancras N.
Suburban Boroughs	Kent, Surrey, Essex	All boroughs in Kent, Surrey and Essex on the fringe of London.
	Middlesex	All constituencies in Middlesex.
South-East England	Kent, Surrey	All constituencies in Kent and Surrey except for the boroughs on the fringe of London.
	Sussex	All constituencies in Sussex.
Wessex	Hampshire Ports	Portsmouth, Gosport and Fareham, Southampton.
	Remainder	The rest of Hampshire, Dorset and the Salisbury and Westbury divisions of Wilts.
Severn	Glos. and N. Wilts.	All Glos. (except Bristol), Swindon and the Chippenham and Devizes divisions of Wilts.
Essex	Essex	All constituencies in Essex except for the boroughs on the fringe of London.
West Midlands	Black Country	All boroughs in South Staffordshire and North Worcestershire.
	Potteries	Newcastle-under-Lyme and Stoke-upon-Trent.
	Salop, Herefordshire, Worcs.	All constituencies in these counties except Dudley and Oldbury and Halesowen.
North-East Midlands	Leics., Notts., Northants	The cities of Nottingham and Leicester are not included.
Lancashire	North Lancs.	S. Fylde, Preston, Clitheroe and all constituencies to their north.
	South Lancs.	The rest of Lancashire, except for Liverpool and Manchester.
North and East Riding	Counties and York	All constituencies in North and East Riding, together with York, except for Hull and Middlesbrough.
North-East England	Boroughs	Middlesbrough, all boroughs in Durham, Blyth, Tynemouth, Wallsend and the Morpeth division of Northumberland.
Border	Border	Cumberland, Westmorland and the Berwick and Hexham divisions of Northumberland.

Area	Sub-Area	Areas included
Wales	Industrial Wales	Glamorgan, Monmouth and the Llanelly Division of Carmarthen.
	Rural Wales	The remainder of Wales.
Scotland	Highlands	Perth and Kinross, Argyll, Inverness and all constituencies to their North.
	North-East	Moray and Nairn, Banff, Aberdeenshire, Angus and Kincardine.
Scotland (contd.)	Clyde	Dumbartonshire, Renfrewshire and Lanarkshire (except the Lanark Division).
	Forth	Fife, Stirling and Clackmannan, West Lothian, and Edinburgh.
	Lowlands	Ayrshire, the Lanark division of Lanarkshire, the County division of Midlothian and Peebles, and all constituencies to their south.

In the tables the capital letters before the main areas of the country serve as keys to the areas in the maps facing p. 316.

NOTE ON METHOD OF CALCULATION.

A. Party Percentages. In the foregoing tables the strength of each party is calculated as a percentage of the total vote cast in the constituencies where it put forward candidates. The purpose is to show the average vote for candidates of each party. It may, however, appear to exaggerate the strength of parties which did not fight all seats. This is illustrated by the following table :

United Kingdom	Conservative	Labour	Liberal	Communist	Other
Number of candidates . .	620	617	475	100	56
% of all votes	43·5	46·1	9·1	0·3	1·0
% of votes cast in constituencies where the party concerned put forward candidates . .	43·7	46·7	11·8	2·0	12·6

This method of presentation makes little difference for the Conservative and Labour parties which fought all but a handful of seats ; but for the Liberals, Communists and Other it does lead to an appreciable change. In the case of the Liberals at least, it may be justified on the ground that, if they had put forward candidates, they would have won a sizeable number of votes in the seats which they left unfought, and that then their aggregate votes would have been nearer to 11·8% than 9·1%.

B. Swing. The simplest way of representing the change in each area since 1945 seems to be to list the average of the Conservative gain and the Labour loss (in percentage of votes won wherever they put forward candidates). It is, however, by no means a perfect index to the rightward movement in political sympathy. The "swing" may be substantially affected by Liberal intervention in constituencies which they left unfought in 1945 ; but there is some reason to believe that on balance Liberal intervention had little effect on the relative strength of the major parties.* In addition to the uncertainty introduced by the increase in Liberal candidatures, there are two other major limitations to the usefulness of the figures for "swing". These are referred to in the

---

* See pages 300–301.

footnotes above. Redistribution makes some areas not strictly comparable; and votes cast for splinter groups on one side or other do sometimes make a contrast between the votes cast for the official candidates of the major parties misleading as an index of the real movement from left to right.

III. Analysis of the Results

Turnout

In the 1950 General Election 83·96% of the registered electorate cast valid votes. This was 10½% more than in 1945 and 7½% more than in any of the inter-war General Elections. However, although there is no doubt that participation in this election was considerably greater than ever before, the improvement over 1945 is deceptive. The register in 1945 was not very accurate. Owing to the system of compilation it contained a large number of " dead " names; the turnout must have been further reduced by failure to reach the service voter and by the general post-war confusion, not to mention the holiday season. The 1950 register on the other hand was much more carefully and accurately compiled and the election took place at a time of much less social dislocation; furthermore the introduction of postal voting facilities enabled 1% to 2% of the electorate to vote who would formerly have been deprived of the opportunity. There is no doubt that people were more active in exercising their suffrage in 1950 than in 1945, but the figure of 10½% is probably twice as much as the real increase.

It is notable how little the turnout seemed to vary between one part of the country and another. In almost every sub-area listed in the tables above it was within 3% of the national average of 84%. The only serious exceptions were the Highlands and Northern Ireland, and four cities—London, Liverpool, Glasgow and Edinburgh. The uniformity in turnout is almost as striking if individual constituencies are considered instead of areas— where, after all, differences may be cancelled out. Diagram I shows how little variation there was from the mean.

The exceptions are interesting. In the two seats won by Irish Nationalists the intensity of the Orange and Green struggle stimulated the highly remarkable turnout of 92%. Apart from this the record was shared by two Lancashire constituencies, Accrington and Clitheroe, where over 91% voted. Nowhere else was 90% exceeded, but the turnout of 89% in the large and scattered constituencies of Montgomery and Merioneth was quite as remarkable. In 37 seats more than 88% voted; 22 of these seats were in the North Country, mostly in Lancashire.

The lowest turnout occurred, not surprisingly, in the Western Isles where less than 56% voted. There were 26 other seats where the vote fell below 75%. These can be divided into two

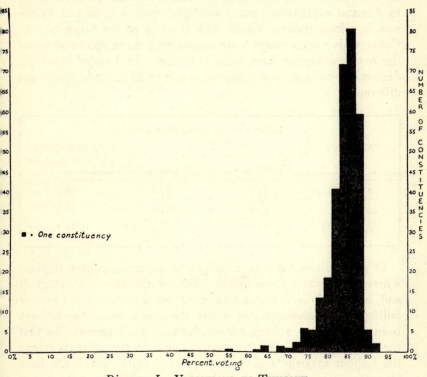

Diagram I.—VARIATIONS IN TURNOUT.

classes—remote rural areas or safe seats in big cities. All but two were to be found either in the Highlands or Northern Ireland, or in one of the eight largest cities. The two exceptions were Cardigan—another remote rural area—and Hexham, which none of the major parties was contesting. It is perhaps worthy of note that, apart from Hexham, the two lowest turnouts in England were in Chelsea and South Kensington (71% each).

Although in 562 of the 623 contested constituencies the turnout fell between 78% and 88%, analysis of the small variations does throw some light on the factors which may influence the number going to the poll.

The turnout appears to be higher in Labour than in Conservative areas. The median in all seats was 84·7%. In seats returning Labour members it was 85·3%. In seats returning Conservatives it was only 84·1%. Perhaps the difference is not sufficient to demand explanation, but a sidelight upon it is offered by the way in which turnout varied with the size of the majority. In Conservative seats voters were appreciably more apathetic when the outcome cannot have been in doubt. In Labour areas the degree of openness in the contest seems to have made much less difference.

Majority	Median turnout in constituencies won by:		Median turnout all constituencies
	Conservative	Labour	
0%–10%	85·7	85·6	85·6
10%–20%	84·2	85·7	85·0
20%–30%	83·0	84·6	83·4
30%–40% } Over 40% }	82·1	84·6 } 85·9 } 85·2	84·5

In general turnout was, as might be expected, higher in seats where there was a close finish. But the difference is not great and, on the whole, it seems surprising that there was not a greater falling off in constituencies where the result must always have been regarded as a foregone conclusion. It is remarkable that the very highest median turnout is found in the 48 seats where the Labour majority was more than 40% of the poll. Of these 48, 33 are essentially mining seats; perhaps in them there is a unique sense of working-class solidarity which has to be demonstrated at the polls.

It has been suggested that many Liberals who had no candidate of their own persuasion must have abstained. In fact the median turnout in the 148 seats where there was no Liberal candidate was 84·7%—exactly the same as in the 475 constituencies where there was a Liberal standing. Even though the Liberals were presumably weakest in the 148 constituencies they did not fight, these must have contained many potential Liberal voters. The fact that there was absolutely no difference between the median turnout in these seats and the median turnout in seats where a Liberal did enter the fray suggests that few Liberals, when it came to polling day, actually shirked the painful task of deciding which was the lesser of two evils. However, this argument is not conclusive. It must be pointed out that the median turnout in the 47 contests where no Liberal stood and where the Conservatives won was 80·7% as against 84·1% in all the 298 Conservative-won seats; these figures too may be misleading, but it can still be argued that in the rural areas (where most of these seats are) a few die-hard Liberals, who will vote for no other party, are to be found.

The physical difficulties in the way of voting in rural areas are obvious and well publicised. But in fact they seem to lead to a surprisingly small reduction in turnout. In the 126 constituencies largest in geographic area the median turnout was 83·4% compared with 85·1% in the other 497 constituencies. It was only in the 20 largest constituencies, constituencies of over half-a-million acres, that the falling off in turnout was marked, the median being only 79·2%. In the 73 constituencies of between (approx.) 200,000 and 500,000 acres the median turnout was just over 83%. In the 33 seats of 150,000 to 200,000 acres the median turnout was 85·5%—above the national average—and there at least the distance to the poll and the difficulty of campaigning over a large area can have had little effect. Indeed the drop in rural turnout was sizeable only in Scotland and Northern Ireland. Of the 126 extra-large constituencies, 96 were in England and Wales, and in them the median turnout was 83·9%. In the 30 in Scotland and Northern Ireland it was only 79·7%. It should, however, be pointed out that the very largest seats were almost all in Scotland and Northern Ireland.

In former elections it is probable that the discrepancy between the turnout in small and large constituencies was slightly greater. The postal voting facilities introduced in 1948 were of particular assistance in rural areas. In these 126 constituencies they were used by 2·2% of the electorate compared with 1·3% in the rest of the country.

In general, it must be considered remarkable that the turnout was so uniformly high and that the factors which might be expected most to influence it had so little effect. The safeness of the seat, the distance to the poll or the presence of a Liberal candidate seem to be less important in deciding how many electors record their vote than the general political temperature in the whole country.

Swing 1945–1950

Despite the limitations set out on pp. 315–316, the figures for " swing " given in the table are revealing.   It is notable that a swing to the left appears in only 3 of the 60 sub-areas listed, and it is probable that each of these three swings is illusory.   Over the whole country the movement really appears to have been to the right—but there were considerable and unquestionable variations in its degree.   The London suburbs, Essex, the Hampshire ports and North Lancashire show swings more than twice as great as the national average.   On the other hand, the Severn area, the West of England, East Anglia, the North-East Midlands, Lincoln- shire, the North-East of England, Wales and the Fife, Stirling and West Lothian area show notably low changes.   Apart from these areas (and one or two others where Redistribution makes the figures suspect) there are no very great deviations from the national average of 3·3%.

The 1948 redistribution which so often hampers area com- parisons between 1945 and 1950 limits far more seriously any investigation of the changes in individual constituencies.   How- ever, the boundaries of 80 seats were left entirely unchanged ; 10 more were created simply by incorporating the whole of two or three former constituencies into one new one ; and in a further 6 the changes were completely negligible.   In 18 of these 96 constituencies comparisons between 1945 and 1950 are imprac- ticable because of differences in party candidatures.   In the remaining 78 the swing varies from 12% to −2%.   The extremes are, on the one hand, Mitcham with a 11½% swing to the right and Hornchurch with 11% and, on the other, four swings to the left, 1% in Merioneth and Ebbw Vale and 2% in Huntingdon- shire and Moray and Nairn.   It is worth noting that of the 34 seats with a swing of 5% or more 29 were in the London area, while the majority of those with a swing under 2% were in country districts.

The Conservative and Labour vote

In the great majority of areas and constituencies the major parties each won between 35% and 65% of the vote.   There were, however, a good many more Labour candidates than Conservatives among the high exceptions and a good many more Conservative candidates than Labour among the low exceptions. Diagrams II and III illustrate this. It appears that the irreducible minimum of Labour supporters in even the safest Conservative areas is higher than the irreducible minimum of Conservatives in working-class strongholds. In only 4 seats did the Conservatives win over 70% of the vote. Three of these were in Northern Ireland; the fourth was South Kensington, where they secured 73%. On the other hand they lost five deposits, and in Bethnal Green (an old Liberal stronghold) their candidate got less than 5%. In 25 seats they failed to win as much as a fifth of the votes. Labour, on the other hand, lost no deposits and fell below 20% in only 6 seats. They did worst in 2 seats, North Dorset (14%) and North Cornwall (15%) where radical Liberals presumably still took the bulk of the left-wing vote. At the other extreme there were 8 seats where they won over 80% of the vote and 37 where they won over 70%. Abertillery with 87% showed the record Labour vote.

If areas instead of constituencies are considered, the variations are of course smaller. The Conservatives fared best in Northern Ireland with 63% of the vote, and in Sussex with 59%. In only 14 of the 60 sub-areas in the table have they over 50% of the vote. Labour fared best in Industrial Wales (ports excluded) with 72%. In only 3 other areas did their share exceed 60%. In 23 of the 60 sub-areas it was above 50%.

At the other extreme the Conservatives did worst in the East End of London and in Industrial Wales (ports excluded) where they secured no more than 20%. But the Durham county divisions provide the only other sub-area where they failed to get 30% of the vote. Labour fared worst in Northern Ireland where they won only 27%. The Highlands, the Border area, Devon, Cornwall, and Sussex were the other areas where they dropped below 30%. In all, in 42 of the 60 sub-areas the Conservatives won between 35% and 50% of the votes. Labour support varied rather more, but in 35 of the sub-areas their vote lay between 40% and 55%. Few of the exceptions were much outside these ranges. On the whole the various parts of the country seem to be less extreme in their partisanship than is sometimes suggested.

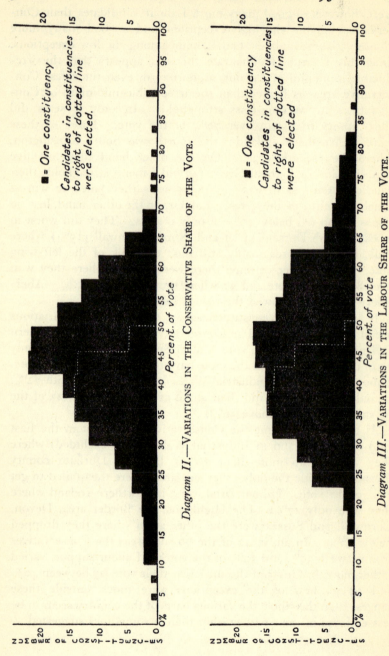

Diagram II.—Variations in the Conservative Share of the Vote.

■ = One constituency

Candidates in constituencies to right of dotted line were elected.

Diagram III.—Variations in the Labour Share of the Vote.

■ = One constituency

Candidates in constituencies to right of dotted line were elected.

The Liberal vote

The Liberals secured 9·1% of the total vote and 11·4% of the votes cast in the 475 seats which they contested. They lost 319 deposits. There were only 24 seats where they won as much as a quarter of the vote. In 14 seats they won a third of the vote and in 9 of these they were successful; there were only 5 seats which they did not win where they came within 10% of victory. Two leaders of the Liberal party, Sir Archibald Sinclair and Mr. Byers, who were defeated by 269 and 97 votes respectively, could complain of ill-fortune, but in general it was the whole working of the electoral system rather than any particular bad luck in individual constituencies that was responsible for the Liberals securing so small a representation in Parliament.

The party fared best in West Huddersfield where there was no Conservative candidate and they won 58% of the vote. Their next highest poll was 52% in Cardigan—the only seat apart from Montgomery where they secured an absolute majority in a three-cornered fight. The party fared worst in West Dundee where their candidate, who entered at the last moment in defiance of a local " pact ", won only 986 votes (1·8%).

All but three of the 24 seats where the Liberals won more than 25% of the vote, were in essentially rural areas with a strong Liberal tradition (and in two of the three exceptions their strength must be attributed to the absence of a Conservative candidate). Of these 24 seats 19 were in Scotland, Wales or the West Country. In the table it will be seen that only in Wessex, the West of England, Suffolk, parts of Yorkshire, the Border area, North Wales and rural Scotland did the Liberals average even 15% of the votes cast in constituencies where they had candidates.

Liberals fared markedly better in seats won by the Conservatives than in those won by Labour. This is illustrated partly by the fact that they left unfought only 49 of the 298 constituencies won by the Conservatives while they neglected 98 of the 315 constituencies won by Labour. The point may be made more sharply by comparing the median Liberal percentage in seats won by Conservatives and in those won by Labour. The median Liberal percentage in all seats was 10·5%. In Conservative-won seats it was 11·4% while in Labour-won seats it was 9·1%. Perhaps this might be restated in the simple proposition that

Diagram IV.—VARIATIONS IN THE LIBERAL SHARE OF THE VOTE.

Conservatives tend to win rural and residential constituencies and that the Liberals, by the nature of their support, tend to be strongest in just those areas. Indeed it may seem surprising that the difference is not more marked.

The Communist vote

Communists stood in 100 constituencies. Of all the votes cast in the country 0·3% were for Communists. On the average each candidate won 917 votes or 2·0% of the votes cast in his constituency. But 78 of their candidates won less than 2% of the vote and the only ones to secure appreciable support were Mr. Gallacher, who got 22% of the vote in West Fife, and Mr. Pollitt and Mr. Piratin, who just saved their deposits in East Rhondda and Stepney. The next highest poll was under 6%. The worst fate befell the candidates in Bedford and Wycombe who, with 207 and 199 votes respectively, secured an even smaller share of the poll (0·4%) than any of the "freak" independents.

The only areas where Communist candidates won on the average over 2% of the vote were the East End of London, South Wales and industrial Scotland. There is perhaps some justification to be found here for the much abused phrase about red Clydeside. The 9 Communist candidates in the area secured a vote nearly twice the national average for their party.

There seems to be a direct correlation between the size of the Communist vote and the size of the Labour vote.

Communist vote	No. of seats	Median Labour vote
0%–1%	28	49·8%
1%–2%	50	56·3%
Over 2%	22	59·6%

It might of course be expected that the Communists would be strongest in working-class areas which regularly return Labour members with overwhelming majorities, but the difference of 10% in the median Labour vote between the strongest and the weakest Communist votes is striking.

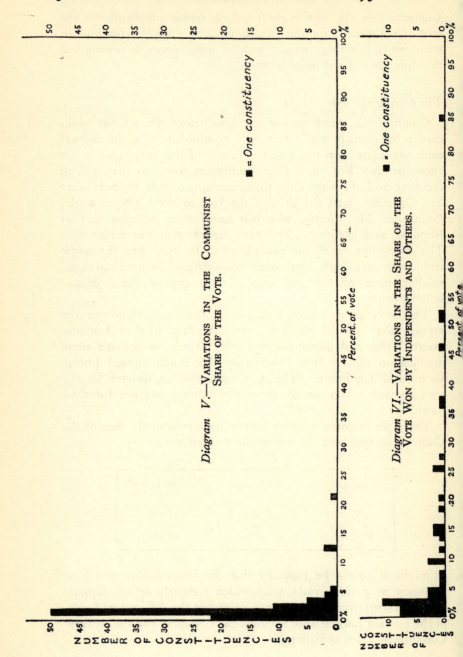

Diagram V.—Variations in the Communist Share of the Vote.

■ = One constituency

Diagram VI.—Variations in the Share of the Vote Won by Independents and Others.

■ = One constituency

Communist intervention probably cost the Labour party 4 seats.

Seat	Communist vote	Labour defeated by:
Bexley	481	133
Shipley	237	81
Glasgow: Govan . .	1,547	373
Scotstoun .	1,088	239

Victory in these 4 seats would have raised Labour's clear majority from 5 to 13.

The vote for minor parties and Independents

There were 56 candidates who could not be classified as Conservative, Labour, Liberal or Communist. They fought under a multitude of designations. The following are the largest single groups :

> 7 Official Welsh Nationalists.
> 5 Labour Independents.
> 4 I.L.P.
> 4 Irish Anti-Partitionists.

Apart from the Speaker and 5 Northern Ireland candidates the only ones to secure as much as 20% of the vote were Mr. Kendall in Grantham (28%), Mr. Lipson in Cheltenham (25%), Mr. Pritt in North Hammersmith (25%), and Mr. Brown in Rugby (20%) ; all these were sitting members at the time of the dissolution. All but 4 of the 29 unclassified candidates who won 3% or more of the vote can be divided into two categories. Seventeen were Nationalists of one sort or another and 8 were Independents or Labour Independents fighting seats which had been held by Independents. The four exceptions were the Speaker and his opponent, an I.L.P. candidate who got less than 6%, and an Independent in Greenock who won 16%, helped perhaps by the absence of any Conservative candidate. The candidates who fared worst were the Independent at Harborough who received only 273 votes (0·5%) and the Socialist Party of Great Britain candidate in North Paddington who received only 192 votes (0·5%).

IV. The Relation of Seats to Votes

The customary excuse for the harsh fate which the British electoral system imposes on minor parties is that it at least trans-

Y

lates a relatively narrow majority in popular votes into a majority in the House of Commons comfortable enough to support a strong Government. In 1950 this excuse did not work. The system very effectively crushed minor parties, but it did not produce a clear-cut decision between the chief contestants, even though one secured 3% more of the vote than the other. Seats were divided between the parties in exactly the same ratio as their votes. Therefore it has been suggested that a change has come over the electoral system and that small majorities in votes are no longer likely to be exaggerated into larger majorities in seats. This certainly has not happened. It can confidently be predicted that the system will continue to produce exaggerated Parliamentary majorities. It is a mere chance that the popular vote in 1950 happened to be divided at the one point where votes and seats would be in the same proportions. There is a bias in the electoral system which favours one party but, if allowance is made for that bias, the turnover in seats for any swing in votes is exaggerated according to a fairly fixed relation.

Before discussing the bias, it is proper to examine this general relation between seats and votes. The exaggeration of Parliamentary majorities is well enough known, but it has been dismissed as a fortunate chance or as " the electoral gamble " and little attention has been devoted to its analysis. An attempt was made to fill this gap in an Appendix to *McCallum and Readman*. There the number of seats a party might expect to win for any given proportion of the national vote was inferred from the 1935 and 1945 results. The general pattern suggested in that Appendix for the relation between seats and votes finds support in an article by M. G. Kendall and A. Stuart appearing in the *British Journal of Sociology*, 1950, Vol. I, No. 3, p. 183. Kendall and Stuart examine a forty-year-old formula for this relation to which attention had been drawn by a reference in the *Economist* during the recent election. The formula was propounded to the Royal Commission on Electoral Systems in 1909 by the Rt. Hon. James Parker Smith. He suggested that under the British electoral system, when there were two parties, the ratio of seats won by the parties might be expected to be at least the cube of the ratio between the votes cast for them; in other words, if the ratio between votes was $A : B$ the ratio between seats would be at least $A^3 : B^3$. Thus, according to this formula, if 600 seats are divided between two

fairly evenly matched parties the Parliamentary majority is likely
to be 15 to 20 seats for every 1% lead in votes. This is shown in
this table.

% Division of Major Party vote	Division of seats	Majority
50–50	300–300	—
51–49	318–272	36
52–48	336–264	72
55–45	388–212	176
60–40	464–136	328
65–35	520– 80	440

The formula was found to fit the results of the 1931, 1935 and
1945 elections with quite remarkable accuracy. It also coincided
very closely with the empirical conclusions about the general
relation of seats and votes offered in the Appendix to *McCallum
and Readman*. Kendall and Stuart offer some statistical justification for the formula. They also tell how they used it, in
conjunction with a slightly inaccurate Gallup poll, to make an
exceedingly accurate prediction of the 1950 result. The inaccuracy of the Gallup poll was fortunate for their prediction,
for it almost exactly compensated for the inaccuracy of the
$A^3 : B^3$ formula on this occasion. If the formula had held good
for this election Labour would have had 18 more seats and the
Conservatives 18 fewer than the actual result.

An undoubted bias in the electoral system is responsible for its
failure to work according to expectations in 1950. The existence
of this bias can be shown very simply. If every member's
majority is expressed as a percentage of the votes cast in his constituency, the number of seats that would change hands as a result
of any given swing between the parties can easily be calculated—
if two not unreasonable assumptions about the evenness of the
swing and the behaviour of the minor party vote are allowed.[1]

[1] The first assumption is that the swing should be universal and equal. It
cannot be exactly fulfilled, although a study of the actual results in 1935, 1945
and 1950 show the assumption of uniform swing to be less unrealistic than
might be thought. However, the argument here does not depend on the swing
being uniform; it merely demands that variations shall approximately
cancel each other. That does not seem unrealistic. It is of course theoretically
possible that the national swing should be concentrated in the marginal constituencies held by one party, while opinion remained static elsewhere. But it
is politically and statistically highly improbable.
The second assumption is that the vote for minor parties is unchanged—or,
equally adequate and much more probable, merely that minor parties remain

There are in fact thirty-five Labour members who hold their seats by a majority of under 4% ; these would be ousted by a swing of 2% of the vote from Labour to Conservative. In the same way a 2% swing from Conservative to Labour would cost the Conservatives 39 seats. The position is illustrated by the following table which shows the approximate number of seats which each of the major parties would have won in 1950 if any given percentage of the voters had transferred their support to the other side.

Swing in % from actual result	% of vote			Seats			Swing in seats from actual result
	Con.	Lab.	Lab. maj.	Con.	Lab.	Lab. maj.	
Cons. to Lab.							Cons. to Lab.
10	33·7	56·7	23·0	124	489	365	174
5	38·7	51·7	13·0	201	412	211	97
4	39·7	50·7	11·0	222	391	169	76
3	40·7	49·7	9·0	234	379	145	64
2	41·7	48·7	7·0	259	354	95	39
1½	42·2	48·2	6·0	269	344	75	29
1	42·7	47·7	5·0	277	336	59	21
½	43·2	47·2	4·0	284	329	45	14
Actual result	43·7	46·7	3·0	298	315	17	Actual result
Lab. to Cons.							Lab. to Cons.
½	44·2	46·2	2·0	305	308	3	7
1	44·7	45·7	1·0	315	298	— 17	17
1½	45·2	45·2	—	324	289	— 35	26
2	45·7	44·7	— 1·0	333	280	— 53	35
3	46·7	43·7	— 3·0	347	266	— 81	49
4	47·7	42·7	— 5·0	365	248	—117	67
5	48·7	41·7	— 7·0	381	222	—159	83
10	53·7	36·7	—17·0	459	164	—295	161

The bias in the system can be clearly seen. If the party votes had been equal at 45·2%—that is to say, if the Conservatives had won 1½% more in every constituency and Labour 1½% less—the Conservatives would have had 35 more seats than Labour. If in every seat just over ½% of the voters had transferred their support

minor parties. In 588 of the 625 seats Conservative and Labour provided the top two at the poll ; in these seats if Liberals or Communists lent their support to one or other side, the major party percentages would be unevenly swelled, but the change would only be tantamount to a swing between the major parties and the argument would not be affected. Of the remaining 37 seats, only 14 were won by majorities of under 15% and need to be considered as marginal. An examination of these 14 seats shows it to be most unlikely under any probable circumstances that all would go one way or the other. Therefore they are not likely substantially to affect the general relation between seats and votes.

to the Conservatives Labour would still have had a majority of almost 2% in votes, but only the same number of seats as their rivals. If in every seat there had been a swing of 3% the position in votes would have been exactly the reverse of the actual result, but the position in seats would have been far more than reversed. In place of Labour's majority of 5, the Conservatives would have had a clear lead of 69 seats,[1] and everyone would have written about the way in which the electoral system had done its duty in producing from an indecisive vote a clear parliamentary majority.

The accompanying diagram sharply illustrates the scale of this bias. It shows the number of seats the parties did win for their actual share of the votes and the number of seats they would have won—assuming an equal swing—for any probable division of the major party vote. For any given vote it is apparent that the Conservatives would get more seats than Labour. In the crucial situation when the parties are separated by less than 10% the Conservatives would get at least 30 more seats than Labour for any given share of the vote.

The probable cause of this bias can be demonstrated almost as simply as the mere fact of its existence. It is no new phenomenon, but its presence used to be concealed by a bias in the opposite direction which has now been eliminated. It has been shown how in 1945, and to a smaller extent in 1935, Labour areas were over-represented for the number of the population and Conservative areas under-represented.[2] In 1945 the average Labour seat contained 51,000 electors while the average Conservative seat contained 57,000. This placed the Conservatives under a heavy disadvantage which was removed by the redistribution of seats under the 1948 Act. Now there is virtually no difference between the number of electors in constituencies which return Labour members and in those which return Conservatives. One bias eliminated, the operation of another and much more ineradicable one can be clearly seen. The Labour party squanders many more votes in piling up huge majorities in absolutely safe seats than the Conservatives whose strength happens to be more effectively spread. Of the 60 largest majorities 50 are Labour and

---

[1] These figures refer to clear majorities over all other parties combined. If, as in the table above, the 12 seats won by minor parties are ignored, a 3% swing in votes would change the Labour lead of 17 seats over the Conservatives into a Conservative lead of 81 seats over Labour.

[2] See *McCallum and Readman*, Appendix III (p. 287).

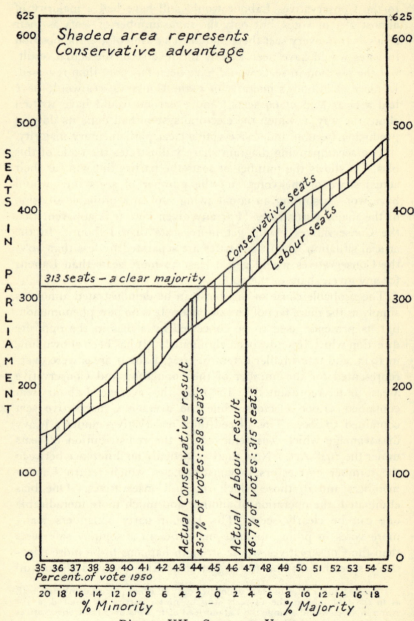

Diagram VII.—SEATS AND VOTES.

10 Conservative. These figures are of course somewhat exaggerated by the fact that Labour did secure 3% more of the popular vote than the Conservatives; however, even if both parties had obtained exactly the same share of the popular vote, it seems that 25 of the 35 safest seats would have been won by Labour.

The extent of this bias can easily be measured. If in every seat just over $\frac{1}{2}$% of the vote had been transferred from Labour to the Conservatives, seats would have been equally divided (306 or 307 for each), but Labour would still have had almost 2% more of the total poll—just over 500,000 votes. It is not intended to press the detailed arithmetic too far but, unless there is a drastic change in the structure of political sympathy, Labour is likely to continue to enter political contests with a handicap of half-a-million votes for some time to come. They will need something like 2% more of the popular vote than the Conservatives to get any given number of seats.

It is interesting that with this 2% discount the $A^3 : B^3$ formula fits with remarkable accuracy not only the actual result but also the hypothetical results which have been calculated here on the assumption of an even swing. However, the extreme accuracy need not be taken too seriously. No formula, whether derived from the evidence of empirical studies or from *a priori* considerations, can be expected to fit the results of every general election with complete accuracy. Nevertheless, if allowance is made for minor chance variations, Diagram VII and the majority columns in the last table probably offer a fair picture of the parliament which would in present circumstances be produced by any likely division of the major party vote. Although a bias exists which is not likely to disappear, no fundamental change has overtaken the electoral system. It retains its tendency to translate even a narrow majority in popular votes into a parliamentary majority large enough to make strong government possible.

INDEX

N.B.—All county constituencies are listed under the counties in which they occur.

PRINTED IN GREAT BRITAIN BY
RICHARD CLAY AND COMPANY, LTD.,
BUNGAY, SUFFOLK.